RELIGIONS IN FOCUS

Religions in Focus

*New Approaches to Tradition
and Contemporary Practices*

edited by

Graham Harvey

LONDON   OAKVILLE

Published by
UK: Equinox Publishing Ltd., Unit 6, The Village, 101 Amies St., London
SW11 2JW
USA: DBBC, 28 Main Street, Oakville, CT 06779

www.equinoxpub.com

First published 2009

British Library Cataloguing-in-Publication Data
A catalogue record for this book is available from the British Library.

ISBN   978 1 84553 217 8   (hardback)
              978 1 84553 218 5   (paperback)

Library of Congress Cataloging-in-Publication Data

       Religions in focus : new approaches to tradition and contemporary
practices / edited by Graham Harvey.
      p. cm.
      Includes bibliographical references and index.
      ISBN 978-1-84553-217-8 (hb) -- ISBN 978-1-84553-218-5 (pbk.)
      1. Religions. I. Harvey, Graham. BL80.3.R43 2009
      200--dc22   2008041769

Printed and bound in Great Britain by Printed and bound in Great Britain by CPI
Antony Rowe, Chippenham

Contents

Acknowledgements

Religions in Focus is the result of the work of many people, all of whom deserve thanks and respect. The idea and the title were suggested to me by our esteemed publisher, Janet Joyce at Equinox. I am greatly honoured that she entrusted me with the task of developing the idea and of inviting colleagues to author chapters and work together as a team in crafting the kind of book that scholars of religion have needed for some time. In most courses about religion it is now normal to discuss religions as the activities performed by people in everyday as well as exceptional circumstances. Until now, however, the majority of the textbooks available to support our teaching and guide our students' learning have privileged the founders, texts, creeds and/or official practices of religious elites. The scholars I invited to become part of the project that resulted in this book were enthusiastic about writing differently.

It has sometimes been a struggle to keep lived religion in focus: sometimes we have found ourselves writing about what the texts or leaders say. But conversations among the authors about, for example, how texts and ideas are used or contested in the actual practice of religions has kept us focused on writing about religions as they are rather than as they once were or as official teachings say they should be. The end result, this book, promises to enrich the study of religions by providing a foundation for studying what people do when they act or live religiously.

I therefore thank the authors of each chapter individually and again as members of a team who have read and commented on each other's drafts in positively enriching ways. Further collaborations in producing the book's companion website are acknowledged on that site. Thanks are due too to our production editor, Chas Clifton, who has further polished our work and expertly prepared it for publication. Illustrations for *Religions in Focus* have been provided by the authors and by other colleagues and friends — these are acknowledged in the relevant places (including, again, those that form an important part of the companion website).

Last but not least, our thanks are also due to our colleagues and students—past, present, and future—who have variously shaped the ways we understand our work as scholars of religion, as researchers, teachers, writers and always as students in the ongoing process of learning. Academic work is about asking questions, about debate and possibilities, far more than it is about claiming to know all there is to know about any topic. Religions, anyway, keep changing so we need to keep engaging with them, learning more, asking more, discussing more. Therefore, we thank you for working with us in this book and in further study for keeping religions in focus.

Graham Harvey

Contributors

Afe Adogame, University of Edinburgh, UK

Shawn Arthur, Appalachian State University, USA

George Chryssides, University of Birmingham, UK

Graham Harvey, Open University, UK

Douglas Davies, Durham University, UK

Hannah Holtschneider, University of Edinburgh, UK

Pratap Kumar, University of Kwazulu-Natal, South Africa

Kenneth Lokensgard, Gettysburg College, USA

Jeffery Long, Elizabethtown College, USA

Sabina Magliocco, California State University-Northridge

Eve Mullen, Emory University, USA

Florian Pohl, Emory University, USA

Jenny Rose, California, USA

Nikky G.Kaur Singh, Colby College, USA

Peter Smith, Mahidol University, Thailand

Katja Triplett, University of Marburg, Germany

Woo Hairan, Hanshin University, Korea

Introduction

Graham Harvey

Religions in Focus introduces the lives and actions of some of the many people worldwide who participate in religious activities. Its focus is on the doing of religion. Its primary interest is in the present day lived reality of religions as they are practiced not only by religious leaders but by a far larger population. Its focus is on what people around us do when they engage in something that scholars of religion call religion. More will be said about definitions of religion and religions in a while. Before that, we invite you to collaborate with us (the authors and editors of the various chapters) in making this book work well.

Six Steps

Religions in Focus is a textbook for use by students and scholars of religion. Producing it has been a collaborative effort by an international team of scholars who are experts not only about particular religions but also about a range critical debates and issues in academia and more widely.

This is an on-going project in which, together, we will improve knowledge and understanding about religion as an important activity in the contemporary world. *Religions in Focus* is supported by a companion web site that includes additional material necessary to a fuller participation in studying religious activities. We anticipate that our colleagues in universities and colleges worldwide will build their teaching around this book and that students will find it a valuable introduction to the vibrant diversity of religious phenomena. All readers, however, will have to do some work. The task ahead is to develop the project of keeping religions in focus.

It is not enough to read any book passively, just taking in the facts and being subtly seduced (perhaps) by our approaches and interests. Nor is it enough simply to be provoked to agree or disagree with what an author writes. Academic study and research at any level is certainly not just about learning facts. Beyond the facts is the art and science of discussion, debate, reflection, consideration, testing theories, asking questions and then asking further questions. *Religions in Focus* is an introduction and all the contributing authors have set out to provide accurate information and analysis about contemporary religious lives. Our goal, however, is to provoke further thought and debate. To that end, we suggest six steps that will maintain and clarify a focus on religions.

Step 1: Contents and Structure

The first step is to be clear about what is in this book. A quick look at the contents pages will indicate something of what we offer and indicate some ways in which you might make the book work for you.

Religions in Focus contains seventeen chapters and, as you've see on the contents pages, they carry titles that name particular kinds of religious people. There are, for example, chapters about Zoroastrians, Pagans and Buddhists. The chapters are organized in reverse alphabetical order: from Z to B. This is the book's only organizing principle. Starting with Zoroastrians (or, more properly, Zarathushtis) and ending with Baha'is says nothing about the age or origins of the religions of these people, nor about their relative size or global spread. It does not group religions by some alleged similarity of regional origin or creed. The *only* point is that we include a selection of the religions practiced in the world today. *Religions in Focus* is interested in what it means to Sikhs, Pagans, Muslims, Jews, Jains, Christians, Baha'is and so on to be members of, or participants in, their religious communities.

You can read the chapters in any order that appeals to you. Our Z-B structure encourages you to pay attention to both diversity and specificity. You should certainly be aware that there are far more religions than those included here. We have not deliberately excluded anyone but we had to make good use of the space available to us. By presenting a wide variety of religious people and activities we hope to provoke readers to think further about even more religions. As you read the following chapters, working with us by taking some further steps as encouraged below, you will gain skills and ideas to apply in further study.

Step 2: Chapter Titles (Again)

Step two involves thinking a bit more about the chapter titles. Calling them by the names of people (e.g. Buddhists or Latter Day Saints) rather than religions (e.g. Buddhism or Mormonism) was no mere whim. Sometimes we do write about the "isms" — the organizations to which some people belong or the systems of ideas or practices to which they adhere in various ways. When we recommend some further reading we will certainly cite other books which use titles such as "indigenous religions" or "Japanese religions". However, by empathizing people rather than systems we encourage you to pay attention to the reality in which religions are made up of the many actions and ideas of all the people who are identified with others in the doing of these religions.

Our interest is in what people actually do, say, think, feel and experience. What people *ought* to do, say, think, feel, and experience is one common aspect of what religious leaders and publications teach. But there is no "official" version of a religion that is separate from how people live. The people who teach about core doctrines, creeds or texts are also members of communities, continuously experimenting with what it means to be an animist, Hindu, or a practitioner of an indigenous religion. Some chapters or parts of chapters say more than others about the kind of teachings or practices that the majority of people within a religion consider central. These are the kind of things that people might tell you if you ask for a quick insight into what's important in their religion. Some will tell you about ideas or beliefs, others about practices. It is important to listen to these specific details. But it is just as important to be aware that you have not heard everything when you have heard the basics.

This second step in keeping religions in focus also entails an invitation for you to do more work. Here we offer you an introduction to the lives and activities of some religious people. In the seventeen chapters that follow you'll meet examples of many religions — but not all. It is in the nature of an introduction, even a careful and expert one, that it cannot include everything and everyone. In academia the point is to discuss issues not to provide the last word; to raise questions rather than fix answers forever. By focussing on these religions and discussing them in these ways we intend to provide a foundation for further study. By noticing the ways in which other scholars of religion write about religions you will pick up skills that can be further refined and applied to ongoing study of whatever religions interest you.

Step 3: Vignettes

The third step in maintaining a focus is to note that every chapter begins with some kind of snapshot, illustration, evocation, or vignette of a real or typical event. This is a further strategy that we have employed to keep the lived reality of living religions in view. These vignettes are not all of the same length or kind. Some form brief introductions to a chapter, others are revisited throughout a chapter. Some are about public ceremonies, others about activities in people's homes. Some are about what religious people do when they visit a sacred site, others about what it is like for students or visitors to observe other people doing their religions. Some imagine the inner thoughts of someone caught in a moment of decision, others attend to everyday acts. Whatever their length or content, these vignettes contribute vitally to the argument of *Religions in Focus*. This book introduces religions and the academic study of religions. To do this it must attend to real life. We hope these encapsulations of what it is like to be a religious person, to perform religious acts, or to observe religious events and places, will not only intrigue you enough to propel you further into studying these and other religions, but will firmly establish the priority of action, doing, performance, observance or whatever you wish to call religion as something people do and live.

One other aspect of these opening narratives is also crucial in our shared task of keeping religions in focus. Vignettes can be defined as brief, elegant but open ended narratives or word-pictures. This "open-endedness" refers to the fact that vignettes are not complete in themselves: they lead to further discussion, not only do you need to move on into the rest of each chapter, and on through the book. *Religions in Focus* can only work if you continue to study these and other religions in more depth. As you do all of this, you need to work with us in remembering that although the chapters present religions as they are practiced today, they cannot say everything about everyone. There are plenty of other things that religious people do that are not mentioned here. Our opening vignettes and further discussions provide valuable starting points.

Step 4: Elsewhere

Yet another fact about the vignettes is an important step in keeping focus. Many (if not all) of them start "elsewhere." In the contemporary world, these religions are practiced in many places far from where they originated. It is entirely possible to encounter practitioners and practices from any of these religions in many countries. Given access to the Internet and the broadcast media it is possible to observe what people do from anywhere. The art and cuisine that was inspired by particular religions is now available in various ways and forms far more widely than ever before. For these and other reasons, it would be a mistake to think of any of these religions as somehow fixed or rooted in one place. It would be a worse error to think that a religion is only performed properly in one place, even in a place where it is the majority religion. Therefore, our vignettes often start in places that are not where the religion came from, nor where it is most visible in a culture. Or they present an activity that is in some other way unexpected. In doing so, not only do we intend to focus on what its like to do religion in various places, we also want to indicate that religions are immensely varied. If a religion is alive (because people live it), it is continuously changing. Even when people assiduously stick to doing the same thing in the same way, the fact that they do so in a world of rapid change is a significant kind of change in itself.

In this step, as in others, we invite you to work with us. Remember that not only are there many more religions to study, there are also many people who do not do things exactly as set out here. We have not described the acts and interests of *all* members even of the religions included here. Just as we are interested in what actually happens rather than what some people say ought to happen, our own presentation should not be misread as saying how things should be. So, when we say what Christians or Buddhists, or practitioners of Chinese, Japanese, or Korean religions do, we are not saying that this is all they do, or that all such people do all these things. We have focused on some common, significant and interesting religious activities and ideas. We invite you to listen in on religious conversations and explanations, to observe religious performances and gestures. But these remain examples from a wider repertoire of what religious people do. By starting "elsewhere" we invite you to wonder what else people do, and whether what we talk about as happening in the United States, South Africa or Korea bears any resemblance to what happens in India, Britain or Saudi Arabia.

Step 5: Labels and Boxes

This step adds a little more to earlier means of maintaining a focus and taking care. Some titles identify religious people in rather odd ways. Because we wanted to talk about religious people doing religion in many places, we had to pick titles that are not always the same as the names people give themselves. Sometimes, in fact, the people we are interested in do not label themselves according to religions as others see them. While there are people who call themselves Christians, Jains or Pagans, it is unlikely that anyone says "I am a Chinese religionist" or "I am an indigenous religionist." However, our labels help us to think about whether there is something distinctive about the way(s) in which Chinese people do religion, or the distinctiveness of specifically indigenous religions. Even if they are an imperfect fit with how people name themselves, they are made for the purpose of introducing significant issues.

It is not only the more convoluted titles that might give rise to some question. Even labels that are commonly used about and by religious people are not really so very different. According to the story Christians tell about their origins, their name was forced upon them by others. The title "Hindu" was not common in India until the British and other European colonial powers thought they needed a name for religious activities that were neither Christian, Muslim, nor Buddhist. As you go on studying religions you will find that there are major debates about these naming and labelling processes. For now, it is sufficient to know that names are useful in making introductions. This is not so different from the way in which one of the first things people do when they are introduced is to exchange names ("hello, I'm Graham"). We know that the name does not say everything, so we go on asking questions or sharing further information. That is exactly what we will do here. Together our task is to use these names only as introductions — polite first steps in gaining understanding of more important matters.

It is also worth noting that just as my name does not tell you everything about me, nor does my job description. Knowing that I am a university lecturer does not tell you what else I do. That is fairly obvious. What might be far more interesting is to wonder how the other things I do interact with the way in which I perform my job as a lecturer. This is, after all, part of what makes me different to other people who do the same thing, and what makes the way I do the job different from the way others do it. Just so, once you know a religious label (whether it is one that practitioners use, like Baha'i, or one that they might not recognise, like "practitioner of a Korean new religion") you still have to find out more. Again, we have been careful in what we say about religions and religious people, but there remains more to be said. It is especially important (even if it is only mentioned here) that many people manage perfectly well to blend ideas and practices that others would insist belong to someone else's religion. In lived reality people are always learning from and reacting to or against other people. Although we cannot write about every religious person, we do want you to remember that religions are not stuck in boxes, each separate from the next, never influencing others. The truth is quite the opposite: religions are as messy as other areas of life. The regular cross-fertilization of acts and ideas is one of the most interesting features of religions.

Step 6: Vernacular Religion and Religioning

Here too, a little more is added to what has already been said. *Religions in Focus* introduces lived religions. As Leonard Primiano implies, lived religion is the only kind there is.[1] He calls this "vernacular religion" not to distinguish it from "official religion" represented by texts, creeds and leaders, but to insist that *all* religion is lived by people. Every religious person, every participant in religious activities, contributes to the current reality of their religion. Similarly, Malory Nye argues that we should talk about "religioning" rather than "religion," pointing to the performative, enacted, practiced nature of what religious people do.[2] Religion is a verb not a noun: an ever evolving activity, not a fixed, essential system.

These are important provocations of further thought and study. They are particularly useful in contrast with most other introductions to religions. These usually focus on founders and texts in preference to what people today do. They commonly divide religions into three categories: "world religions", "new religions" and "indigenous religions". The first alleged type suggests a small club of elite, "world class" religions – usually with a long history and texts that require expert interpreters. Do not mistake it for a label that simply says that these religions have a global presence. Almost all religions now have a global presence: there are, for example, Maori performing indigenous religious activities in London.[3] "World religions" are just as integrated into the contemporary era as any other religions, the antiquity of their origins is really not that influential in how people actually engage in them. "New" religions are rarely new by any means of counting — some were founded more than a hundred years ago, others evolved from far older traditions. The label "indigenous" can be mistakenly thought to limit the changeability, diversity or spread of such ways of being. All this is unhelpful.

Religions in Focus is only structured by a reverse alphabetical list, Z to B. While it includes religions that others might class as "world," "new," or "indigenous", the discussions resist such labels. Only in a few chapters do these labels appear—and that is only ever to show that reality is far more rich, exciting, and problematic than these seemingly neat distinctions suggest. In fact, what look like descriptive labels are polemical propaganda. On the occasions where *Religions in Focus* refers to them it is to demonstrate that there are better ways to engage in the study of religions.

1. Leonard N. Primiano, "Vernacular Religion and the Search for Method in Religious Folklife", *Western Folklore* 54, no.1 (1995): 37-56.

2. Malory Nye, "Religion, Post-religionism, and Religioning: Religious Studies and Contemporary Cultural Debates," *Method & Theory in the Study of Religion* 12 (2000): 447-76.

3. Graham Harvey, "Performing identity and entertaining guests: Maori diaspora in London," in *Indigenous Diasporas and Dislocation*, ed. Graham Harvey and Charlie Thompson (Aldershot: Ashgate, 2005), 121-34.

Defining Religion

Nowhere in this book do we offer a definition of religion. Although we insist that whatever religion is it is something that people do, we want to open rather than close this debate. Obviously we have included seventeen groups (of various kinds, with fluid boundaries, and so on), from Z to B. Scholars of religion (the authors of these chapters in particular) include these among the religions they teach about. As you read each chapter, it might be interesting to ask "what definition of religion arises from this religion?" or "how do *these* people define religion?" Often religion is defined from a Protestant Christian perspective as a set of beliefs in a divine being and as an activity focused on salvation. (Religious terms like "salvation" themselves need almost as much discussion.) Applying this to other religions has led to considerable confusion and misunderstanding. That alone is a good reason for not starting with a definition of religion, even a scholarly one!

In addition, the academic study of religion embraces a wide range of approaches that are also part of many other disciplines (e.g. anthropology, art history, cognitive science, gender studies, history, philology, philosophy, migration studies, ritual studies, sociology, theology). Some of these invite strong use of particular definitions of religion, for example, sociologists of religion offer definitions that privilege social activities. The religious people that we are interested in can be approached in many ways. *Religions in Focus* demonstrates the value of some (perhaps not all) approaches and invites an expansion of conversations between those with interests in specific aspects of religious realities.

In short, although we do not offer a definition of religion, nor do we apply only one approach to religion (whatever that is), all the authors in this book agree that as a foundation it is enough to begin by saying that "the activities studied by scholars of religion are religions." *Religions in Focus* is not, in the end, primarily a book about religions (and it is especially not only about seventeen religions!), but it offers itself as an introduction to the academic study of religions that invites further work. Although we do not raise flags, blow trumpets, or bang drums to alert our readers to the large methodological, theoretical, or critical questions that are an important part of the study of religions today, we do (explicitly or subtly) introduce significant issues in the chapters that follow. Our purpose is to encourage you (our readers and fellow students of religions) to contribute to these debates and to the increase of knowledge.

Going Further

Now it is time to engage with the chapters that follow. Many chapters cite other books that usefully continue this project of studying religions. We also offer a companion web site that provides more resources to enrich and enable your studies. This includes photographs and links to further web sites with texts and recordings. Religions are vibrant and fascinating phenomena that play vital roles in the lives of the majority of the world's population. The study of religions can be exciting and enjoyable as well as important. The hard work of keeping religions in focus is immensely rewarding, and we wish you well as you work with us.

1

Zoroastrians / Zarathushtis

Jenny Rose

Chisti and Bijan[1] celebrated their fortieth wedding anniversary in southern California in 2005. That in itself is an uncommon statistic in today's world. Another unusual aspect of the couple's marriage is that they belong to a religious tradition that at the beginning of the twenty-first century numbers only about 150,000 adherents. Both Chisti and Bijan are Zoroastrians. The Zoroastrian religion traces its origins to an Iranian is known in the West as Zoroaster, a name derived from Greek tradition. Nowadays, most Zoroastrians prefer the Iranian form of the name and refer to themselves as *Zarathushti* or *Zardushti*.

Chisti and her husband Bijan had different experiences growing up in the religion, since she was born in Iran of Iranian Zarathushti parents, while he was born in India of Parsi parents. The term "Parsi," meaning "Persian," refers to a Zarathushti whose family came to India in the centuries following the arrival of Islam in Iran.

Chisti's grandfather was a carpet merchant, who moved his family to India when Chisti's mother was still a baby. When Chisti's mother married a cousin from Tehran, she returned to Iran, where Chisti and her siblings were born. Chisti attended secondary school at the Anushirvan-e Dadgar in Tehran, a Zoroastrian school founded with financial assistance from the Parsi community in India. The school had a good reputation and was not restricted to Zoroastrians, but accepted girls from all religious backgrounds.

Although Chisti had already learnt many of the prayers by heart at home, it was in high school that her formal education in the teachings of her religion began, with weekly lessons conducted by a priest (*mobed*).

---

1. Both names have been changed at the participants' request.

These early experiences continue to shape many of her daily and seasonal religious practices.

From a young age, Chisti made yearly visits to Bombay (Mumbai) and Pune to spend summers with her aunts. As a young adult, she was sent to learn English at a Christian missionary school in a hill station[2] near Mumbai. During this time, she lived with a Parsi "auntie," who was on the lookout for a suitable husband for her charge, and who pushed Chisti to attend social functions in order to meet eligible men. On one of these occasions, she met Bijan, a young Parsi from Navsari in the Indian state of Gujarat, who had gone to college in the United States to study first engineering, then microbiology.

Navsari is one of the oldest Parsi communities in India. It was settled by Zarathushtis from Iran sometime around the twelfth or thirteenth century CE. Bijan was raised in an orthodox Parsi family on the west coast of India, but spent his early adult years as a student in a foreign country. Both he and Chisti grew up in a polyglot environment, learning English at school, speaking another language at home (Gujarati and Persian respectively), and using yet another language in prayer (Avestan). Because Chisti had lived in India sporadically for several years she was comfortable in the Parsi culture, a fact that facilitated the couple's relationship. In 1965, the two became engaged and married a month later.

Following Parsi tradition, the wedding rituals lasted seven days. They included planting a mango tree in a pot at the homes of both the bride and groom; the exchange of gifts between the couple, the ceremonial anointing of Chisti with milk and rose petals by three married women; and a bachelor party that involved Bijan being carried through the streets of his home town, Navsari, in a public declaration of his impending marriage. The couple was married in a *baug*, an open area belonging to the community, so that non-Parsi guests could attend. They sat facing each other with a cloth between them on a dais next to an *afargan*—a fire-holder containing a burning fire—and two Zarathushti priests wound a piece of thread loosely seven times around the seated couple to enclose them in a circle. As the seventh round was finished, the couple threw rice over each other. The senior priest fastened the ends of the thread together and then twisted it around the joined right hands of the couple seven times, whilst reciting the most sacred Avestan prayer, the *Yatha Ahu Vairyo*. After the final blessing the couple, now seated next to each other, paid reverence to the fire.

The day following the marriage, they each took a ritual shower before

---

2. A settlement in the hills of the Indian subcontinent where the temperate summer climate attracted government officials and civilians wishing to avoid the heat of the cities.

going to the Atash Behram, the highest grade of fire temple, to make an offering of sandalwood to the fire. On the third day after the wedding, Bijan and Chisti took the colorful hanging strings of flowers (*torans*) that had decorated the *baug*, some rice, sugar and rose petals and, standing on a bridge over a stream in Navsari, threw them into the water, whilst reciting a prayer to the waters (the *Aban Nyayesh*). This invocation of the vigor, fertility, and completeness that the waters represent appears to be an ancient custom amongst the Zarathushtis.

Bijan did not require the customary dowry[3] from his bride, as he felt the idea was old-fashioned and undignified. The couple experienced few cultural differences in the early years of their marriage, but some cultural preferences remain, even after forty years. Fortunately food is not one of those preferences, since Chisti prepares both Persian and Indian cuisine, sometimes in combination. Such culinary adaptability is not universal, however. One of the most contentious issues today at social gatherings of Parsis and Iranian Zarathushtis is that the food is either too spicy for the latter or not spicy enough for the former! The language difference also remains a source of division between the two groups, with the former using Gujarati and the latter Persian as their predominant language of prayer.

From the outset of their married life, the couple chose to celebrate the Zarathushti festival of Nav Ruz (New Day) in the spring, as it is in Iran, rather than in August as most Parsis do. Bijan feels that the current Parsi practice of adhering to a non-seasonally based calendar disregards the fact that most Zarathushti festivals are related to the cycle of the year. The spring equinox is the point in the earth's yearly turning when daylight begins to be longer than the night. It is regarded as a symbolic victory of light over darkness.

Zarathushti cosmological myth as recorded in the Middle Persian (Pahlavi) text, the *Bundahishn* (Creation), refers to the world as being made originally in a state of perfection, with all elements created first in "conceptual" or "mental" (Pahlavi, *menog*) state, and then embodied in "existent" or "living" (Pahlavi, *getig*) form. Before time began, the sun stood at noon in the sky and eternal spring prevailed. Although not all Zarathushtis accept this myth as dogma, they do recognize its metaphorical significance, and regard the festival of Nav Ruz as representing the possibility of the eventual renewal of the world—when the whole of creation will be restored to its original state. This concept is reflected in

3. A dowry is a sum of money or other goods brought by a woman to her marriage. In the case of the Parsis, the dowry is money or a portion of wealth given by the bride's father to the bridegroom's family.

Figure 1.1: *A* Nav Ruz *table with the* Haft Sin—*seven items beginning with the letter "s" that represent health and growth. (Photo courtesy of Jenny Rose.)*

the Parsi reference to the festival as Pateti, from *Patet*, meaning "Repentance." Classical authors indicate that the Ancient Persians held a festival at the time of the vernal equinox, and across the centuries Nav Ruz has remained the quintessential Iranian celebration, observed across various religions and Persian-speaking groups in the region.

When I approached Chisti and Bijan with the idea of writing about their personal experiences of the Zarathushti religion, they reacted with incredulity, claiming that they do not represent a "normative" approach to the religion, because their thinking and practice has changed significantly since their respective childhoods in Iran and India. But it is because of that very breadth of experience that such a case study as theirs provides an accessible introduction to the Zarathushti religion as a lived faith within the contemporary world. Not only do Chisti and Bijan offer a microcosmic view of the religion as a living actuality, they represent both the "gendered realities" of the male and female perspectives. Together, they also embody the two long-established Zarathushti communities—the early homeland of Iran and the subsequent place of refuge and resurgence, India. The move to India is sometimes referred to as "the first diaspora." The couple's relocation to America with the consequent demands and pressures of a new majority environment and its impact on their belief and practice, reflects the issues confronting the religion as it becomes established in the New World.

The relationship between Chisti and Bijan thus incorporates the range of customs, practices and beliefs found throughout the Zarathushti community at the beginning of the twenty-first century. The key concerns and issues facing the couple and their immediate community occur within the wider context of the development of the religion in the past couple of centuries, particularly in relation to the influence on both belief and praxis by the prevailing cultural dynamics of Iran and India and by Western thought and mores. Given their small numbers, Zarathushtis are a minority group everywhere, but in diaspora—that is, initially removed from the community institution of the anjuman (lay council responsible for community affairs) and a ritual life centered on an agiary/atashkadeh (fire temple)—they have been increasingly confronted with new questions concerning self-definition and normative practice.

What is "Zoroastrianism"?

Although traditional ways of life have changed radically for Zarathushtis in the last century due to the increase in education and urbanization and the shifts in family structure and employment, nonetheless many Zarathushtis in both rural and urban settings, in both Eastern and Western contexts, continue to profess beliefs that go back three millennia to the time of Zarathushtra and to perform ritual practices that date back at least fifteen hundred years if not earlier. To talk about "Zoroastrianism" is to use a late-nineteenth-century construct that has been imposed on the adherents of the religion by outsiders. Previously, Zarathushtis referred to themselves as "those of 'the good religion' or 'the good vision'" (*daena vanguhi*) or as *Mazdayasnian*, that is, "those who worship [Ahura] Mazda, the Wise [Lord]."

During the lengthy history of the Zarathushti Din the religion has morphed considerably to become the "ism" it is today. It is now impossible to recreate the original, "pristine" form of the religion or to presume to know the mind of its founder, but one can explore some aspects of the development of the religion through later written texts, both sacred and secular, and through ritual observance, both private and public. One must also consider the significance of centuries of interaction between the Zarathushti Din and other cultures, religions and philosophies.

It has been said that the religion of Zarathushtra "has probably had more influence [on humanity] directly and indirectly, than any other single faith."[4] Indeed, much has been written concerning the relation-

---

4. Mary Boyce, *Zoroastrians: Their Religious Beliefs and Practices* (London: Routledge, 2000), 1.

ship of Zoroastrian beliefs, particularly in the spheres of cosmology and eschatology, with those of other religions.[5]

In his philosophical poem *Also Sprach Zarathustra* (Thus Spoke Zarathushtra) one of the questions Friedrich Nietzsche[6] asks of his readers is "Who is Zarathushtra to us?" Throughout successive epochs Zarathushtra has appealed to European scholars and literati as the archetypal Wise Man who presents transformational or revolutionary answers to those difficult, ultimate questions concerning human existence. Although some readers might not have heard of "Zoroaster" until just now, the name has been known to Europeans since the Greeks first referred to his teaching in the mid-fifth century BCE. Nietzsche's work, however, was the first popular text to use the proper Iranian name, Zarathushtra, as opposed to the Greek version. When translated, Zarathushtra means something like "[driver of] old camels," although popular translations include "golden light/dawn" and "gold star." The latter held particular appeal for Nietzsche, who discovered this meaning coincidentally, after writing part 1 of *Also Sprach Zarathustra*.[7]

Zarathushtra is now thought to have lived around three thousand years ago in the steppe lands of Central Asia, and his teachings to have taken root amongst the Iranian people before they moved south and west towards what became the country of Iran. Those teachings became the religious basis for the three great Iranian empires, which spanned over a thousand years from the mid-sixth-century BCE to the mid-seventh century CE, until the incursion of Islam. The three empires are the Achaemenids or Ancient Persians (550-330 BCE); the Parthians (c. 250 BCE -224 CE); and the Sasanians (224-651 CE). Middle Persian works concerning the life of Zarathushtra, such as the *Denkard* and *Wizidagiha-i Zadspram* reflect a legendary, rather than historical, representation of Zarathushtra. Late ninth- and early-tenth-century texts celebrate such qualities of Zarathushtra as "wisdom," "compassion" and "the performance of good deeds." He is perceived as one who advocated moderation—"the right measure" (Pahlavi, *payman*)—in all things, emphasizing justice and morality, rather than extremist revolutionary or ascetic behaviour.

Until the end of the twentieth century, most scholars accepted as a

5. See, for example, John R. Hinnells, *Zoroastrian and Parsi Studies: Selected Works of John R. Hinnells* (Burlington: Ashgate, 2000), 45-92.

6. Friedrich Wilhelm Nietzsche (1844-1900) was a German philosopher and classical philologist who criticized what he considered to be the stultifying impact of traditional philosophy and religion.

7. Jenny Rose, *The Image of Zoroaster: The Persian Mage through European Eyes* (New York: Bibliotheca Persica), 176, 190 n17.

given that the *Gathas*, the "songs" ascribed to Zarathushtra, were the work of a single mind. This remains the position of Zoroastrians and of the majority of scholars, as epitomized in recent linguistic analyses of the composition of the *Gathas*.[8] But some philologists contend that the *Gathas* were composed by a group of ritualists led by Zarathushtra, and this approach has in turn led to a challenge to the historicity of Zarathushtra.[9] Zoroastrians are understandably perturbed by this development, and in the summer of 2006 the newly formed Society of Scholars of Zoroastrianism organized a conference in Chicago at which community members and academics discussed their various approaches to the religion.

By the 1880s, when Nietzsche was writing *Also Sprach Zarathustra*, many of the teachings ascribed to Zarathushtra had been translated from their original Iranian languages of Avestan and Pahlavi into English, French and German. Such teachings, along with equally ancient Hindu texts, had particular appeal for authors such as Nietzsche, who were looking for dramatic protagonists outside the Jewish and Christian tradition.

In Nietzsche's work, Zarathushtra is presented as an enlightened guru—a teacher from an eastern background, who descends from his solitary contemplation in the mountains to challenge received notions of Greek philosophy and Christian morality. Although Nietzsche manipulated the image of Zarathushtra to meet his own needs as a literary construct, he states at one point that his motive for choosing Zarathushtra was because he recognized him as "being more truthful than any other thinker," and "as the first to see in the struggle between good and evil the actual wheel in the working of things."[10]

This ethical dualism—the constant struggle between good and evil played out in history—is, in fact, a key Zoroastrian teaching. The *Gathas* speak of the primordial existence of "two fundamental spirits (*mainyu*) of existence," one of which is incremental, the other evil. The Avestan word *mainyu* (Pahlavi *menog*) can be translated as "mental impulse," or "(religious) inspiration." Later texts identify these two impulses as *Spenta Mainyu*, the "bounteous spirit" that promotes wholeness, increase, and

8. For example, Almut Hintze, "On the Literary Structure of the Older Avesta," *Bulletin of the School of Oriental and African Studies* 65 (2002): 31-51, and Martin Schwartz, "How Zarathushtra Generated the Gathic Corpus," *Bulletin of the Asia Institute* 16 (December 2006): 53-64.

9. For example, Jean Kellens, *Essays on Zarathustra and Zoroastrianism* (Costa Mesa: Mazda Publishers, 2000); P.O. Skjaervø, "Zarathushtra: First Poet-Sacrificer," in *Paitimana*, ed. Siamak Adhami (Costa Mesa: Mazda Publishers, 2003),157-94.

10. Friedrich Nietzsche, *Ecce Homo*, trans. R.J. Hollingdale (Harmondsworth: Penguin, 1983), 3.

life, and *Angra Mainyu* (Pahlavi: *Ahriman*), the "destructive spirit" that is the source of all suffering, lies, pollution, and death. *Angra Mainyu*, as the spirit of counter-creation, or not-life, threatens the good creation of *Ahura Mazda* (translated as "the Wise [Lord]"), who exists eternally. The emphasis of the teaching in the *Gathas* is that human beings were created to take part in the personal, social, and cosmic battle against the onslaught of such destruction, particularly in its form of "bad thoughts, bad words, bad deeds," until eventually the world will be rid of evil and "revitalized" (Avestan, *frasho.kereti*).

At the core of the Gathic presentation of the cosmos and humanity's place within the world is the concept of *Asha*, a term cognate with Sanskrit *Rta*, meaning cosmic, social, or ritual "order." In the *Gathas*, *Asha* becomes linked with moral order, with its idea of rightness as concrete and knowable—the concept of "truth." This is contrasted with the concept of *Druj*, the "lie"—that cosmic deception that brings chaos and confusion to the good creations of *Ahura Mazda*.

Everyone, regardless of status or gender, is constantly faced with a choice between following the path of *Asha* or that of *Druj*. One verse of the *Gathas* begins:

> Listen with your ears to the best things
> reflect with a clear mind,
> each person for himself
> upon the two choices of decision… (*Yasna* 30.2)

The one who chooses *Asha*—the *ashavan*—is a just, upright, "truthful" being, one who exemplifies "good thoughts, good words, good deeds" (Avestan: *humata, hukhta, hvarshta*). This short, but powerful maxim is considered to be a succinct summary of the Zarathushti ethic. The *Gathas* tell how the *ashavan* shall, at the end, enter into the "foremost existence" and dwell in the "house of song" (*Y.* 51.15).

In contrast, the *dregvant*, who chooses *Druj*, is someone who utters untruthful statements about *Ahura Mazda* and the constituents of the ordered cosmos, bringing chaos. The acts of wrath, violence, and oppression of the *dregvant* shall lead to the "worst existence" (*Y.* 30.4) forever in the "house of deceit" (*Y.* 46.11). This state is described in the *Gathas* in terms of darkness, bad nourishment, misery, degeneration and destruction (*Y.* 30.10f.; 31.20; 53.6-9). The notion that one has a choice in this life as to the decisions one makes implies that the worst existence is initially experienced in the here and now by those who make the wrong choice. For those Zarathushtis who believe in an afterlife, the life of degeneracy and delusion, if unchecked, is thought to lead the soul to cry "woe" even after death. The concept of separate domains of heaven and hell are expounded in later texts, beginning with the Young Avestan *Videvdad* and *Hadokht Nask*.

This contrast between two moral choices is echoed in the inscriptions of Darius I (reigned 521- 486 BCE), where the king describes his institution as ruler by the "great god" *Ahura Mazda* whose role as establisher of the good is celebrated. Darius emphasizes that he received the support of *Ahura Mazda* because he was "not hostile, nor a lie-follower," nor a wrongdoer, "acting crookedly," but because he had behaved with rectitude, "following the straight path," treating all equally and with justice. A short time later, the Greek historian Herodotus (484-c. 425 BCE), in his description of the Persians, mentions that above all things they consider telling lies the most disgraceful (*Histories*, I.136).

The choice between "order" and "chaos," "truth" and "deception," is understood by Zarathushtis to relate not just to a mental decision, but also to physical action. The *Gathas* reflect an understanding that both the conceptual and material spheres of existence are part of the realm of *Ahura Mazda*, which is prone to be assaulted by destructive forces.

Some Zarathushtis understand these negative impulses to be purely the products of human mentality, rather than an external cause. They take the position that *Ahura Mazda* creates humans with the freedom to choose between two fundamentally opposite ways of thinking—the one incremental (*spenta*) and good, the other detrimental (*angra*) and bad. This is the position of the "*Gatha*-only" school of thought: that is, those for whom the *Gathas* are the only authoritative teachings, since all later texts are considered to include extraneous material, particularly relating to ritual.

Other Zarathushtis maintain that there is allusion to a cosmological as well as ethical dualism in the *Gathas* that is elaborated upon in later texts, such as the *Bundahishn*. This perspective construes evil as a distinct reality in both the *menog* and *getig* realm, deriving from a source that is completely separate from and opposed to the good creation of *Ahura Mazda*.

In the ninth century CE, a Zarathushti theologian, Mardanfarrokh, wrote in his *Shkand Gumanig Vizar* (Doubt-Dispelling Exposition) that the very essence of *Ahura Mazda* was of absolute goodness, and, as such, was completely antithetical to, and apart from, the nature of evil. Such an understanding leads to the theological postulation that *Ahura Mazda* is omniscient, but is not responsible for any of the afflictions in the world, since good can never give rise to evil. By this account *Ahura Mazda*, although perfect, will not become omnipotent until the forces of evil, which have a finiteness and limited power, have been overcome through the aid of the faithful.

Debate between these so-called "monotheist" and "dualist" cosmol-

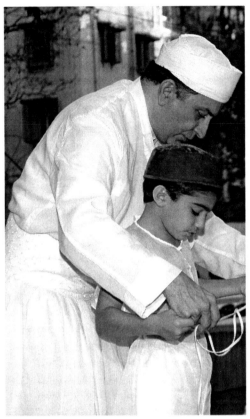

Figure 1.2: *A child's* navjote, *performed in Dallas. Photo courtesy of the Balsara family.*

ogies has been divisive in the past, but a joint Parsi-Iranian collaboration published by the Federation of Zoroastrian Associations of North America (FEZANA) in 1998 entitled *The Zara-thushti Religion: A Basic Text* incorporated the range of perspectives in a teaching resource that was intended for widespread use.[11] The two main perspectives are also discussed in a 2002 FEZANA supplement entitled *The Legacy of Zarathush-tra.*[12] Such materials leave the way open for a non-prescriptive approach to the religion, which is appealing to many young Zara-thushtis, particularly those in the western diaspora.

Despite their diverse interpretations as to the source of evil, all Zara-thushtis recognize the ethical imperative of the *Gathas* for the *ashavan* to be alert at all times to withstand the urge to think, speak or act negatively. One of the ways that ethical conduct has been encouraged amongst Zarathushtis through the centuries has been through the donning of the distinguishing garments of the initiate: the *sudreh*, the white cotton shirt worn under one's daily clothing; and the *kusti*, the cord worn around the waist over the shirt.

For many Zarathushtis, the practice of wearing the *sudreh* and *kusti* acts as a constant reminder of their duty to heed the teachings of Zarathush-tra. The Parsi initiate is referred to as the *Navjote*, meaning "new person who offers prayers." The equivalent Persian term for the initiation cer-

---

11. Khojeste P. Mistree and Mobed Fariborz Sohrab Shahzadi, *The Zarathusti Religion: A Basic Text* (Chatsworth, Calif., FEZANA), 1998.

12. "The Legacy of Zarathushtra: An Introduction to the Religion, History and Culture of the Zarathushtis (Zoroastrians)," FEZANA *Journal*, Summer 2002.

emony is *Sedreh pushi*, "the putting on of the sacred shirt." The *navjote/ sedreh pushi* ceremony is the same for boys and girls. Once initiated, the Zoroastrian child is meant to be responsible for her or his own actions, thoughts and words. Traditionally, the Zoroastrian age of religious maturity was fifteen years old, but since initiations are now usually performed in public, they take place before a child reaches puberty for reasons of modesty.

The *sudreh* symbolizes simplicity and purity and is worn as an undergarment like a vest. It has a small pocket at the front to remind the initiate that she should store up good deeds during her lifetime. The *kusti* is a cord woven from seventy-two strands of lamb's wool and blessed by prayers. It is tied in a special way during ritual prayer. A knot in the front affirms the importance of performing good actions, and the knot in the back affirms that the wearer will champion the cause of truth. If worn constantly, the *sudreh* and *kusti* are removed before having a bath. Both garments are washed regularly and replaced when they become worn out.

Such public observance of tradition has become one of those issues of "normative practice" that Bijan and Chisti have had to confront personally. Although Bijan discarded the wearing of the sacred garments for a time during his early student days in the United States, he chose to resume this tradition after marriage, at a time when he became more interested in studying the faith for his own spiritual development. Bijan's choice to wear the sacred garments and say the accompanying prayers is an action that helps to focus his intentionality. He provides a cosmological basis for his decision to observe the *kusti bastan* (*kusti* tying), referring to a Pahlavi passage in which a father explains to his son the reason for tying the cord around the waist with the words: "The body of man is a world in miniature" (from *Chem-i-kusti Bastan*; another Pahlavi text, *Denkard* 3.263, reiterates the idea that humans are a kind of summary of the world). Bijan recognizes that humans are a microcosmic representation of the macrocosm; what each human does both reflects and has an impact on the cosmos. Most Zarathushti ritual can be viewed as an activity that humans engage in to revitalize both themselves and the cosmos. This conception of humans as agents of healing in the world is an ancient notion, found in the *Gathas* and integral to the Zarathushti ethos.

Parsis in general tend to be more punctilious than Iranian Zarathushtis about wearing the *sudreh* and *kusti* every day, but then the Parsi community in India has not had to survive the depredations experienced by their Iranian co-religionists in the past few centuries. The threat of taunts or worse from the majority community caused most Iranian Zarathushtis to put on the *sudreh* and *kusti* only when they visited the *atashkadeh* (fire temple). Most fire temples in Iran have a separate room, where spare garments are kept for those who do not own them or who forget to bring them. For Chisti, however, the regular donning of the *sudreh* and the tying of the *kusti* are physical acts that she finds morally and emotionally supportive. When she wraps the *kusti* around her like a belt, she says that she feels "surrounded with God's blessing."

It is because they do not always wear the sacred garments that Iranian Zarathushtis have occasionally been barred from some Parsi *agiaries* (fire temples) in India. The regular exclusion not only of non-Parsis but also the spouses and children of intermarried Parsi women remains a cause for tension within the community in India, where some consider the religion to be patrilineal. This means that the children of Parsi fathers are initiated, but not those of non-Parsi fathers. In August 2005, the newly created Association for the Revival of Zoroastrianism (ARZ) opened a prayer hall in Mumbai designated specifically for the families of Parsi women who have married out. This enabled the *navjotes* of the latter to be performed in a public, congregational ceremony, rather than in private at home, as they had to date.

Anxiety concerning discrimination has affected public observance within the diaspora community. Bijan and Chisti's son was teased at grade school for wearing the *sudreh* and *kusti*, and Chisti remembers one incident when her son had removed his *kusti* for physical-education class, and the other boys picked it up to use as a skipping rope! In such circumstances, many choose to abandon the garments altogether, since opportunities for combating such ignorance and disrespect are considered to be limited or futile.

But decisions concerning observance are not only made for pragmatic reasons. Many Zarathushtis today claim that the wearing of the *sudreh* and *kusti* has no material value but is more of a psychological prop or a symbolic gesture, and for that reason choose not to wear the garments at all after initiation. Such attitude tends to go hand in hand with the rejection of anything that could be construed as superstition or that is not compatible with modern science. The same approach applies to covering the head during prayer. Bijan recalls that older or more traditional women amongst the Parsi community, such as his grandmother, wore a headscarf (*mathubanu*) at all times, but that his own mother did not cover her hair, except with her sari, when she attended the fire temple. The California Zoroastrian Center in Westminster provides head coverings for anyone who wishes to wear them, but they are not compulsory.

When my own grandmother—a Parsi who had left India in the early twentieth century to train as a nurse in London—was well into her eighties and experiencing short-term memory loss, she nonetheless recalled with great clarity the rituals and practices associated with her childhood in Rawalpindi and Mumbai. She remembered in particular the *kusti bastan* and other daily devotional prayers. The most important and therefore well-known prayers that form a central part of a Zarathushti child's education date back to the time of the *Gathas*. The *Yatha Ahu Vairyo* (or *Ahuna Vairya, Ahunvar*) and the *Ashem Vohu* are mantric utterances in Old Avestan that are still taught orally from one generation to the next. The *Ahunvar* is a short prayer in honour of *Ahura Mazda* and is spoken at every act of public or private devotion. It is said to be so holy and powerful that it may, in need, replace all other acts of worship. The *Ashem Vohu* is a highly poetic text that often functions as a meditational prayer.

The tradition of oral recitation dates back to before the time of Zarathushtra, when the correct intonation of a mantra (Old Avestan: *manthra*) was believed to reveal the power and vision it embodied. Since oral transmission was an integral part of the religion until recently, it did not matter that the laity could not read the prayers as they could recite many of them by heart, despite their limited knowledge of Avestan. In both Iran and India a child's education in these prayers was often undertaken by the mother or grandmother in the home, or sometimes by a priest at the local fire temple. This changed somewhat with the introduction of Zoroastrian schools in the mid-nineteenth century, when teachers would also undertake basic religious education. In diaspora, Zarathushtis now receive most of their teaching concerning the religion at local Zoroastrian centers, where introductory classes are offered for both children and adults in aspects of Zoroastrian history, the *Gathas*, and the Avestan language. Such was the case for Bijan and Chisti's children, although they learnt to recite their prayers with their parents. These classes are supplemented by lecture series and talks. Similar programs are offered through the *anjumans* in Iran and India.

Most older Zarathushtis are not accustomed to reading their prayers, since they learnt them by heart as children. Those who do use a text often cannot read Avestan, so they rely on a transcription of the prayers in Gujarati, Arabic or Latin script. Several American Zarathushti Associations have produced translations of the prayers in English, so that the young can understand them and feel that they are participating in a devotional dialogue, rather than just reciting incomprehensible words by rote. This approach is somewhat at variance with the ancient perspective that it is only by reciting the prayers in the original language of Zarathushtra, with devotion and intent, that one can activate the spiritual energies to which they refer.

Since the latter part of the twentieth century, the education of the laity in the basic tenets and practices of the religion has become a pressing matter, as Zoroastrians in both their ancestral homelands and in diaspora confront the reality that there are not enough people training for the priesthood, and that few members of the community are qualified or willing to undertake the education of the laity in religious matters.

The priesthood in both India and Iran, which traditionally has been a hereditary male profession, has lost much of the respect that it had in previous generations. Wages for priests are relatively low compared with other professions, and the role is demanding, particularly in terms of its require-

Ashem vohu	ٱٮڒڰ؏ ٮڛٮٯ
Vahishtem asti	ٱٮٮڛٯ ٮڛٮٯ٭ٯٮٯٲ
Ushta asti	ٲٮٯٮٯ ٮٯٮٯٮٯ
Ushta ahmai	ٮٯٮٮٯ ٮٯٮٯٮٯ
Hyat Ashai	ٮٯٮٮٯ ٷٮٯٮٯ
Vahishtai Ashem	ٰٰ ٮٯٮٯٮٯ ٮٯٮٯٮٯٮٯٲ

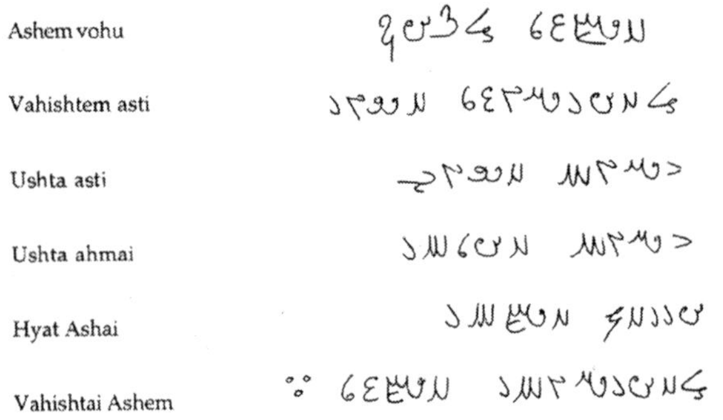

Figure 1.3: *The Ashem Vohu prayer in Avestan script.*

ments regarding personal purity and education in the sacred texts, which are composed in long-dead languages. Fewer men from priestly families are opting to become full-time priests. Some receive enough basic training to meet the needs of their local community as an "assistant priest" (*mobedyar*), but choose to pursue a lay career in the outside world as their source of income and status. Pahlavi texts make the distinction between various categories of priests and the laity, who are referred to collectively as *behdinan*, the Middle Persian form of *vanguhi daena*. Many *behdinan* feel that even those who do become fully qualified as priests often lack the requisite communication skills to convey the inner meaning of the rituals they perform, let alone address the plethora of questions raised by the laity concerning the spiritual application of the faith.

For several decades, communities in both Iran and India have had no residential priest, and the laity have increasingly assumed responsibility for conducting certain rituals. Although not from a priestly family, Bijan is a *mobedyar* by training, and in this capacity he performs initiation ceremonies, weddings, and *jashans* (ceremonies of thanksgiving and praise) and helps to guide the ritual life of the local community. Bijan trained for his priestly duties in Mumbai, but was initiated in America by two Parsi *mobeds* (priests).

The community remains divided in terms of its attitude toward the acceptance into the priesthood of candidates from non-priestly background. Several self-designated "traditionalist" groups, such as the Athravan Educational Trust in India, have raised funds to be allocated to the training of boys from priestly families and their subsequent full-time employment and commensurate remuneration. "Reformists," on the other hand, often dispute the notion that Zarathushtra was himself a priest and claim therefore that any member of the laity, with the proper education, can assume the role of religious teacher and leader. According to one Pahlavi text, *Shayest ne Shayest*, there is no prohibition against women reciting the liturgy (*Yasna*) or other Avestan scriptures, and some do; but no woman in the modern period has yet attempted the performance of priestly functions, although the possibility was hotly debated at the Second World Youth Congress held in London in 1997.

Bijan considers ritual to be a crucial dimension of the religion, bringing individuals in the community together whether to celebrate or to console. He maintains that humans need ritual and prayer to make sense of their place in the world, and that it is important to bring people together

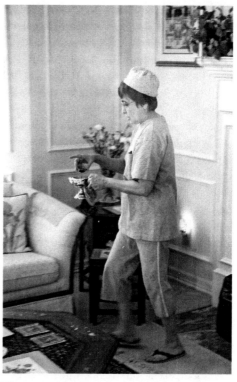

Figure 1.4: *A Parsi woman performing the* loban *ritual around the house. Each day, Chisti's mother would take a small fire-holder* (afargan) *with incense* (loban) *around each room of the house. She would chant a prayer for the well being of the family. The sweet, pungent smell of the incense was intended to imbue the house and its occupants with good thoughts—and also to keep the bugs away. This practice incorporates the understanding that both the* menog *and* getig *worlds are to be cared for and sustained by the faithful. (Photo by Jenny Rose).*

to encourage both learning and personal spiritual growth. Others regard ritual as not original to the teachings of Zarathushtra, but an element from earlier Iranian practice that was reintroduced at a later stage in the development of the religion. Apart from a handful of seasonal celebrations, and community gatherings on special occasions, the religion tends to be one of personal acts of devotion for the laity.

For Chisti, these community rituals such as the celebration of *gahambars* (seasonal festivals) provide a sense of *hambandegi*, that is, a "connectedness in prayer" with her co-religionists. This idea is expressed most obviously in the *jashan*, a communal ceremony that helps to bring people closer together in times of sadness as well as times of joy. Sometimes a *jashan* is performed in a large hall, so that as many of the community as possible can gather together. But sometimes it takes place in a person's home, when only the family and close friends are invited. During the *jashan*, Zarathushtis give thanks to *Ahura Mazda* for all the blessings they have received and pray for more blessings in the future. Participants in the *jashan* recognize that the objects used in the ceremony have a symbolic connection with the elements of creation, such as water, plants, fruit, milk, and fire. These are all set out on a large white cloth, which represents the earth itself. The *jashan* is not, then, just celebrating the well-being of humans, but also the conceptual and material (*menog* and *getig*) well-being of the world and all its elements. Bijan interprets the ritual as generating a link between the mundane and the divine.

A more formal priestly liturgy, conducted on a regular basis at a fire temple with a source of natural water such as a well or stream, is the *yasna* ceremony. The *yasna* is performed in the morning during the *havan gah* (the period from dawn until noon), and takes about two and a half hours to complete. At least two priests officiate, and both must be in a state of ritual purity, just as the physical location and all the ritual implements used in the act of worship must be ritually cleansed and consecrated. Such emphasis on purification expresses the belief that that which is sacred and good is metaphysically different from that which is polluted. From this perspective, devotion and ritual practice can only be efficacious if personal and communal purity is ensured.

The focus of the *yasna* revolves around the preparation of consecrated elements to be offered to the waters at the end of the liturgy. In India, this libation consists of dried *hom* twigs, the sap of pomegranate leaves, and milk, plus consecrated water: it thus includes elements from both the plant and animal realms. The ritual relates to an ancient understanding of the waters as bringing nourishment and vigour to all the waters of creation, which in turn sustain all life. Zarathushtis have always displayed reverence for the waters as a source of "wholeness" (Old Avestan: *haurvatat*) and life. In his comments regarding the religion of the Ancient Persians, Herodotus notes their self-imposed restrictions to keep the waters pure by not urinating, spitting, or washing their hands in them (*Histories* 1.138). This concern for the living waters of the rivers, lakes and oceans is repeated across the centuries by foreign observers, as well as in the Pahlavi texts, and is continued by Zarathushtis today.

In the Old Avestan liturgical text, the *Yasna Haptanhaiti*, several physical elements, including the cosmic waters and fire, are invoked as divine beings. Although *Ahura Mazda* is the only divinity mentioned by name in the *Gathas*, the concept of friendship (*Airyaman*) appears to be hypostatized in the ancient prayer, *Airyemo ishyo* (*Y.* 54.1), and several other abstract concepts are referred to in this manner in Old Avestan. In later texts, these entities come to form a fixed series of six, which, along with *Ahura Mazda*, both reflect the divine qualities that guide the faithful, and also act to protect the seven elements of creation. Together this group is known as the *Amesha Spentas*, the "Life-increasing Immortals." They consist of the following concepts and their respective creations: *Vohu Manah*, "Good Thought" (cattle/animals); *Asha Vahishta*, "Best Order/ Right" (fire); *Khshathra Vairya* "Worthy Rule" (sky); *Spenta Armaiti*, "Life-increasing Faithfulness" (earth); *Haurvatat*, "Wholeness" (water); and *Ameretat*, "Continuity of Life" (plants). These qualities are said to "form the core of the ethical infrastructure of the religion," which incorporates the belief that each Zarathushti should strive "towards generating harmony within creation." [13]

Although all the elements of the world are important in Zarathushti teaching, fire is the most significant in the rituals that take place in the home and the temple. In the *Gathas*, fire is linked explicitly with *Asha*, the order that pervades and regulates the world, and is thus the emblem of *Ahura Mazda*, providing strength and courage to the faithful. One verse refers to "the fire that possesses strength through *Asha*," which is "of clear help to the supporter of *Ahura Mazda*" (*Y.* 34.4) As a visual index, fire has been central to Zarathushti worship since the earliest stages of the religion.

As expressions of a personal vision, the *Gathas* do not refer much to ritual, but they do make frequent reference to fire, which is a common Indo-Iranian motif, present at all rituals. Even today, wherever possible, Zarathushtis say their dawn and sundown prayers facing the sun, the greatest natural fire. Otherwise, a lamp or the hearth fire can substitute: at one time the latter was the main source of light and warmth inside the house.

This focus on the natural elements was first recorded by Herodotus, who related that the Persians had no temples or statues, but worshipped outside on mountains, and that for them God was "the whole circle of the heavens." Excavation at Pasargadae, the administrative center established by Cyrus the Great around 540 BCE, revealed two white stone fire-holders that stand just above waist height, with a three-tiered top and base. It is thought that rituals were conducted outside in front of the burning fire, and this is supported by the iconography on Persian royal tombs,

---

13. Mistree and Shahzadi, *The Zarathusti Religion*, 14ff., 178ff.

Figure 1.5: *Fire in modern* atashkadeh *(fire temple) in Yazd, Iran. (Photo by Jenny Rose.)*

which depict the king standing on a three-tiered raised platform in an attitude of reverence before a blazing fire in a similar kind of fire holder. More formal buildings to hold established fires seem to have been introduced around the fourth century BCE.

Fire remains a powerful symbol for Zarathushtis throughout the world, although they are concerned to point out that they are not "fire worshippers" and resent being referred to as such. Most Zarathushtis are still careful not to defile a burning fire in any way. Priests will cover their mouth with a cloth *padan* when engaged in any ritual, so as not to pollute the fire with their breath or saliva. Even though social attitudes have changed considerably in the last century, and many of the purity laws advocated in later texts are no longer rigidly adhered to, women in menses may also take particular care not to come into contact with fire. Many women do not visit the fire temple during this time, nor attend public festivals when fire is present, such as marriages, initiations, or funeral ceremonies.

Chisti chose not to participate in public prayer when menstruating and to maintain a respectful distance from the fire, whether in the *agiary* or at a community ritual in a *baug* or a private home. Some menstruating women do not perform any daily domestic rituals that involve being near fire, such as cooking or lighting the lamp for the daily prayers at dawn. Chisti's avoidance of touching sacred books or objects whilst on her cycle is also quite common.

Bijan describes how his mother and sisters slept on a mattress on an iron bed frame in a separate room during menses, and that the women in his family would keep apart for forty days after childbirth. During this time, a mother would place her newborn child on a cloth on the floor. Other women then picked up the baby to care for it, avoiding direct physical contact with the new mother. The maintenance of physical distance, and the use of a non-porous metal bed and utensils for food, and old clothes and bedding kept for these times all relate to an understanding that menstruation and childbirth involve pollution of the material world. Such restrictions are elaborated upon in the Young Avestan *Videvdad* and later Middle Persian texts, which teach that everything leaving the body—including blood, urine, hair cuttings, nail clippings, and saliva—is ritually impure.

Despite the decline of the notion that such bodily discharges are polluting not just of the individual, but potentially of the community and other created elements, many Zarathushtis still adhere to certain practices of separation and reintegration following these transitional moments. For instance, some women still isolate themselves for a month or so after childbirth, and couples will often take a shower after intercourse. Most women, such as Chisti, would say that they do this primarily for reasons of hygiene and health, since they regard the stringent regulations of the Videvdad as outdated and having little to do with their understanding of the Zarathushti Din. Some Zarathushtis, however, retain the belief that the body is as susceptible to assault as the mind and must therefore be kept in as pure a state as possible. This approach is particularly observed by the Kshnoomist Zarathushtis, who belong to a mystical movement that originated in Mumbai in the nineteenth century.

The ancient belief that dead matter is polluting has affected Zarathushti funerary practices since early times. Both Greek and Iranian texts indicate that it was a Persian custom to expose the dead to birds and animals, so as not to pollute the elements of creation, particularly fire, earth, and water. Herodotus states that the Persian practice concerning the burial of the dead "is something of a mystery" in that a body of a male was not buried until it had been "torn by a dog or a bird" (*Histories*, 1.140). He then adds that in general, the Persians "cover a body in wax and then bury it." From the time of Cyrus the Great, the kings of all three Iranian dynasties were entombed in stone. It seems that the practice of exposure was an eastern Iranian custom (as evidenced by ossuaries found in Central Asia and Khorasan) that existed alongside western practices of embalming and primary burial. Cyrus' impressive stone tomb is still standing at Pasargadae, and those of Darius and later Achaemenid kings near or at Persepolis.

Until the mid-twentieth century, the most common funerary practice in both Iran and India was to place the body of a dead person in the stone *dakhma*, called by European travelers "Towers of Silence," where vultures would strip the flesh in about twenty to thirty minutes. The remaining bones would be bleached clean and dry in the sun, then collected by designated Zarathushtis and placed in a central pit to await the final physical resurrection.

As the Zoroastrian community modernized or moved away from India and Iran, so the practice of burial in stone or cement tombs was adopted, and death rituals were modified accordingly. In 1862 Brookwood Cemetery, located about thirty miles southwest of London, was the first private burial ground to allocate a separate section to Zoroastrians. Many Zarathushtis from Europe are buried there, including several members of the prominent Tata family.

In 1937, the Tehran Zarathushtis built a cemetery (*aramgah*) and abandoned the *dakhma*, which had been built nearly a century earlier under the aegis of the Society for the Amelioration of the Conditions of the Zoroastrians in Persia. The *dakhmas* established by the Amelioration Society in Yazd and Kerman continued in use until the 1960s, when they too were relinquished in favor of nearby Zarathushti cemeteries.

A further impetus for change occurred towards the end of the twentieth century, as the area around the *dakhmas* in Mumbai became more built up. One *dakhma* had to be closed because the residents in a nearby tower block could see right into it. Then the number of local South Asian vultures began to decline to the extent that the corpses were not being disposed of in a timely fashion. It is now thought that this sudden decrease was due to the vultures' exposure to the anti-inflammatory drug Diclofenac, used to treat both humans and cattle. Traditionalists have introduced various methods to address this problem, including funding studies into the feasibility of breeding vultures and the placement of solar panels around one of the towers in order to desiccate the bodies. Zoroastrian journals have devoted many editorial columns and letters pages to the discussion of this delicate and emotionally charged topic.

Although burial is now the preferred method of disposal for most Zarathushtis outside Mumbai, some Parsis feel that since cremation is still practiced by the Hindus, with whom they share the closest common ancestry, this means of disposal is also acceptable. When Bijan's mother passed away in Mumbai in 2006, her body was cremated according to her wishes, and a priest conducted her funeral rituals. Such was also the case with Freddie Mercury (born Farrokh Bulsara), lead singer of Queen, who died in 1991 and was cremated following a funeral conducted by a Zoroastrian priest.

Perhaps the major issue facing Zarathushtis at the beginning of the twenty-first century is their own steady decline in numbers, highlighted in a worldwide census collated and published in *FEZANA Journal* in the winter of 2004. This decrease is caused by several factors, the most noticeable being the low birth rate. The Parsi community in India is predominantly an older population (in 2001, 31 percent were over sixty years old), partly because many younger Parsis go abroad for their tertiary education and stay to pursue careers in other countries. Those Parsis who do remain are being encouraged to have two or more children, but not all couples are persuaded to take up this mission.

Editorials in that issue of *FEZANA Journal* and subsequent Zarathushti publications, such as *Parsiana*, published in Mumbai, suggest that the demographic crisis now facing the worldwide Zarathushti community could be resolved on two fronts. The first, and least controversial approach, involves providing the impetus for those who were born of Zarathushti parents to remain within the faith, in order to sustain its growth. The second course of action entails a re-definition of who a Zarathushti is. This is the topic that causes the most anguish, particularly for Parsis, since access to the community infrastructure on the Indian subcontinent is through one's Parsi or Irani Zarathushti heritage. By its very existence, the ARZ challenges the notion that birth to a Parsi father is a necessary pre-requisite to being a Zarathushti, through its assertion that the mother is equally a practitioner of the Zarathushti Din, and that any child of a parent of either gender should have access to the rituals of the religion. In Iran and parts of Central Asia, the self-identification of a Zarathushti has been broadened wider to include individuals who claim Zoroastrian ancestry from ancient times. And amongst certain groups in America and Europe the definition has extended even further, to include individuals who have no Zoroastrian "ethnic" heritage, but who have personal conviction and have been initiated.

Despite their conventional upbringings in devout Zarathushti homes, Chisti and Bijan recognize and embrace the fact that there have been many changes in their religion during their lengthy marriage to one another. They regard this as part of the natural development and progress of any religion in the modern world, and take a sanguine view of the future advancement of the Zarathushti Din. They are optimistic that those who choose to follow the teachings of Zarathushtra in the New World will do so with a consciousness and attentiveness that will galvanize the spiritual awareness of Zarathushtis "back home." On a personal level, they believe that their personal practice and community ritual, informed by the teachings of the *Gathas*, provide a balanced model of faith: the outward expression of inner prayer.

Suggestions for Further Reading

Boyce, Mary. *Textual Sources for the Study of Zoroastrianism.* Chicago: University of Chicago Press, 1990.

Clark, Peter. *Zoroastrianism: An Introduction to An Ancient Faith.* Brighton: Sussex Academic Press, 1998.

Godrej, P., and F. Mistree, eds. *A Zoroastrian Tapestry: Art, Religion & Culture.* Ahmedabad, India: Mapin Publishing, 2002.

Hinnells, John. *The Zoroastrian Diaspora.* Oxford: Oxford University Press, 2005

Kreyenbroek, Philip. *Living Zoroastrianism: Urban Parsis Speak about Their Religion.* London: Routledge, 2001.

Mehr, Farhang. *Zoroastrian Tradition: An Introduction to the Ancient Wisdom of Zarathustra.* Rockport, Mass.: Element., 1991.

Stausberg, Michael. *Zarathustra and Zoroastrianism.* London: Equinox, 2008.

2

Sikhs

Nikky-Guninder Kaur Singh

For our Wellesley College alumnae tour of India last year, the highlight was the visit to the Golden Temple in Amritsar. It was a cool January evening. We took off our shoes. Covered our heads. Washed our feet. Walked through a marble gateway—and suddenly came upon a breathtakingly spectacular scene. Facing us was the luminous Golden Temple. How to describe it? A sparkling star in the vast dark evening? A brilliant lotus emerging out of a shimmering pool? A dazzling ship sailing on breezy waters? The festive *palki* service (part of the daily evening *sukhasan* ceremony) was in process: the Guru Granth was being taken in a gold and silver palanquin (*palki*) from the central shrine for its nightly rest. The devotees (and visitors) in a procession were taking turns—offering their shoulders—to carry the revered book. Guru Nanak's hymn "Arati," replaying the cosmic choreography, sonorously echoed. The sights and sounds of the ceremony left my Christian, Jewish, and atheist friends, as well as our Hindu tour guide — equally mesmerized. What we participated in was the quintessential intersection of sacred verse and sacred space in Sikh religion, and we therewith experienced a moment in which the Sikhs' cumulative past and dynamic future powerfully fused together.

The Guru Granth

The 1,430-page text that was being reverently carried in the palanquin forms the quintessence of Sikh metaphysics, ethics, and rituals. In Sikh consciousness, their scripture is the living body of their Ten Gurus. The text as "body" indeed is a very unique and innovative phenomenon in the history of religions. The Hebrew Bible, the Vedas, the New Testament, the Quran, are absolutely significant in their respective traditions. But in no case do they embody the Jewish Prophets, or the Rishis, or the Evangelists or the Prophet Muhammad. In the Sikh instance the Granth is literally the Guru: *"guru granthji manio pargat guran ki deh*—know the Guru Granth as the visible body of the Gurus" constitutes the daily liturgical hymn.

This textual Body germinated in the literary matrix of the founder Guru, Nanak (1469-1536) who was born in the town of Talwandi, now in Pakistan. Every Sikh knows that Nanak had a very sensuous experience of the Divine. One day, as Nanak went for his usual bath, he was ushered into the divine presence. He heard the divine voice, he received a cup of nam (*nam piala*), he held it in his hands, and he drank. *Nam* (the cognate of the English word name) is the identity of the transcendent One. By sipping the drink, Nanak gets to *know* the Ultimate Reality. As the contents enter his blood stream, Nanak bursts into rapturous exaltation of the wondrous infinity he beholds. He saw the singular light in each and every body, for "there is a light in all and that light is that One" is his resounding melody. During this aesthetico-religious experience, Nanak recited three hymns, which form a part of the daily Sikh prayers: *Japu, Arati*, and *Sohila*. Soon thereafter he started traveling and spreading his message of the singularity of the Ultimate Reality and the consequent unity of humanity. Poetry became his medium of expression, heightened sensitivity to the singular Divine, his message.

Guru Nanak's *Ikk Oan Kar* (One Being Is), an articulation of his revelatory experience, is the embryo that bodied forth the Guru Granth. In fact, the large textual body begins with it. *Ikk* is literally the numeral One, the singular Divine. *Oan* is the primal syllable of Indian thought. Nanak's distinct character for *oan*, with an arc flying off, physically recollects the infinity of the numeral 1 that he intensely experienced. Over the course of history Nanak's primal conception grew into the Body that has become the core of Sikh belief and conduct. Nanak's fifth successor Guru Arjan (1563-1606) compiled the Granth in 1604. The Sikh Guru's editorial lenses did not demarcate boundaries between Sikh, Hindu, or Muslim: the spiritual language was common to them all. The skeins, tissues, and membranes of the Granth consist of the poetic utterances of the Sikh Gurus, Hindu Bhaktas, and Muslim Sufis.

Here the divine One is embraced in a plurality of languages from the Arabic, Sanskrit, and Persian. The Formless One is addressed as *Ram* and *Khuda*. Whatever resonated philosophically and artistically with Guru Nanak's vision, Arjan included it in the Granth. But he did not model the Sikh text on either Muslim or Hindu scriptures, nor did he include passages from either of their revered scriptures. Against a divisive backdrop in which God was either *Ram* or *Rahim*, the worship was either *namaz* or *puja*, the place of worship *mandir* or *masjid*, and the language of scripture either Sanskrit or Arabic, the Sikh Guru brought together voices that expressed a common spiritual quest. What governed Guru Arjan's choice was not a syncretism or synthesis of concepts and doctrines from prevailing religious traditions but rather his penetrating insight into the Divine. Like his predecessors, Guru Arjan believed that knowledge of the Transcendent is attained neither through servitude to a god of the Hindu pantheon (*sevai gosain*) nor through worship to Allah (*sevai allah*). It is received through an active recognition of, and participation in, the Divine Will (*hukam*):

> Some address Ram, some Khuda,
> Some worship Gosain, some Allah . . .
> Says Nanak, those who recognize the Divine Will
> It is they who know the secret of the Transcendent One. (GG: 885)

Most of the Guru Granth is set to the 31 classical Indian *ragas.* Each *raga* has a season prescribed for its singing, it has a prescribed time of the day, an emotional mood, and a particular cultural climate, for each measure evolved in a specific region. In this way the verses are harmonized with the natural rhythm of the day, season, and region, and correspond with inner moods and psychological states. Along with the classical *raga* system, there are folk musical patterns with elemental beats, as well as regional Bhakti and Qafi forms with their own primal rhythms, and other musical styles extending from Afghanistan to the South of the Indian peninsula. The meaning of *raga* is embedded in the brilliant blush (*rang*) of emotions produced by their symphony. Rather than theological treatises or ethical injunctions to be debated or obeyed, the ideal is to eat *(khavai)* and savor *(bhunchai)* the divine verse. Daily Sikhs recite the epilogue to the Granth penned by their editor Guru:

> they who eat this, they who relish this
> they are liberated…

The Guru Granth is imaged as a *thal* (large metal dish) on which lie truth *(sat)*, contentment *(santokh)*, and contemplation *(vicaru)*. The epistemological value of these dishes is savored and absorbed by the readers, reciters, and hearers. The Fifth Guru made Nanak's aesthetic experience the quintessential practice for the growing Sikh community.

In 1708, Guru Gobind Singh (Nanak X, 1666-1708) invested the sacred book with Guruship. The role of the "Guru" is to apply the eyeliner of knowledge (*gyan anjan*) to enhance human vision so that it can recognize the infinite One permeating the cosmos (GG: 610). Before Guru Nanak passed away, he appointed Angad as his successor, bequeathing him his inspired utterances. The second Guru continued the tradition of sacred poetry, which he felt was important for the knowledge it brought to human life. The transference of Guruship from Nanak to Angad was repeated successively through to the installation of the Tenth Guru, Gobind Singh. A day before he passed away, Guru Gobind Singh ended the line of personal gurus by conjoining his physical self and that of his predecessors with their metaphysical utterances. The Guru did not pass on the Guruship to any of his disciples; he passed it to the Granth. There were to be no battles of ego against ego to climb patriarchal ladders; the Guru embodied in the Granth was to be the center of their thought and action forever. Thus the message and the mission begun by Guru Nanak continued through nine more gurus and culminates in the Guru Granth. Sikhs celebrate the identity between their Gurus and their poetic utterances: "Bani (voice) is the Guru, the Guru is Bani, within Bani lie all elixirs" (GG: 982).

Their Gurus' enchantment with the corporeality of the text has systematized into Sikh daily practices and rites. For it was this Body we saw being taken for its nightly rest. Its sonorous breath melodiously wafted as the devotees recited Nanak's hymn "Arati." Its title conjures *arati*, the beautiful Hindu mode of worship, in which devotees encircle a platter decorated with lamps, incense, flowers, and fruit around their favorite deities. Guru Nanak transforms this traditional mode of worship into a cosmic choreography of the planets: the spacious and ethereal skies serve as the platter *(thal)* on which the sun, moon, and twinkling starry lamps perform *arati* around the infinite One! His fifth successor reconfigures this universal platter *(thal)* as the literary Body filled with dishes that have to be eaten and relished. The Sikh ethical ideal is to connect the human mode of worship with that of nature, the food on the kitchen tables with the Guru Granth itself, so that we are constantly nourished and fed physically, emotionally, intellectually, spiritually.

The Harmandar (Golden Temple)

The three dimensional Harmandar is the Sikhs' central shrine. Sikh tradition crystallized within its very precincts, for it was here that Guru Arjan ceremoniously placed the Granth compiled by him on August 16, 1604. He had built the shrine in the centre of a pool that his father had begun. Later patrons, including Maharaja Ranjit Singh (1780-1839) employed Sikh, Muslim, and Hindu craftsmen to build upon and embellish the unique Sikh aesthetic designs cherished by Guru Arjan. Emerging from the shimmering waters, the structure appears to stand without any solid borders or boundaries. The innumerable abstract patterns on its walls set the imagination in motion. The panoramic view of the building merging at once with transparent waters and radiant sunlight sweeps the visitor into a sensory swirl. Here Sikhs visually encounter the infinite One envisioned by Guru Nanak.

Just as the sacred text transcends all either/or distinctions, so does the Golden Temple. The art of the Golden Temple utilizes Hindu and Islamic forms. We find the Hindu *kalsas* just as we find the Islamic domes. We see the Hindu square pillars supporting the roofs just as we see the Muslim arches. We recognize the beautiful geometric patterns that decorate the Jama Masjid, just we recognize the blooming lotuses afloat in the Bhagavad Gita. Central features of Islamic architecture (domes and minarets) and art (calligraphy, complex geometric designs, de-naturalization, arabesques, mirror-work...) pervade the Golden Temple complex. Hindu designs and motifs like fish, crocodiles, lions, elephants, and deer vigorously decorate its walls as well. In the communal memory, Guru Arjan invited Mian Mir, a Muslim saint, to lay the foundation for the Harmandar—a powerful psychological acknowledgement of their Guru's real and enduring relationship with Islam. In our religiously torn society we need to remind ourselves that Sikh sacred architecture is grounded in kinship with people of "other" faiths.

Yet neither Hindu nor Islamic characteristics are consciously added together to produce syncretic models, be it the Guru Granth or the Harmandar. Till very recently books on religions targeted Sikhism as a prime example of "syncretism." Such presumptions miss out on the revelation, uniqueness, and originality of the Sikh Gurus. Guru Arjan did not try to add two disparate traditions to reproduce a hybrid Sikh text or space. Whatever was in harmony with Guru Nanak's revelatory experience of Oneness, Guru Arjan included — be it Hindu or Muslim. The Sikh Gurus were not insular or exclusive in their approach to the transcendent One. Therefore the Guru Granth is fully respectful of the Quran, the Vedas, the Puranas; it fully encompasses the verses of the Bhaktas and Sufis. But it is *not* modeled on either Muslim or Hindu scriptures. Nowhere does it include passages from either of their revered scriptures. It does not piece together their philosophical ideals. It is an entirely different literary narrative with its own set of values. It does not even utilize their language. It is, however, remarkable that in a religiously torn society, Guru Arjan included the voices of Hindu Namdev and Muslim Farid into his own revered Sikh text. Through his profoundly personal sensibility, he heard their human longing for the Divine—he did not get stuck on external differences in accents, intonations, grammar, or vocabulary. And he did not merely assemble their passages and market it as a new product.

Similarly, while sharing many features with mosques and temples, the Harmandar is an entirely different space. The utter feeling of submission to an omnipotent creator felt in the mosque is taken over by the feeling of elation in the Gurdwara. Fundamental aspects of mosques such as the *mihrab* (prayer niche), *minbar* (pulpit), and the tombs of saints (especially popular in Sufi sacred spaces), have no place in Sikhism. Nor is there anything particularly potent about the topology of the Harmandar in the traditional Indian sense. Unlike Hindu temples, which are built at very specific places — "where the gods are seen at play" — the site for the Harmandar was not chosen for any specific reason. The idea for the pool within which Guru Arjan built the shrine goes back to the time of the third Guru Amar Das when Goindval was the Sikh centre.

The Gurdwara is not constructed on any traditional diagramatic plans either. It does not draw upon the highly elaborate Hindu science of architecture with its technical blueprints that secure a deity into the site. The Sikh shrine does not attempt to install the Divine into its structure. Its landscape is not deified in any sense. The Gurdwara is simply a door (*dwara*) towards enlightenment *(guru)*. Having completed and lined the pool begun by his father, Guru Arjan wanted to set a building within it. He may have imagined the construct as a "lotus" sitting serenely on the waters or even as a "ship" sailing across the ocean as Michael Ondaatje describes in his fascinating novel, *The English Patient*. Guru Arjan's pluralist model rises about provincialism and narrowness into a vaster and more profound perspective. It is not "syncretic" by any means.

The entry into the Golden Temple complex requires a downward motion. The physical descent ensures that the precincts are entered with a sense of humility. Guru Nanak had said, "getting rid of ego, we receive the word" (GG: 228). In order to absorb the Divine, the selfish, egotistical "I" must be emptied. Guru Arjan reiterated the pathogenic effects of egocentricity: "by getting rid of arrogance we become devoid of hatred" (GG: 183). The poison of arrogance and egocentricity fills arteries with hostility towards the human family, and the mind with inertia and ignorance.

The four doors of the Harmandar were Arjan's architectural translation of his ethical injunction: "Kshatriya, Brahmin, Shudra, and Vaishya, all four classes have the same mandate"(GG: 747). Rejecting societal distinctions, the Granth declares that religion succeeds "when the entire earth becomes one color" (GG: 663). "Color" (*varna*) is the standard Indian word for the four classes, so by calling for the world to be of "one color" it is demanding an end to class discrimination. The four doors opened up to welcome people from all castes and complexions. Walking through the doors Sikhs could understand what Nanak meant: "accept all humans as your equals, and let them be your only sect" (Japu, 28).

Guru Arjan's three-dimensional Harmandar is therefore a visual and tactile reminder of the access to the infinite matrix. For Sikhs it is the place where their blurred vision, muffled hearing, and numbed senses can be recharged; they are freed from all sorts of fears and phobias, and are inspired to recognize the Infinite One. The weaving, circulating, and colorful *text*ure of their scripture is visible on the floors and walls and ceilings. The black and white marble slabs upon which one walks are repeated rhythmically. So are the stylized flowers and birds and vines and fruits and arabesques and lattice-work on the walls and sides. The structure itself repeats its arches and domes and pillars and kiosks and windows and storeys. Amongst the unending repetitions that one walks upon, touches on the sides, and sees on the building, the melodious words are heard. The rhythmic repetitions create a dynamic movement for the senses and imagination. Together they are impelled onwards. Any feeling of uneasiness gives way to harmony; doubts and dualities begin to dissolve; the ignorant psyche seeks to discover its essential spark. Through its finite structures the Golden Temple creates an energetic movement towards the Infinite Transcendent.

Worship

The pattern of worship in the Golden Temple is the paradigm for Sikhs in all parts of the world. If we visit any Sikh home, we find that reading the Guru Granth, hearing it, singing it, or sitting in its presence constitute the core of their worship. Every Sikh family wishes to have a room in their home enshrining the Guru Granth. Both in private and in public places of worship, the Guru Granth is treated with the highest respect and veneration. The visitor will find it draped in cloth (called *rumala*), placed on quilted mats, and supported by cushions. A canopy hangs over it for protection, and a whisk is waved over it as a sign of respect. Sikhs everywhere bow before the Guru Granth and seat themselves on the floor. They remove their shoes and cover their heads in the presence of their holy book. The Guru Granth is opened at dawn. This act of opening the holy book is called *prakash*, "making the light manifest." *Vak* or "the order of the day" is obtained by opening the Book at random and reading the passage on the top of the left-hand page. That passage resonates with the reader for the rest of the day. After dusk, the Guru Granth is closed. The closing ritual is called *sukhasan*, which means "to place at rest." The Guru Granth is read for all rites of passage, for any family celebration — a new house, a new job, birthdays, engagements, and for all times of uncertainty and difficulty—sickness or death. Usually, the reading at these events is *akhand*, a forty-eight hour, nonstop reading of its 1430 portfolio pages, during which several readers take turns. Any Sikh, male or female, who can read Gurmukhi script may read the Guru Granth.

In public, the worship takes place in a Gurdwara; literally, the doorway *(dwara)* to the Guru, which is designed on the open and inclusive architectural patterns of the Harmandar. There is no central chamber from which any male or female is excluded, for the Guru Granth is the focal point to which everyone has equal access. The shrines serve as a central point for the local Sikh community, and especially in diasporic communities, they are the source of information, assistance, food, shelter, and fellowship. For the newly arrived Sikhs—whether in Southall or San Jose or Paris or Dublin, locating the Gurdwara is an important initial step. The Sikh community creates and maintains its social, cultural, intellectual, and political links through the Gurdwara. Where there are large Sikh populations, Gurdwaras are being designed to accommodate huge gatherings. A spacious Gurdwara like the Ontario Khalsa Darbar with 38 acres and over 35,000 square feet of building (located close to the airport in Toronto) allows Sikhs to celebrate their special festivals in thousands. Simultaneously, it enables a person living in the neighborhood to pay daily homage before starting off for their job — just as many Sikhs do back in India. Even for an occasional visitor, the Gurdwara offers a wonderful opportunity to pay homage, listen to *kirtan* (singing of scriptural verses), partake of the delicious *langar* (community meal), visit the library, and meet with fellow Sikhs. With exactly the same sights, sounds, accents, smell, and spirit as the Gurdwaras in the Punjab, Gurdwaras in "foreign countries" take immigrants back home, back into the recesses of their deepest self.

Besides the Golden Temple, there are five popular pilgrimage sites. They are called the five *takhts*, the five seats of temporal authority. The Akal Takht in Amritsar faces the Golden Temple and is regarded as the supreme seat of religious and temporal authority. The other four are associated with the tenth Guru: Patna Sahib in Bihar, where he was born; Keshgarh, in Anandpur, where he created the Khalsa; Hazur Sahib in Nander where he died; and Damdama, near Bhatinda where he took rest and where a center of Sikh learning later developed. Even if they cannot make the pilgrimage in person, devotees send through their families and friends, money for the *langar* and upkeep of the shrine, and gifts like *rumalas* (cloths that are draped over the Guru Granth).

Whether we visit a home or a Gurdwara, Sikh ritual consists primarily of the singing of scriptural verses (Kirtan). Harmonium and *tabla* (a set of drums) are the most common musical accompaniments. As the verses of infinite love mingle with the music they seep deep into the unconscious, awakening our essential humanity.

Special social functions and rites of passage are marked by the Bhog Ceremony. The word *bhog* literally means "pleasure." In Sikhism it signifies the gratification attained by having concluded a reading of the scriptures. *Bhog* involves reading the concluding pages of the Guru Granth, saying *ardas* (in which a congregation stands up to remember the Ultimate Reality, the ten Gurus, their mergence with the Guru Granth, and events of Sikh heroism, devotion and martyrdom), and partaking of the Sikh sacrament of *karahprashad*, which concludes every religious ceremony. *Karahprashad* is the sweet sacrament consisting of equal portions of butter, flour, sugar, and water. I should specify that these ingredients are vigorously stirred on a stovetop, because when students from my Sikh seminar at Colby College baked the ingredients, the *karahprashad* turned into a giant cookie! It should be moist and sticky. During its preparation, men and women keep their heads covered, their feet bare, and recite the verses of the Gurus. When the *karahprashad* is ready, it is put in a large, flat dish and placed on the right side of the Guru Granth. After scriptural readings, the warm and aromatic sacrament is distributed to the entire congregation, which is received in the cupped palms with both hands joined together.

Daily Rhythms

Lived reality for Sikhs centers on remembering the One Reality as often and as intimately as possible. The daily spiritual routine (*nitnem*) consists of recitations of hymns from the various Gurus. Every morning and evening Sikh sacred spaces and homes (and even cars and trucks!) resonate with the melodious sounds of their daily hymns. Children hear them from the lips of their parents, and some adults hear them on tapes and CDs.

The morning hymn is Guru Nanak's Japu (frequently called Japuji, as *ji* is a suffix for respect). It is the first hymn of the Guru Granth. It is the core of Sikh metaphysics, and simultaneously, highly artistic. Japuji's very first stanza celebrates the One Truth pervading time past, present and future, but it immediately raises the question: "*kive sachiara hoi hai? Kiv kure tute pala?*—How to become Truth? How to break the walls of falsity?" (Japuji: 1). There is thus a quick shift from the focus on the Divine to the individual; from the timeless Creator to life lived truthfully here and now; from the praise of divine virtues to their absorption. While extolling the One, the Japuji is profoundly contemplative and self-analytic. How are we to live "truthfully" in our complex world? Guru Nanak's morning hymn charges Sikhs to gather their human facultiesand actively to search for ways of living truthfully amongst family, friends, and community. It serves as a mirror through which Sikhs see not their superficial blemishes and wrinkles, but their intrinsic reality. Like the rest of the Guru Granth, the style of the Japuji is interactive. The Guru-poets do not preach. They do not give any do's or don'ts. There is no authorial figure or doctrine that Sikhs are commanded to follow. Rather, the poetic text subtly, most aesthetically, trains readers and hearers to use their intellectual gifts and discover new tracks. Mothers can be heard reciting the Japuji as they prepare breakfast or comb and braid the hair of their children.

Besides hearing the daily hymns in the laps of their parents and grand-parents, children learn about their faith through narratives called the Janamsakhis. These are literally birth (*janam*) stories (*sakhis*) about Guru Nanak. They provide Sikhs their first literary and visual introduction to their heritage. Combining myth, legend, and history, they portray the divine dispensation of Nanak, his concern for kindness, social cohesiveness, and his stress on divine unity. The Janamsakhis disclose the illustrious advent of Nanak's birth. In their central concern and luminous descriptions, the accounts of Nanak's birth have a great deal in common with those of Jesus, Buddha, and Krishna. Just as baby Jesus' stable was lit up by the bright Star of Bethlehem, the humble mud-hut in which Nanak was born was flooded with light at the moment of his birth. But Mata Tripta goes through normal pregnancy, and her Muslim mid-wife Daultan is struck by the extraordinary qualities of the child she delivers.

The Janamsakhis continue to provide fabulous details of Guru Nanak's entire life. They depict scenes in which dreadful and dangerous elements of nature either protect him (like the cobra offering his shade to a sleeping Nanak) or are controlled by him (with his outstretched palm Nanak stops a huge rock hurled at him). They depict Nanak's divine configuration: at his death, the shroud is left without the body; flowers are found instead of his body; and both Hindus and Muslims carry away the fragrant flowers— to cremate or bury according to their respective customs. The quick and vigorous style of the Janamsakhis lent itself easily to oral circulation, and they became very popular. They have also been painted and brightly illustrated. As babies, Sikhs hear and see the illustrated Janamsakhis about their first Guru, and are nourished by them throughout their lives.

For the millions of Sikhs living around the globe, Nanak is a continuing reality. Their day begins by reciting his sublime poetry. Sikh homes, places of business, and their sacred spots display his images. Wearing an outfit combining Hindu and Muslim styles, his eyes rapt in divine contemplation, and his right palm imprinted with the symbol of the singular Reality, Guru Nanak inspires his viewers to experience the One reality, the foundation of Sikh Religion.

Sikhs try to bring the Divine into the daily rhythms of their lives. Even the simple greetings welcome the Divine, for whenever they say hello or goodbye, they join their hands and say "Sat Sri Akal" (Truth is Timeless). Their frequent exclamation "Waheguru" (before a meal, after a sneeze etc.*)* surges with a sense of wonder and echoes Guru Nanak's awe (*wah!*) as he experienced the transcendent One. The secular and the sacred aspects of life are not bifurcated in the Sikh way of life. In fact, Sikh scripture validates normal activities: "while laughing, playing, dressing up, and eating we attain liberation" (GG: 522). Marriage, family life, and social participation have consistently been affirmed. As a result, Sikhs have developed a strong work ethic, which is summed up in the popular maxim: "work hard (*kirat karni*), remember the Divine (*nam japna*), and share your enjoyment with others (*vand chhakna*)."

Celebrations

Annually, Sikhs celebrate Gurpurabs (the days of the Guru). These days commemorate the birthdays of their ten Gurus, important historical events, and the martyrdom of their heroes. All over the world Sikhs joyously celebrate the birth of Guru Nanak, the installation of the Guru Granth in the Harmandar, and the birth of the Khalsa. Baisakhi, which is also the first day of the Sikh calendar, commemorates Guru Gobind Singh's creation of the Khalsa in 1699. During Gurpurabs, uninterrupted readings of scripture take place, intellectual symposiums are held, and musical performances are organized. Gurpurab celebrations also include huge Sikh processions with colorful floats carrying the Guru Granth, and depicting different aspects of Sikh life. The spirit of hospitality during Gurpurabs is amazing: on the roads in India, Sikhs will stop fast moving cars and buses, and offer *langar* to the public in the form of meals and snacks, and hot and cold drinks depending on the season.

The Punjabi folk dances Gidda and Bhangra are popular performances during Sikh celebrations. Gidda is choreographed by women in gentle and lithesome movement. Together they celebrate nature and her bountiful gifts through the seasons of spring, summer, monsoon, autumn, and winter. Amidst sparkling agrarian scenes, Gidda captures simple activities: how they milk cows, cook mustard seeds, do needlework, fan in the summer, buy glass bangles, churn milk in the morning, carry water in earthen-ware pitchers sturdily balanced on heads, help with ploughing and harvesting. Bhangra is traditionally performed by a group of men. It dates back to the 14th century, originating in West Punjab (now a part of Pakistan). But in modern times, Bhangra has become extremely popular with both Sikh men and women. Dressed in bright colors, the group dances in an elemental rhythm to the beat of a large drum, and everybody joins in the songs celebrating Punjabi village life. With the migration of Sikh communities to the west, this Punjabi folk dance has become the latest rage with young music lovers in Britain, Europe, and North America. The modern form of Bhangra combines North Indian folk music with a kaleidoscope of contemporary styles including reggae and western pop. In the postcolonial and diasporic reality, Bhangra, with its complex cultural webs, has become a crucial marker of Sikh memory and identity.

Rites of Passage

In Sikhism there are four rites of passage: name-giving, amrit initiation, marriage, and death. The name-giving ritual can be extremely simple or elaborate, but it is essentially the naming of the child in consultation with the holy Book. While the spine of the Guru Granth rests on the cushions, a reader (a family member if the rite is at the home, an official reader if it is at the Gurdwara) holds the Guru Granth closed with both hands and then gently lets it open at random. The child is given a name that begins with the first letter appearing at the top of the left-hand page where the Guru Granth opens. Sikhs do not have different names for boys and girls. The addition of the name Kaur or Singh indicates the gender of the child. The child also receives its first *kara* or steel bracelet. The recitation of *kirtan* (hymns of praise) readings from the Guru Granth, recitation of *ardas* (the daily prayer), and the partaking of *langar* are the central activities, just as they for all Sikh rites of passage.

Amrit initiation replays the memorable event of Baisakhi 1699. That day the tenth Guru and his wife prepared the *amrit* drink (mixture of water, sugar, iron, and sacred verse), and five men from different castes in front of a large Baisakhi gathering sipped the drink from the same bowl. Their sipping together was a bold gesture of spitting out divisions of caste, class, and hereditary profession. The five "beloved" as they are called were adorned with the five physical symbols: *kesha* (long hair), *kangha* (comb to keep the hair tidy), *kirpan* (sword), *kara* (bracelet) and *kaccha* (underwear) and entered the new family of the "Khalsa." They were also given a new name as a mark of their new identity. The pattern established by Guru Gobind Singh is followed in contemporary practice. No particular age is prescribed for this initiation rite. It may be as soon as a boy or a girl is old enough to be able to read the scripture and comprehend the articles of the Sikh faith. Or it may be later in life — some people even wait until their own children are grown up. The initiation is open to all. According to the Sikh Ethical Code (the Rahit Maryada), "Any man or woman of whatever nationality, race, or social standing, who is prepared to accept the rules governing the Sikh community, has the right to receive amrit initiation."

Anand Karaj (*anand*=bliss, *karaj*=event) is the Sikh rite of marriage. No words or gestures are directly exchanged between the bride and groom, nor any legal formalities performed between their families. The wedding takes place either in a Gurdwara or in the home of the bride with everyone seated on the floor in front of the sacred Book. Anand Karaj begins with the father of the bride handing one end of a scarf (about two and a quarter yards in length) to the groom, and the other to his daughter. Through the auspiciously colored scarf (pink, saffron, or red) the couple is bonded together. Each holding one end of the scarf, the groom and the bride then walk around the holy book four times. The four circumambulations by the couple correspond to the four *lavan* (circle) passages read by the official reader of the Guru Granth. After each circling of the Book, the bride and the groom touch their foreheads to the ground, and rejoin the congregation by seating themselves on the floor in front. Bowing together to the Guru Granth marks their acceptance of each other. They are solely — and equally — bound to the sacred word rather than to any legal or social authority. The rite concludes with Guru Amar Das' rapturous hymn, *anand* (bliss) — the name of the wedding ceremony itself. This popular scriptural hymn by the Third Guru is liturgically recited at the conclusion of all Sikh congregational services and joyful ceremonies. But with its focus on the bliss that results from the union of the individual with the Divine, *anand* is particularly appropriate for the wedding ceremony.

Life and Death are regarded as natural processes, and just as each day that dawns must set, so must all people depart. The dead body is carried on a stretcher by the closest male relatives and friends of the family to the funeral grounds where it is cremated. As customary from ancient times, the pyre is lighted by the eldest son. The body returns to the elements it is made up of: the fire of the person merges with the crematory flames, their breath with the air, their body with the body of the earth, and their ashes and bones (called *phul*, literally, flowers) are immersed in the flowing waters of a river or stream. Death in the family is marked by a reading of the Guru Granth. A *bhog* ceremony takes place on the tenth day with the final prayers recited for peace to the deceased. At the death anniversary, the family supplies *langar* to the community.

Gender, Sex, and Sexuality in Sikh Religion

By designating the Divine as numeral "One" at the very outset, Sikh scripture discards centuries-old images of male dominance and power, and opens the way to experiencing the Transcendent One in a female modality. The text offers a vast range of feminine symbols and imagery: the ontological ground of all existence is *mata*, the Mother; the divine spark within all creatures is *joti*, the feminine light; the soul longing to unite with the Transcendent One is *suhagan*, the beautiful young bride; the benevolent glance coming from the Divine is the feminine *nadar*, grace. Sikh scripture continuously provides readers with a multivalent and complex feminine imagery. This variety in turn presents a host of options through which men and women can become who they choose to be.

We find men and women participating equally and enthusiastically in the fundamental Sikh institutions of *seva* (voluntary labor), *langar* (community meal where everybody cooks together and eats), and *sangat* (congregation). On our tour of the Golden Temple community kitchen, we saw men and women chopping vegetables, cooking lentils, rolling thousands of *chappatis* (flat bread), and cooking them over the fire. We were proudly shown an expensive "foreign machine" (a big oven bought from the Middle East) that automatically made *chappatis*, even though it was "out of order" at that time! We did get to taste some fresh bread and cauliflower anyway. Sikhism rejects notions of celibacy and asceticism, which denigrate women. Single women, married, and widows are equally welcome. The various institutions promote spiritual engagement while being full members in family and society. There is no priesthood in Sikhism, so both men and women are free to read and recite the sacred verse at home or in public, and anybody from within the congregation can be chosen to lead worship.

Both Sikh men and women wear the five symbols of their identity: *kangha, kesha, kara, kirpan*, and *kaccha*. These were given to mark the new family of the Khalsa and dissolve caste and class categories. While Sikh men wear turbans, Sikh women have their hair either neatly braided or put up in a bun. We can distinguish Sikh women by their *salwar* (loose pants), *kameez* (shirt till the knees) and the *dupattas* (long sheer scarves). Sikh men have the last name "Singh" (meaning lion); Sikh women have the last name "Kaur," meaning princess, which remains the same whether they are married or unmarried, thus freeing them from the lineage of fathers and husbands. The first name can be the same for men and women; Singh and Kaur mark their gender.

The Gurus envisioned a common humanity and rejected biological hierarchies. In fact images of conception, gestation, giving birth, and lactation are unambiguously and powerfully present in their verse. They remind us that we are created from the mother's blood, we are lodged in her womb, and we are first nurtured by her milk. They denounce taboos against menstrual blood and blood of parturition—both stereotyped by their society as impure and dangerous, and ritually avoided. In contrast, the Guru-poets celebrate women's sexual and maternal processes, and even honor the womb as our first home. Acutely aware of their oppressive patrilineal north-Indian society in which the family name, caste, and profession came down through birth, they honor her womb as a social utopia free from all sorts of "isms" and androcentric hegemonies: "in the dwelling of the womb, there is neither name nor caste" (GG: 324). Sikh scripture resonates with numerous positive images of the fetus gaining physical, intellectual, and spiritual nourishment in the mother's body.

Though heterosexuality or homosexuality is not explicitly addressed, sexuality is regarded as an important aspect of humanity and spirituality. Female sexuality — denigrated in society and victim of male fears, phobias, anxieties, and disgust — is voiced as healthy and wholesome. The scriptural paradigm is female. She incarnates physical beauty and spiritual awakening. And she rapturously makes love with her divine lover. In the words of Guru Nanak, "The woman abides in truth, and sleeps soundly locked in the Divine embrace" (GG: 843). The tenth Guru gave the *kaccha* (underpants) to both Sikh men and women as a reminder of their moral responsibilities: bodies, male and female alike are the home of the Divine; sex is not to be abused, and that no*body* is to be exploited or abused.

It is also interesting to note that the male Sikh Gurus expressed their love for the Divine from a female perspective. They do not repress or stunt themselves in male-female dualisms. Feeling the Infinite intensely within, they openly identify with the female person, her psyche, her tone, her sentiments, and trace the Transcendent as both father and mother, male and female.

Gender, Sex, and Sexuality in Sikh Praxis

Unfortunately, the liberating momentum of the Sikh Gurus lies buried under ancient discriminations against girls. The radically uplifting female concepts, symbols, and images permeating the Guru Granth are simply neglected. The fundamentally patriarchal culture of the Punjab has continued to reproduce "malestream" interpretations and translations, and so the One is invariably translated into a "He Lord," and the inspiring female imagery is neglected. Even public worship continues to be led by men. Such sexism has negative impact because the superior role and privilege of men is unconsciously reproduced in the family, home, and Sikh society at large.

Several other factors have contributed to produce a hyper-masculine society. For instance, during the flamboyant regime of Maharaja Ranjit Singh, male dominance increased, and practices of *purdah* and *sati* condemned by the Gurus, found their way into the upper echelons of Sikh society. British admiration for the "martial" character and strong physique of Sikh men (who were recruited in the British imperial army in disproportionately large numbers) generated a vigorous new patriarchal discourse.

From the moment of birth the son and daughter are chartered out different roles and given a whole different set of obligations. Sons are privileged in all spheres of Sikh life. Calendrical festivals are celebrated with extra verve in Sikh homes where a boy is born. It is taken for granted that the daughter leave her natal home at marriage and join her husband and his family, and that her biological parents be responsible for all major events in her life, even after marriage. Marriages are mostly arranged. They have become extremely opulent, dowries extravagant, and gifts to the daughter and her in-laws for every rite, ritual, and festival, exorbitant. The Sikh scriptural verse "bride and groom are one spirit in two bodies" has grown into an elaborate commercial racket and ends up in the bride's family's oppression. Whereas the daughter depletes her family's earnings, the son accrues: along with a wife, the gifts for lifetime flow to him and his family. When a daughter dies, no matter what age or stage of life she may have been in, it is *her* natal family's responsibility to supply the meal following the cremation. From her birth till her death, the daughter is a debit. The son's family enjoys a status that the daughter's family simply does not.

The cultural and economic codes have made the obsession with sons so great that modern technology is abused profusely to perform sex-selective abortions and maintain India's traditional anti-female bias. Even though the Government of India has banned the use of sex determination techniques, the law is not enforced. Sikh leaders are beginning to take initiatives against this grave tragedy: 250 of them recently met at a Sikh shrine in Fatehgarh Sahib, where the ratio of females has dwindled to 750 per 1,000 males.

While globalization is offering some men and women exciting new opportunities and success in business ventures, professions, and arts, many others are becoming its victims. Women who earlier followed their husbands and fathers are now migrating on their own to study, teach, and enter business, fashion, medicine, or law. But Globalization has also triggered a trend in the Punjab to marry off daughters to men settled in distant lands as a means of sponsoring their entire families for immigration. Sociologists interpret this phenomenon as "sacrifice of the daughter for the sake of the son." How to preserve Sikh identity in the modern world is a vital concern for Sikhs across the globe. Since women are literally the reproducers of the community, the preservation of "Sikhness" falls primarily on them. As a result, Sikh women are subjected to manifold restrictions. Control over their reproductive rights leads to the reproduction of the family's identity and that of the Sikh community at large. "Honor" or *Izzat*, which is identified with manliness and belongs to hierarchical and patriarchal systems, has come to be a central code of Sikhs.

Counteracting Sexism: the Sikh Rahit Maryada

In its attempt to formalize the message of the Gurus, an ethical code was developed by Sikh reformers in the middle of the twentieth century. It provides several rules to combat female oppression:

> Twice it makes the point that Sikh women should not veil their faces.
> Prohibits infanticide, and association with people who would practice it.
> There is no prohibition against abortion.
> Allows widow remarriage, and underscores that the ceremony be the same as that of the first marriage.
> Sikhs should be free of all superstitions, and not refuse to eat at the home of their married daughter.
> Prohibits dowry.

Such a sensibility did have an impact: Sikh women were the first Indian women granted the right to vote by the Gurdwara Act of 1925. But sadly, many of the explicit rules from the Sikh ethical code are simply not followed. Though divorce and widow remarriage are legal, they carry stigmas, and dishonor the family. Out of "respect" for their daughters, Sikh parents will not accept a penny from their working daughter nor sip water in her married home. She is their prized "object," and so the ancient gender codes and sexist attitudes continue to govern Sikh life.

The economic and social demands of Sikh masculinity are so strong that the teachings of the Gurus go unheeded. Living in their doubly patriarchal society, the Sikh Gurus might not even have been aware of all the liberating implications of their words and actions. But they set them in motion. They made the Shudra (anybody from the lowest caste) equal with the Brahmin (a priest from the highest caste). They made Singh and Kaur equal. They created an opening through which women could achieve liberty, equality, and sorority. They were not stuck up to a macho mode of sexuality and offered a plurality of ways of relating with the singular Divine. The Sikh community needs to match up their daily practices with the egalitarian and pluralistic vision of their Gurus.

Sikhs Abroad

There are about 22 million Sikhs worldwide, and although the vast majority live in the fertile plains of the Punjab (with agriculture as a major occupation), many with their spirit of adventure and entrepreneurship skills have migrated to other parts of India and around the world. The British annexation of the Punjab in 1849 offered Sikhs opportunities to become a part of the imperial work force and migrate to distant lands. A substantial number served in the British army in a variety of countries, and many were employed as soldiers and clerks in British colonies on the Malay Peninsula and in East Africa. In the late nineteenth/early twentieth centuries, advertisements by steamship companies and recruitment to work on the Canadian Pacific Railroad attracted many Sikh men to the North American Continent. There were barely any Sikh women in this early group of immigrants, and Sikh men often married Spanish-speaking women on the western rim, creating a biethnic community erroneously termed "Mexican-Hindus" (also "Mexidus"). There was a lot of discrimination against them, and because they wore turbans as their Sikh symbol, they were called "rag heads." Since the relaxation of immigration laws after World War II, and especially after the elimination of national quotas in 1965, there has been a dramatic surge in the Sikh population, both male and female, all across North America. The new family-reunification policy opened doors to a second wave of Asian immigration through which Sikh men and women from all strata of society arrived in increasing numbers. Political crises in India have also impelled the increase in migrations over the last few decades. In the 1980s, the Sikh quest for an independent Khalistan led to a tragic political situation, driving many young Sikhs to find homes abroad. Another example is the case of the "twice migrants" who were initially settled in Uganda, Kenya, and Iran, but due to political turmoil in their adopted countries, families were forced to migrate, and many settled in North America. Although the Punjab-like terrain of California still attracts Sikhs (Yuba and Sutter counties form the largest and most prosperous Sikh farming communities outside India), recent Sikh men and women migrants are highly urban-based and very successful.

Sikhs are becoming deeply involved in exposing their faith to the larger society. Throughout my high school, college, and even graduate school in America, there were no course offerings on this north Indian religion. Books on religions seldom had chapters on Sikhism and if they did, they missed out on its uniqueness and originality. Invariably, Sikhism was tucked under Hinduism, or Islam, or presented as the perfect model of "syncretism" between a monotheistic Islam and a polytheistic Hinduism. The first generation of Sikhs had been concerned about social and economic success, and they pretty much kept their religion in their homes and places of public worship. But now they are more confident about themselves and concerned that they be correctly understood. The overall interest has generated the establishment of Sikh Chairs at American universities like Santa Barbara, Hofstra, Riverside, and Ann Arbor; the creation of a permanent art gallery at the San Francisco Asian art Museum; and a fairly steady flow of books and journals.

Sikhs abroad maintain their links with the homeland, and the establishment of institutions like the Punjabi University (in Patiala) and Guru Nanak Dev University (in Amritsar) has spurred academic interest in the West. I was quite impressed by the undergraduates at Stanford University who took the initiative and organized a course on Sikhism by inviting visiting lecturers from across the continent! The second generation of Sikhs care about their rights in the land of liberty and equal opportunity, and following the discrimination faced by many Sikh Americans after 9/11, they are taking the responsibility to educate the general public. Mainstream media projections instilled such fear and hate for anybody with turban and beard that more than two hundred Sikhs have been victims of hate crimes in America since 9/11. In the mind of the attackers, Punjabi Sikhs are the same as Afghani Muslims and Afghani Muslims are the same as al-Qaeda terrorists. In Phoenix, a Sikh gas station owner was murdered in that blinding rage. In response, young Sikhs are enthusiastically providing legal assistance, educational outreach at the federal and state levels, and legislative advocacy to protect the civil rights of American Sikhs. Sikh organizations, foundations, filmmakers, and web sites are emerging to rectify past errors and deletions, and to promote new channels of inter-religious understanding.

Today Sikhs celebrate their heritage with great jubilation across the globe at numerous cultural and academic venues. The air is especially abuzz with excitement around Baisakhi, the Sikh new year (in the spring) and for Guru Nanak's birthday (in the autumn). During festive parades, colorful floats carry their eternal Guru through villages and cities, including the metropolises of North America. Clearly, the religious celebrations at the Harmandar are reaching the far corners of the world. A moment like the one with my Wellesley alumnae group in Amritsar can be experienced on the American soil itself! As a member of the community, I sense vibrant new patterns adding to the dynamic Sikh tradition; as a scholar of religion, I see the "forgotten" north Indian tradition making its mark as a vital mosaic in the religious plurality of our global world. It is an exciting time for Sikhs.

Suggestions for Further Reading

Axel, Brian Keith. *The Nation's Tortured Body: Violence, Representation, and the Formation of a Sikh "Diaspora".* Durham: Duke University Press, 2001.

Barrier, N. Gerald, and Verne A. Dusenbery. *The Sikh Diaspora: Migration and the Experience Beyond Punjab.* Columbia, Mo: South Asia Books, 1989.

Barrier, N. Gerald, and Pashaura Singh. *Sikhism and History.* New Delhi: Oxford University Press, 2004.

Bhachu, Parminder. *Twice Migrants: East African Sikh Settlers in Britain.* London: Tavistock Publications, 1985.

Brown, Kerry. *Sikh Art and Literature.* London: Routledge, 1999.

Cole, W. Owen, and Piara Singh Sambhi. *The Sikhs: Their Religious Beliefs and Practices.* London: Routledge, 1989.

Coward, Harold G., John R. Hinnells, and Raymond Brady Williams. *The South Asian Religious Diaspora in Britain, Canada, and the United States.* Albany: State University of New York Press, 2000.

Fenech, Louis E. *Martyrdom in the Sikh Tradition: Playing the "Game of Love".* New Delhi: Oxford University Press, 2000.

Goswamy, Brijinder N. *Piety and Splendour: Sikh Heritage in Art.* New Delhi: National Museum, 2000.

Grewal, J. S. *From Guru Nanak to Maharaja Ranjit Singh: Essays in Sikh History.* Amritsar: Guru Nanak University, 1972.

Hans, Surjit. *A Reconstruction of Sikh History from Sikh Literature.* Jalandar: ABS Publishing, 1988.

Jakobsh, Doris. *Relocating Gender in Sikh History: Transformation, Meaning and Identity.* Delhi: Oxford University Press, 2003.

Juergensmeyer, Mark, and N. Gerald Barrier. *Sikh Studies: Comparative Perspectives on a Changing Tradition: Working Papers from the Berkeley Conference on Sikh Studies.* Berkeley: Graduate Theological Union, 1979.

Khushwant Singh. *A History of the Sikhs.* Princeton: Princeton University Press, 1963.

King, Noel Quinton, and Gurdev Singh. *Perspectives on the Sikh Tradition.* Chandigarh: Siddharth Publications for Academy of Sikh Religion & Culture, 1986.

Kohli, Surindar Singh. *A Critical Study of Adi Granth.* New Delhi: Punjabi Writers' Cooperative Industrial Society, 1961.

La Brack, Bruce. *The Sikhs of Northern California, 1904-1975.* New York: AMS Press, 1988.

Macauliffe, Max Arthur. *The Sikh Religion: Its Gurus, Sacred Writings and Authors.* Oxford: Oxford University Press, 1909.

MacLeod, William Hewat. *Exploring Sikhism: Aspects of Sikh Identity, Culture and Thought.* New Delhi: Oxford University Press, 2001.

———. *Textual Sources for the Study of Sikhism.* Chicago: University of Chicago Press, 1990.

Mahmood, Cynthia Keppley. *Fighting for Faith and Nation Dialogues with Sikh Militants.* Philadelphia: University of Pennsylvania Press, 1997.

Mahmood, Cynthia Keppley, and Stacy Brady. *The Guru's Gift: An Ethnography Exploring Gender Equality with North American Sikh Women.* Mountain View, Calif: Mayfield Publishing, 2000.

Madanjit Kaur. *The Golden Temple, Past and Present.* Amritsar: Guru Nanak Dev University Press, 1983.

Mann, Gurinder Singh. *The Making of Sikh Scripture.* Oxford: Oxford University Press, 2001.

Mann, Jasbir Singh, and Kharak Singh. *Recent Researches in Sikhism.* Patiala: Punjabi University, 1992.

Nripinder Singh. *The Sikh Moral Tradition: Ethical Perceptions of the Sikhs in the Late Nineteenth/Early Twentieth Century.* New Delhi: Manohar, 1990.

Oberoi, Harjot. *The Construction of Religious Boundaries: Culture, Identity, and Diversity in the Sikh Tradition.* Chicago: University of Chicago Press, 1994.

O'Connell, Joseph T., Milton Israel, and Willard Gurdon Oxtoby. *Sikh History and Religion in the Twentieth Century.* Toronto: University of Toronto, Centre for South Asian Studies, 1988.

Pashaura Singh. *The Guru Granth Sahib: Canon, Meaning and Authority.* New Delhi: Oxford University Press, 2000.

Shackle, Christopher, Arvind-pal Singh Mandair, and Gurharpal Singh. *Sikh Religion, Culture and Ethnicity.* London: Routledge, 2001

Singh, Harbans. *The Encyclopaedia of Sikhism.* Patiala: Punjabi University, 1992.

———. *The Heritage of the Sikhs.* New Delhi: Manohar, 1983..

Singh, Nikky Guninder Kaur. *The Feminine Principle in the Sikh Vision of the Transcendent.* Cambridge: Cambridge University Press, 1993.

———. *The Name of My Beloved: Verses of the Sikh Gurus.* San Francisco: HarperSanFrancisco, 1995.

———. *Sikhism.* New York: Facts on File, 1993.

Singh, Pashaura, and N. Gerald Barrier. *Sikh Identity: Continuity and Change.* New Delhi: Manohar, 1999.

Singh, Patwant. *The Golden Temple.* Hong Kong: ET Pub. Ltd, 1988.

Stronge, Susan, ed. *The Arts of the Sikh Kingdoms.* London: Victoria & Albert Publications, 1999.

Tatla, Darshan Singh. *Sikhs in North America: An Annotated Bibliography.* New York: Greenwood Press, 1991.

3

Shamans and Animists

Graham Harvey

A man in a bird mask is playing a steady rhythm on a bodhran (pronounced "bow-rahn," an Irish-style frame drum) on a high ridge overlooking a wide plain. As he dances himself into a light trance, the drum beat gets quieter and he settles himself down at the roots of a tall tree. He has come to this place to renew his friendship with what he calls the "spirits of the place" and to "enter the dream of the land." Later he will drink tea from a thermos flask before driving back to his home in a nearby city in England. He will have found new energy and enthusiasm to pursue his job as an environmental educator working with groups in schools and country parks. He may even have received fresh ideas about ways to do his work. He is a shaman, a mediator between the human and other-than-human communities. Shamans are also healers: this man tries to heal relationships, especially helping people to restore good relations with the other inhabitants of the places in which they live—that is, the animals, plants and other living beings. He does not teach a religion called "shamanism." Most of the people with whom he works have no idea that he is a shaman. Indeed, many have never heard the word or, if they have, it was on a TV programme about Siberia or the Amazon. Few associate what this man does with what they know about shamans. He does not advertise his title or worldview but encourages and enables people to live ecologically responsible and celebratory lives. He has colleagues who are not shamans but are also committed environmental educators. But, he says, all his inspiration, commitment, and passion come from his shamanic engagement with empowering beings whom he visits in the otherworld he accesses while in trance on that high ridge away from the city.

This chapter is about shamans and their communities. It introduces the world or the nature of reality as it is understood by two loose groups of people. (These are not organised groups, and the differences between them are not fixed.) The first group can be labelled "animists" (a term that will be explained later) whose worldview and lifeways make shamans necessary for certain purposes. The second can be called "self-religionists" (again, this will be explained soon) for some of whom it is desirable to become a shaman. The animists are the chief focus of the chapter, along with animist shamans. Some attention is devoted to self-religion shamans in the later part of the chapter. The conclusion will note that in reality people often shift back and forward between the two groups— which, anyway, only exist as broad categories of academic study.

First, we must confront the problem that until recently there was no religion called "shamanism." In fact, the recent idea that shamans and those who employ them practice "shamanism" might surprise many of those so labelled. It is not just that the label is strange to them: it is common for strangers, visitors. and academics to feel they need to label something that locals or insiders take for granted as part of their everyday lives. But in this case, as far as some of those involved are concerned, the title "shamanism" might seem as strange as if Christianity were called "priestism" or Buddhism "monkism." What shamans, priests, and monks do is of great importance to many people, but their technical activities (doing what shamans, priests. and monks do) are far from the whole of these religions. It is also important to note that shamans are not the only religious officials that animists might approach or employ. Indeed, to identify people as members of a religion called "shamanism" when they might only rarely call upon shamans pays far too much attention to such matters.

Nonetheless, that there is now a religion called shamanism is evidenced by the large number of books and websites with "shamanism" in their titles. Many of these are devoted to helping people become shamans, and it is now possible to train to do so almost anywhere. There has been a massive, rapid, and widespread increase in global, popular, positive interest in shamans and their worldviews and practices. While I will argue that these new shamans are not the same as the other kind (the ones I'm calling "animists"), and while it is true that "shamanism" is a new phenomenon, this does not mean that new ways of being a shaman are not religious or interesting. The two kinds of shaman are just different, existing in different cultural contexts—and the difference between them helps us understand both.

The first part of the chapter is about animists, then something will be said about the shamans they employ. In fact, these shamans are themselves animists who work for other animists. This is a label that is now applied to people who understand the world to be a community of persons, most of whom are not human, but all of whom deserve respect. Animists are people who are involved in learning how to be a good person in respectful relationships with other persons, whether or not they are human.[1] They resort to (animist) shamans when they need someone who is good at mediating with various other-than-human persons, or who can help restore the well-being of individuals and communities by various means.

The following vignettes are about a community of First Nation Canadians or, more accurately, indigenous Newfoundlanders. They offer some insights into what animism means to a community when things are going reasonably well, when there is no need to call in shamans to solve problems. Later we will discuss the kinds of problems that make shamans necessary to animists and what they do about it.

Conne River Powwow

Eagles are quite common along Newfoundland's Conne River. They live among the forested rocky crags across the river from the Mi'kmaq town of Miawpukek (a First Nations reserve recognised by the Newfoundland and Canadian governments). They often take fish from the community's fishery in the Bay d'Espoir. Local people, therefore, see them every day. However, when the inhabitants of Miawpukek held their first traditional, non-competitive powwow in 1996, an eagle flew one perfect circle over the central drum group during the final honor song, and then flew back to its treetop eyrie across the river. Everyone, locals and visitors, noticed. Cries of *"kitpu"* or "eagle" simultaneously greeted the eagle, expressed pleasure at its beauty and participation, and declared that its flight demonstrated approval for the event. The flight of this eagle, in this way, at this moment, was celebrated as an encouragement to the Mi'kmaq community to continue the process of returning to their observance of traditional lifeways. Several people told me that what was happening at Miawpukek was not a "revitalisation movement" because traditional ways did not need revitalising: the eagles and bears had always maintained them. Now that significant numbers of the indigenous human population of the area, and of the island more generally, were returning to participate in traditional ways of life and traditional understandings of the world, a representative of the eagles was honoring them for coming home and joining in.

Powwows are indigenous North American cultural festivals with a particular stress on dancing. Sometimes dancers compete for prizes (best costume, best dancer of a particular style), but at Conne River this

---

1. Graham Harvey, *Animism: Respecting the Living World* (London: C. Hurst & Co., 2005).

first powwow was not competitive. The drum groups and dancers were part of a celebration of the recovery of pride in being indigenous or native. The dances were not thought of as "religious" or "sacred," except perhaps for the "honor songs" which paid respect to elders and veterans and involved the use of eagle feathers and eagle-bone whistles, which are considered sacred by many native people in North America. Near the powwow dance grounds were a series of more explicitly sacred places. A fire was kept alight throughout the three days of the powwow and was the focus of ceremonies each dawn. People would gather and smoke a pipe of tobacco or kinnikinnick (a mixture of local herbs) together, always offering smoke to the six directions (east, south, west, north, above and below). They would also make small offerings to the fire. When they talked about this they would say that it was important to feed the fire not only with wood but also with gifts of sacred herbs and even with the first portion of the food prepared for all powwow participants. "Feeding the fire" was obviously not just a metaphor, the fire was understood to desire food and to be grateful to those who made offerings, as well as those who gave it wood.

On the same promontory on a bend in the river, the organisers had constructed four sweat lodges. These were temporary domed structures in which about a dozen people could sit around a central hole in the ground. Stones were heated up in a large fire outside between the four lodges, and at appropriate moments in a long ceremony they were brought in and placed in the hole. Water poured on the hot stones immediately turned to steam and raised the temperature dramatically. The coverings on the lodges kept the heat in and the light out. The ceremony in the darkness and the heat was not undertaken for individual health (lodges are not like Scandinavian saunas) but in order to pray for the well-being of all living beings. Some people talk about "stone people lodges" rather than "sweat lodges," implying that the most powerful participants in the ceremony are not the sweating humans but the rocks who are understood to be giving up their lives for the benefit of all other living beings. They are addressed as "grandfathers," a term of respect and kinship.

One day during the powwow I was talking with the leader of one of the sweat-lodge ceremonies about everything that was happening that week. He started to talk about how Conne River was not only home to human people, but to a wide range of other-than-human people including the bears, eagles, fish, trees, rocks, and the fire. He said that there were also people who were only seen in visions, people who might come to teach someone how to live a better life, or to give them some piece of knowledge that they could use to help others. He said that the craggy rock across the river was home to a community of "little people." But as

Figure 3.1: *A sweat lodge or "stone people lodge" with a corner of the covers lifted to reveal the framework. (Photo by Joyce Gannon.)*

soon as he said this, he stopped talking to me, walked to the river bank and seemed to speak to someone over the river. Later he told me that it was not appropriate to speak about such powerful people without their permission and without offering respect. He apologised but insisted that no more should be said about them. The important thing, he said, was to talk with them if they showed themselves to you, but otherwise to leave them in peace. Having been given similar advice in Ireland, I suspect that the "little people" are not little; rather, this term is used to speak about powerful beings without distracting them from whatever they may be doing at the time.

These four short stories about my experiences at Miawpukek's first powwow (the eagle's flight, the fire being fed, the sweat lodge ceremonies, and the "little people") illustrate facets of a way of living that can be called "animism." The Conne River Band of the Mi'kmaq Nation are not the only animists in the world. Many indigenous peoples share animist understandings of the nature of the world and practice animistic ceremonies. Animism has also been a factor in the revival of Paganism, especially among those who stress the importance of belonging to particular places, those who have sought advice from indigenous people, and those are the forefront of Pagan eco-activism.

It is important to remember that there are many different kinds of animists. Animism is not a single religion, but a label for a kind of religion or a trend recognisable among religions. This chapter provides an introduction to the flavour of animism using real (or slightly fictionalised) examples from many places, but it does not claim that all animists are the same or that they agree on everything. This is particularly true because animism (like all living religions) arises from and is expressed in particular relationships. Animists in particular places engage with *specific* living beings, or "other-than-human persons," who live in the same area.

The intention of these introductory stories is to suggest issues that most, maybe all, animists would recognise as being important. At the heart of each story is knowing that the world is a community of living beings—persons—most of whom are not human, but all of whom deserve respect and are willing to communicate. In sweat lodges, people often end each round of prayers by saying "all our relations," recognising that all living beings (which might include rocks) are related. (There are many different sweat lodge traditions, and not all of them use "all our relations" as a refrain, but all address other beings in kinship terms). This is the common ground that animists share. The precise question of how one recognises a living being and how one actually engages in relationships with other-than-human persons generates the diversity of local styles of animism. Later we will discuss the problems caused by animist ways of life that require shamans to act as mediators and healers. The following two sections, however, address two contrasting uses of the word "animism." These will not only enrich our understanding of how animists engage with the world, but will also prevent confusion caused by later reading of different interpretations of animism.

Edward Tylor's Old Animism

Many dictionaries define animism as a "belief in souls and spirits" or as the "attribution of soul or life to inanimate or natural objects." Sometimes animism is said to be the belief in a supernatural force animating natural objects, the world or the cosmos. The problem with these definitions is that they suggest, if not state, that animism is wrong because it does not match the modern notion that "natural objects" (such as trees and animals) do not have souls or life in the same way that humans do. These dictionaries also define "soul" as some part of humans that is different to their bodies, possibly combining consciousness, will, and emotion. It might be seen as the part of humans that is immortal. Certainly it is said to be distinct from physical or material form. More detailed discussions would show that in some cultures it is understood that people have more than one "soul," each performing a different function. Despite the complexity of these systems of knowledge, dictionaries often allege that animists are simply and childishly confused about the nature of the world, projecting human attributes (life, soul, consciousness, immortality, mind) on to inanimate, "natural" (i.e. merely physical) objects.

The dictionaries are following a tradition established by Edward Tylor in the late nineteenth century. Tylor is sometimes called the "father of anthropology." He was interested in a remarkable range of human activities. In his two-volume work *Primitive Culture*, Tylor argued that religion is a "belief in souls or spirits."[2] He asserted that these are mistaken beliefs: such entities do not really exist but came to be believed in because their existence would explain strange dreams and feverish hallucinations. Also, he thought, such beliefs were persuasive because they comforted people in the face of death. That is, if you dream of someone whom you know to be far away, perhaps your "soul" is travelling to meet them. If you know that someone possesses a "spirit," you can hope that when they die you may meet them again in another form or in another realm. Tylor drew on evidence provided by travelers, missionaries, colonial officers and many other sources from around the world. He was not chiefly concerned with offering a careful ethnographic description of particular people and their cultures and knowledges. He thought that the mass of data that he collected was evidence of particular local types of a common, global phenomenon called "religion." He also argued that it was possible to use this information to discover the first creation of religion and to trace its evolution throughout history. Thus, he claimed to have defined the one thing that all religious ideas and practices have in common. His conclusion was that at an early stage in human cultural evolution people adopted the mistaken belief in souls and spirits, and that only modern rational science could correct the error and discover the real world.

Much of Tylor's work was challenged as soon as it was published, and now it survives only as an example of superseded Victorian scholarship. His work cannot be cited as an accurate description of any particular culture, and no one is convinced by his claim to have defined the essence of religion. Nonetheless, dictionaries still echo his assertion that there are people called animists who believe in souls and spirits. Perhaps this is related to the fact that Tylor's views coincide closely with the modern notion that only humans possess mind while everything else is mere matter. This notion, too, has been challenged from many perspectives but remains generative and pervasive for some.

---

2. Edward Tylor, *Primitive Culture* (London: John Murray, 1913 [1871]).

The New Animism

The term "animist" has been adopted in some places as a self-designation, a label by which people are happy to identify themselves. For example, many West Africans who observe traditional religious practices but are not Christians or Muslims call themselves animists. Increasing numbers of British Pagans call themselves animists, especially those who stress the importance of respecting the diversity of life in their immediate surroundings. What these people mean by "animism" is not what Edward Tylor meant. Contemporary scholars use the term in a new way that fits better with evidence provided by conversations with animists and participation with them in relationships in particular places.

The new use of the term animism labels ways of living in the world that understand it to be a community of living persons, most of whom are not human, but all of whom deserve respect and engage in relationships of various kinds. In contrast with Tylor's stress on beliefs in souls and spirits, the new animism is concerned with behaving towards other beings with respect—or "caution and care" as Mary Black says.[3] The key words are different: "souls" and "belief" in the old animism, "persons" and "behaving respectfully" in the new animism. Many of the scholars interested in animism draw on the work of Irving Hallowell, who spent time with the Ojibwa of Beren's River in southern central Canada in the 1930s and 1940s.

In the Ojibwa language a grammatical distinction is made between animate and inanimate genders but not between masculine and feminine genders. A suffix, –g, is added to nouns and verbs that refer to animate persons rather than inanimate objects. For example, the plural form of the word *asin* (stone) is *asiniig*, identifying stones as grammatically animate.[4] Ojibwa speakers use the same personal pronoun (*wiin*) for masculine and feminine persons, not making much of the difference between masculine and feminine (grammatically anyway), but they use animate gender terms for a wider range of beings than the English language officially recognises. In practice some English speakers do talk about their ships, cars or computers as if they were animate beings rather than inanimate objects, giving them names and applying the personal pronouns "he" or "she" rather than the impersonal "it." In the French language, tables are marked as grammatically feminine, *la table* rather than *le table*. Do French speakers treat "female" tables as animate female persons?

---

3. Mary B. Black, "Ojibway Power Belief Systems," in *The Anthropology of Power*, ed. Raymond D. Fogelson and Richard N. Adams (New York: Academic, 1977), 141-51.

4. John D. Nichols and Earl Nyholm, *A Concise Dictionary of Minnesota Ojibwe* (Minneapolis: University of Minnesota Press, 1995), 14.

Perhaps they do in poetry and children's stories, but what about in everyday reality? Just so, the question arises, do the Ojibwa treat grammatically animate stones as animate persons? Do they speak with stones or act in other ways that reveal intentions to build or maintain relationships?

Irving Hallowell asked an old Ojibwa man, "Are *all* the stones we see about us here alive?" [5] Grammatically all stones everywhere are animate, but did the old man actually think that particular rocks around him were alive? The man (who is never named) answered, "No! but *some* are." He had witnessed a particular stone following the leader of a shamanic ceremony around a tent as he sang. Another powerful leader is said to have had a large stone that would open when he tapped it three times, allowing him to remove a small bag of herbs when he needed it in ceremonies. Hallowell was told that when a white trader was digging his potato patch, he found a stone that looked like it may be important. He called for the leader of another ceremony who knelt down to talk to the stone, asking if it had come from someone's ceremonial tent. The stone is said to have denied this. Movement, gift-giving and conversation are three indicators of the animate nature of relational beings, or persons.

Hallowell makes it clear that the key point in each account is not that stones do things of their own volition (however remarkable this claim might seem) but that they engage in relationships. For the Ojibwa the interesting question is not "how do we know stones are alive?" but "what is the appropriate way for people, of whatever species, to relate?" This is as true for humans as it is for stones, trees, animals, birds, fish, and all other beings that might be recognised as persons. Persons are known to be persons when they relate to other persons in particular ways, more or less intimately, willingly or respectfully. (This is not to forget that enmity is also a relationship, and we will think about this in a while.) The category of "person" is only applicable *when* beings are relating with others. This is quite different to the understanding of ontology (the way being is understood) in most European-derived cultures, in which personhood is an interior quality, a fact about an individual (human) who is self-conscious. Hallowell recognised this by insisting that we are not talking here about different "belief systems"—epistemologies—but about different ontologies, different ways of being in the world, different ways of living. Indeed, we could say that the Ojibwa old man lived in a different world from Hallowell's until the latter learnt to see the world as his teacher showed it to be.

5. A. Irving Hallowell, "Ojibwa Ontology, Behavior, and World View," in *Readings in Indigenous Religions,* ed. Graham Harvey (London: Continuum, 2002), 24. Originally published in *Culture and History: Essays in Honor of Paul Radin,* ed. Stanley Diamond (New York, Columbia University Press, 1952). Citations are to the Continuum edition.

The World Is a Community

Having learnt from his Ojibwa hosts, Hallowell coined the phrase (used several times in this chapter already) "other-than-human persons" to refer to the animate beings with whom humans share the world. He has been criticised for privileging humanity, as if he were saying that what makes something a person is their likeness to humans. In fact, he is clear that "person" is not defined by human characteristics or behaviours. The term is a much larger umbrella than "human." All beings communicate intentionally and act towards others relationally: this makes them "persons." It is useful *for us* (humans) to speak about "human-" and "other-than-human" persons only because (a) we are humans talking to humans (if we were bears we might speak of "other-than-bear persons"), and (b) because the English language encourages people to hear the word "person" as a reference to humans. It is a common problem in speaking of religions or of cultures other than our own that we do not have words that translate exactly what other people say in their language. If the phrase "other-than-human person" seems clumsy, this is only because it derives from a world that speakers of English and other European languages do not easily inhabit. A great weight of history and accepted ideology encourages us to think that humans are different from all other beings. Our uniqueness has been asserted so often that we find it difficult to see ourselves as related to all other living beings. We easily speak of our "environment" as if we were surrounded by a heap of resources available for the taking. "Nature" is like the blank page on which humans write significant "cultural" words. But animists live in a different world: a community of persons all of whom are capable of relationship, communication, agency and desire. There is no mute or inert "nature," but only the many competing conversations of cultural life. Perhaps some more examples will enrich understanding here.

All Our Relations

Another of Hallowell's informants told him that he had been visiting with an elderly couple during a thunder storm. He said, "There was one clap of thunder after another. Suddenly the old man turned to his wife and asked, 'Did you hear what was said?' 'No,' she replied, 'I didn't catch it.'" Hallowell comments that

> The casualness of the remark and even the trivial character of the anecdote demonstrate the psychological depth of the "social relations" with other-than-human beings that becomes explicit in the behavior

of the Ojibwa as a consequence of the cognitive "set" induced by
their culture.[6]

In other words, after a lifetime living as animists this couple assumed that
thunder is an act of communication.

On a short visit to the midwestern United States, I was invited to
go sage-picking with a group of Lakota and Ojibwe (a variety of spell-
ings and different names are used by the people: not only Ojibwa and
Ojibwe but also Anishinaabeg, Chippewa and others). They use sage in
their prayers throughout the year, burning some when they seek purification, and making up small bundles to offer as gifts to helpful other-than-
human persons. We drove out of the city to a location where sage grew
plentifully. Before cutting any sage, or even entering the field, everyone
took pinches of sage left over from the previous year and held it to their
hearts while introducing themselves to the field of sage, and requesting
permission to cut some leaves for the following year. After a pause each
person placed their sage offering on the ground. Once these gifts were
given and one of the elders had indicated that permission was given,
everyone gathered new leaves, being careful not to destroy entire plants
and expressing gratitude each time they cut.

A similar experience was told to me by a Pagan couple who cut holly,
ivy, and yew annually in order to decorate their home for their midwinter
Yule festival. Their common practice had been to introduce themselves
and their purpose at a spring in the heart of a wood near their home.
They lit a candle and some incense by the spring while offering season's
greetings to the wood and its inhabitants. Then they offered gifts to each
tree from which they cut greenery, sometimes pouring libations of some
drink at the roots of the trees, or tying strands of wool around a branch.
One year, as they were leaving the wood, they saw a holly tree burdened
with ripe berries. What they had cut until then held few berries, and
they thought that just a few sprigs with their red fruit would enhance
their celebrations. In too much of a hurry, or thinking that they had
already addressed the whole wood, they attempted to cut from a branch.
Although there was no wind that day, the prickly tree swiped the couple.
Chastened, they apologized and left, being careful in future visits to pay
particular attention to that tree.

In one of her excellent discussions of Aboriginal Australian relationships with their land and other-than-human neighbours Debbie Rose
writes that not only humans, but also "other animals like kangaroos have
their own rituals and law, and ... they too take care of relationships of

---

6. Hallowell, "Ojibwa Ontology," 34.

well-being" among all the inhabitants of an area or "country." All related beings share rights and responsibilities, and are expected to be committed to and concerned for each other's "flourishing in the world."[7] Rose uses the term "totemism" to refer to these relationships and commitments that cross species boundaries, involving high degrees of mutual care. The word "totem" originated among the Ojibwe and refers to clans that include humans and particular animals and plants. It has come to be used more widely, but Rose demonstrates that many Aboriginal Australians understand totemic clans similarly to Ojibwe, i.e. as close inter-species kindreds. The title of one of her books points to the central importance of these relationships in making (human/Aboriginal) people what they are: *Dingo Makes Us Human*.[8] Rose is careful to point out that relationships are not always harmonious: they can lead to tension, conflict and competition. There is often a need for mediators or diplomats to intervene between groups and individuals to sort out problems (the kind of intervention that might be the main activity of shamans in some communities, as we'll see). But in a community that privileges respect and seeks cooperation there is likely to be a bias towards trying to resolve differences amicably rather than destructively.

This series of short narratives illustrates a variety of points about animism. First among them is that animists treat the world as a community of living beings. Animists assume or expect that other-than-human persons might speak with them, give and receive gifts, and in other ways act intentionally as members of a local cross-species community. On occasions these relationships can be made tense or even aggressive by the competing desires and needs of particular beings or species meeting others. These various ways in which particular animists act towards other persons, human or otherwise, imply too that not all animists are alike; there are different kinds of animism. This diversity is hinted at in the vignettes by the inclusion of different groups of indigenous people and of British Pagans. But there is more: the indigenous people include both those who hold "traditional" worldviews and those who identify as Roman Catholic Christians. As was said earlier, "animism" is not a label for a single religion but for a style of religious activity. It is a style that seems appropriate not only to those commonly labelled "animists" but also to many other people.

These short narratives should also make it evident that animists do not

7. Deborah B. Rose, "Totemism, Regions, and Co-management in Aboriginal Australia," draft paper for the Conference of the International Association for the Study of Common Property, Vancouver, June 10-14, 1998, http://www.indiana.edu/~iascp/Drafts/rose.pdf

8. Deborah B. Rose, *Dingo Makes Us Human: Life and Land in an Australian Aboriginal Culture* (Cambridge: Cambridge University Press, 2002).

privilege a supernatural or spiritual realm over material, physical reality. The phrase "other-than-human persons" embraces plants, rocks, animals, and thunder storms. Contrary to what Tylor's version of animism suggested, there has been only one reference, so far, to any animist belief in spirits and souls. But when the shaman whose story introduces this chapter speaks of "spirits of place" it is likely he does so only because he thinks that is easier than naming the specific beings of different kinds with whom he relates. Possibly, too, he is speaking of what others call the *genius loci*, a Latin term that refers to the powerful guardian of particular places.[9] Interestingly, he is not in the least interested in "believing" in such beings. He says he is far too busy talking (and sometimes arguing) with the other-than-human inhabitants of the place to worry about belief and believing. Although some interpreters of animism insert the word "spirit" into their discussions, speaking of "tree spirits" or "rock spirits," the word hardly aids our understanding of what animists mean when they assert that trees and rocks intentionally communicate.

Otherworlds and Spirits

Having said all this, and without weakening the statement at all, it is important to note that animists might also assert that there are more elusive, less robustly material beings whom it is possible to encounter. According to Ojibwe animists, one of the signs that someone is a powerful person is that they are able to change their shape or transform their appearance. What may look like a thunder cloud one minute may appear as a rock or a bear or a human at another time.

Many animists say that there are beings in the world unrecognised as yet by rational scientists. In common with many other people they might continue to talk with their deceased relatives. In elaborate ceremonies or in casual everyday comments, people tell the dead what they are doing and seek advice and help. In many communities it is deemed appropriate to speak to any and every deceased person. In others, only those who were wise or powerful people before death are revered as ancestors after death. Especially wise or powerful ancestors might become the focus of ceremonies conducted only by people who have trained in the use of trance to be able to access an other-than-everyday reality in which they can converse with the elite among the ancestors. Just as animists give gifts when cutting plants, seeking reciprocal gifts in return, so they make culturally appropriate offerings to the ancestors.

9. For example, Barry Patterson, *The Art of Conversation with the Genius Loci* (Milverton: Capall Bann, 2005).

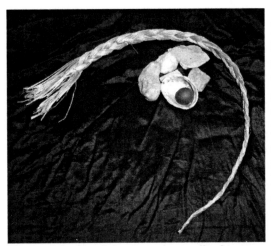

Figure 3.2: *One of these stones is reputed to be a transformation of a thunder-being. Intimate (relational) knowledge is required to distinguish between them. The braid of sweet grass is an offering to the stones. (Photo by Graham Harvey.)*

Traditionally, the Inuit of the Arctic live by hunting seals and other sea creatures in the winter and caribou and other land creatures in the summer. Like many hunting groups, they say that animals have a leader, a Mistress or Master of Animals, who controls the number of animals taken by hunters. Not only is it important to offer respect to this leader, but it is vital that particular animals are treated respectfully too. Any insult is likely to lead to failure in hunting, and thus to hunger and maybe even starvation. But even respectful hunting and eating has its dangers. Animists do not see the world as a resource given to them to exploit but as a community of persons, relational beings worthy of respect. Also, death might not be the end of existence, but a particularly dramatic transformation into another stage of life. If the world is a community of persons, how is it possible to eat? Ceremonies in which animists request permission to take lives for the purpose of eating are not romantic decorations of an otherwise hard life. They are key elements of the relationships that animists work hard to maintain between themselves and other-than-human persons. Animists are taught by their elders (people responsible for inculcating appropriate ways of acting towards others) that relationships involve reciprocity. This can be wonderful when you are busy offering respectful gifts, but sometimes relationships go badly wrong. By accident or intention someone gets insulted. One insult or act of violence is likely to be reciprocated with more insults or violence unless someone steps in to mediate. Animists often need shamans.

Shamans and Shamanism

The word "shaman" derives from the Tungus language family spoken in Siberia. Among the Tungus-speaking Evenk, for example, it refers to religious ceremonial specialists whose job it is to serve their (animist) communities in particular ways. They deal with some of the problems caused by living in animist ways. They are the diplomats who negotiate between human communities and the wider other-than-human community. If someone gets injured, shamans are called upon to find out if there is a personal cause or if this is "just an accident." Illnesses are often thought to be caused by aggrieved or aggressive otherworld beings, diseases are persons (just as bacteria and, perhaps, viruses may be). There are also predators in the world who consider humans to be prey, desirable sources of food. If animals feel insulted they will make sure that the hunters will fail to find anything to eat. In each case, shamans are necessary.

There has been considerable debate about whether the term "shaman" should be used with reference to anyone outside of Siberia, or anyone apart from Tungus-speakers. The problem is that by applying the label one might make the mistake of thinking that what one shaman does is the same as what all shamans do. In fact, there are differences even between Evenk shamans. Interestingly, these differences are caused by the fact that they are animists. That is, each shaman is involved in more or less intimate relationships with particular other-than-human people, especially those from otherworlds (dimensions of reality normally alien to most humans). They are part of a group (the shaman and other-than-human and otherworld persons) who work together to heal people from particular illness-persons, to deal with particular animal-persons who may need persuading to become available to humans as food, or to gain knowledge otherwise inaccessible but necessary to the continuity of life or the well-being of society.

What makes some scholars sure that it is necessary to use the term "shaman" more widely is that there are religious experts in many parts of the world who perform ceremonies for similar (not always identical) purposes and do so in similar (but never identical) ways. The most common practice that leads some ritual leaders to be identified as shamans is the ability to enter trance states deliberately.

One scholar, Mircea Eliade, has dominated the study of what he called "shamanism." He placed techniques for altering states of consciousness, achieving trance or "ecstasy," the sense of being outside one's body and especially the sense of journeying to other dimensions, at the heart of what shamans do. Those who have followed Eliade's lead have used the phrase "altered state(s) of consciousness," or its abbreviation "ASC," so much that it is hard to see shamanism as anything but the deliberate manipulation of inner states, the quest for ecstasy.

Eliade asserted that there is a world-wide phenomenon, originating in the earliest phases of human evolution, in which people set apart in some way (at birth or in a life-threatening illness or accident) are trained by more experienced shamans or by otherworld persons to control their conscious states in order to perceive and enter other realities. Once there, they gain knowledge and power to help their communities. The title of Eliade's book summarises his whole argument: *Shamanism: Archaic Techniques of Ecstasy*.[10] The echoes of Edward Tylor's claims about animism ring loudly here. Eliade has not been rejected quite as decisively as Tylor, but there are few scholars who support his argument or approach without significant qualifications. Leaving aside the idea that we could know what the earliest "archaic" religion of humanity was like, there is just too much about Eliade's work that reveals it to be his own wished-for edifice. It is not acceptable to dismiss as "degenerate" those who do not quite fit Eliade's package—failing to journey into otherworlds using one or more of Eliade's preferred techniques, or not privileging a putative upper-world as Eliade did. In the end, there is too much Eliade in his construction of "shamanism" to be an acceptable lens through which to examine what shamans do.

Rejecting the notion that there was any such (systematised) thing as "shamanism" before Western travellers and scholars invented it out of the various practices and worldviews they observed (or imagined) among indigenous people, we are helped to see that what animist shamans do is rooted in what animists need them to do. Instead of paying so much attention to the strange practice of trance or "ecstasy" we might use the acronym "ASC" to talk about "altered styles of communication" rather than "altered states of consciousness." This aids understanding because it pays attention to the purposes for which shamans alter consciousness rather than to unusual techniques. Shamans communicate (with words and rituals, and sometimes with aggressive actions) with other-than-human persons, particularly the powerful ones, especially those from other dimensions of the world. They do so for the benefit of their human community but always in relationship with other-than-human helpers. They are called upon to act as shamans when things go wrong.

Other animists can and do talk with the other-than-human persons to whom they are related in totemic clans (cross-species kin groups). In many places animist adolescents are sent out into places less frequented by humans to seek a vision of a personal helper. This other-than-human or otherworld person may be with them for the rest of their lives and be the subject of continuous relational encounters and rituals. Animist elders (not shamans) may be responsible for making regular offerings to

10. Mircea Eliade, *Shamanism: Archaic Techniques of Ecstasy*, trans. Willard R. Trask (New York: Pantheon, 1964).

a wide range of other-than-human persons to maintain the health of the whole, diverse inter-species community of a particular place. (In addition to Debbie Rose's work, cited earlier, see Caroline Humphrey and Urgunge Onon's discussion of the different roles of shamans and elders among Daur Mongols.[11])

Shamans are deemed most valuable in many places when they cooperate with a range of allies in conflicts with beings who prey on or otherwise assault their human community. Piers Vitebsky writes of this risky business that "the shaman is a hero who makes a bold and necessary intervention into cosmic processes. The power to act is precarious and this human action is fraught with danger."[12] The willingness of shamans to take on their risky ventures and maintain high-risk relationships is deemed necessary in many animistic communities or contexts because someone has to deal with conflicts of interest between human and other-than-human persons who, altogether, make up the living world.

Contemporary Shamans and Core Shamanism

Contrary to Eliade's polemic, contemporary shamans are not (by definition) degenerate heirs to a once more noble, archaic tradition. Like members of other religions, they are the contemporary performers of living and evolving practices. Their worldviews, like their rituals, develop as new situations, needs, desires, knowledges and ideas arise. They, and the wider animistic communities for which they work, not only respond to outside or alien pressures, they actively seek the tools they need to deal with the world today.

Examples of mutual interaction between animists, shamans, and practitioners of a remarkable array of religious and cultural movements abound. In Siberia (the putative heartlands of "shamanism"), and elsewhere in central and north Asia, the fall of the Soviet empire has led to new possibilities for shamans as, for example, employees in various national, regional, or ethnic heritage performances. Amazonia continues to produce new movements inspired by animistic, Catholic, Spiritist, and other worldviews and lifeways. Shamans incorporate chants to their outboard motors in their repertoire of healing and empowering ritual songs. Elsewhere, animistic shamans, as the opening vignette of this chapter illustrates, confront the hierarchical separation of humans

11. Caroline Humphrey with Urgunge Onon, *Shamans and Elders: Experience, Knowledge, and Power among the Daur Mongols* (New York: Oxford University Press, 1996)

12. Piers Vitebsky, "From Cosmology to Environmentalism: Shamanism as a Local Knowledge in a Global Setting," in *Shamanism: A Reader*, ed. Graham Harvey (London: Routledge, 2005), 279.

from the world induced by Cartesian modernism. They blend ritual and educative expertise in entertaining and profound acts of creativity that aim to reinvigorate human relationships with other beings. Perhaps they answer Ronald Grimes' incitement to imagine a ritual performance that will be suitable to the need for humans to "root themselves in the planet like old trees."[13]

Contemporary animist shamans (and their animist neighbours)—who drive cars, design websites, run fish farms, use credit cards, vote in political elections and otherwise share and contest modern global culture— are the current exponents of one way of being and acting as shamans. There is another way. Although this way of being a shaman is now commonly called "shamanism" it too is fluid, changeable and dynamic. Some people shift (more or less easily) between the two forms—demonstrating again the need to be careful not to imagine that academic distinctions are anything more than useful ways of seeing patterns.

What I have called "self-religion shamans" may sometimes also be animists. But the key feature that invites us to see them differently is that what they do has a particular purpose. In common with a significant number of other people worldwide, they aim to enhance their knowledge of themselves, and improve their self-expression and personal well-being. Paul Heelas's encapsulation of New Age as a "self-religion" is applicable here too.[14] Following Eliade and particularly Michael Harner's "core shamanism,"[15] self-religion shamans employ "the techniques of ecstasy" to understand, improve and heal their inner selves. This shamanism is a therapeutic movement entirely suited to the modern age. Its concept of the self and its purpose is largely that of modernity: there is an inner core to each individual that can be accessed and more fully realised by a variety of techniques drawn from meditative, psychotherapeutic and other practices as well from animist shamanic performances. The various alienations and losses of soul that seem endemic in modern life can treated in what may then be seen as a path towards wholeness and maturity.

This brief sketch of the emerging phenomenon of modern shamanism is in no way meant to suggest that it is of less value or interest than the animism which has been the focus of most of this chapter. For that matter, the brevity of this introduction might misleadingly suggest that the two kinds of shaman have nothing in common. Again, let me emphasise that

13. Ronald Grimes, "Performance Is Currency in the Deep World's Gift Economy," *Interdisciplinary Studies in Literature and Environment* 9 (2002): 162.

14. Paul Heelas, *The New Age Movement: Religion, Culture and Society in the Age of Postmodernity* (Oxford: Blackwell, 1996).

15. Michael Harner, *The Way of the Shaman* (San Francisco: Harper & Row, 1980).

people can and do shift between the two styles. However, there are differences of purpose, performance and philosophy that are worth attending to. The foundation of this difference is the understanding of what it means to be a person. By trying to see the specifics of particular practices of both animist shamans and self-religion shamans we begin to see what attracts people to each. For animist shamans the world is an interrelated community and a person is a being made up of many relationships. For self-religion shamans the world is a collection of individuals and the true self is found within. Shamans of both kinds offer therapies appropriate to both worlds. They intervene to attempt to deal with the difficulties of living. If the animist shaman tends to work for others and the self-religion shaman seeks to work on their inner self, both do so because they understand these to be the most significant arenas of need.

There are, then, broadly speaking, two kinds of shaman. Each kind is actually lived out in a multiplicity of different styles in particular localities. This must be true given that the broader contexts in which shamans perform their religious acts also vary enormously. There is no one way to be an animist. There is no one way to be a modernist. Variety of experience as well as expression are common to followers of all living religions, including shamans and animists.

Suggestions for Further Reading

Harvey, Graham, ed. *Shamanism: A Reader*. London: Routledge, 2003.
————. *Animism: Respecting the Living World*. London: C. Hurst & Co., 2005.

4

Practitioners of Indigenous Religions of Africa and the African Diaspora

Afe Adogame

It is not unusual for a casual observer walking on the streets of a traditional Yoruba town or village to confront certain objects such as cooked or raw food, a decapitated bird or animal, eggs, cowry shells, coins, candles, etc., in a clay bowl or pot, conspicuously displayed at a road junction, road intersection, or at the foot of a gigantic Iroko tree. While such sights and objects may convey little or no meaning for non-Africans, many indigenous Africans will immediately recognize and contemplate the religious and ritual significance of these objects. They may have been deposited at the spot within a specific ritual time, mostly at midnight. This may be perhaps in compliance with a specific ritual instruction emanating from a religious adept, diviner, traditional healer, sorcerer, or by the decision of the individual. The act of ritual sacrifice and offering indicates the intersection of the visible and the invisible worlds and a human intent to project into the spiritual cosmos. It is the symbolic presentation of material or physical objects to the spiritual entities through ritual action. The import of sacrifice and offering is partly to avert a calamity or an impending danger, or to atone for offences, attract the benevolence of spiritual forces, or to show appreciation and thanksgiving for favor received from benevolent spiritual agencies. Thus ritual sacrifice is meant both to counteract the evil machinations of the malevolent spiritual beings on humans and to invoke the benevolence of the deities, ancestors, and spirits in order to ensure and maintain cosmic balance and cohesion in the society. For that reason, many people would not dare to remove such objects nor play with them, as such action is believed to have negative repercussion

Figure 4.1: *Sacrificial offering by a road in Brazil (Photo by Kelly E. Hayes)*

for both the one who places it there as well as the one who removes it.

As I walked down New York's Harlem 148th Street adjoining Malcolm X Boulevard on a hot summer afternoon in June 2007, I was suddenly distracted by a small crowd that had formed a semicircle beside makeshift kiosks and street vendors stretching along the busy commercial street, reminiscent of Paul Stoller's vivid description of New York's informal economy and "commerce-from-below."[1] Although I was at the time undertaking religious ethnography in specific sites in Harlem, the scene created an additional site as the event unfolded. Squeezing through the growing crowd to get a good view, I saw a white-bearded, dark-skinned man (ostensibly of Yoruba ethnic extraction as his facial scarification suggested), whom I later learnt was an Orisa priest/diviner from West Africa. He wore completely white apparel and sat on a low stool mumbling some unintelligible words (incantations) that synchronized with the beating of a traditional drum by his young apprentice. The third person was a middle-aged African woman swaying, dancing ecstatically until she slumped to the ground jerking intermittently with eyes tightly closed. Instantaneously, the Orisa priest/diviner alerted the now-panicky crowd

1. Paul Stoller, *Money Has No Smell: The Africanization of New York City* (Chicago: University of Chicago Press, 2002).

that she was one of his several clients who had patronized him for spiritual solutions to life problems. He added, in a matter-of-fact way, that his client had taken a momentary journey in trance to the spirit world in order to discover her spiritual potentials. It was only after a quarter of an hour when she gradually opened her eyes that the priest's explanation began to go down well with the crowd. As I gathered later on, this trance-like state marked the climax of a ritual enactment that had commenced over an hour earlier. While I do not describe here the ritual process of explanation, prediction, and control that transpired, the event nevertheless suggests an instance of the globalization of indigenous African forms of spirituality and the exportation and mobility of a diviner/priest in Harlem, New York.

Such ritual actions that continue in traditional, modern African societies on the one hand but also in the African diasporic context—in this case in Harlem—are indicative of the resilience and continual transformation of indigenous cosmologies and ritual systems. African religious systems are dominated by cosmologies and ritual enactments to the supersensible entities in order to ensure successful life and well-being. Rituals sustain cosmic harmony at individual and collective levels. The pursuit of health, fertility, and a balance between humans and with nature constitute some of their basic concerns. This makes indigenous religions more lived and experiential traditions than simply compendia of doctrines.

Diversity and Commonality

Indigenous African religions encompass phenomena that are primarily defined in terms of their orality and their cosmological and ritual orientation towards specific geo-cultural landscapes. These traditions are not characterized by any historical foundation. Their beliefs and practices are transmitted from one generation to another through oral traditions, myths, legends, art, paintings, sculpture, songs, and dances.

Indigenous African religions are not monolithic. They vary from traditions of remote societies, hunter-gatherers, mountain and cave dwellers, settled agricultural communities, nomadic peoples and large, complex societies. They encompass the Yoruba, Zulu, Azande, Akan, Nuer, Xhosa, Shona, Massai, Chewa, and the religions of the Kalahari Bushmen among other ethnic groupings that are spread across several countries. Hitherto, some existed as nations, empires and kingdoms until their artificial re-merging into new states by the European colonial system. Since African societies and their religious collectivities are complex and diverse, it is problematic to homogenize all indigenous religions into a single whole. However, indigenous African societies share some affinities in their religious worldviews, their belief in spiritual entities, in the use of concepts to represent them, and in ritual attitudes towards their manipulation and control. Cosmologies or oral narratives transmit their worldview values and describe the web of human activities within the spiritual cosmos. Their social structures and cultural traditions are infused with a spirituality that cannot be easily separated from the rest of the community's life. Therefore, to analyze indigenous religions as a separate system of beliefs and practices apart from subsistence, kinship, language, politics, and the landscape is to misunderstand them. This chapter will therefore focus on aspects of Yoruba and Akan indigenous religions and their manifestations in the African diaspora across space-time. It explores the dynamic nature of indigenous African religions as they negotiate resilience, transformation, and change in a fast globalizing era.

Sacrifices, Divination and Other Rituals

Ritual sacrifice to divinities or ancestors is common. Sacrifice, in its ritual or ceremonial use, means "a making sacred, an offering that becomes divinized." Whatever is sacrificed crosses from humans to the divine, and objects are empowered to facilitate the process. Indigenous Africans speak and think of sacrifice essentially as a religious act, which takes the form of rendering something to a supernatural being or beings, and with various intents and purposes. For instance, it could be the decapitation of an animal in honor of a deity or the provision of food, fruits, drinks and other items. While sacrifice usually involves the shedding of blood of animals and birds such as chicken, goats, cows, and sheep, offerings on the other hand include ritual objects and artifacts such as foodstuffs, water, money, and farm implements. All these materials and victims of sacrifice have symbolic meanings, and as such they are not ends in themselves but means to an end.

Different categories of sacrifice can be discerned at individual, family, community, and corporate levels. Sacrifice may be enacted during individual rites, family feasts, or communal festivals and is usually partaken of first by the divinities or ancestors and then by the individual, family, or community of worshippers. Thanksgiving, communion, votive, propitiatory, preventive, substitution, and foundation rites characterize virtually all indigenous African religions. Through divination, an individual finds out what type of sacrifice will ensure that a predicted good fortune will actually come to pass or, alternatively, mitigate the worst effects of a predicted bad fortune. In almost every case, divination ends in the prescription of sacrifice to the spiritual entities. The persistence of these rites and ceremonies in indigenous socio-religious milieus makes clear the strength

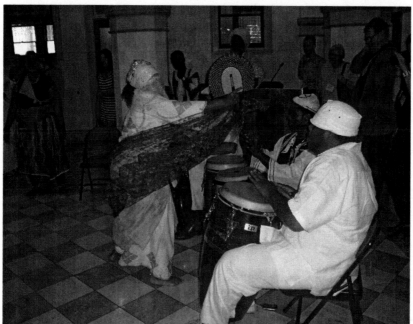

Figure 4.2: *Orisa devotees drum and dance at the reception held at the University of Florida's Thomas Center, Gainesville, as part of the 14th Triennial Symposium on African Art.*

of the belief that humans are in active touch with the supersensible world and that right relationship with these benevolent powers is a prerequisite for human progress, happiness, and total well-being. Sacrifice can be transmuted and made to bring blessing, or it can remain "unsanctified" and uncontrolled to wreck havoc on individuals or groups or to counteract the powers of destruction.

Rites of passage are a common feature of religious life. Their ritual structures draw largely upon a philosophy of relationships. Rites of passage create a bond between temporal processes and archetypal patterns in order to give form and meaning to human events. An individual's passage through life is monitored, marked, and celebrated from pre-birth, parturition, naming and circumcision, puberty and initiation, childhood, transition to adulthood, adulthood, marriage, old age, death, and arrival among the living-dead (ancestors). Other rites are associated with planting and harvesting; natural calamities such as drought, rain, earthquakes; sickness or illness; passing examinations; quest for employment; search for marriage partners; or embarking on journeys. They acknowledge that life is worth living and death worth dying.

Rites and ceremonies therefore characterize each stage of existence.

These elaborate rituals and sacrifices—involving processes of explanation, prediction, control, petition, adoration, praise and thanksgiving—
are facilitated by people with special religious roles. Some of the many
special roles in indigenous religious practice include those of the priest,
diviner, medicine man, sorcerer, and witch. Spirit mediums, spirit-pos-
session cults, diviners, and medicine men form a large section of the
indigenous health care system. In some of the sacred spaces such as
communal shrines or sacred groves, there are ritual specialists or priests
who undertake special roles in the ritual enactment processes. These religious functionaries serve as caretakers of the communal sacred spaces,
as consultants and facilitators of the ritual sacrifices and offerings, and
also protect the space from desecration and misappropriation. There is a
strong link between gender, spirit possession and mediumship: women fill
an overwhelming majority of these roles. Women's roles and statuses are
defined by what is deemed to be wholesome to the welfare of the entire
community of men, women, and children. Women carry out crucial
ritual functions. In most Yoruba communities women are in charge of
some shrines where they carry out cultic functions.

Divination is an important activity and the role of the diviner is
widespread. "Divination represents the central organizing mechanism
through which the world of Yoruba practitioners is understood."[2] Africans employ divination through the diviner, medicine man, and healer.
It also involves, in many cases, the enactment of sacrifice. The diviner or
medicine man is a pivotal force for order and rapprochement between
humanity and the spirit world. The Yoruba people perform divination to
know the wishes of a supernatural being and to inquire about their own
destinies. Divination is performed in all existential circumstances such
as illness and death; in situations of loss, calamity, or unresolved conflict; in the corroboration of a marriage choice; in seeking employment,
promotion in the work place, or admission into schools; embarking on a
journey; and in all other life crisis and circumstances.

Ifá is the most widespread means of Yoruba divination. It is based
on *Odu* (a large repertoire of poems, correlated with a set of 256 divination figures). Other systems include the casting of kola nuts, sixteen
cowries, and *Opele* (divining chain). *Ifá* and the other systems of divination provide confidence and certainty in a world of anxiety and doubt,
a world populated by evil and mischievous spiritual forces. Orunmila
(the oracular divinity) is not only prescient but also prescribes antidotes
against any contingency, and pleads an individual or group's case before

2. Kamari M. Clarke, *Mapping Yoruba Networks: Power and Agency in the Making of Transnational Communities* (Durham: Duke University Press, 2004), 20.

Olodumare/Olorun (the supreme deity). In this way, divination and sac-rifice are inseparably linked.

Osun Festival

We started with an example of a rite that may have been enacted by an individual or a few people, but rituals of a communal and even larger scale continue in the contemporary era. Some communal rituals in com-memoration of specific local divinities are becoming internationalized. The annual Yoruba Osun Os(h)gobo festival and kingship ritual (lasting fourteen calendar days, usually in the month of August) now attracts devotees and tourists from around the world, thus transforming the ritual event from an ethnic-based one to one with an international audience and participation. The naming of one of Nigeria's thirty-six states as Osun is symbolic, marking the resilience of the goddess Osun in local religious thought.

Amidst pomp and pageantry, the Osun festival is associated with offer-ing of sacrifices at the Osun shrine, drumming, dancing, and feasting. The festival commences with the traditional cleansing of the town (*Iwopopo*), followed three days later by the lighting of a 500-year-old sixteen-point-lamp (*Olujumerindinlogun*). On the fourth day, sacrifices are offered for the deceased rulers (*Ijuba fun awon Oba to ti waja*, "the head and crown"), and for the deceased wives of the past Obas (*Iborariade* and *Ijo-ayaba Isale*), and blessings are requested from the assemblage of the crowns of deceased rulers (*Ataojas*). A procession to the Osun grove marks the peak of the fes-tival. "The main attraction of the Osun festival is the ritual procession and pilgrimage of the king and the Oshogbo people to the Osun River to present their sacrificial offerings to the goddess."[3] This procession to the Osun grove is led by the oratory or votary (virgin) maid (*Arugba*) who carries on her head a calabash containing materials for sacrifice.

Indigenous religions are often described as non-missionizing reli-gions or as religions that adherents are born but not converted into. This, however, is fast changing. Non-Africans are both converting into indigenous religions and also assuming roles of religious adepts. Since the 1960s for instance, the Austrian-born artist, painter, and sculptor, Suzanne Wenger has been living as an initiated priestess *(adunni olorisha)* to the gods Osun and Obatala in the sacred groves of Oshogbo, the traditional home of the river goddess Osun. Instructed by high priests, Wenger was inaugurated into the content and form of Yoruba religious

---

3. Jacob K. Olupona, ed., *African Spirituality: Forms, Meanings and Expressions* (New York: The Crossroad Publishing Co.), 57.

life in an initiation process lasting ten years.[4] An oracle determined that she should be the one to reconstruct the derelict ritual sites, shrines and symbols in the sacred groves of Oshogbo. Together with her ritually adopted children, Shangodare and Doyin, she has become an important part of the traditional cult life in Oshogbo. Wenger's work has brought about a revitalization and modernization of the sacred Osun groves. Her shrines and sculptures in Oshogbo are artistic and architectural manifestations that are unique in the way they combine traditional and new styles.

The historical and cultural significance of indigenous African religious traditions is partly discerned in their plurality and multivocality both in Africa and the African diaspora. The centrality and authority of the various orisas (divinities) as vice-regents of Olodumare/Olorun is evident in Yoruba religious thought and practice. However, we must recognize the diversity of aspects of orisas layered in any single Yoruba tradition as well as the multiple traditions of each Orisa thriving in Africa and the diaspora. For instance, Sandra Barnes' *Africa's Ogun* explores the complex nature of Ogun, the Orisa who transforms life through iron and technology,[5] while Murphy and Sanford's *Osun Across the Waters* espouses the dynamism and texture special to Orisa Osun, showing how Osun traditions continue to grow and change as they flow and return from their sources in Africa and the Americas:

> Osun and Ogun present dynamic examples of the resilience and renewed importance of traditional Yoruba images in negotiating spiritual experience, social identity, and political power in contemporary Africa and the African Diaspora.[6]

These brief references to Orisas Osun and Ogun indicate the dynamism and resilience of various indigenous African religions in the context of change and transformation. Whether in the local context in which these traditions are found or in the diasporic context to which elements of these traditions have been transmuted, indigenous African religions have never been static but continually change, adapt, and transform themselves. Their resilience is witnessed today, although the renewed visibility of Islam, Christianity, and other religions is transforming indigenous

---

4. *Living with the Gods*, a documentary film by Suzanne Wenger is available online at http://www.willkefilm.de/index.html?willkefilm/englisch/wenger.html

5. Sandra Barnes, *Africa's Ogun: Old World and New* (Bloomington: Indiana University Press, 1997).

6. Joseph Murphy and Mei-Mei Sanford, *Osun across the Waters: A Yoruba Goddess in Africa and the Americas* (Bloomington: Indiana University Press, 2001), 2.

African religions considerably, introducing new ideas and practices. This proliferation of Islam and Christianity has also produced new religious movements, with some appropriating indigenous ritual symbols and giving them new meanings. Continuing to focus on Yoruba and Akan groups in sub-Saharan Africa, we shall demonstrate how this encounter helped to transform indigenous religious thought and praxis, but did not supplant them. Indigenous African peoples preserved aspects of their belief and ritual cosmos but also adjusted to a new socio-cultural milieu. Now a cross-section of Africans is experiencing something of a religious revival and becoming concerned with the preservation of their religio-cultural heritage.

Afrikania Mission

The Afrikania Mission, also known as the Afrikan Renaissance Mission or Sankofa Faith, marks one striking example of this tendency towards indigenous religious revival. Founded in Ghana in 1982 by Rev. Dr. Osofo-Okomfo Kwabena Damuah, a Ghanaian theologian and former ordained priest of the Roman Catholic Church of Ghana, the Afrikania religion took a reformist stance towards the traditional religion. As the founder remarks:

> Afrikania religion is a way of life that promotes godliness, truthfulness, goodness, justice and liberation from the Afrikan perspective... God did not make us Afrikans by mistake. He has made us Afrikans so that we can serve Him in an Afrikan way... it is the duty of the Afrikan to study it, promote it and revive it for the benefit of Afrika and all mankind.[7]

The name "Afrikania" derives from two Akan words, *afri* and *kania*, meaning literally "has come out of light." The composite connotation of the term means "bringer of civilization."

> Afrikania is a concept of life and more importantly, a spiritual revolution that aims at creating a new world order based on *Amen-ra* (the Creator), positive consciencism [sic] and spiritual equilibrium.[8]

(The ancient Egyptian word for God, *Amen-Ra* was adopted because it

---

7. Osofo-Okomfo K Damuah, *The Introduction to Afrikania* (Accra: Afrikania Mission, 1998) 2. See also Azasu Kwauzi, *African Traditional Religion: Afrikania. A Brief Exposition* (Accra: Afrikania Renaissance Books, 1999, 4).; Osofo Kofi Ameve, *The Divine Acts: Holy Scriptures for the Sankofa Faith (Afrikanism)* (Accra: Afrikan Renaissance Mission, n.d.), 11.

8. Kwauki, *African Traditional Religion*, 4. See also "Afrikania in Brief," Afrikania Mission, http://members.tripod.com/afrikania/id2.htm

was believed to have been preserved by the ancestors.)

> It is called Afrikania because it is rooted in Afrikan experience. Its
> foundation and its goal is the creator. It is the restructuring of the
> Afrikan traditional concept which is the first recorded religion of
> mankind and the mother of all religions.[9]

Sankofa, on the other hand, means "going back to our roots." Thus, as
the movement claims, "the Afrikania mission or Sankofa is the re-activa-
tion, renewal, rebirth and re-organization of the African traditional religion to make it relevant to our times" The Afrikan Renaissance Mission
has set itself "the task of redefining, reforming and renaming the Religion of Afrika." Its function includes "to study and interpret Afrikan
culture and to teach and promote Afrikan religion or Afrikanism. It is
here to teach the Afrikan to respect and accept Afrikanism as the true
religion of the Afrikan ancestors." [10]

Quite unequivocally, the group discountenances any claim of Afrikania as a new concept and asserts that it is "the rebirth, revival and reor-
ganization of the Afrikan traditional religion, so that it can contribute
effectively toward human development for the glory of *Amen-ra.*" Such a
religious innovation, with its teaching and modus operandi, were meant
as a form of critique of Christianity and other religious forms considered
as external to African sensibilities, but which were also inherently intol-
erant. Afrikania indicts slavery and colonization for the loss of African
traditional spirituality and criticizes government, foreign diplomatic mis-
sions, and non-governmental organizations for corrupting and demoniz-
ing traditional values and imposing foreign religious beliefs. However, the
Catholic background of its founder seem to leave significant Christian
imprints in Afrikania's belief and ritual systems, thus producing a religious synthesis. The attempt to re-brand or reposition indigenous African
religious traditions has also resulted in the tendency to universalize, can-
onize, and institutionalize it. As the group claims, "It is the practice of
Afrikan divinity based on the unique diversity of African cultures." [11]

In 1983, the founder ordained nine young priests to start propagating
"the message of the holy ancestors." Following the founder's demise in
1992, Osofo Kofi Ameve headed Afrikania Movement from 1993-2003.
Since 2004, the mantle of leadership has fallen on Osofo Atsu Kove.
From its international headquarters, the Afrikania House in Accra-

---

9. "Afrikania in Brief," http://members.tripod.com/afrikania/id2.htm

10. Ameve, *The Divine Acts*,11. See also "Afrikania Mission," http://members.tripod.
com/afrikania/id2.htm and "Afrikan Life Ways," http://home.btclick.com/jabu/afri-
kania.htm

11. Damuah, *The Introduction to Afrikania*, 2.

Ghana, the movement has gradually spread to other regions of Ghana as well as into the diaspora. Afrikania leaders claim that the movement has more than a million followers worldwide. The group's websites claim that "the purpose of the Afrikania Mission is to create a new world order for the children of *Amen-Ra* based upon the Nubian-Khamitic principle of Maat which is righteousness, justice and truth—the structural foundation of our ancient Afrikan spirituality and the divine law of nature that our Holy Afrikan ancestors lived by for thousands of years." They indicate their target audience: "The Afrikania Mission is seeking to communicate with the thousands of our continental and diasporan brothers and sisters worldwide (regardless of their religious or social affiliation) who would like to learn more about their ancient Afrikan spirituality; any member of our extended Afrikan family is welcome to come and serve the Creator from the Afrikan perspective."[12] The Afrikania Mission is not simply a set of doctrines; the movement has become more popular through its experiential dimension. It is the emphasis on rituals that serves as a major point of attraction for its clientele. "Spiritual community services" (rituals/ceremonies) are held in temples in Ghana just as in the diaspora. For instance, a monthly service takes place in Montreal, Canada. Initiation, purification, and healing rituals are frequent features of these services. The Afrikania religion follows a liturgical structure. "Guidelines for Community Worship" are laid out in the *Nwoma Kron Kron* (Spiritual Book), and their philosophy and belief system is partly based on the 42 Admonitions of Maat, the Divine Law of Universal Order, believed to be the first spiritual scriptures of mankind given by *Amen-Ra* and the holy Afrikan ancestors in 3500 BCE. Altars are erected and prayer rituals are enacted through the ancestors to *Amen-Ra*. Pouring of libations to ancestors, sprinkling of water over people, healing rituals, fumigation of incense, drumming, and blowing of horns are characteristic of Afrikania services.

African Diaspora

The global dimension of indigenous African religions is manifest in varied forms, being introduced to new geo-cultural contexts through migration, tourism, and new communication technologies. The African diaspora influences cultures in Brazil, Cuba, and Haiti, partly leading to the development of African-derived religions such as Santeria, Candomblé, Vodun, and Yoruba-Orisha traditions across the Americas. In 1981, an Act of Parliament in Trinidad and Tobago raised the Yoruba religion

12. "What is Afrikania?" http://members.tripod.com/afrikania/id18.htm

to the status of an official religion. In the diasporic context, orisa veneration has developed on different levels. While the veneration of a singular orisa may have produced a distinctive group or clientele linked to Ogun, Shango, Orunmila, Oya, or Osun, there is a certain tendency in which orisa veneration, as compared to that in Africa, is becoming increasingly institutionalized and universalized. In this light, adherents venerate or patronize a legion of orisas contemporaneously. As Efún Moyiwá noted, "it was decided that for the religion of the Orishas to survive as a whole, it was necessary for each person, upon being consecrated as a priest, to receive a majority of the orisas at that time (Elegba or Eleguá, Ogun, Oshosi, Obatalá, Oya, Oshun, Yemajá and Shangó). This is opposed to the practice in West Africa, where a priest of Obatalá would receive Obatalá and Elegba and no other orishas... Here, the orishas become interconnected more than in Africa"[13].

Without any clear-cut demarcation between these spiritual forces, adherents have adopted a generic, universal name such as orisa to embrace all or some of these deities. In contemporary Cuba, orisa veneration exists as part of a larger continuum of religious change in the Americas in which religious practices, now known as Santeria but also referred to as Lukumi and *regla de ocha*, have transformed the shape of orisa veneration outside of West Africa.

These religious forms are proliferating in the diasporic context with their practitioners and clientele widening ethnically and racially. Ifá priests and devotees now include Yoruba, Africans, African-Americans and non-Africans alike. "African-derived religions have entered a new phase with the growing presence of western adepts. These have become part of an evolving tradition. Several outsiders broke the mold, and their scholarship is impeccable."[14] These include Pierre Verger, Odette Mennesson-Rigaud, Zora Neale Hurston, Suzanne P. Blier, Robert Farris Thompson, Karen McCarthy Brown, Henry J. Drewal, Judith Gleason, and David G. Wilson (Falo'kun Fatunmbi). As Kamari Clarke aptly notes, "Santeria practitioners—some claiming Hispanic roots, others claiming Afro-Cuban national identities, and still others claiming American or African heritage—are active participants in the production of Yoruba-based practices in America."[15]

The founder and first leader of the Yoruba Oyotunji Village in South

---

13. Efún Moyiwá, "The Religion in Africa and Cuba: How Different are They Really?" OrishaNet, http://www.orishanet.org/africa.html.

14. Patrick Bellegarde-Smith, ed., *Fragments of Bone: Neo-African Religions in a New World* (Chicago: University of Chicago Press, 2005), 5.

15. Kamari M. Clarke, *Mapping Yoruba Networks: Power and Agency in the Making of Transnational Communities* (Durham: Duke University Press, 2004), 17.

Carolina, His Royal Highness Oba Adefunmi I, was a white American. The former and current Oyotunji chiefs of the *Ile Onisegun* (Oyotunji temple), Chief Alade and Dr. Adelerie Onisegun are African-Americans. In the 1990s, Olufadeke the Iyanifa (formerly Vassa) and Oluwo Fagbamila (formerly Philip John Neimark), a white American couple, became Ifá priestess and priest respectively. Oluwo Fagbamila is the prolific leader and founder of the Ifa College and The Ifa Foundation of North America Inc ("the Home of American Ifa"). The Ifa College mission statement, summarized as "Bringing the Wisdom of Ancient Africa to the Modern World," describes its work thus:

> To provide advanced learning center for Ifa Foundation initiates. It will also, as time unfolds, become a valuable source of learning and growth for all Orisa followers.... The College will offer continual on-line learning in all aspects of the philosophy in order to help create wiser and more skilled practicing priests. The subtleties, observations, and methods of divination, ceremonies, healings, initiations etc. will be part of both classroom settings and group discussions by the Ifa Scholars of the College.[16]

Clarke notes that "the college is opening parameters of orisa membership to a broader clientele—this time, predominantly white American students and professionals—thereby creating a university mechanism for the teaching and accreditation of orisha practices as well as an Internet resource for potential converts."[17] This tendency is leading to a kind of "faculty-culture" intellectualization of Yoruba orisa religion. As these practices are increasingly being experienced outside of Africa, they are in a way contributing to the growing decentralization of indigenous knowledge production in diverse local contexts.

The twentieth and twenty-first century proliferation of groups of orisa practitioners outside of West Africa continues to attract millions of adherents of Yoruba and Santeria religious practices.[18] Increasing numbers of these orisa adherents are contributing to the growth of multiple networks of knowledge outside of the African continent. Knowledge institutions such as the Ifa College, which espouse particular interpretations of orisa practices, are becoming increasingly widespread. Ifá College provides orisa religious training to a new generation of practitioners, some who were formerly excluded from participation in African ritual practices. Boasting a wide spectrum of faculty members from the United States and Africa, Ifa College is creating increased horizontal linkages across Africa

16. Ifa College Mission Statement, http://www.ifacollege.com/.

17 Clarke, *Mapping Yoruba Networks*, 18.

18. Ibid., 5.

and the United States. The website parades a wide array of practitioners—faculty and scholars—reflecting a diversity of nationality, gender, background, experience, and sexual orientation. Membership includes white Americans, African-Americans, and Africans. The diversity of this group is further evident as Javier Lujan (adopted name Fajuitan), who was initiated as an Osun priest subsequently became the first openly gay man initiated as a *babalawo* (traditional priest) at the Ifá Foundation of North America Inc.

An interesting feature of the Ifá Foundation and other orisa practitioners is the conscious adoption of religiously symbolic Yoruba names such as Fagbenle, Fasegun, Ifánike, Ifáleye, Ogunjobi, Ifábukonla and Fajuitan. Some of the practitioners are priests/priestesses and initiates of Ifá, Oya, Ogun, Obatala, and Osun. Most of their names associated with a prefix of Orisa Ifá and Ogun—a common feature of naming among the Yoruba. Such names reveal their meanings and significance but also indicate the specific deity venerated by the recipient. In most African societies, newborns are named based on specific situations surrounding their birth. Naming a child is taken very seriously because it is believed that a name can make or mar a person. Thus, a name that conveys no concrete meaning, no links to a spiritual source, and evokes neither narrative nor links to any historical events and landmarks is perceived as meaningless. To most Africans, a name represents an essential component of human spiritual anatomy and could serve as an indicator of destiny. Names are often circumstantial, and historical narratives are woven around them. The symbolism, meaning, and power of naming, and several elements of the indigenous naming ritual have been transposed within indigenous and Christian worldviews in Africa and the African diaspora. In Africa and the diaspora, names not only give meanings but also serve as an identity marker in a new multicultural context. Further, they connote personality and build ties to culture and ancestry.[19]

Institutionalisation and Other Trends

As I have indicated above, there have been significant changes and transformation in the form and content of orisa veneration in Yorubaland, West Africa, the Americas, and elsewhere, particularly in the last two centuries. Today, orisa practitioners in West Africa, the Caribbean, and

19. Afe Adogame, "Contesting the Ambivalences of Modernity in a Global Context: The Redeemed Christian Church of God, North America," *Studies in World Christianity* 10:1 (2004), 25-48; "African Instituted Churches in Europe: Continuity and Transformation," in *African Identities and World Christianity in the Twentieth Century*, ed. Klaus Koschorke (Wiesbaden: Harrassowitz, 2005), 225-44.

South America are increasingly in conversation with practitioners from the West. Now, more than ever, vast numbers of Americans in the United States are converting to Yoruba religious practices and playing central roles in reshaping how orisa traditions are to be practiced.[20] As the various Yoruba and Yoruba-derived Orisa traditions in the West are assuming alternative forms of spirituality for Africans and a growing number of non-Africans, this development is also leading to the importation of indigenous priests/diviners abroad. In the 1990s, Wande Abimbola was officially appointed delegate to Boston from Nigeria to represent and transmit the tradition of Ifá. He was a professor of African religions at Boston University and taught courses on Ifá, Yoruba religion and culture at Harvard, Colgate University, and at different locations in the United States at both academic and practitioner levels. Abimbola was initiated a *babalawo* in 1971. In 1981, he was installed as *Àwise Ni Àgbáeé* (spokesperson and ambassador for Ifá and Yoruba religion in the world) by *babalawos* in West Africa and as president of the International Congress of Orisa Tradition and Culture.

The commodification of indigenous art and religious objects is on the increase. "Electronic technologies, circulating publications, and films about orisha religious and cultural practices have played a critical role in enabling the expansion of Yoruba transnational religions in North and South America, England, and Canada; the formation of Ifá College is one example."[21] The proliferation of Internet web pages with advertising products or services, coupled with the growing visibility of African arts and craft markets in major Western cities, provide one avenue for the commodification of indigenous knowledge, art, and crafts. This partly suggests how indigenous and transnational Yoruba religions are negotiating, but are at the same time taking part in, the production of African modernity.

The growth of transnational Yoruba institutions has promoted the widespread availability of self-help books and videos, online orisa chat rooms, and Internet-based services, by which people with differing levels of familiarity with Yoruba practices are attaining the knowledge to become orisa worshippers. "These forms of knowledge production circulate within private ritualistic and public forums and are becoming increasingly embedded in global circuits of exchange and local sites of historically relevant variation."[22] For instance, Yoruba Oyotunji Village generates income through the sale of prophetic divinatory consultations,

20. Clarke, *Mapping Yoruba Networks,* 6.
21. Ibid., 18.
22. Ibid. 7.

African market souvenirs (such as cloth, books, candles, and carvings), and through fees for community-based tours and dining services. There is a growing production of practices performed in the name of African traditions. The proliferation of Yoruba drumming circles throughout New York communities is a case in point. In several American urban centers, male and female drummers "perform Africa" through these practices.

Internet Information and Practice

African and African-derived religions are also increasingly appropriating new communication technologies in transmitting their religious ideologies. The character of indigenous Africans and their religions in conditions of globality will continue to be determined and shaped by how and to what extent they negotiate continuity, identity, and change. The role of new media technologies in contributing to the production and spread of new African images for Western consumption cannot be underestimated. "With the consequent growth of various electronic technologies, new forms of access to information and video and films about Yoruba religious cultural practices globally are contributing to the institutionalization of African-derived cultural identities being invented and procured for the reproduction of religious life outside of Africa."[23] Thus, one way in which orisa traditions and other African-derived religions are inserting themselves into global religious landscapes is through the proliferation of Internet sites. Virtual religiosity is assuming a central feature of their modus operandi since the establishment in 1995 of the Orishanet by Frank Baba Eyiogbe, one of the highly respected *babalawos* of the orisa traditions in the African diaspora.[24] Orishanet became the first orisa website on the Internet and the premier web resource for Ifá, Santeria, Lukumi and the orisas.

The Internet has also provided an interactive space where priests, devotees, students of the indigenous religions of Africa, and the public engage in virtual, sometimes intellectualistic, discourses of traditional African religion. OrisaList is the oldest Internet forum that brings together list members from a variety of indigenous African traditions and cultural backgrounds.[25] These links document impressive lists and biographies of outstanding priests of traditional African religions serving religious communities worldwide.

23. Ibid., 22.
24. Its website is http://www.orishanet.org/.
25. Its website is http://groups.yahoo.com/group/orishalist/. See also http://www.geocities.com/priestmemorial/living.htm

The Ibile Faith Online Congregation was established to provide online spiritual and religious services to members world-wide, and a forum to spread Yoruba traditional religion all over the world. Yoruba traditional religion and Yoruba language lessons are offered via Internet, mails and telephone for beginners, intermediate, and advanced learners for a fee.[26] These interactive spaces become a medium through which members affirm, reconstruct old identities but also invent new ones. Although the Orisa mailing list appears open to the public, they are however quick to alert users about membership prerequisites and limitations of scope of discourses. As they assert, "we do not entertain questions or inquiries about paganism, Wiccan or new age movements as these are outside of the scope of this group,"

Media (Mis-)Representations

The global stature of African and African-derived religions is demonstrated in the way they form part of global discourses and lend their voices in issues of public concern. A case in point is the infamous "Torso in the Thames" case of September 2001, in which the decapitated body of a five-year-old boy, named Adam by Scotland Yard detective, was found floating in the Thames River, allegedly the victim of a ritual murder or a human sacrifice.[27] Media and public speculations of the sources of killing were tied severally to African religions, indigenous African churches' rituals, voodoo invocation, black magic, child trafficking, and witch-doctor killing rituals. While indications of the possible perpetrators still remain largely speculative, the "Thames Torso" case took on a new twist as sensationalized media reporting received harsh criticisms from varied constituencies.[28] Some disaporic groups reacted and condemned this kind of media sensationalism. In correspondence with orisa devotees and sympathizers globally, they remarked:

> We are writing to you out of concern for what is becoming an internationally significant media event that affects all of us as Orisa/Ifá people and sympathizers. In September 2001, a child's torso was found in the Thames River in London. The ongoing police investigation and

26. Its website is http://www.yorubareligion.org.

27. BBC News, "Ritual killing link to dead boy," 25 January 2002. http://news.bbc.co.uk/1/hi/england/1780990.stm; "Thames Torso was Human Sacrifice', 29 January 2002. http://news.bbc.co.uk/1/hi/england/1788452.stm; "Thames Torso was ritual murder," 30 January 2002. http://www.mysouthwark.co.uk/southwark/community-localnews-jan02.htm.

28. Afe Adogame, "Engaging the Rhetoric of Spiritual Warfare: The Public Face of Aladura in Diaspora," *Journal of Religion in Africa* 34, no. 4 (2004): 511-13.

media reporting are committing some of the most fallacious racism against Africans, and, for us, against the Yoruba and the Orisa, specifically Osun and Sango. The crux of the matter is that the police and the media perceive the death of this child not as a murder but as a "ritual sacrifice" by which they are condemning Africans and Orisa religion. Both Yoruba culture and the Orisa religion are being represented as primitive and savage which conforms to a Euro/American racist expectation of Africa rather than truth. And the weak excuse of saying it is done by a "deviant cult" does not relieve the media of responsibility for its portrayal of all Orisa traditions, indigenous African traditions as a whole, as deviant and savage from the assumed civilized gaze of the West. We must respond with consistent and organized effort to hold journalists and filmmakers and their publishers/producers accountable…To date, it is mostly the BBC that is churning out the racist portrayal. The main point to make when writing a response is that murder is not a part of African religious practices and this murder should be treated the same way as any other murder, not as a cultural persecution through invented "cultural profiling." Social deviancy and pathology is not the same as cultural norms! This ethical point must be demanded for African cultures, not just those of developed nations!...We are encouraging the global communities of Orisa and Ifá devotees to flood the BBC with emails and letters about their offensive and incorrect representation of this murder and to demand its correction along with a public apology to the communities damaged.[29]

The group also interpreted the BBC Scotland mini-series program *Sea of Souls*, as clearly based on the Thames Torso murder and the subsequent hysteria towards African religion.[30] These examples are pointers to how Orisa traditions are appropriating the new media to negotiate their status and existence on the one hand, but also as a tool for self-repositioning and self-packaging.

Reinventing Twins

There are several indications of how African discourses and ritualisms are reinvented and rehearsed in diaspora narratives and spiritualities. The importance of twins in Africa and the African Diaspora is linked to the fact that the recorded twinning rate in Africa is higher than anywhere else in the world. Wherever African populations have settled in the New World, be it Cuba, Brazil, the United States, or Haiti, the importance and

29. Afe Adogame, "Engaging the Rhetoric," 493-522; "Orisha and Child Murder," Awo Study Center, 26 April 2004, http://www.awostudycenter.com/Current/Orisha_Child_Murder.htm.

30. For a synopsis of this series, see http://www.bbc.co.uk/seaofsouls/episode_guide/episode3_1.shtml and http://www.bbc.co.uk/seaofsouls/episode_guide/episode3_2-shtml.

frequency of twin births leave its imprint.[31] The birth of twins and the religious significance they attract in many indigenous African societies, such as among the Yoruba where they are called *ibeji*, appear in virtually all religious reconstructions in the Americas —such as in the Yoruba and Yoruba-derived religions.

The symbolism of twins as ancestral figures that inhabit transitional spaces where the worlds meet becomes a central example here. As Bellegarde-Smith aptly notes, "Houlberg's essay situates itself at the crossroads of Yoruba, Fon, Ewe, Kongo, Haitian, Cuban, and Brazilian mythology, the old and the new—an African discourse embedded in diasporic narratives."[32] Haitian Vodou is one of the many African religions in the New World that venerates twins. In Brazil, the Yoruba attitude toward twins is salient in the Afro-Brazilian religions of Candomblé, Macumba, and Umbanda,

Figure 4.3: *Toys, sweets, Saints Cosmas and Damian, and some tranquilizing oil for the Marassa Twins. Home altar of Haitian vodou priestess living in Montreal, Canada. (Photo by Heike Drotbohm.)*

where twins are called *beji* (ellipsed from the Yoruba *ibeji*). Twins are also sacred in the context of the Afro-Cuban religion Santeria, which closely follows the Yoruba model. For Santeria practitioners in Cuba and the United States, Oshun, the Yoruba goddess of love and children, is considered the mother and guardian of twins. On the last day of the Oshun initiation ceremony, parents who have *ibeji* bring them to

---

31. Marilyn Houlberg, "Magique Marasa: The Ritual Cosmos of the Twins and Other Sacred Children," in *Fragments of Bone: Neo-African Religions in a New World*, ed. Patrick Bellegarde-Smith (Chicago: University of Chicago Press, 2005), 16.

32. Bellegarde-Smith, *Fragments of Bone*, 6.

the shrine for blessing ritual. It is through ritual and ceremony that the veneration of twins and sacred children has been transmitted over time and space. Ritual, art, and symbol interact in an elaborate dialogue surrounding twins and sacred children. The effigy or imaging of twins, *ere ibeji*, becomes a significant symbol object, which is conspicuous in shrines, altars and even homes of devotees. Special altars are erected and sacrificial foods and drinks are offered to propitiate them. Among the Yoruba, beans and palm oil are the favorite foods for twins and are considered to control their power and anger. A similar concept applies to the twins in Haitian Vodou and in other parts of the African Diaspora. Special days are set aside for ceremonies and feasts in commemoration of twins and sacred children. In the African diaspora, the imaging of twins and the ritual calendar have undergone a synthesis in which, for instance, several Catholic saints are now correlated with twins in Vodou. As Houlberg aptly concludes, "the importance of twins and other sacred children in Africa and the African Diaspora continues to be a significant grounding factor in the growing importance of African-based religions in the New World."[33]

Sacred Spaces

Ritual and sacrifice operate within sacred space and time and occupy a conspicuous place in indigenous African religious life. The symbolism, sustenance, and reconstruction of sacred spaces have become significant not only as a context for ritual action and performance; they are now also preserved for their socio-cultural, political, and touristic value. The Osun grove in Oshogbo is a tangible expression of Yoruba divinatory and cosmological systems. Its annual festival is a living, thriving and evolving response to Yoruba beliefs in the bond between people, their ruler, and the goddess Osun. It now represents Yoruba sacred groves and their reflection of Yoruba cosmology. The increasing religious, cultural, socio-political, and economic significance of the Osun grove and its annual festival has translated the constructed space into a national and an international center for tourist attraction in Nigeria. The Nigerian federal government acquired it in 1986 as a national monument, where tree-felling, bush-burning, hunting, farming, building, and dumping of refuse are strictly forbidden. In 2005, UNESCO declared the grove as a World Heritage Site.

The recreation of sacred space and sites has remained a common feature of adherents of African and African-derived religions in the

---

33. Houlberg, "Magique Marasa,"31.

Americas. Sacred space is largely reconstructed and improvised for religio-cultural reasons. Although it is rare among the orisa practitioners in the Americas to have orisa groves (*igbo orisha*), a common feature in West Africa, private garages and basements are now consecrated and set aside for ritual purposes. However, one of the most conspicuous examples is the Yoruba (African) Oyotunji Village, which represents a conscious attempt to refashion Yoruba religion, culture, and history within a prototype reconstruction of a Yoruba indigenous village settlement. Located sixty-five miles southwest of Charleston in the rural region of Beaufort, South Carolina, the Oyotunji Village is a Yoruba "revivalist'"community founded in 1970. The founders reconstructed this multi-complex space as a means of finding their way back to Africa, back to a "homeland." Oyotunji residents use reconfigured temporal and spatial notions of ancestral continuities to recast their conceptions of homeland as Africa in America.[34]

These sacred spaces and towns such as the Osun grove and Oyotunji Village have been transformed into pilgrimage sites. Oyotunji residents and other orisa practitioners in the Americas embark on annual pilgrimages and heritage tours to Yoruba towns such as Oyo, Ife, and Oshogbo, contexts they perceive as their African homeland. In a bid to strengthen their ties to Nigerian Yoruba clan groups and to gain the ritual legitimacy of Nigerian rituals, founder Oba Adefunmi joined in the heritage tours by traveling to Nigeria in 1972. During his four-month sojourn, he was initiated into the cult of Ifá, a ritual act which provided him with the legitimacy he sought.[35] These visits are usually made to coincide with major religious festivals to commemorate the orisas such as Osun, Ogun, Shango, and Oya. Pilgrimages, coupled with the religious activities that are enacted in specific ritual times, help to bridge the gap between original homeland and the diaspora, and between local and global spaces. Pilgrimages, particularly to Nigeria and other Yoruba-speaking parts of West Africa, have had a huge impact on Yoruba indigenous religious thought and practice. This had resulted in a renewed interest in indigenous religions by the local people. The increasing significance of indigenous religions as an academic subject is becoming more evident.

Daily life in Oyotunji Village revolves around calendrical celebrations of Orisa gods and goddesses known to have originated in West Africa.[36] The Yoruba Oyotunji Festival Calendar is largely indicative of how virtually all months of each year are dotted with festivals in honor

34. Clarke, *Mapping Yoruba Networks*, xxii.
35. Ibid., 77.
36. Ibid., 58.

of deities including Olokun, Esu, Ogun, Osun, Egungun, Ifá, Yemoja, Sango, Obatala, and Oya. It involves other life cycle and seasonal rituals.[37] Each ritual is organized by a religious priesthood and is technically referred to as an annual religious ceremony or festival. Usually a priest presides over the ceremony, leading the placement of offerings on the altars to the respective deity, or hosting and organizing prayer rituals, dancing, and general festivities. Such monthly rituals or periodic festivals are no longer limited to Africa; they are now largely reenacted outside of Africa. On September 30, 2001, the Ile Ise Ejiogbe Ifá Temple celebrated the beginning of its 2001-2 festival season with its first ever Ifá festival.[38] The festival took place outside the Ile Ise Ejiogbe Ifá Temple in Washington, D.C. under the leadership of Chief Ifálade Babaegbe Omoawo Ajampo and Mama Tunde Akinyele, both chief priest and priestess of Ile Ise Ejiogbe Ifá Temple. Participants that gathered from Washington, D.C., Delaware, and Maryland, partook in rituals as they congregated around the Ifá Oke Orere (mound of Ifá or Ifá's Staff). In the same year, the Ifá Temple also celebrated the Egungun and Esu festival in Baltimore and Philadelphia respectively.

International conferences and conventions on the promotion and standardization of Yoruba (African) ritual practices have become a common feature. Orisaworld, founded in 1981, appears to be the world's largest organization of practitioners and scholars that research or teach topics related to orisa tradition, religion, and culture. With individual and institutional members from more than fifty countries in Africa, Europe, North and South America, the Orisaworld partly "aims to revitalize and rejuvenate the Orisa culture and all its traditions."[39] The biannual World Congress of Orisa Tradition and Culture inaugurated in Ile-Ife (Nigeria) in 1981 is now being rotated internationally between Brazil, Cuba, Trinidad and Tobago, the Unites States and Nigeria. In June 2004, Ostbevern (Germany) hosted the Irunmole Festival, the "8th Festival of Yoruba traditional religion." This event was the brainchild of the Ibile Faith Society-Irunmole Followers (Friends of Yoruba Culture), a self-defined neo-Yoruba religion established in Germany by Prince Adigun Olosun in the 1990s.[40] The Ibile Faith Society draws much of its belief and ritual practices from Osun veneration. The founder himself hails from Oshogbo, where he is a traditional priest of Osun. The festival was

---

37. Ibid. 291.

38. *Ile Ise Ejiogbe Ifá Temple Newsletter*, 2, no. 1 (October 2001).

39. International Congress of Orisa Tradition and Culture, http://www.orisaworld. org.

40. Prince Olosun, personal communication, 14 September 2002; see also http://www.yorubareligion.org.

marked with dancing, drumming and procession through the town of Ostbevern. Symbolic rituals were also enacted at the River Bever, while Yoruba food was served to participants to mark the end of the festival.

Changing Divination Practices

Orisa practitioners in the African diasporic context are witnessing the changing face of divinatory practices and the institution itself. The act of divination continues to represent a significant pivot on which the ritual world of Yoruba religion or orisa practitioners revolve. The special role of a diviner in ritual thought and practice has remained quintessential, although the rigorous, indigenous training mode that produces the religious functionary is gradually being transformed. The Ifá Foundation in America recognizes "the imperative of educating initiates into the philosophy in a long term and meaningful way," but as its leader Oluwo Fagbamila remarks,

> unlike the African model, where an individual might apprentice for five or ten years before initiation, and where, during that process a firm foundation of knowledge and experience were acquired, here in the West you come for a week and "poof" you are a priest. Well, the actions, judgment and character of too many that have been produced from that paradigm point clearly to its failure.[41]

Apparently, it was as a critique of the proliferation of this practice that the Ifá College emerges to instill in-depth knowledge about the cosmology and praxis of orisa. As Fagbamila asserts, "It is our goal to return the philosophy to the intellectual standards that created it, rather than the anti-intellectual, superstitious, illogical paradigms that have attempted to co-opt it."

One way in which we can discern the changing face of divination is in its computerization or digitization through the Internet. In addition to traditional modes of divination highlighted above, Ifá Foundation now enacts divination both over the phone and through email communication. Ifa Foundation claims to be the first to recognize the logic and validity of divination over the phone or Internet. In spite of its transformation from a personal to an impersonal mode, the leader of Ifa Foundation insists that Ifá has

> not changed at all in its capacity as a series of universal, timeless, truths that automatically adjust to, and become contextually relevant

41. Ifá Foundation, http://www.ifafoundation.org. For divination, see http://ayodele_fadele.tripod.com/index.html

to the situation to which they are applied. It is when we try to apply out of context observations—either as a result of societal differences or freeze frame mentality—that these differences appear.

The vast numbers of transnational orisa institutions, many of which are either mainly Internet-based religious groups or others who have hosted own websites, provide new, alternative avenues for clients to obtain online divinatory readings; explanation, prediction and control of existential problems. Through this medium, "online diviners" prognosticate and limp into the future on behalf of their clientele.

The globalization of Yoruba religious practices is at the same time confronted with significant challenges based on issues of resilience, continuity, and change on the one hand, but also on questions of authenticity and originality. The institutional production of African-American reinventions of Yoruba traditional practices is sometimes generating corresponding contestation of such practices by West African Yorubas. Narratives gleaned from several Yoruba orisa Internet websites such as in the Ifa Foundation website and Ifa College web chat room point to enigmatic discourses revolving around the reconstruction, contestation and negotiation of Yoruba indigenous religious practices between Yorubas in Nigeria and the Diaspora on the one hand, and orisa practitioners in the Americas. The perceptive critique of traditional divination techniques was also an attempt to legitimize the Americanization of Ifá/Orisa. American Ifá is claimed to be the result of more than twenty five years of study and examination of the ancient philosophy of the Yoruba culture of West Africa. The Foundation enthused:

> American Ifa is Ifa for today's world... the basis of American Ifa is to re-unite the intellectual capacity with the spiritual power in the partnership they were originally intended to be. To strip away the encroachment, malignancy, and manipulation of Western religions that sought to usurp and control these universal truths...to suppose that the client had to be seated across from the Diviner in order for the external vision and wisdom of Orunmila who, by definition, is the witness of fate, and to whom all past, present and future probabilities are clear, simply was illogical. To suggest that prayers are only valid if they are uttered in the original Yoruba is equally illogical... To suggest that Ifá is limited to a certain culture, skin colour or sexual orientation is equally illogical... This is not to say that the traditional methods were wrong. They were right... for the time, culture and circumstances of Africa. Many are not right, for Americans today. More complex is the structure and initiation process of priests in this hemisphere.[42]

42. "What is American Ifa," Ifa Foundation, http://www.ifafoundation.org/en/class-

On the other hand, many Yoruba in West Africa and the Diaspora consider this practice of "American Ifá'"as inauthentic Yoruba religious practice. Some are even skeptical about the status of non-Yoruba, white Americans and African-Americans as devotees and adepts of orisa religion. The Vodoun and other African traditional and diasporic religions have been criticized for "experiencing an influx of Neo-pagans, Thelemics, Wiccans, Satanists and other non-Diaspora who are misinterpreting, and revising its core philosophy and cosmology to reflect their own beliefs and spiritual agenda."[43] Meanwhile, ritual recipes and procedures gleaned from several orisa-based Internet websites are indicative of the influence of Eastern-related forms of spirituality.

Conclusion

Indigenous African religions pose an interesting, complex problem of description and interpretation. In spite of the complex diversity that characterizes African peoples and their religious collectivities, there exist some common denominators in terms of their historical specificities, cosmological systems, and ritual dimensions. We have explored how the global dimension of these religions, introduced to new geocultural contexts through migration and media technologies, is manifesting in varied forms. These religious forms are now proliferating in the diasporic context, with practitioners and clientele assuming a multiethnic and multi-racial character. The internationalization of indigenous African religions therefore opens new challenges about their nature, scope and identity; issues of terminology, originality, or authenticity; but also renewed contestations of resilience, continuity, and change between local and global contexts.

Suggestions for Further Reading

Adogame, Afe. "Contesting the Ambivalences of Modernity in a Global Context: The Redeemed Christian Church of God, North America." *Studies in World Christianity* 10 no. 1(2004): 25-48.

———. "Engaging the Rhetoric of Spiritual Warfare: The Public Face of Aladura in Diaspora," *Journal of Religion in Africa* 34 no. 4 (2004): 493-522.

———. "African Instituted Churches in Europe: Continuity and Transformation." In *African Identities and World Christianity in the Twentieth Century*, edited by Klaus Koschorke, 225-44. Wiesbaden: Harrassowitz, 2005. pp. 225-244.

room/what-is-american-ifa.html.

43. "The New Age Trend to Obscure a Sacred Birthright," Mami Wata West African and Diaspora Vodoun, http://www.mamiwata.com/voodoo3.html.

Ameve, Osofo Kofi. *The Divine Acts. Holy Scriptures for the Sankofa Faith (Afrikanism).* Accra: Afrikan Renaissance Mission, n,d,

Barnes, Sandra. *Africa's Ogun: Old World and New.* Bloomington: Indiana University Press, 1997.

Bellegarde-Smith, Patrick, ed. *Fragments of Bone: Neo-African Religions in a New World.* Urbana: University of Illinois Press, 2005.

Clarke, Kamari M. *Mapping Yoruba Networks: Power and Agency in the Making of Transnational Communities.* Durham: Duke University Press, 2004.

Damuah, Osofo-Okomfo K. *The Introduction to Afrikania.* Accra: Afrikania Mission, 1998.

Houlberg, Marilyn, "Magique Marasa: The Ritual Cosmos of the Twins and Other Sacred Children." In *Fragments of Bone: Neo-African Religions in a New World,* edited by Patrick Bellegarde-Smith, 13-31. Urbana University of Illinois Press, 2005.

Kwakuzi, Azasu. *African Traditional Religion: Afrikania. A Brief Exposition.* Accra: Afrikania Afrikan Renaissance Books, 1999.

Murphy, Joseph and Mei-Mei Sanford. *Osun Across the Waters: A Yoruba Goddess in Africa and the Americas.* Bloomington: Indiana University Press, 2001.

Olupona, Jacob K., ed. *African Spirituality: Forms, Meanings and Expressions.* New York: Crossroad Publishing Co., 2001.

Stoller, Paul. *Money Has No Smell: The Africanization of New York City.* Chicago: University of Chicago Press, 2002.

Websites

Roots and Rooted: Traditional African Religion. (http://www.rootsandrooted. org/).

Mami Wata West African and Diaspora Voudon. (http://mamiwata.com/ voodoo.html).

Temple of Nyame Dua. (http://web.mac.com/loveasante/iWeb/Temple/ Welcome.html).

Afrikania Mission. (http://members.tripod.com/afrikania/id2.htm).

Ifa College. (http://www.ifacollege.com).

Ifa Foundation. (http://www.ifafoundation.org).

OrishaNet Articles. (http://www.orishanet.org/africa.html).

Orisha and Child Murder. (http://www.awostudycenter.com/Current/ Orisha_Child_Murder.htm).

5
Pagans

Sabina Magliocco

On a sunny afternoon near the first of May, Pagans from all over the San Francisco Bay area are gathered in Berkeley's Live Oak Park for the Beltane celebration of the members of the New Reformed Orthodox Order of the Golden Dawn, or NROOGD. At the center of this ritual is the hobby horse, or "Oss," a large round frame covered in black fabric worn by a hooded dancer, with a brightly painted horse's head attached to it. NROOGD members borrowed this character from a Cornish May Day tradition that appeared in a 1953 documentary by folklorists Alan Lomax and Peter Kennedy.[1] To NROOGD Pagans, the Oss represents an ancient spirit of the land linked with a Celtic horse deity, symbolizing the land's cyclical fertility and sustaining qualities.

Like all NROOGD rituals, this one begins with a dance—a chain that becomes a circle in which the ritual will take place. An altar has been set up in the north, and the priestess, dressed in white, stands over it. She blesses the water, oil and salt inside a large crystal bowl. Picking up the bowl and sprinkling the circle to purify the space, she chants, "Three from me, of five alive, by nine makes mine." She takes the ritual knife from the altar and holds it extended towards the circle, moving clockwise, and traces a circle in the air. Next, the priest, striking in his black attire, moves to the center of the circle carrying a great sword, which he holds vertically. He begins by facing east and calls upon the element air to be present. Next, he turns south and calls upon fire; in the same way, he turns west and summons water, then north and calls forth earth. Now he calls in the May Queen, a young woman dressed in green and white with flowers in her hair, who is led into the circle by her two attendants. Invoking the goddess to embody her, the participants chant:

> Lady, come, come in, come through
> Lady, join the work we do.

1. *Oss Oss Wee Oss*, directed by Alan Lomax, Peter Kennedy, and George Pickering (1953).

Figure 5.1: *The Berkeley Oss is a "hobbyhorse" costume supported on the shoulders of its wearer, with a drapery hanging from an oval rim and a small head and tail attached. The wearer looks out through eyeholes in the conical mask. The "teaser" guides the horse's motions. (Photo by Sabina Magliocco.)*

> Come down, Lady; now she is near.
> She is coming, she is coming,
> She is here!

The May Queen calls in her consort, Jack-in-the-Green, a young man dressed in fabric leaves, who runs into the center of the circle and kneels at her feet. He whistles, and his attendants arrive, bearing the maypole, decorated with ribbons and garlands; as it passes by, many hands reach out to touch it, to gain for themselves a little of its magic—the power of the returning spring. The pole is erected in the center of the circle, and each participant takes a ribbon and begins to dance, weaving the ribbons over and under, to the accompaniment of music and song.

The May Queen and Jack-in-the-Green hold the maypole between them as they kiss and caress one another. To the crowd's delight and amusement, Jack occasionally strokes the maypole, which appears to be rising from his groin. For modern Pagans, Beltane, or May Day, is the celebration of the union of the masculine and feminine principles in nature that leads to the fruitfulness of summer's bounty, and the actors take pleasure in performing their assigned roles. Soon the whole maypole is covered in a brightly braided sheath of ribbons. At the May Queen's signal, all move forward towards the pole, willing the energy into the earth for the fruitfulness of the soil and crops.

Now Laurel, who plays the part of the teaser, or guide for the Oss, moves into the center of the circle. "You know what time it is, don't you?" she teases the crowd. "It's time to call him in. Oss, Oss!" she calls.

"Wee Oss!" the crowd roars in response.

"Oss Oss!"

"Wee Oss!"
"Oss Oss!"
"Wee Oss!"

Suddenly from the far end of the meadow the Oss emerges from his hiding place. He moves majestically over the green grass, black skirt and mane rippling as he advances. Although up close the heavy wood-and-metal frame is cumbersome and awkward, from a distance the Oss looks powerful and otherworldly; there is something profoundly stirring about him. The crowd is hushed, and the circle opens to let him in.

Now the Oss and teaser begin their mirroring dance. Inside the Oss costume, the bearer cannot see past the end of the large frame he carries on his shoulders, so the teaser's crucial role is to guide him by moving as she wants him to move, ensuring that he does not strike people with the heavy hoop or trample those who dart in and out under his skirt—for it is good luck to be caught under the Oss. Women who wish to conceive, or participants seeking other forms of prosperity, will try to duck under him as he dances. It is the teaser who tells the Oss when to twirl, when to go forward and back, dodge or feint, and this is done entirely through body movements.

The performance of the Oss and teaser is accompanied by the sound of the choir singing a traditional Cornish May song:

> Unite and unite and let us all unite
> for summer is a-comin' today
> And whither we are going, we shall all unite
> In the merry morning of May.
> Oh where is King George? Oh where is he now?
> He's out in his long boat all on the salt sea-o....

When the chorus sings the "King George" verse, the Oss stops and settles to the ground. The teaser pretends to coax him and finally in exasperation kicks him. At last a little girl is called forth to kiss the Oss; only this persuades him to rise again, enacting the yearly drama of death and resurrection played out in the rhythm of the seasons. Finally a bucket of water is brought in for the Oss; he dips the beard on the end of the horse head into it and twirls, spraying the crowd. People eagerly rush forward to catch the droplets, which are considered a blessing.

At last the ritual is winding down. Jack and the May Queen bless a loaf of bread and a cup of ale, and carry them around the circle so all can have a taste. The priest salutes the spirits attending, and the priestess unwinds the circle, saying: "Around, around, it shall go to ground and not rebound." All gather around the priest's staff in the center of the circle; those who can, reach out to touch it, and those who are too far away touch someone next to them who can touch another person whose hand is on the staff. The energy is driven into the ground with a chant:

> Let the power pass from me
> To end where it was begun.
> As I will so mote it be;
> Chant the spell and be it done.

Seasonal ritual and celebration are at the heart of modern Paganism (or Neopaganism, as it is sometimes called). These terms designate a variety of religions that share certain basic characteristics, but do not have sacred texts, religious hierarchy, or even a collective form of organization. Modern Pagans are inspired by the pre-Christian religions once practiced by peoples of Europe, the Near East, and North Africa, as well as by indigenous religions from other parts of the globe. They re-create, revive, and experiment with elements from these religions in order to create meaningful ways of relating to nature and the sacred.

For modern Pagans, the sacred is both immanent and transcendent. It is present in every living thing, including humans, as well as in nature. At the same time it goes beyond the material world to include unseen entities such as gods and goddesses, elemental spirits, nature spirits—and for some Pagans, a universal force that manifests through these other spirit forms. The idea of nature as sacred is central to modern Pagans; for this reason, modern Paganisms are sometimes referred to as "nature religions" or "earth-based religions." Most forms of Paganism recognize the sacredness of four principle elements—air, fire, water and earth—and some see the planet itself as a living organism, an embodiment of a nurturing goddess. Humans are seen as partaking of this sacredness: the body is perceived as holy, and human sexuality as a manifestation of the creative, generative force that lies at the center of existence. Modern Pagan religions generally celebrate all forms of sexuality, and have few rules restricting its expression. This emphasis on the body extends to a search for an embodied spirituality: Pagans seek spiritual experiences they can feel in their bodies, through such activities as dancing, drumming, chanting, sacred sexuality, and occasionally through the use of mind-altering substances. Contemporary Pagan religions also share a search for a direct, personal, individualized experience of the sacred, an emphasis on spirituality as a path to personal development and self-realization, a distrust of religious hierarchy and dogma, and a tendency to borrow elements from a variety of different cultural and religious sources in their quest to construct a personally evocative spirituality.

"Pagan" comes from the Latin word *paganus*, meaning "country-dweller." There are currently two theories on how it came to designate non-Christians. The first, older, and more accepted of the two is that because Christianity diffused first through the urban centers of the Roman Empire, those who lived in rural areas were among the last to accept the new religion; thus the word became associated with those who were not Christian, lived in contact with nature and the agro-pastoral cycle, and saw themselves as local (belonging to a *pagus*, or rural territory), rather than identifying with a larger state. The second, more recent theory is that the word had acquired the slang connotation of "civilian," in contrast to a member of the Roman army. It was used by Christians to refer to those who had not joined the army of God.[2] Modern Pagans perceive sacredness in the earth and the cycle of the seasons, and believe ancient pagans lived in greater harmony with nature and the sacred than modern, post-industrial Westerners. While there was probably no sense of shared religious identity that united ancient pagans, modern Pagans have reclaimed the term and infused it with their own associations and with new life. Modern Pagans trace the roots of their religious practices back to ancient religions, or at least to European folk practices that maintained pagan elements during the centuries of Christian domination. However, this group of new religions arose in Europe during the early twentieth century and is now diffused throughout the globe. On one level, contemporary Paganism is a reaction against the excesses of modernity: Pagans tend to see contemporary life, especially in Western urban centers, as alienating human beings from nature and the cycle of the seasons, and from a feeling of kinship to other human beings and life forms. Their rituals and other forms of religious practice, which will be examined below, are attempts to heal this rift, to re-create the harmony and connectedness they see in indigenous religions and imagine once existed in the religions of their own ancestors. Yet Paganism is itself a product of modernity, urbanization, the development of individualism and modern concepts of personal growth and self-realization. This paradox lies at the heart of contemporary Paganism.

Modern Pagan religions offer their adherents direct, unmediated contact with the sacred and a chance to create an individualized spirituality apart from the strictures of organized, mainstream religions. No single belief unites practitioners: Pagan religions are orthopractic, rather than orthodox, unified by a set of attitudes and praxes, but not sharing common beliefs or sacred texts. The most widely shared outlooks are a feeling of connection to the natural world, and a search for ecstatic, embodied spiritual experiences. The most important shared practice

2. Robin Lane Fox, *Pagans and Christians* (San Francisco: Harper and Row, 1986), 30-31.

is ritual. Pagans tend to ritualize many aspects of life, both as a way of sacralizing the everyday, and as a pathway to religious ecstasy and embodied experiences of the sacred. Most celebrate a number of seasonal rituals, and some denominations also mark the cycles of the moon. Many modern Pagan traditions also mark changes in the life cycles of their members, including the arrival of a baby, a young person's coming of age, a formal union with a romantic partner, and the remembrance of life upon an individual's death. Some traditions of Paganism are mystery religions that require members to undergo initiation in order to fully participate; these constitute another type of rite of passage. Finally, at times of crisis, Pagans may either singly or in groups perform rites to address the situation and bring about a resolution. These will be addressed in greater detail below.

Most Pagans believe that rituals can bring about transformations, though they differ in their interpretations of how this takes place. Some think the rites themselves have power, while others see them as symbolic statements that work mostly on the psyches of the individuals concerned. This range of attitudes also applies to sacred figures such as goddesses, gods, and nature spirits: while some Pagans see them as having an independent existence, others interpret them as human projections, symbols, or aspects of the self. Modern Pagans emphasize life in the present, rather than life after death. There are few shared beliefs about the afterlife. Some Pagans believe in a form of reincarnation: after a period of rest in a pleasant after-world, sometimes called the Summerland, souls are reborn into healthier bodies in the company of those whom they loved in previous lives. Others believe that the dead become part of some greater spiritual force or energy, but lose individuality and personality. Still others have no particular beliefs about life after death, although many think that the dead can occasionally communicate with the living, particularly with loved ones and descendants. Absent from Paganism are narratives about afterlife rewards or punishments for deeds done in this life. In this group of religions, ethical breaches have consequences in the present.

Folklore plays a significant role in modern Paganism, in that it is regarded as a repository for bits and pieces of ancient religion that survived to the present day. Because Pagans locate authenticity in ancient religions, folklore becomes an important index of authenticity, and a way to reconnect with the past. Many modern Pagans are knowledgeable and well-versed in folklore, especially European lore, which has been collected and documented since the late eighteenth century. Significantly, the Romantic, survivalist approach of the early collectors, who saw in folklore the remnants of knowledge and customs from ancient pre-Christian societies, appeals to Pagans today because it allows them to use folklore to attempt to reconstruct the practices of ancient pagan religions and cultures.

The Roots of Modern Paganisms

The roots of contemporar Paganisms lie in concepts of an animated universe common to all indigenous religions, also found in the ancient religions whose written records remain to us. But that link is indirect and complex, interrupted by a series of movements, both religious and secular, that separated Westerners from local, nature-based spiritualities for many centuries. Some of these traditional concepts and practices continued to exist in everyday practices such as folk magic and healing. Until quite recently, many Western societies had specialized healers, sometimes known as cunning folk, who used herbs, magic and prayers to cure everyday ailments, and who occasionally were called upon to lift curses or undo magical spells. Their systems drew on principles of magic that can be traced to very ancient times, but these were generally inserted into a Christian religious framework, even when their structures and techniques hearkened back to earlier worldviews.

Modern Paganisms have been called revitalizations—social movements that emerge during periods of marked social transformation and attempt to change society by introducing new worldviews, new religious movements, and revived religions, presupposing a link to past religions.[3] In effect, they have some characteristics of each of these. Loretta Orion, one of the earliest ethnographers to describe the movement, compared it to Wallace's "nativistic cult," a type of revitalization movement that re-values everything that is indigenous, local, and free from foreign influence,[4] while journalist Margot Adler, whose comprehensive study *Drawing Down the Moon* provided the first published account of modern Paganism, noted its use of folklore to connect with lost roots.[5] Religious studies scholar Catherine Albanese has examined the movement within the context of what she calls "nature religions": popular spiritual movements that value what is natural, unaffected, and homegrown, share liberal political tendencies and millenarian beliefs, engage in various forms of alternative healing, and make extensive use of alternate states of consciousness.[6]

3. Anthony F.C. Wallace, "Revitalization Movements," in *Culture and Personality*, ed. Anthony Wallace (New York: Random House, 1970).

4. Loretta Orion, *Never Again the Burning Times* (Prospect Heights, Ill.: Waveland Press, 1995) 25-27.

5. Margot Adler, *Drawing Down the Moon* (Boston: Beacon Press, 1987 [1979]), 253.

6. Catherine Albanese, *Nature Religion in America* (Chicago: University of Chicago Press, 1990), 6.

Historian Ronald Hutton has called them "revived religions," emphasizing their presumed link to the past and similarities with other kinds of revival movements.[7] Modern Paganisms have in common the practice of reclamation, the re-valuing and re-casting of discarded or devalued traditions for the purpose of creating a new identity. Reclamation, part of the process of tradition, encompasses revitalization and revival as well as the creation of new cultural forms out of what was previously rejected.[8]

Precursors to modern Paganism began to emerge in Europe during the Enlightenment, when many elements of Classical culture were in vogue. In England, various orders of Druids re-interpreted the ancient priests of Britain and Gaul as keepers of arcane wisdom and forces of resistance against Roman domination. While these early druid societies were not primarily religious in orientation, they nevertheless had a strong spiritual component. They created a link in the popular imagination between the ancient Celtic order and prehistoric monuments by conducting rituals at Stonehenge.[9]

The nineteenth-century Romantic revival provided two additional important elements that contributed to the emergence of modern Paganism: the re-valuation of nature and its personification in the Greek god Pan and an earth mother goddess, and the revisionist interpretation of European witchcraft as the vestige of an ancient pre-Christian nature religion. According to this explanation, the witch persecutions that had racked the early modern period were based on misinterpretations of what was an ancient pagan religion based on fertility magic that venerated a horned god and an earth mother goddess. Medieval clerics had mistaken the horned god for the devil, fertility rites for perversions, and healing philters for evil spells. While it originated with the Frenchman Jules Michelet, this interpretation was popularized by British folklorist Margaret Murray through her books *The Witch Cult of Western Europe* (1923) and *The God of the Witches* (1935). These in turn influenced Gerald B. Gardner, a British civil servant who had spent much of his life in Borneo and Malaysia, but returned to England in the mid 1930s. In 1954, he published *Witchcraft Today*, a book in which he claimed to have

7. Ronald Hutton, *The Triumph of the Moon: A History of Modern Pagan Witchcraft* (Oxford: Oxford University Press, 1999), 145-16.

8. Sabina Magliocco, *Witching Culture: Folklore and Neopaganism in America* (Philadelphia: University of Pennsylvania Press, 2004), 8-9.

9. Prys Morgan, "From Death to a View: The Hunt for the Welsh Past in the Romantic Period," in *The Invention of Tradition*, ed. Eric Hobsbawn and Terence Ranger (Cambridge: Cambridge University Press, 1992) 43-100; Ronald Hutton, *The Druids* (London: Hambledon, 2007).

discovered a coven of witches practicing in southern England according to the pattern described by Murray, and made their practices known to the world. There is much scholarly controversy over whether such a group actually existed. Gardner was a member of several amateur theatrical groups around Bournemouth, as well as being a Co-Mason, and it is possible that some of his acquaintances may have formed a society devoted to exploring occult practices before Gardner came upon them and took them for a witch cult. Two things are certain: the first is that if such a group indeed existed, its history did not go back much further than the early twentieth century. The second is that by the mid-1950s, Gardner had himself formed such a group. Gardner was a great promoter of his new religion, appearing on many popular radio and television programs and even founding a Witchcraft Museum on the Isle of Man (which has since been moved to Boscastle, Cornwall).[10] By the time of his death in 1964, there were several covens in existence in England, and a few of his followers had migrated to the United States, bringing what came to be called "Gardnerian" Craft with them.[11]

The 1960s proved a pivotal decade for the new Paganism. The counterculture, with its rejection of all that was staid, conventional, and mainstream, created an atmosphere in which groups were eager to experiment with new ways of worship, including many forms of Pagan revival. Colleges and universities, as centers of learning, free speech, and liberal ideals, became centers around which interest in modern Paganism flourished. A number of new Pagan groups were formed by university students: at Carleton College in Northfield, Minnesota, a group of students who resented the requirement of attending Sunday morning worship services formed the Reformed Druids of North America. While the organization began as a spoof, eventually some members decided they enjoyed the weekly meetings on the college green, and began to systematize a set of practices. NROOGD, the Berkeley group that enacts the yearly May Day games described at the beginning of this chapter, was formed by a class of students at San Francisco State University who were studying ritual. And Wisconsin priestess Selena Fox of Circle Sanctuary got her start in the Classics Club at the University of Virginia, where she re-enacted Dionysian rites.

Because Witches venerate a goddess as well as a god, and because of the central role of the priestess, Witchcraft appealed to feminists who were searching for religious expressions that valued the feminine divine and gave important liturgical roles to women. The second-wave feminist

10. Museum of Witchcraft, http://www.museumofwitchcraft.com
11. Chas S. Clifton, *Her Hidden Children: The Rise of Wicca and Paganism in America* (Lanham, Md., AltaMira Press, 2006), 11-36.

movement inspired authors Zsuzsanna "Z" Budapest and Starhawk to create variants of Pagan Witchcraft that foregrounded feminist ideals and women's spiritual development. Budapest's Dianic Witchcraft featured women-only covens, where women could experience freedom from male dominance and explore their personal spirituality, centered on the worship of the goddess Diana. Starhawk, a key founder of the Reclaiming tradition, saw the oppression of women as linked to a patriarchal system of domination that also included the exploitation of the earth. In Reclaiming mixed-gender covens, women and men work together to bring about political and social change, with ritual as an important tool in changing consciousness.[12]

New Pagan religions continued to expand and produce new varieties throughout the 1970s, 1980s, and 1990s. The arrival of the Worldwide Web in the mid 1990s further expanded modern Paganisms, making them one of the fastest-growing new religious movements of the late twentieth and early twenty-first centuries.

Who Are Modern Pagans?

It is difficult to generalize about such a broad and individualistic group of religions, but studies have shown that at least in North America, Pagans are predominantly Euro-American, slightly more likely to be female than male (about 60 percen to 40 percent), better-educated than average, and earn less than the average income for their high degree of education. This may be because modern Pagans tend to study subjects like the humanities, in which high-paying jobs are not easily available; because many prefer to make a living at creative endeavors, such as the arts, that do not provide high salaries; and because they often value creativity and service to others over high earnings. In the United States, many are employed in the computer and health-care industries. While Pagans may live in cities, suburbs, or the countryside, they are concentrated in urban areas and university towns, where there is greater tolerance for non-conformism. More Pagans than the national average tend to identify as other than heterosexual. This may be in part because these religions lack judgmental attitudes towards non-mainstream sexuality which characterize some established religions, and thus attract gay, lesbian, bisexual, and transgendered individuals searching for religious community; but it

---

12 Cynthia Eller, *Living in the Lap of the Goddess: The Feminist Spirituality Movement in America* (Boston: Beacon Press, 1995); Jone Salomonsen, *Enchanted Feminism: The Reclaiming Witches of San Francisco* (New York: Routlege, 2001).

could also reflect the generally non-conformist and experimental nature of contemporary Pagans, who may have partners of both genders over the course of a lifetime. Some Pagans also embrace alternative practices such as vegetarianism, naturism, holistic and herbal healing, astrology, yoga, and unconventional sexual practices such as polyamory and poly-fidelity. Although some Pagan intentional communities do exist, for the most part, they do not live separately from the surrounding populace.

Most modern Pagans are not born into these religions, but come to them as young adults, as a result of reading, political and social interests, friendships, and, increasingly, the influence of the Internet. Today, there is a growing number of second and third-generation Pagans who grew up in Pagan families. The basic unit of Pagan social organization is the small group. These groups, called covens, circles or groves, typically consist of between three and fifteen individuals who meet regularly to worship in each other's homes, public parks, or rented spaces, such as community halls and church basements. They may affiliate with larger denomina-tional groups with whom they share a liturgy, practice and ritual style. There are also a number of Pagan networking organizations that bring together many different denominations to pursue common interests, engage in political and social activism, and do charitable work; three of the most prominent include Covenant of the Goddess, the Pagan Alli-ance, and the Pagan Federation. Many Pagans choose not to affiliate with any group or organization, preferring to practice their spirituality indi-vidually. Occasionally, these "solitaries," as they are called, may attend a ritual, festival, or fair organized by one of the larger groups or network-ing organizations. "Moots" are another feature of Pagan social networks; these informal but regularly occurring meetings in coffeehouses and pubs are generally open to all interested parties, and are a way for Pagans to get to know one another before committing to joining a particular group or denomination. The Internet plays a significant role in Pagan social interactions as well, with over 20,000 web sites and chat rooms devoted to Pagan topics.[13]

There is no single charismatic leader or unifying Pagan authority. Modern Pagan religions are non-exclusive and informal; members may belong to a variety of Pagan groups and denominations, attending only the rituals and events that interest them. Some belong simultaneously to other religious communities; for example, it is not unusual to find Pagans of Jewish heritage who feel culturally Jewish, but spiritually Pagan. At

13. Douglas Cowan, *Cyberhenge: Modern Pagans on the Internet* (New York: Routledge, 2004).

the same time, Paganism often overlaps with, or borders on, other communities, including historical re-enactment societies, fantasy role-playing gamers, fans of science fiction and fantasy literature, folk musicians, feminists, environmentalists, the Goth subculture, and the New Age movement. Because of the fluidity and informality of the movement, it is difficult to estimate the exact number of practitioners. According to some estimates, there are about 1 million Pagans world-wide with perhaps 700,000 living in North America.[14]

Types of Modern Pagan Religions

Contemporary Pagan religions as a whole are eclectic and syncretic, combining material from a wide variety of sources, including Western occultism, Eastern religions, science fiction and fantasy novels and television programs, popular psychology, and academic research on anthropology, archeology, and folklore. Most, however, are inspired by one particular pre-Christian religion, or by the traditions of a specific national or regional group. Thus there are Celtic, Egyptian, and Norse Pagans, as well as those inspired by ancient Greek and Roman religions and those of the ancient Near East. Some Pagans are neo-shamanic, while others are inspired by Native North American traditions. Often, Pagans are attracted to traditions with which they feel a connection because of their own ethnic background, but the majority of Pagan groups do not require members to have a cultural link to religious practice.

Pagans are strongly influenced by surrounding cultures: those who live in cities with a large Afro-Caribbean population may incorporate elements of *orisha* worship into their work, while throughout California, the strong Latino presence makes itself felt in local Paganisms through elaborate ancestor altars inspired by Mexican *Día de los muertos* observations. In Europe, modern Paganism is often tied to national and regional notions of identity, although there, too, the movement is eclectic, drawing upon a variety of sources for inspiration to reconstruct lost aspects of religious practice.

One of the most important distinctions Pagans make among themselves is between those who consider themselves Witches and those who do not. Witches, also known as Wiccans, constitute the largest percentage of modern Pagans. Some modern Pagan Witches consider themselves to be the spiritual descendants of medieval witches who were persecuted for practicing a non-Christian religion. While only a small percentage can

14. Online sources for membership include www.adherents.com/Religions_By_Adherents and www.pluralism.org.

trace their lineage directly to Gerald Gardner's covens, the majority have been strongly influenced by Gardnerian Craft in the structure of their rituals, their ritual year, and their general liturgical patterns. Witches generally recognize a goddess and a god as embodiments of the feminine and masculine principles in nature. The goddess is associated with the Moon; her triple nature as maiden, mother, and crone is linked with the Moon's monthly cycle, from new to full to waning. The god is often thought of as both her son and consort. In his horned aspect, he is associated with herd animals, while in his aspect as the Green Man, he symbolizes the yearly cycle of vegetation and fertility. Their symbolic union is celebrated at monthly coven meetings, which take place at the time of the full Moon, and at eight yearly sabbats, which occur on the solstices, equinoxes, and on the days falling roughly between them: November 1, February 1, May 1, and August 1. Of all the modern Pagan groups, Wiccans are the most magically oriented, in that they recognize magic as a natural force and regularly incorporate it into their rituals.

There are various denominations, or "traditions," of modern Witchcraft. British traditional Craft, which includes Gardnerian and Alexandrian Witchcraft, traces its ancestry directly back to either Gerald Gardner or Alex Sanders, promoters of the religion who lived in mid-twentieth century England. There are also various ethnic varieties of Witchcraft, each claiming descent from the folk practices of a specific European ethnic or national group; for example, Seax Wicca draws from Anglo-Saxon religious practices, while Stregheria claims a connection to Italian and ultimately Etruscan polytheism. On the other hand, eclectic Witchcraft traditions may draw from the pantheons and folk practices of a variety of peoples, combining them according to their own aesthetic pleasure. Some types of eclectic Witchcraft, such as the Reclaiming tradition, are strongly eco-feminist in their orientation and encourage members to become politically active for environmental and social change. Other feminist traditions, such as Dianic Witchcraft, are for women only, and recognize only a goddess in their ceremonies.

There are also a substantial number of non-Wiccan Pagan groups. While some, like the Church of All Worlds, are eclectic in their orientation, others center on the traditions of a specific culture area or ancient tradition. Thus, for example, the Fellowship of Isis focuses on an Egyptian pantheon; various Druid orders are inspired by the practices of the ancient Celtic priestly class; and Heathenry comprises a group of Pagan traditions reviving a Norse heritage. Some Pagan traditions are lighthearted and imaginative, drawing inspiration from science fiction television programs such as *Star Trek* and *Buffy the Vampire Slayer*, comic strip characters like Berkeley Breathed's Bill the Cat, and pop culture items such as troll dolls. Others are more strictly reconstructionist, seeking as much authenticity as possible in their recreations of ancient pagan ceremonies.

Finally, some modern Pagans pursue shamanic paths inspired by the healing traditions of indigenous peoples. Here, shamanism is broadly interpreted as any practice involving communication with the spirit world, usually in an alternate state of consciousness, for the purpose of healing. Modern Pagan shamans generally interpret healing to include personal spiritual growth and development, as well as larger goals such as healing the ecological damage humans have done to the earth. They may communicate with spirit helpers, who often take the form of animals, in their ceremonies.

Pagan Practices

Modern Pagans seek nothing short of the re-enchantment of the universe—to re-create the kind of relationship they imagine their ancestors had with the sacred, in which the universe was animated by forces that could be influenced through ceremonies, rituals, and prayers. Many traditions use magic, which they interpret as a natural force, to create and develop this sense of enchantment. Definitions of magic vary within the movement, but a commonly accepted one is "the art of changing consciousness at will." Modern Pagans believe that by changing human consciousness, the true, enchanted nature of the universe can be revealed, and humans can align themselves with it and live in greater harmony. Some believe that magic can directly affect the outcome of events, beyond just changing individuals' consciousness and perceptions. Most Pagans see everything in the universe as infused with a life force, or energy, which can be raised, manipulated, and directed by knowledgeable practitioners. Pagans may perform magic in order to enhance their chances of getting the results they want—for example, to help them find a job, sell their house, or undertake an important project, as well as to heal the sick or bring about planetary harmony and healing. The majority also recognize that magic alone is not enough to bring about results, though, and that actions must be taken in the material world in order to effect change. An ethical code governs the practice of magic in most traditions. It is often summarized by two principles: "Do what you will, but harm none" and the Threefold Law, a principle whereby what one puts out into the world is believed to return threefold. Therefore, generous and caring actions will eventually bring positive consequences, while selfish and immoral ones will have serious negative repercussions. Nearly all modern Pagan religions forbid the use of magic to coerce or manipulate others.

Because Pagans see the universe as interconnected, they may practice forms of divination such as tarot-card reading and astrology, believing that larger patterns mirror smaller ones, and vice-versa. Divination is sometimes interpreted as reflecting the will of the gods regarding some matter. A number of Norse Pagan traditions have revived an oracular practice known as *seidr*, in which a priestess answers questions and makes predictions in a trance state. Her pronouncements are understood to be divinely inspired.

As we saw at the beginning of this chapter, ritual is central to the practice of most modern Pagans. Even those denominations that do not practice magic hold regular rituals, or worship services. Much of the purpose of monthly and seasonal festivities is to help re-create a sense of connection between practitioners and the natural cycles around them, imparting a sense of mystery to natural processes and connecting them to human development and desires. Thus the cycle of the seasons, with its rhythms of birth, growth, fruitfulness, death, and regeneration, is equated to phases in the human life cycle, and to the natural progression of any project or undertaking. Rituals also connect modern Pagans with their predecessors in history, even if they understand that the rites were not practiced in exactly the same way. They form a bridge through time and space, connecting the modern world with the ancient, technology with nature, and human with divine.

The majority of modern Pagans do not have a specially designated place to worship, such as a temple or church; they hold rituals in private homes and gardens, in public parks, and rented halls. Ordinary space must be consecrated for the spiritual work that will take place, so most rituals begin by creating sacred space. This may be done through purification, for example by sprinkling the perimeter of the location with salt water that has been blessed, then purifying it with incense. Pagans usually worship in a circle, and many traditions cast the circle by having a priestess or priest walk its perimeter bearing a sacred knife, sword or staff and physically marking off the sacred space for all to see. Once the space has been purified and marked, the four elements (air, fire, water, and earth) and cardinal directions (east, south, west, and north) may be invoked, goddesses, gods, and other spirits may be called into sacred space, and practitioners may interact with them in various ways, depending on the rite's purpose. The core of the ceremony usually involves what Pagans call "raising energy" and directing it towards a specific goal. That goal may be summarized in a statement of the rite's intent, such as "Today is Midsummer's Day, and we dance to celebrate the bounty of the earth at the peak of the growing season," or "We work today to send healing energy to [name of person] and to all others who need it at this time."

Energy may be raised in a variety of ways: through body movement, dancing, chanting or singing, meditation, drumming, or some combination of these. All rituals have a strong participatory element, which often aims to personalize the rite's message and allow for individual input. Pagans greatly value this participatory, egalitarian aspect of their ceremonies; it is part of what connects them with the sacred. Once the work of ritual is done, and the energy has been directed towards a specific goal, the deities and other spiritual forces are thanked and released, the circle is opened, and all return to ordinary time and space. Many traditions, especially Wiccan ones, include a ceremonial meal of cakes and wine at the end of the rite.

The search for direct contact with the sacred is central to many rituals. To this end, rituals are frequently designed to bring about alternate states of consciousness in which participants enter the realm of their imagination and commune directly with the gods and the spiritual world. As illustrated above, rituals can be colorful, stimulating, and filled with music, dance, dramatic performances, storytelling, and other cues that transform the everyday world and encourage participants to enter into a mild trance state. At these times, Pagans may experience religious ecstasy, a feeling of being outside of the ordinary world and in touch with something sacred, mystical, and profound. Each individual experiences this differently, and experiences may likewise differ greatly from one ritual occasion to the next. They range from deep insights into the practitioner's life and spirituality, to messages perceived as coming directly from the gods, to states in which the individual becomes filled with divine spirit. Some Wiccan traditions practice deity possession: the spirit of the goddess or god is invoked into the body of a priestess or priest, and the practitioner then speaks and behaves as the deity for the duration of the rite. Ecstatic states are central to many Pagan rituals: while not everyone achieves religious ecstasy during every ritual, individuals yearn for and look forward to this aspect of ceremonies. Religious ecstasy makes beliefs real for practitioners; it also personalizes the religion, allowing each participant to be a priestess or priest and communicate directly with gods.

Many Pagans are extremely creative, artistic individuals, and modern Pagan rituals can be elaborate pieces of performance art, complete with costumes and props. For this reason, religious material culture is important to modern Pagans. Some make their own robes to wear in ritual, as well as liturgical tools such as cups, plates, wands, staffs, and other symbols. Most traditions have at least one altar present inside the sacred circle which holds holy symbols and acts as a threshold between the material and spiritual worlds. Some have multiple altars, each dedicated to an element or deity. The objects on the altar have specific meanings that help Pagans connect to and interpret the meaning of the ceremony. Wiccan altars typically hold symbols of the four elements: salt (earth), water, incense (air), and a burning coal (fire). At the beginning of the rite, the priestess blesses the elements and combines salt and water, incense and flame. These mixtures symbolize the magical transformations at the center of the life process and foreshadow the ceremonial meal of cakes and wine (again, transformed by the processes of leavening and fermentation) that ends Wiccan rites. Altars may also hold symbols of the deities; these may consist of statuary or abstract objects, such as a flower, a stone, a seashell, or anything else that suggests the sacred to the individual practitioner.

In addition to ritual altars, which are ephemeral, in that they are taken down at the end of each rite, many Pagans keep permanent altars in their homes, where they perform personal ceremonies and commune with their gods. Domestic altars serve as portals between the human and divine worlds—places where relationships to the deities are imagined, negotiated and maintained. Practitioners may leave offerings there for their tutelary spirits, work magic spells, meditate, pray, and perform other religious activities. Domestic altars are always changing, in that they reflect the current concerns of their makers. Some become quite elaborate; quite a few contemporary Pagans have transformed their entire homes and gardens into sacred spaces that reflect their personal spiritual paths.[15]

Like members of other modern subcultures, Pagans create identity through consumption, and may recognize one another through their jewelry, clothing, music, books, home décor, and other material culture. To keep Pagans supplied with the accoutrements for their religious practice, a large industry has sprung up providing everything from sacred statuary and jewelry to liturgical robes and music, not to mention necessary altar items such as incense, charcoal, candles, anointing oils (to bless candles and other items), pentacles, wands and knives. Much of this is produced by Pagans, for Pagans, and consists of hand-crafted objects; other items, such as musical CDs and books, are mass-produced and marketed, but also originate as divine inspiration. Pagans buy these items through the Internet, at local occult and craft shops, and at Pagan festivals and camps, where the vendors' stalls are always popular destinations.

Most contemporary Pagans live surrounded by what they sometimes call "mundane" culture—people who do not share their practices and views, and who may not even know their neighbors, co-workers, and asso-

---

15. Sabina Magliocco, *Neo-Pagan Sacred Art and Altars: Making Things Whole* (Jackson: University Press of Mississippi, 2001).

ciates are Pagan. In many cases, they must keep their religious identity concealed in mainstream settings because of intense prejudice: Pagans have been fired from jobs, had their homes and businesses destroyed, and lost custody of children because of their unconventional religion. However, they have recently won a number of court victories that illustrate their religions are becoming more accepted, or at least that the principles of religious freedom in modern liberal democracies are working in favor of these religions. For example, in 2006 Wiccans won a battle against the Veterans Administration of the United States allowing the pentagram, a five-pointed star within a circle that symbolizes the four elements plus spirit, to be engraved on the tombs of Wiccan soldiers who had lost their lives in service to their country.

Pagan festivals and camps serve as contexts in which they can freely express their religious identities in a setting that celebrates and glories in them. These events typically take place in the warmer months, and are usually outdoor events at primitive camping facilities (although one of the largest, Pantheacon, takes place every February in a California hotel). They feature daily workshops on topics such as scrying (looking into a mirror or crystal as a form of divination), dancing one's inner animal, natural herbal healing, and connecting with the Dark Goddess within, as well as scholarly or historical lectures, musical performances, dances, and, of course, rituals. These events play a key role in the diffusion of ritual elements, chants, songs, and magical techniques, and act as important venues for networking. They are usually sponsored by Pagan networking organizations or by regional councils of organizations such as Covenant of the Goddess. Reclaiming's Witch Camps have now acquired a global presence, with branches all over North America, in Europe and Australia.[16] Away from the pressures of their workday lives and surrounded by the beauty of the natural world, Pagans are more able to fully experience religious ecstasy, spiritual growth, and communion with the sacred and with community. Camps and festivals are also places where Pagans can fully perform their religious identities, wearing elaborate robes and jewelry (or nothing at all, at clothing-optional retreats), decorating their campsites with altars and shrines to their tutelary deities, and using sacred names that connect them to their religious and spiritual beliefs.[17]

Ultimately, most Pagans believe religious convictions must be taken beyond the confines of the sacred circle, festival, and campsite and into

16. Witch Camp, http://www.witchcamp.org.

17. Sarah Pike, *Earthly Bodies, Magical Selves: Contemporary Pagans and the Search for Community* (Berkeley: University of California Press, 2001).

the world in order to bring about real, lasting change. Some traditions include among their teachings a directive that members contribute to the world in proportion to what they have received. For this reason, a large number of Pagans participate in volunteer activities of various sorts, from community clean-ups in parks and reservoirs, to political actions and demonstrations, to Interfaith work that allows them to work with clergy from other faiths to achieve humanitarian goals. Many feminist and environmental organizations draw Pagan participation, as do community health-oriented projects such as soup kitchens and clean needle exchanges for drug addicts. Pagans who feel a strong connection to animals may work on animal conservation and welfare issues. For modern Pagans, there is no contradiction between the practice of magic and involvement in grass-roots political causes and volunteer work; political action is in fact a form of magic, a way to change consciousness and reality, and an extension of religious expression.

Suggestions for Further Reading

Adler, Margot *Drawing Down the Moon: Witches, Druids, Goddess-Worshippers, and Other Pagans in American Today.* Boston: Beacon Press, 2007 [1979, 1986].

Albanese, Catherine. *Nature Religion in America.* Chicago: University of Chicago Press: 1990.

Bado-Fralick, Nikki. *Coming to the Edge of the Circle: A Wiccan Initiation Ritual.* Oxford: Oxford University Press, 2005.

Berger, Helen. *A Community of Witches.* Columbia: University of South Carolina Press, 1999.

Berger, Helen, ed. *Witchcraft and Magic: Contemporary North America.* Philadelphia: University of Pennsylvania Press, 2005.

Clifton, Chas S. *Her Hidden Children: the Rise of Wicca and Paganism in America.* Lanham, Md.: Alta Mira Press, 2006

Cowan, Douglas. *Cyberhenge: Modern Pagans on the Internet.* London and New York: Routledge, 2004

Eller, Cynthia. *Living in the Lap of the Goddess: The Feminist Spirituality Movement in America.* Boston: Beacon Press, 1995.

———. *The Myth of Matriarchal Prehistory.* Boston: Beacon Press, 2000.

Fox, Robin Lane. *Pagans and Christians.* San Francisco: Harper and Row, 1986.

Greenwood, Susan. *The Nature of Magic: an Anthropology of Consciousness.* Oxford: Berg, 2005.

———. *Magic, Witchcraft and the Otherworld: an Anthropology.* Oxford: Berg, 2000.

Hanegraaf, Wouter J. *New Age Religion and Western Culture.* Albany: State University of New York Press, 1996.

Harvey, Graham. *Listening People, Speaking Earth: Contemporary Paganism.* London: Hurst, 2005.

Hutton, Ronald. *The Triumph of the Moon: a History of Modern Pagan Witchcraft.* Oxford: Oxford University Press, 1999.

———. *The Druids.* London: Hambledon, 2007.

Magliocco, Sabina. *Neo-Pagan Sacred Art and Altars: Making Things Whole.* Jackson, Miss.: University Press of Mississippi, 2001.

————. *Witching Culture: Folklore and Neopaganism in America*. Philadelphia: University of Pennsylvania Press, 2004.

Orion, Loretta.. *Never Again the Burning Times*. Prospect Heights, Illinois: Waveland Press, 1995.

Oss Tales. DVD. Directed by John M. Bishop and Sabina Magliocco. Portland, Oregon: Media-Generation Productions, 2007.

Pike, Sarah. *Earthly Bodies, Magical Selves: Contemporary Pagans and the Search for Community*. Berkeley: University of California Press, 2001.

————. *New Age and Neopagan Religions in America*. New York: Columbia University Press, 2004.

Salomonsen, Jone. *Enchanted Feminism: the Reclaiming Witches of San Francisco*. New York and London: Routledge, 2001.

Strmiska, Michael, ed. *Modern Paganism in World Cultures: Contemporary Perspectives*. Santa Barbara, California: ABC-Clio, 2006.

York, Michael. *Pagan Theology: Paganism as a World Religion*. New York: New York University Press, 2005.

Websites

Adherents.com (http://www.adherents.com/Religions_By_Adherents.html).

Covenant of the Goddess (http://www. cog.org).

Pagan Federation (http://paganfederation.org/).

The Pluralism Project (http://www.pluralism.org/resources/statistics/tradition.php#Paganism).

The Witches' Voice (http://www.witchvox.org).

6

Muslims

Florian Pohl

It is before 4:30 in the morning at Pondok Pesantren Sunan Pandanaran, a Muslim boarding school on the Indonesian island of Java, when the muezzin intones the call to prayer known as the *adhan.*

الله أكبر (4x)

أشهد أن لا إله إلا الله (2x)

أشهد أن محمدا رسول الله (2x)

حيّ على الصّلاة (2x)

حيّ على الفلاح (2x)

الله أكبر (2x)

لا إله إلا الله (1x)

Allahu Akbar (God is most great) (four times)
I testify that there is no god but God (twice)
I testify that Muhammad is the messenger of God (twice)
Come (alive) to the prayer (twice)
Come (alive) to flourishing (twice)
Allahu Akbar (God is most great) (twice)
There is no god but God (once)[1]

The muezzin's is not the only voice to be heard this morning, which is hardly surprising considering that the Southeast Asian nation of Indonesia is the world's most populous Muslim-majority country. Every day at dawn a multitude of chants issues forth from the countless neighborhood

---

1. Michael Sells, *Approaching the Qur'an: The Early Revelations* (Ashland: White Cloud Press, 1999), 150.

mosques surrounding the school and breaks the silence of the night. Each mosque's muezzin independently calculates the time for the *adhan* so that different callers will begin at slightly different times. Their voices intermingle and entwine for some minutes filling the crisp morning air with the distinctive sounds that for those who have experienced them are unforgettably associated with living in a Muslim community.

The combination of many individual voices during the period of the *adhan* suggests some of the heterogeneous qualities of the Muslim community. But the distinctiveness of the call's cadence and sound patterns, the fact that it contains important Qur'anic passages, and the regularity with which it permeates life five times daily in Indonesia and elsewhere also reveals more universal characteristics such as the belief in one God and the Prophethood of Muhammad.

Educating Muslims: Pondok Pesantren Sunan Pandanaran, Java

Almost 1,500 students at Sunan Pandanaran wake to the predawn *adhan*, which reminds them of their obligation to perform the dawn prayer, the first of the five daily prayers. Participation in these prayers is required of both female and male students, who attend the *pesantren* in equal numbers. Some have been up for a while, performing the voluntary night prayer or *tahajjud*. It is still dark, but activity on campus begins to pick up and with it the noise level. There is still some time before the dawn prayer. Sleepy voices can be heard mixing with the sound of splashing water from students completing ablutions. The ritual washing of face, arms, and feet, including wetting one's hair, is an essential part of the morning routine before the prayer for which a state of ritual purity is required. Some students join others for the prayer in one of the two large mosques on campus where the female students sit behind the rows of their male peers; others prefer to perform the daily prayers in one of the smaller prayer rooms that can be found in every dormitory complex. While many leave their places of prayer after the completion of the pre-scribed number of prostrations, more than a few remain behind to recite additional devotional prayers.

Prayer remains a prominent element of *pesantren* life throughout the day. Its significance is reflected in the students' schedule that structures all learning units in relation to the five prayer times. The first activity after the dawn prayer is instruction in Qur'anic recitation known as *tajwid*. It forms an important part of the educational life at Sunan Pandanaran since the memorization of the thirtieth and final part of the Qur'an, Juz Amma, is a minimum requirement for all students who want to graduate from the *pesantren*. Recitation classes are followed by regular classroom instruction that extends to the noon prayer, after which lunch is served. With the afternoon prayer start the co-curricular activities such as Arabic and English language clubs; and, finally, advanced instruction in the Qur'an is given between sunset and evening prayers.

The status of prayer reveals the importance attributed to spiritual practices at Sunan Pandanaran. Various devotional exercises such as voluntary fasts and communal devotions infuse *pesantren* life. Prominent among these is the practice of *dhikr*, the remembrance of God. For extended periods of time and in conjunction with specific breathing exercises, the students will chant God's name in an attempt to focus their spiritual awareness solely on the divine presence in the world. In its communal and often more elaborate fashion such exercises are also known as *wirid* and *mujahada*.

At Sunan Pandanaran a *mujahada* with all students as well as with members from the local community is held every Thursday in the mosque. It is usually led by the *pesantren* director who is addressed by the honorific title *kiai*. The charismatic leadership of the *kiai* extends beyond the *pesantren* to the local community in which he commands great respect. In addition to his role as religious expert, he in some cases assumes the functions of a political leader, counselor, or that of a spiritual healer. His authority rests on his erudition in Islam and is often coupled with the conviction that he possesses special spiritual and mystical powers that make him a source of blessing or *barakah*. Inspired by the belief that his *barakah* extends beyond his earthly life, a *kiai*'s death will be commemorated with an annual pilgrimage to his grave site which remains a preferred place for spiritual exercises of both students and the local community throughout the year.

As these spiritual practices indicate, students and staff at Sunan Pandanaran understand that the purpose of education is not just to convey knowledge, be it religious or otherwise. Rather, life and learning in the school are aimed at building a student's character with refined morals in addition to a sharp mind. Spiritual, intellectual, and moral aspects in the school's life thus combine into a holistic educational concept, the goal of which is to lead to piety or *taqwa*, a consciousness of God characterized by obedience or submission to the divine will.

Few, if any, self-identifying Muslims are likely to disagree that this is, generally speaking, what it means to be a Muslim. After all, the Arabic term "Muslim" literally means someone who submits to God's will. It derives from "Islam," Arabic for "submission" or "surrender" with the implied notion of submission to God. Still, just how one accomplishes this submission in one's life is a matter of considerable discussion, and Muslims associated with traditional schools such as Sunan Pandanaran have no monopoly over answers to this question. Some within the Indonesian Muslim community criticize many of these schools' spiritual beliefs and practices, arguing that they contain many heterodox elements influenced by local religious practices or Hindu and Buddhist traditions. Contesting the "Muslimness" of such practices, they advocate instead a return to a pure and orthodox Islam based exclusively on the textual traditions of the Qur'an. Debates over what it means to be a Muslim point to diversity within Islam. Such contested Muslimness is a theme to which we will return throughout the chapter.

The Qur'an

Although sometimes charged with the heterodoxy of their practices, it is imperative not to overlook that the Qur'an plays a central role in the daily life and self-understanding of Muslims in the traditional schools. Particularly prominent is the study of *tajwid* as the science of Qur'an recitation is known. Under the guidance of a teacher, students memorize parts of the Qur'an and practice proper recitation which includes attention to pronunciation, intonation, breathing patterns, and the distinctive sound quality of the Qur'anic text. The focus on the recited text is anything but accidental. In the daily piety of most Muslims worldwide, be they Arabic speaking or not, the Qur'an unfolds its beauty first and foremost as a recited text.

The recited Qur'an

The Qur'an is the foundational sacred text for Muslims, believed to have been revealed to the Prophet Muhammad in seventh-century Arabia. Considered the Word of God, its status for Muslims is aptly compared to that of Jesus as the Word of God for Christians. It is through the Qur'an, its meanings and sounds charged with divine power, that Muslims experience God's activity in the world most immediately. Copies of the Qur'anic text are thus treated with the greatest respect. When one visits the home of a Muslim family, it is quite common to find the Qur'an wrapped in a special cloth or a finely stitched bag and placed high on a shelf, elevated above other books.

It would be difficult to exaggerate the significance and influence the Qur'an has in the life of Muslims individually and socially. The five daily prayers and other devotional practices contain Qur'anic passages, and many private as well as public events, such as the opening of a parliamentary session in some Muslim countries, are marked by readings from the Qur'an. The text also serves as a vehicle for literacy education beyond the level of religious instruction. For many children, Arabic speaking or not, the Arabic script of the Qur'an is the first alphabet they learn. Qur'anic themes, sounds, and rhymes permeate literature and the arts. Arabic calligraphy, the preeminent visual art form, is deeply grounded in Qur'anic calligraphy and features in the architecture throughout the Muslim world. Even expressions of popular culture bear the Qur'an's influence. Perhaps the most famous Egyptian singer of the twentieth century, Umm Kulthum, was celebrated for her vocal artistry which was influenced strongly by the distinctive style of Qur'anic recitation.

It is crucial here to realize that the Qur'an exerts its influence in the daily life and piety of Muslims primarily as spoken or recited text. Although the revelations the Prophet Muhammad received came to be written down and were later collected in the form of a book, it is the aesthetic experience of hearing the Qur'an that has remained fundamental in the encounter with the text. The Arabic word "Qur'an" quite literally means "reading" or "lection," thereby indicating that the Qur'an is the reading or recitation of the eternal, divine word revealed to the Prophet Muhammad. Among Muslims those who have memorized the entire Qur'an and are able to recite it from memory enjoy high status and respect. It will be clear that not everyone can commit the text in its entirety, some 6,000 verses, to memory, but learning even parts of the Qur'an by heart is considered meritorious and praiseworthy, and boys and girls alike start committing to heart passages from the Qur'an often at an early age. It is through memorization that the Divine Word of the Qur'an is taken in most deeply, God's presence inscribed on one's tongue and assimilated in the heart.

The religious significance of Qur'anic recitation is reflected in the popularity many professional reciters enjoy. Particularly prominent among them are Egyptian reciters such as Sheikh Ahmed Amir. Their recitations are broadcast on radio and TV; CDs, and DVDs of their performances are sold throughout the world and on the Internet. Their public recitals attract large audiences, and many beyond Egypt have come to consider the melodious Egyptian style the paradigm of Qur'anic recitation. Although Muslim women and men alike commit the Qur'an to memory, many versed female reciters may perform their art mainly at private gatherings or before other women.

The Indonesian Hajjah Maria Ulfah is among the few female reciters to travel the world and perform at public events. She is widely known beyond Indonesia for her compelling and highly embellished recitational style that has earned her titles at numerous national and international Qur'an recitation competitions. Such competitions, widely popular throughout the Muslim world, reinforce the public character of the recited Qur'an. The popularity of these contests that often are broadcast nationally gives further testimony to just how significant the oral, performative dimension of the Qur'an is in Muslim piety. To be sure, these public recitations and contests are joyous events throughout which one will hear repeated outburst of enthusiasm for the performance. But it is equally common to see many a listener moved to tears by the beauty of the Divine Word, realized most profoundly in the encounter with the recited rather than the written Qur'an.

The written Qur'an

The importance of the Qur'an's oral dimension can also be gleaned from the organization of the written text which is divided into 114 suras or chapters. They are arranged neither topically nor in a strict sense chronologically but according to length. After the first sura, Al-Fatihah (The Opening), which is a short incantation, the suras are organized from longest to shortest in descending order. Additionally, liturgical divisions can be found that divide the text into seven sections or thirty parts of equal length, allowing recitation of the whole to be completed within a week or a lunar month upon which the Islamic calendar is based. Neither of these divisions relates to the meaning of the text or its narrative structure. Instead, they can be seen as sign of the Qur'an's significance as an oral, recited text rather than one that is studied or read in solitude and silence.

The short suras of Juz Amma, the thirtieth and final part of the Qur'an, are the ones learned first by Muslims all around the world when they begin reading, memorizing, and reciting the Qur'an. Their powerful lyricism, often compared to the poetic qualities of the Hindu Upanishads and the Psalms of the Bible, sets forth existential themes that outline the Qur'anic worldview, relating most immediately to a person's life. Sura 112, alternatively known as Al-Tawhid (The Unity) or as Al-Ikhlas (The Sincerity), furnishes a fitting example. It reads as follows:

> In the name of God the Compassionate the Caring
> Say he is God, one
> God forever
> Not begetting, unbegotten
> and having as an equal none.[2]

On the level of doctrine, Sura 112 is a clear affirmation of divine oneness or *tawhid* and the uncompromisingly monotheistic character of Muslim faith. Its alternative title, Al-Ikhlas or The Sincerity, gives expression to

2. Ibid., 136.

the moral dimension implied in the affirmation of God's unity. Humans are exhorted to make this one divine reality their sole focus. Just like any other sura of the Qur'an (except for Sura 9), it is prefaced by the *bismillah*, an appellation that is also often translated as "In the name of God the Compassionate the Merciful." Divine compassion and mercy, however, are balanced by God's justice through which humans are held account-able for their actions in the world on the Day of Judgment. The message of human moral responsibility is particularly prevalent in those passages of Juz Amma that repeatedly denounce social injustices brought on by the accumulation of wealth and disregard for the well-being of the less fortunate such as the poor, the widowed, and orphans.

It must be emphasized here that the theological and ethical dimen-sions in Sura 112 and in the Qur'an in general do not nearly exhaust the interpretive possibilities of this fundamental sacred text for Muslims. The stress on divine oneness in Sura 112 also invites a concentration on spiritual aspects and the internal dimensions of faith. Here the affirma-tion of divine unity is seen as urging the believer to seek spiritual union with the divine, a state in which one realizes that ultimately only God truly exists. While the principle of *tawhid* is central to each reading of Sura 112, the doctrinal, ethical, and spiritual understandings indicate the polyvalent nature of the Qur'anic text that invites interpretative differ-ences. A similar situation presents itself with respect to the ritual obliga-tions enjoined in the Qur'an.

Ritual Practice: Orthopraxy and the Importance of Prayer

Among the acts of worship mentioned in the Qur'an, five have gained particular prominence. First is the profession of faith or *shahadah*, which we encountered above as part of the call to prayer asserting the divine unity and the prophethood of Muhammad: "There is no god but God and Muhammad is the messenger of God." It is spoken during each of the five daily prayers known as *salat*, the second prescribed act of worship. The Qur'an's condemnation of a life dedicated to the acquisi-tion of wealth and the moral directive to care for the poor and margin-alized is reflected in the third practice, the giving of alms or *zakat*. It is seen as an obligatory act of worship through which the divine injunction to take responsibility for the poor and destitute in the community can be fulfilled. Fourth, Muslims are obliged to fast during daylight hours for the entire month of Ramadan, the ninth month in the Islamic calendar. From sunrise to sunset they are to abstain from food, drink, smoking, sex, and, ideally, from all evil or impure thoughts. Lastly, all financially and physically able adult Muslims should undertake the annual pilgrimage or *hajj* to the city of Mecca in today's Saudi Arabia at least once in their lives.

These five acts of worship are commonly referred to as the Five Pillars of Islam. The significance placed on these Five Pillars of Muslim practice has led observers to describe Islam as "orthopraxy," a religious tradition in which outward practice takes center stage over the inner dimensions of faith. Most Muslims are likely to agree that the Five Pillars are a basic requirement for every Muslim, although the level of individual conformity will differ as much as ideas about just how they should be carried out. The example of the proper form and meaning of *salat* demonstrates this diversity.

Prayer occupies a position of prominence in the Qur'an, particularly in Juz Amma where its continual performance is urged with great frequency. Yet little in terms of detailed description is offered. Is *salat* to be performed in community or by oneself? Should the words during prayer be audible or spoken silently? Who can join or should be excluded from participation in the prayer? Still more basic, what is the purpose of prayer and what does it achieve? Looking at the living reality of Muslims, a commonly held position stresses the performance of *salat* as a means to enhance self-discipline and to gain control over worldly passions and desires. Communal prayer is favored as it is seen to reinforce unity and mark the equal status of each individual in the community and before God. Although such an understanding of the obligatory prayers fits well with the notion of orthopraxy, it is imperative to realize that an emphasis on the external or practical aspects of Muslim life does not indicate the absence of spiritual dimensions and the cultivation of inner attitudes and virtues.

Muslims who emphasize the spiritual dimension of prayer describe the prostrations that are part of the prayer ritual as an outward sign of inner humility before God. Not denying the significance of the external aspects, prayer provides above all an opportunity to draw closer to God and to increase one's inner awareness of the all-encompassing presence of the divine. Reflecting the spiritual dimension of prayer, many mosques around the world bear inscriptions that speak of prayer as "the believer's ascension to God." The phrase goes back to a prominent tradition about the Prophet Muhammad, who is believed once during his life to have ascended into heaven and into the presence of God. Through prayer, the individual believer is afforded a similar opportunity of closeness to God.

Muhammad: Messenger of God

Next to the Qur'an as the primary textual foundation, the personal model for Muslim piety is that of the Prophet Muhammad to whom the Qur'an was first revealed. Muhammad was born in the year 570 into the changing socio-political milieu of late sixth-century Mecca. The city had long been the site of an annual pilgrimage during which people from all over Arabia came to worship at its sacred place, the shrine of the Ka'ba, which housed statues, images, and paintings of tribal deities. Mecca's spiritual significance was paralleled by its economic importance. It was strategically located in the center of the Arabian Peninsula's western part along a major trade route running from north to south. With the steady influx of pilgrims and caravans Mecca had become a burgeoning economic center. But the new wealth brought its own challenges as social cleavages and economic disparities within Meccan society intensified.

Orphaned at an early age, Muhammad grew up in the custody of his uncle. His experience as an orphan in a society that strongly relied on family and tribal bonds caused him to be particularly sensitive to the needs of those most vulnerable to the social and economic exploits of the mercantile Meccan elite. In his own dealings with others he exhibited a rectitude of character that earned him the title al-Amin, "the trustworthy"; it was coupled with a strong spiritual-mindedness that led him frequently to seek solitude and contemplation in the hills surrounding Mecca. During one of these retreats when he was about forty years of age, Muhammad received what was the first in a line of divine revelations that would henceforth come to him regularly until his death in 632. The revelations persuaded him that he was called upon as prophet by the one and only God to communicate the divine message to his people.

The message Muhammad brought bore a direct challenge to both the polytheistic ways of the Meccans and the economic interests of their elites. The unyielding monotheism of his message demanded individual moral responsibility in this life and ultimate accountability before God on the Day of Judgment. Muhammad's message championed the rights of the poor and exploited, such as widows and orphans, and demanded that the rich and powerful fulfill their social and moral obligations to ease socioeconomic inequalities. Resistance to Muhammad and his message grew among the Meccans to the point that he and the small group of his followers were forced to leave the city.

In 622, they migrated to Yathrib, an oasis community to the north of Mecca, from where Muhammad had received an invitation to help settle the disputes among the city's tribes. With the migration or *hijrah* to Yathrib, later renamed Medina, the political fortune of the Muslim community changed decisively. Within Muhammad's lifetime, the majority of Arab tribes in Medina became Muslim, and a stream of converts from among the Meccans and other Arab tribes steadily increased the number of followers. When Muhammad died in 632, Mecca, despite its initial hostility, had become integrated into the Muslim community which extended throughout most of the Arabian Peninsula, uniting its people in a religiously bound community that transcended earlier tribal loyalties.

Muhammad as moral authority

Muslims do not worship Muhammad. Worship belongs to God alone. Yet Muhammad's centrality in orienting Muslim life can hardly be overestimated. Notwithstanding his success as political and military leader, to Muslims he is first and foremost known as *rasul Allah*, the Messenger of God. The profession of faith and the call to prayer affirm his status as God's prophet and messenger to humankind. Throughout the centuries Muhammad has been the exemplar of Muslim piety. Muslims consider Muhammad's life, his words and deeds, the ideal to be emulated. In addition to the revealed message of the Qur'an, he is regarded by many Muslims as the "living Qur'an" whose every deed illustrates how God wants Muslims to act in this world.

For the most part, the Qur'an contains general moral principles awaiting concretization and interpretation. It is not surprising then that the early Muslim community turned to the words and deeds of the Prophet Muhammad, his Sunna or tradition, as a second source of guidance. After all, the Qur'an speaks of Muhammad's authoritative status when it says, "He who obeys the Messenger, obeys Allah" (4:80). Accounts about Muhammad's Sunna, his sayings and practices, were transmitted early on in the form of anecdotes or reports, each one of them called a hadith. Tens, even hundreds of thousands of these were known to the early generations of Muslims. First preserved in oral and later in written form, many were subsequently brought together in hadith collections. Some of these collections have achieved canonical status, most famous among them the compilation by al-Bukhari (810-870) and the one by Muslim (817-875).

The scope of these collections is truly comprehensive, touching on practically every aspect of concern to individual and communal life, such as ritual, moral, political, legal, and even medical practices. Still, not everybody can be expected to sift through the voluminous material contained in these collections. Abridgments and compilations of a smaller numbers of hadiths thus are available to illustrate important Islamic

130

beliefs and practices. One such work is the popular *An-Nawawi's Forty Hadith*, a collection of actually forty-two hadiths by Imam Nawawi, a thirteenth-century Syrian scholar.

From the way to hold one's hands during prayer and what food to eat when breaking the fast to settling disputes with neighbors, Muhammad's practice as conveyed in the hadith literature provides the community with a normative example of Muslim life. Indeed, so important is the role of the Sunna that it has become a central element in the self-identification of the largest sectarian group within the Muslim community. About eighty percent of Muslims worldwide identify as Sunni Muslims or "People of the Sunna" and describe themselves as traditionalists because of the normative role the Prophetic tradition plays next to the Qur'an.

Muhammad as beloved intercessor

It would seriously impoverish our understanding of the Prophet Muhammad's role in Muslim life if we relegated his religious significance solely to his relationship with the Qur'an and to the ethical directives gained from his life. As important at these aspects are, Muslims throughout history also have been engaged with the Prophet on a personal, devotional level. The standard hadith collections contain numerous traditions that have inspired love and veneration of the Prophet Muhammad. Popular among these is the saying that anyone who blesses the Prophet will be rewarded ten-fold by God.

Muslim devotion to the Prophet Muhammad is visible in calendrical feasts as well as in works of literature and the arts expressing intense love for the Prophet, who is believed to intercede with God on the believer's behalf. A rich tradition of poetry exists in many Muslim languages from Arabic to Urdu and Persian that praises the Prophet Muhammad, his beauty and kindness. More elaborate compilations of prayers for the Prophet are prominent from North Africa to Southeast Asia. Among the most famous of poems is *Qasida al-Burda* or *Ode of the Mantle*. Written in thirteenth-century Egypt by Iman Busiri, the Burda contains accounts of the Prophet's life from miraculous events surrounding his birth and wondrous later deeds to his intercession with God on behalf of humankind. Its verses adorn mosques throughout the Muslim world, and properly recited, it is believed to have healing powers.

The Burda's most prominent place in Muslim piety is during the Mawlid celebrations in observance of the Prophet's birthday, which most countries with a Muslim majority population consider a public holiday. Processions in the streets and special events in mosques and public places give this holiday a particularly celebratory, near carnival-like character. Stories about the Prophet's life are told along with recitations of poetry and prayers which may be accompanied by simple percussion. In some places, such as the city of Srinaga in northern India, the display of relics believed to be from the Prophet is part of the Mawlid celebration as well.

A further artistic creation that is especially prominent in Turkey and other parts of the Near East is the portrayal of the Prophet in the form of a calligraphic icon known as *hilya*. The calligraphic portrayal of the Prophet's appearance is most often based on an account given by Ali, his cousin and son-in-law. It describes the beauty of his physical form as well as his generosity and kindness along with Muhammad's exalted position in the universe. Through calligraphy, the dominant mode of religious art in Muslim cultures, the *hilya* provides a legible representation of the Prophet without having to portray him visually. Highly embellished copies of these calligraphic icons adorn mosques and homes where they are used by many Muslims for devotional purposes and to pray for the Prophet's blessings and grace.

Modes of Piety: Legal-Moral and Spiritual-Mystical Orientations

Many of the aforementioned traditions are influenced by local custom and as a result show a great variety from one place to the other. Although these practices often date back more than a thousand years, their Muslimness has come under explicit criticism by modern reformist groups which reject as idolatry the concept of an intercessor with God, even Muhammad, and focus instead on the Prophet's role as ethical model and legal authority.

Historically one must note that the two perspectives hardly have been mutually exclusive. They are, however, indicative of two distinctive modes of Muslim piety, one that emphasizes a legal-moral orientation and another in which spiritual-mystical aspects are accentuated.

Legal-moral orientation

Muhammad's role as moral authority directs our attention to the significance of religious ethics and law in Muslim piety. The centrality of religious practice to which we referred above as "orthopraxy" is reflected in the remarkable intellectual accomplishments of Muslim ethical, moral, and legal thought. Rather than the abstract metaphysical speculation of theology, the science of Islamic law has occupied a prominent place in Muslim intellectual history

The sacred law stipulating God's will that is to be followed by humans is known as *Sharia*. It literally means "path to (life-giving) water," thereby implying that those who abide by its regulations are traveling on a path to life in this world and the world to come. The Sharia has become a normative element in the self-understanding of many Muslims. Marshall Hodgson, an eminent scholar of Islam, has described this dimension of Muslim piety that stresses behavioral aspects as "Shari'ah-mindedness."[3] It is characterized by an understanding of Islamic law as the central expression of Muslim piety and by a practitioner's attempt to make her or his all actions conform to the behavioral norms prescribed by Islamic law.

Over the first centuries of the Muslim community, scholars developed the methodology of Islamic law by defining the sources, principles, and rules to derive moral and legal rulings. Next to the Qur'an and the Prophet's Sunna, these included the use of independent reasoning by learned scholars and their consensus of opinion, the authority of customary practices, as well as considerations for the social welfare of the community. Through the application of these principles to cases not explicitly addressed in either the Qur'an or the Hadith literature, scholars spelled out concrete regulations for every area of life which were codified in legal manuals and books of law. Despite the comprehensive scope of these works, the legal methodology has given Islamic law a degree of flexibility and openness to address new ethical and legal challenges brought on by changing historical and social circumstances of Muslim life.

The modern period has witnessed an intensifying debate among Muslims over the proper role and status of Islamic law, particularly in majority Muslim societies. Political groups such as the Muslim Brotherhood of Egypt call for the establishment of an Islamic state on the basis of Islamic law. As powerful and attractive as such political claims to the exclusivity of Islamic law may be, they have little precedent in Muslim history but are rather a phenomenon of the modern period. As such they are indicative of a trend to view Muslimness solely in terms of Islamic law. Not only does such an exclusively legal orientation distort the historical experience of the Muslim community, but it also obscures the existence of another, spiritual mode of piety central to the self-understanding of many Muslims.

3. Marshall Hodgson, *The Venture of Islam: Conscience and History in a World Civilization*, 3 vols. (Chicago: University of Chicago Press, 1974), vol. 1, 351.

Spiritual-mystical orientation

Next to the legal-moral dimension that stresses behavioral aspects of Muslim piety has developed another mode of being Muslim, which is popularly associated with Islamic mysticism or Sufism. Rather than regulating one's outward actions and behavior in the world, the mystics seek to cultivate inner, mental, emotional, and spiritual dispositions in an effort to achieve direct, unmediated experience of the divine. Often quite rigorous spiritual exercises, including prayer, fasting, and bodily discipline, are undertaken through which detachment from the material world is sought. Leaving behind the concerns of the world and its passions is often understood as a precondition for experiencing the presence of the divine in one's life.

Mystical practices are varied but share as their ultimate goal a union with the divine, the realization that ultimately only God exists. The Five Pillars of worship—supplemented with devotional exercises such as prayers, fasts, visits to the tombs of Sufi masters, and poetry—became a central medium to communicate the mystic's intense spiritual longings and experiences. Perhaps most famous is the Persian poet Jalal al-Din Rumi (1207-73), whose words describing the soul's loving longing for God are read by Muslims and non-Muslims around the world today.

Music and dance are central to many Sufi practices. In South Asia, devotional music known as *qawwali* is a popular way to generate ecstatic experiences for artist and listener alike. A *qawwali* performance at a shrine or holy place can carry on for many hours; indeed, it is common for an individual song to last for more than twenty minutes, starting slowly and building up in energy, tempo, and passion as it progresses. Especially through the late Pakistani singer Nusrat Fateh Ali Khan (1948-1997), *qawwali* has achieved some popularity beyond South Asia in Europe and America.

Among the most distinctive mystical practices, however, is the *dhikr* or remembrance of God. In its basic form it entails the rhythmic repetition of God's name, sometimes in conjunction with the words "*la ilaha illa Allah*," "There is no god but God." For extended periods of time and accompanied by specific breathing exercises, the devotees will chant God's name in an attempt to focus their spiritual awareness solely on the divine presence in the world. Although it is a basic practice, various Sufi orders have different ways of performing *dhikr*. For instance, the Naqshabandi order practices a silent *dhikr*, while the Rifa'i order is known for its loud performance which has earned its followers the somewhat disparaging title "howling dervishes." Still different, the "whirling dervishes" of the Turkish Mevlevi order seek to experience God's nearness in their *dhikr* through intoxicating dance.

The existence of discrete mystical orders is an organizational characteristic of Sufism. Common to all is the spiritual authority of the master or *shaykh*, many of whom trace back their spiritual lineage directly to the Prophet Muhammad. Particularly, the founders of mystical orders are venerated as saints and their *barakah* or blessing and intercession before God are invoked beyond their death. The tombs of Sufi saints are therefore central institutions in the spiritual life of many communities. Pilgrimages, devotional gatherings, and celebrations occur throughout the year and are particularly festive on a saint's anniversary.

Pilgrimages to the shrines of saints and the idea of their spiritual mediation are by no means the monopoly of Muslims who identify with Sufism. The practices and beliefs of the various Shi'i groups—constituting the second-largest sect of Muslims next to the Sunni majority—include many such features as well. Central to the Shi'i worldview is the belief in the charismatic leadership of the imams, who are thought to be endowed with divinely inspired wisdom to guide the community. Although Shi'i Muslims consider Muhammad the final prophet, his spiritual powers and authority were passed on through the line of imams starting with the Prophet's cousin Ali and continuing with his sons Hasan and Husayn to subsequent imams.

The belief in the imams as saintly intermediaries has engendered a colorful tapestry of Shi'i spirituality. Their birthdays and the anniversaries of their deaths are commemorated with elaborate celebrations, many of which exhibit a mournful quality. Sacrifice and atonement are common motifs since many of the imams suffered persecution, oppression, and violent death. Particularly the martyrdom of Imam Husayn is remembered during the month of Muharram with celebrations culminating on the Day of Ashura. Pilgrimages and devotional visits to the tombs of the imams in the shrine cities of Iran and Iraq are popular throughout the year and in some cases eclipse the *hajj* to Mecca in popularity. Beyond the annual pilgrimages, plays of mourning and lamentation, poems, and recitations of stories about the imams provide entertainment and at the same time sustain popular Shi'i piety on a daily basis.

The Relationship between the two modes of piety

Questions about the proper relationship between the two orientations described above have occupied Muslims throughout history. More recently, however, Sharia-minded reformist movements vehemently have challenged the Muslimness of many practices and beliefs associated with the spirituality of Sufi and Shi'i Muslims. The Wahhabi destruction of the shrines of Shi'i imams and Sufi saints in Saudi Arabia in the early twentieth century furnishes a telling example in this regard.

Accusations such as the Wahhabi reproaches of Sufism, however, are a relatively recent phenomenon. Throughout much of history mystical practices and beliefs have been standard expressions of Muslim piety alongside legal-moral interpretations. Indonesia's *pesantren* tradition, as exemplified in our case study of Sunan Pandanaran, is a good example for a piety that combines the study of classical religious texts with mystical and devotional practices. It would thus be mistaken to draw too bold a line between these two modes of piety or to suggest that they are mutually exclusive. Most Muslims throughout history have seen no inherent contradiction between the two orientations but rather conceived of them as two complementary and balancing orientations of Muslim life.

Diversity and Contentious Issues: The Public Role of Religion

The debates concerning the proper relationship between Islamic law and mysticism indicate the interpretative diversity of belief and practice that characterize the Muslim community and show that, despite a strong sense of unity among Muslims worldwide, there exist divergent ways of being Muslim today. These differences are reflected in many of the contemporary debates among Muslims concerning issues such as the proper relationship between religion and politics, support for democracy and pluralism, the status of women, as well as science and education.

Muslim resurgence and the Islamic state

Many Muslim countries have seen a growing Muslim self-assertiveness over the past decades. Commonly described as "Muslim resurgence," Muslim organizations have assumed key roles in the public life of many contemporary Muslim societies, and religious issues have increasingly influenced the public debate. This has intensified debate over religion's role in the public life of Muslim societies and raised aspirations among some for the transformation of society along religious lines.

A newly emerging ideal in this debate is that of the Islamic state in which politics and law are tied exclusively to religion. "The Qur'an is our constitution!" is the call of Muslim political groups such as the Egyptian Muslim Brotherhood seeking to establish what they consider the pure and original Islam of the early Muslim community in the seventh century. Although the model of the early Islamic society to which these groups aspire serves as a powerful symbol to mobilize support, Muslim history offers sparse precedent for organizing individual and social life solely in relation to Islam. Consequently, the current political realities of states that purport to be Islamic differ rather drastically.

Saudi Arabia and Iran, two of the most visible examples of states in which Islamic symbols ground political discourse, espouse quite different political structures. The world's foremost exporter of petroleum, Saudi Arabia is a tribal monarchy that claims the Qur'an as its constitution. A central government has been developed over the past decades, but authoritarian monarchic rule generally has recognized neither political parties nor national elections, and in instances of local elections, women usually have been excluded from the right to vote. Iran's political structure, on the other hand, combines clerical rule with a modern constitutional system. The Iranian Revolution of 1979 has been followed by parliamentary and presidential elections with universal suffrage, and the rights of women as well as those of non-Muslim minorities are spelled out in the constitution.

Not only are the actual political systems to which Islamic symbols give rise marked by a great diversity but also the strategies with which Muslim political movements seek to transform societies towards their religious ideals vary significantly. Some seek a strengthening of Islam through education programs aimed at a deeper profession of faith while others carry out attempts to capture and change the political system itself. Even in this latter group, however, the approaches range from seizing the state through violent means to working through Muslim parties within the established political system.

Social activism and democracy

Despite the media attention that political movements advocating the establishment of an Islamic state receive, their popular appeal is limited. Looking at election results in Muslim countries such as Kuwait, Egypt, Sudan, Tunisia, Malaysia, and Indonesia, one can see that Muslim political parties running on a platform that includes the goal of an Islamic state or the implementation of Islamic law have rarely done well. Where they received a substantial share of the vote, as was the case with the Indonesian Prosperous Justice Party (PKS), which gained about 7.5 percent of the national vote in the 2004 elections, electoral success was achieved by pushing to the background the demand for an Islamic state and instead running on an anti-corruption platform with a promise to provide social services that the current government has failed to deliver.

The provision of services in the fields of health care, education, and economic assistance by a growing number of Muslim voluntary organizations around the world draws attention to the fact that the promotion of Islam on the political level is neither the only nor the most popular way to assert a public role for religion. Over the past decades Egypt, like other Muslim societies, has seen a proliferation of voluntary organizations offering social services from schools and professional training centers to medical and childcare facilities. Numerous microfinance institutions support community development projects through small business loans to individuals, many of whom are women. Among the latter, the Grameen Bank, started in Bangladesh, received international attention when it was awarded the 2006 Nobel Peace Price for its work among the rural poor.

Different from the more rigid formalism of some political movements, central strands of this social activism are democratic, pluralist, and deeply suspicious of the idea of an Islamic state. Still, many Muslim activists are committed to a holistic understanding of religion and reject the notion of a purely privatized faith. Instead of insisting on fixed Islamic legal structures in the form of an Islamic state, however, they demand that the tradition's general ethical principles such as equality and justice provide the basis for public morality.

It is important to realize that Muslim activists often draw on resources within Islamic tradition and history to contend that Islam has an inherently democratic character which makes it not only compatible with but in fact necessitates the affirmation of individual freedom and equality. Although voices of intolerance and unreason continue to be heard as in any religious tradition, Muslim social activists exert a pervasive influence in all spheres of society where they uncover and scale up the rich resources of their texts and traditions to promote issues such as democracy, human rights, freedom of religion, and gender equality.

Gender and women's dress

It is worthwhile to remember that most of the fundamental concepts associated with modern life such as democracy, women's rights, or human rights more generally, are not mentioned explicitly in the pre-modern sacred sources of the world's religious traditions. They are rather late developments in human history that have been accommodated quite recently, and often only after tumultuous resistance, in many religious traditions. Few, if any, religious symbols are self-evident or can mean only one thing. As seen above, Islamic symbols can accommodate political systems as diverse as tribal monarchies and modern democracies. Similar diversity is reflected in some of the ambivalences concerning women's roles and rights in Muslim societies today.

In many Muslim countries such as Saudi Arabia and Iran, women constitute the majority of university graduates, yet their participation in other areas of public life is restricted. Muslim women have been heads of state in countries such as Indonesia, Pakistan, Turkey, and Bangladesh. Yet in other instances, Muslim women may be required to ask permission to travel from a male relative, are legally obliged to wear Islamic dress in public places, and suffer from unequal rights of inheritance and divorce.

It would be shortsighted to attribute all of this to the influence of religion alone. Indeed, many Muslims point out that the Qur'anic revelation and the Prophetic Sunna contain rights for women that substantially improved their status compared to pre-Islamic Arabia in such matters as marriage and divorce rights as well as economic and legal capacity. In many parts of the Muslim world, however, the dominance of patriarchal customs and male-dominated cultural interpretations have scaled back reforms and rights introduced in early Muslim history.

The question of Muslim dress for women is particularly sensitive and controversial. The Qur'anic text enjoins modesty for Muslim men and women alike but contains only vague injunctions concerning dress. Veiling became customary about a century after the Prophet's life, possibly influenced by Persian practices. Moreover, the practice of veiling seems to have been an upper-class phenomenon among urban women and was adopted more slowly in rural areas. Cultural customs as well as issues of education and economic class continue to influence the ways in which Muslim women dress today. The various styles of women's clothing from a simple headscarf or *hijab* that one finds next to European fashion in the streets of Cairo to the Iranian *chador*, which is worn like a cloak covering the women from head to feet, make it impossible to speak of a single Islamic style of dress.

While some Muslims and non-Muslims alike criticize the custom of veiling as oppressive, others point out that a growing number of young and educated Muslim women have adopted traditional garb over the past decades voluntarily and as a sign of protest, liberation, or cultural self-determination. In other instances the adoption of Islamic dress has enhanced women's access to education. This in turn has afforded them opportunities to reevaluate critically the sources of their tradition and to challenge androcentric interpretations. Instead of abandoning their tradition, these examples indicate that many Muslim women struggle from within an Islamic framework to overcome patriarchy and advance gender equality.

Modernization and Muslim education

Over the past centuries, many Muslim educational systems worldwide have been characterized by a secularizing trend, often caused by the implementation of Western-style schools during the period of European colonialism, roughly from the seventeenth to the twentieth centuries. Some Muslim educators have reacted with a defensive withdrawal into a religio-educational subculture by focusing entirely on traditional subjects of Muslim learning. In other cases, however, the responses have been more varied. Changes were introduced into Islamic schools that saw many of them gradually adopt new educational models in addition to the classical religious system of learning. Some implemented new teaching methods and a graded class system but retained the religious nature of instruction. Others took up the teaching of secular subjects in addition to religious curriculum content.

The Muslim resurgence of the past decades has also led to a renewed interest in Islamic education. Many countries have seen the creation of religious colleges and universities such as the International Islamic University in Kuala Lumpur, Malaysia, established in 1983. Similar energy is visible on the level of primary and secondary education. Turkey's Imam Hatip schools, which operate as middle and high schools, have proliferated in the recent past. The establishment of Muslim religious schools also accompanies the presence of a significant Muslim population in many European countries. Increasingly these Muslim schools become integrated into the national systems of education, often through the incorporation of formal schools with government-accredited curricula. Our initial case study, Sunan Pandanaran, is representative of these developments. Since 1986 it has featured a formal middle and high school in which students study subjects such as mathematics, biology, literature, English, and computer science alongside subjects of a religious nature. Upon graduating they will be eligible to pursue studies in many of Indonesia's private and state institutions of higher learning.

The goal of a school such as Sunan Pandanaran is to take seriously the expansion of all fields of knowledge and to educate young Muslims for the intellectual, social, economic, and technological demands of the modern world while retaining at the same time a religious framework to guide the educational process. That many Muslim schools accommodate modern social and epistemological changes in their teaching routines does not mean that these schools and their curricula are identical to western schools, but they are also not completely different. The challenges of finding appropriate ways to incorporate the teaching of religion into the curriculum of modern schools are debated around the world and point to the shared dilemmas and overlapping concerns of finding a religious path in today's world.

Conclusion

Muslims, like all human beings, are subject to multiple and often disparate influences that shape their actions and beliefs in the world. Only at the cost of de-humanizing people could one assume they are entirely determined by their religious identity and thus exclude from consideration factors such as politics, history, geography, language, culture or ethnicity. More than 1.5 billion Muslims live in more than forty countries with a majority Muslim population and as sizeable minorities in countries around the world. In this diversity there is no single perspective that all Muslims recognize as the true Muslim view on any given issue. Rather, there are only multiple expressions of Muslim identity, each articulated in its specific context and time.

It would be impractical, maybe even impossible, to identify a set of core practices and beliefs that could function as a template against which to establish the Muslimness of contending interpretations. It is more enabling instead to describe religious beliefs and practices as an expression of Muslim identity if and when practitioners relate them to Islamic texts and traditions such as the Qur'an and the Sunna of the Prophet. The multivalent nature of these sources, however, and the different or even contradictory ways to understand them ensure that the unity and universality of Muslim faith is balanced by a diversity of interpretations.

Sugestions for Further Reading

Arberry, Arthur John. *The Koran Interpreted*. New York: George Allen & Unwin, 1955.

Ernst, Carl. *Following Muhammad: Rethinking Islam in the Contemporary World*. Chapel Hill: University of North Carolina Press, 2003.

Esack, Farid. *On Being a Muslim: Finding a Religious Path in the World Today*. London: Oneworld, 1999.

Geertz, Clifford. *Islam Observed: Religious Development in Morocco and Indonesia*. Chicago: University of Chicago Press, 1968.

———. *The Religion of Java*. Chicago: Collier-MacMillan, 1960.

Hefner, Robert W. *Civil Islam: Muslims and Democratization in Indonesia*. Princeton: Princeton University Press, 2000.

Hodgson, Marshall. *The Venture of Islam: Conscience and History in a World Civilization*. 3 vols. Chicago: University of Chicago Press, 1974.

Knight, Michael Muhammad. *The Taqwacores*. Brooklyn: Autonomedia, 2004.

Kurzman, Charles, ed. *Liberal Islam: A Sourcebook*. Oxford: Oxford University Press, 1998.

———. "Bin Laden and Other Thoroughly Modern Muslims." *Contexts* 1, no. 4 (Winter 2002): 13-20.

Lawrence, Bruce. *The Qur'an: A Biography*. New York: Atlantic Monthly Press, 2007.

Mernissi, Fatima. *The Veil and the Male Elite*. Reading, Mass.: Addison-Wesley, 1991.

Rahman, Fazlur. *Islam*. Chicago: University of Chicago Press, 1979.

Sells, Michael. *Approaching the Qur'an: The Early Revelations*. Ashland: White Cloud Press, 1999.

Wadud, Amina. *Qur'an and Woman: Reading the Sacred Text from a Woman's Perspective*. Oxford: Oxford University Press, 1999.

Woodward, Mark R. *Islam in Java: Normative Piety and Mysticism in the Sultanate of Yogyakarta*. Tucson: University of Arizona Press, 1989.

7

Latter-day Saints

Douglas J. Davies

Many people are familiar with the scene of two young people in smart clothes involved in work for their church. Whether visiting homes or speaking to people in public places, these missionaries of the Church of Jesus Christ of Latter-day Saints (LDS) are engaged in a two-year period of their lives supported by their own families. It is an important time of their life when, probably, they have left home for the first time, have undergone a period of basic training, and set out to seek to spread the message of what they call the Restoration of the Gospel to the world. For many this involves learning a new language and for all makes great demands upon personal discipline in rising early to pray and study the scriptures and then work in close partnership with another missionary. Most of the time people will not accept their message, but occasionally, someone will, and then the missionary has the joy of baptizing that person by total immersion and then laying hands on that person's head so that they can receive the gift of the Holy Spirit. And those things are all done in the local Mormon church where those visiting missionaries attend on Sundays and some other days along with the local LDS congregation. When they complete their mission period they return home and often either go to university or marry and start a family. Mormon families are very proud of their sons and daughters when they accept a "call" from the church leaders to "serve a mission" and the church itself benefits a great deal from the experience and maturity gained from those periods.

This brief account of the missionary period of these young people provides a window into the world of Mormonism and highlights the place of youth that echoes the boyhood of Joseph Smith, the founder and first prophet of Mormonism. The image of the missionaries also marks the importance of spreading the message of the restored Gospel to the world, and their early life as returned missionaries highlights the importance of the family within this religious movement. If we followed a missionary in the months or early years after returning home we would find ourselves looking through another window into the Mormon world, that of the Mormon temple. For on completing a mission and finding a marriage partner it is very likely, and regarded as most desirable, that these young men have a temple marriage. Unlike the local Mormon churches or chapels that are open to everyone, the temples are accessible only to Latter-day Saints in good standing within their community. As we will see, the marriages held in them are believed not only to be for this life—"til death do us part"—but for all eternity. In the temple, too, these young people are likely to conduct ceremonies on behalf of their dead relatives. So it is that missionary work for living people and, in a sense, work that helps the salvation of the dead are brought together in the life-experience of members of the Church of Jesus Christ of Latter-day Saints.

Temples

For those looking at the LDS account of the world and human destiny, the temples can be thought of as a kind of middle point that links the past, the present, and the future because in them there take place special rituals that link the past, present, and eternal future. The "past" is, however, a complex idea in Mormonism because of the belief that all people have, in one sense, always existed. From all eternity there have been what early Mormon leaders called "intelligences." Mormons then tell how the one who is now identified as God the Heavenly Father and who is the father of Jesus Christ was in some way more mature and insightful than the intelligences he saw around himself and set about helping them to develop their potential. Indeed, "potential" is a crucial aspect of LDS philosophy and belief about people. So it was that the Heavenly Father took these intelligences and made them his Spirit Children. Sometimes the process is described as "begetting." This was all achieved long before the earth came into the form in which we know it, in a phase of "pre-existence" before the time of human beings. These Spirit Children of God the Father inhabited a kind of heavenly domain. Mormon thought then gives an account of what is called the Plan of Salvation. It starts from the assumption that many such spirit children existed in a fairly heavily populated heavenly domain. Then, just as God the Father had looked around him and seen many intelligences in need of development, so he and these Spirit Children looked around and saw a material world in need of development. So it was that they decided to develop these relatively formless places into habitable domains. This desire to develop the potential of things brings us to the earth and to the divine desire to fashion it into a world full of opportunity. So it is that Mormons speak of organizing the earth and not creating it, just as Spirit Children were begotten from intelligences and not created anew. We will return to this plan later; for the moment it is only important to know that in the "pre-existence" many decisions were made about what would happen to the earth. From those eternal "past-times" we move to the earth and its religious history, for it was here that the Spirit Children of God moved into a new stage of their development as they were given physical bodies. In Mormon terms that differ from many other religious and philosophical understandings, the spirit comes to the body and it becomes a living "soul." These human beings now have opportunity to develop their potential much further. In particular they have the opportunity to be obedient to the laws and principles of existence of their Heavenly Father. But this earthly life is only part of the total scene of existence, for after death and after a future resurrection there exist new worlds of eternal opportunity. And it is the temple that provides the means for using earth-opportunity to prepare for eternal-opportunity. The basic means of doing this lies in special forms of ritual that will be described below, especially baptism for the dead which relates to the historical past of earthly life, and the Endowment rituals that focus on the eternal future. But first, we move from these abstract aspects of the Plan of Salvation to the historical time when the Mormon Church first came into being

Founding a Church

The Church of Jesus Christ of Latter-day Saints was founded in America with six members in 1830. It is better known to non-members as the Mormon Church, athough its leadership would prefer to have people call it the Church of Jesus Christ. In the early twenty-first century it has some twelve million members spread across the world. Its growth from small beginnings has been matched by important changes in emphasis on belief and practice over the years, but these would not be well-known to ordinary members today.

So, let us begin by imagining a dedicated Mormon family in contemporary England. It might well have two or three children and parents whose main concern lies on their home and life together. They have often heard the story of how their teenage founder, Joseph Smith, was confused by the differing claims for truth made by many Christian churches in his part of New York state during a time of religious revival. Young Joseph decided to pray secretly to God to ask which one to join. Some years later Joseph looked back and told how, as he knelt in the woods, he was overcome by a terrible sense of fear and felt that he was going to be destroyed by some great force of evil. As he prayed for one last time he sensed a pillar of light descending upon him, dispelling the dark evil, and revealing two figures. One pointed to the other as his beloved son, telling Joseph to "listen to him." As time passed, Joseph received other visions as a result of which he told that he had been directed to find some hidden metal plates that turned out to be an account of the life and times of ancient American peoples written in strange characters. He was able to translate these through special spectacle-like objects and finally publish them as the Book of Mormon in 1830.

Other visions instructed Joseph to found a church. At first it was called The Church of Christ and later The Church of Jesus Christ of Latter-day Saints. He was also given authority to organise it through two priest-hoods, one called the Aaronic and the other the Melchizedek. These apply to males in the church. Boys begin in the Aaronic Priesthood when they are twelve years old and pass through the grades of deacon, teacher and priest. When they are about nineteen, they can become Melchizedek priests. All this information is contained in special texts called The Doc-trine and Covenants and The Pearl of Great Price, and many Mormons would own a set of these bound together with The Book of Mormon. Along with the Bible, usually in the King James Version, these are called the Standard Works of the Church, are important for teaching and understanding the faith, and will probably be used as part of a Latter-day Saint's personal prayer as well as in public teaching.

The main church meeting occurs on a three-hour block of events on Sunday morning when Mormons the world over gather for the sacra-ment meeting, when they eat bread and drink water and ask their Heav-enly Father that they may always follow his Son Jesus Christ and have the Holy Spirit to be with them. They also hear talks, sing hymns and pray, and once a month also have time when people can give their testi-mony and tell what their faith and membership in this church means to them. One night of the week is set aside for the Family Home Evening, which is a kind of religious meeting in each home and which stresses the importance of the home for Latter-day Saints.

It is this centrality of the home that helps make sense of another whole aspect of Mormon Church life, not that focused on the local chapel which is a gathering place for the local Mormon community, but of the temple. Temples are very special and relatively rare—there are only two in Great Britain. They exist for reasons that bring together very dis-tinctive Mormon doctrines and practices whose goal is to create eternal families in which people experience a fullness of salvation, called exaltation, not available to others. Joseph Smith believed that these teachings and rituals were very ancient in origin, even going back to the days of Adam, but had been taken from the earth by God shortly after the time of Jesus because of human disobedience. The priesthoods, too, had also been removed from the earth by God. The fact that these priesthoods, the truths they taught, and the rites they had the authority to administer were returned to earth in the 1820s-1840s was the prime reason for describing Mormonism as "the Restoration."

The key elements of this restoration, then, begin with the priesthoods and the authority they have to conduct the special temple rites. We can best see these as a pattern of family ritual aiming at the ultimate salvation of the family itself. From today's perspective it affects a dedicated Mormon family, as a young couple is married in a temple. They can only attend the temple for this rite if they are Mormons in good standing and hold a special recommendation certificate. This reflects the fact that they support the teachings and leaders of the church, pay a tithe on their surplus income, and live a morally worthy life. In their temple union they kneel at each side of a prayer-altar and clasp hands while a high priest of the Melchizedek order seals them together for time and all eternity. For this is not a marriage only until death. Temple marriage transcends death.

But marriage is not the only rite that makes that eternal existence possible. As dedicated Mormons the couple also need to receive their "endowments" in a ritual that involves being washed and anointed with oil, wearing special temple clothes, learning distinctive teachings, and making certain vows in covenant with God. The result is that they are given power to conquer death and enter into the highest of the three major afterlife worlds, that of the Celestial Kingdom. Two other domains, the Terrestrial and Telestial Kingdoms are for other people who are given rewards according to their deeds but are not of the highest order. These different "degrees of glory" are based on Paul's First Letter to the Corinthians in the Bible where his Chapter 15 distinguishes between the glory of the sun, moon, and stars. It was an image that meant a great deal to early Mormons and underlies much Latter-day Saint symbolism.

In that future celestial glory the family will continue to grow under the authority of the father who is in the process of becoming a godlike person himself along with his wife as his goddess. They will also experience the presence of God the Heavenly Father. In order that their eternal family should grow, it is the duty of families while on earth to discover their family tree and be baptized, married, and ordained for their deceased relatives in a special ceremony of baptism for the dead that also occurs in the temple. The circular baptismal font is large enough for several people to stand in it, and it itself stands on the backs of twelve life-sized oxen whose heads point outwards. This remarkable ritual object is a replica of the structure described in the Bible as part of Solomon's Temple built in Jerusalem in which the priests should wash (2 Chronicles 4: 2-6). Other interpretations associated with these oxen are that they symbolize the twelve tribes of Israel. Through the baptisms occurring in these modern baptisteries the ancestors now have the opportunity to accept the baptism done on their behalf or indeed to reject them if they so wish. This is an important part of the LDS belief in individual "agency," the right of each person to decide for themselves. And as with baptism so with the other rites of Mormonism: any rite that can be performed for a living person can also be carried out, vicariously, for the dead. This way of thinking allowed Mormons to answer what can be the difficult theological question of the ultimate destiny of those who lived on earth before the Christian message emerged or who simply did not encounter it during their lives.

Mormons believe that once somebody dies, their spirit separates from their body and goes to a special place of spirits. If one's ancestors had never heard the message of the Church, they could not gain the benefit of it and could not move from that spirit-world on into a more heavenly sort of existence. But if living family members are baptized on their behalf, then the ancestor could in the afterlife accept the teachings of Mormonism and gain salvation from their sin. This means that at some time in the future, when the resurrection of the dead takes place and spirits be rejoined with a new body to be judged by God, they will be in the right position to gain the reward for all the good things they had done during their life on earth. Then, the church believed, they would be given a place in one of those three heavens. This meant that everyone got what they deserved, with the reward of a particular "degree of glory," as it was sometimes called. It also reinforced the bonds of family membership.

This family aspect of Mormonism is reflected in the way Jesus is sometimes described not only as our "Elder Brother" but also as "Father" of this earth, a title linked to that of Jehovah described below. One aspect of this emphasis on family life is the fact that for much of the nineteenth century Mormons accepted and some practised what the LDS call celestial or spiritual marriage, and which others call polygamy. Its essential significance lay in the idea of the eternal family with a male at its head whose status or degree of glory could be enhanced by the size of his overall family. This practice, irrespective of its religious significance, brought Mormons into sharp conflict with American federal authorities with the result that in 1890 the president of the church, Wilford

Woodruff, made an official declaration calling the Saints to obey the law of the land and not practise polygamy. A small number of breakaway groups did not obey and have been excommunicated; they are often called Mormon "fundamentalists." Other groups from early Mormonism also exist. The largest, now called the Community of Christ, based at Independence, Missouri, never adopted polygamy or temple ritual and is largely orthodox in theology. For years it was led by Joseph Smith's descendents.

There is one aspect of the overall Mormon view of their church that helps explain the significance of polygamy for some early Mormons and which also explains a teaching that may come as a surprise to Mormon converts from other Christian denominations. It is that Jesus is also identified as Jehovah, the divine figure of the Old Testament of the Christian Bible. Underlying many Christian traditions is the fundamental doctrine of the Holy Trinity. This understands God to consist of three persons, the Father, Son, and Holy Spirit. Many then associate the Old Testament and the religion of ancient Judaism with the Father, who is also identified as Jehovah. They then speak of the life and work of Jesus in the first century, and finally refer to the Holy Spirit as the major influence in the emergence and ongoing history of the Christian Church. On this scheme, Mormons are unusual in describing the period of the Old Testament and the ancient history of the Jews as a time under the major influence of Jesus, whom they name as Jehovah. This teaching is important because Mormons encounter it in the temple ceremonies, which offer a dramatic expression of what the church calls the Plan of Salvation. This describes a scene in heaven when divine figures talk about fashioning the earth into a place for humanity and then, with considerable foresight, consider what to do when human beings become disobedient to God. Jesus has his plan on how to atone for people's sin accepted, and Lucifer has his plan rejected. It is here that Jesus begins to take responsibility for the earth and its future. Both the practice of polygamy and the doctrine of Jesus as Jehovah reflect an early Mormon idea, one that was important for most of the nineteenth century, that Mormons saw themselves as God's specially chosen people. This view has several dimensions to it. It starts in the belief in Joseph as a prophet of God and of all his successors as being "prophets, seers, and revelators" for the Church. Such prophets stand in line with the prophets of the Old Testament and give the Saints a sense of continuity. This is reinforced by the epic story that forms the narrative of the Book of Mormon, which has several key prophetic figures in it who come to America in a series of waves of migrants from the Holy Land starting about six hundred years before the time of Jesus. They give rise to great civilizations that continue the story of people being obedient and disobedient to God, who continues to address them through prophets. Even Jesus came to America after his resurrection to address these people and made twelve new disciples there. Nevertheless, these people, especially the Nephites and Lamanites, end in a final battle to the death which is recorded and then hidden away by a person called Mormon. It is that record to which Joseph Smith believed he had been directed by God. It became his Book of Mormon. In other words, ancient America had Jewish origins. Joseph Smith was inspired by this, and his early message was properly prophetic in calling people to obedience and, in a very Christian way, to come to join him in America to prepare for the Second Coming of Christ.

Many thousands did so, including many from Britain and Scandinavia who experienced much hardship in their journey to America. One of the great shocks they received, in 1844, was Smith being killed by a lynch mob while he was being held in jail over a dispute about a printing press and a newspaper that opposed some of his views. Nevertheless, they migrated on to present-day Utah and began to settle the land. They also began to build temples, because it was believed that Jesus would need somewhere to stay at his second coming, when the world would be changed for the good. Ultimately there would be a final battle with Satan, who would be defeated and cast out for ever. (This Adventist and millenarian position was widely shared by other Christian groups that believed Christ would come again on the clouds of heaven and inaugurate a thousand year reign along with his specially chosen saints.) After that period there would be a final battle between good and evil, when Satan and his wicked hosts would be finally defeated by God. Mormons acted on these beliefs in such large numbers that they produced a culture and community of their own. They identified this new world of theirs with the world of ancient Israel, for now they possessed their own promised land, prophets, scriptures, priesthoods, and temples: they were their own kind of Zion. Though Jesus did not come again as expected, the Saints were able to develop a sense of identity as Zion through their temples and priesthoods and with a developing idea of Jesus as Jehovah.

In the middle of the twentieth century there began a program of evangelism and world expansion. Instead of a heavenly kingdom coming on the clouds of heaven, such a kingdom could grow throughout the earth by means of church-growth. Though polygamy had been given up for the earthly survival of the church, a renewed emphasis on the family developed as described above.

Behind all this human organization lies that most influential Mormon way of thinking about human destiny already introduced earlier as the

Plan of Salvation. It is now time to tell more of this plan as the most basic Mormon account of salvation, especially of the way in which it saw how humanity, once coming into existence, would disobey the rules of God and be in need of salvation. Lucifer, one of the heavenly inhabitants, offered a plan to do this, but God the Father rejected it in favour of what Jesus would do. While Lucifer's option involved an element of force that would abuse human "agency," Jesus saw a way of salvation that would involve his own self-suffering. The Father's preference for this led to Lucifer's rebellion, and he is cast from heaven and becomes Satan, whose future lies in tempting human beings into disobedience.

All this is dramatically enacted or presented in the temple rites of endowment so that today's believers come, in a sense, to play a part in the original Plan of Salvation as their covenant to be obedient. Having made these covenant promises with God, men and women are given a special item of clothing called a temple garment. Quite apart from the special clothing worn only in the temple, this garment is worn all the time in everyday life and reminds them of the promises they made and of the good lives they should lead. These are personal garments and not to be shown to non-members. When worthy and temple-active Latter-day Saints die they are prepared for their funeral in the special temple ritual clothing, and their grave is specially dedicated to hold and preserve them until the resurrection. The sacredness of the temple clothing and belief in the resurrection had led the LDS Church in the twentieth century to favour burial over cremation whenever possible.

Gethsemane and the Plan

While the Plan of Salvation plays an important part in the religious education that accompanies the temple ritual of endowment, there is one other descriptive account, another theological story, that also plays an important part in Mormon life. In fact, it complements and spells out the Plan in a deeply moving fashion. It describes Jesus in the Garden of Gethsemane and tells how he encountered evil and experienced within his own person the wickedness of all time. So great was his involvement with this load of sin that he sweated what seemed to be great drops of blood. Latter-day Saints have often spoken of this as "the Gethsemane experience" and seen in it the outworking of part of the Plan of Salvation. For it is here that Jesus makes atonement for sin and does so at great cost to himself and without forcing or abusing the free agency of human beings.

The LDS emphasis does not ignore what also happened to Jesus on the cross, but they stress the Garden experience much more than any other Christian denomination. The result of that pained suffering is that all people are guaranteed a resurrection of their own. This is where divine grace becomes apparent: by grace all will be resurrected without regard for their own level of goodness or wickedness. After resurrection comes judgement, and this is where a person's own life-work comes into focus, for it is as a result of each person's obedience and moral achievement that they will be granted a place in one of the three great afterlife kingdoms.

In the middle and later twentieth century Mormons came increasingly to think of Jesus less as the Jehovah figure of the Old Testament and of themselves as a special kind of "Israel" and more of Jesus as Jesus Christ, the Saviour. In this sense, they resembled much Protestant religion with its emphasis on Jesus as the central figure of religious concern. This meant that from the middle and later twentieth century, Mormonism was more easily seen as a Christian movement than as a group overshadowed by Jewish-like interests. At the same time, the Book of Mormon came to be thought of much more as "another testament of Jesus Christ." Still, just as the missionary program grew in strength, so too did the number of temples, with one appearing in many major nations across the world. Some Saints starting talking about the possibility of Mormonism becoming a world religion of its own.

In practice the church can be seen as a combination of the ideas that have influenced it up to the present. It is, in part, a special people like the people of Israel, but it is also a restored church with a complex hierarchy and organization that resembles a global corporation. The one point at which these images come to sharp focus is in each Mormon family. Though Mormons do not see it like this in any explicit way, there is a sense in which the family and its eternal destiny replaced both the idea of Mormons as a kind of Israel and the belief in the second coming of Christ. And this family is serviced and enhanced in two ways, first by the local church organization, arranged as a ward with its own church leadership and, second by the temple, which prepares it to conquer death and obtain celestial glory. This is why the church leadership, which begins with the Prophet-President and his two counsellors, followed by Twelve Apostles and then by groups of Seventies, encourages family life and participation in temple activities. For it is through those temple rites that Mormonism brings to the world what it believes to be the distinctive truths of human and divine life.

It is against that background of becoming gods in eternal families and in being worthy of such a destiny that church leaders press the importance of obedience to church teaching and ritual or ordinances. Repentance and faith, baptism and receipt of the Holy Ghost—Mormons mostly say Ghost, not Spirit—and then temple marriage, genealogy and work for the dead, along with receiving endowments and any other higher ordinances—all underlie eternal glory. Respect for the church leadership also accompanies this concern for doctrine and is reflected in respect in the Church for the seniority of people, especially the prophet, the Twelve and the Seventies, many of whom live in America but who sometimes pay visits to other parts of the world and always appear at the large church conferences that are televised. Deep respect also extends to local leaders, making respect part of the atmosphere of the Church.

Mormons are very practical people and would see such respect as one aspect of the importance of authority that underlies the belief in this church as the true church. What is more, its doctrines of obedience are given shape through other rules and customs of life, the best known of which is called the Word of Wisdom. This originally instructed members not to drink alcohol or hot drinks and not to eat too much meat but has now come to include ideas of not drinking tea and coffee or drinks containing stimulants. This instruction developed in its application throughout the twentieth century and serves as an identity marker of Mormons, especially if living amongst non-church members. A similar strong code of ethics has developed with a strong emphasis on sexual control and trust between marriage partners. This extends, in some places, to an understanding of the kinds of clothes that both young men and women should wear and the kind of music they should listen to, on the basis that some of these behaviours encourage indiscipline and detract from the high code expected by family and church. This comes to a very practical focus when people wish to go to the temple for any of the reasons mentioned above. They must first have an interview with their local bishop who has to assure himself that they are living a "worthy" life, in all these ways. Only then will they be able to receive their temple recommendation, and this is important for those who wish to live as active participants in Mormon community life.

Within the congregational life of Mormonism one of the most important ideas is that of a "call." In many wider Christian denominations it became customary to speak of a "calling" or through a Latin derivation of a "vocation," as something that applied to ordination as a priest. To have and follow a vocation was to live life not in any random or accidental way but in a way directed and approved by God. The Reformation in the sixteenth century opposed the idea of vocation as applying, for example, to monks, nuns, or only to priests, preferring to speak of what was called the priesthood of all believers, which made every Christian's life into a "calling." In LDS thinking we find a kind of combination of these ideas in the sense that all worthy males over the age of twelve may be ordained into the two priesthoods recognized by the Mormon Church, the Aaron and Melchizedek priesthoods. More than this, even, all members of the Church, women as well as men, may be given a special "call" to carry out a particular job or to hold an office in the church. This applies to the great majority of leadership positions from the senior hierarchy down to the local congregation. The way this works is interesting, especially when, for example, a person may be given a calling for a senior position which is held for, say, three years, and is then released from that calling and given another one in what might be viewed as a much less desirable or high-profile task. Except at the very top layers of the Church hierarchy, where posts are held for life, this relative movement of people from junior to senior to junior posts fosters the ideal of doing well whatever it is one is called to do. It also fosters the spirit of collaboration that is vital in a movement that is led at local levels by people who are not professional religious leaders. As the church grows, with many millions of members across the world, this ideal of "calling" and "release" from calling is increasingly important in maintaining an efficient and dedicated organization. One aspect of such organization involves a degree of discipline, and this is something that is also carried out at the local level as church leaders meet with individuals whose lives may be problematic in terms of the high moral ideals and degree of activity within the church.

Complementing this disciplinary side of official Mormon life—and many Latter-day Saints would see such discipline as a very positive and not a negative feature—is the personal and more intimate realm of religious experience and emotion. This is apparent in some Mormon church services, especially in the testimony meetings when individuals may show signs of being touched by their feelings of gratitude to God and the church. Some Saints also tell of feelings at the temple when undergoing vicarious rites for the dead, times when they feel close to their departed relatives and speak of the veil between the departed and the living as being thin. And there is an even more personal context in which Latter-day Saints have a sense of the closeness of God in what is called the patriarchal blessing. This can be given by a person's father, for every father is a patriarch to his family, something that echoes Mormon-ism's earlier sense of itself as a kind of Israel. But it can also be obtained from an official church officer, actually named as a patriarch, and there is one in each local area. Such a patriarch lays hands on a person's head in a private context and gives a blessing to the individual in words that are believed to be under the direct influence of the Holy Spirit. These are recorded by a secretary with copies for the individual and for church records. Many Saints seek such a blessing at key moments in their lives, perhaps when going to college or on a mission, or when ill.

For most Mormons it is this combination of family, local congregation, and temple involvement that gives a sense of identity amongst a people with a distinctive history and sense of mission in the world. A major issue for Mormons, however, is that this identity always has to be played out in relation to ancient Israel and to other Christian churches. The Mormon story started with young Joseph Smith's confusion over which church was the true church. Much of its subsequent doctrine was worked out in disagreements over parts of the doctrine of already-existing churches and always with the key question of who had the best authority over religious issues. In practical terms, this means that many Mormons see something of their own position and perhaps their major competitor in the Roman Catholic church with its world-wide organization. Yet one of the areas of Mormonism's growth in the twenty-first century lies in parts of South America and parallels the success there of many Protestant evangelical groups, often at the expense of the Catholic church. However people might evaluate the Church of Jesus Christ of Latter-day Saints, it offers a magnificent example of the birth and growth of a religious movement whose history is better known than practically any other.

Suggestions for Further Reading

Bushman, Richard. *Joseph Smith: Rough Stone Rolling*. New York: Random House, 2007.

Davies, Douglas J. *Introduction to Mormonism*. Cambridge: Cambridge University Press, 2003.

———. *The Mormon Culture of Salvation: Force, Grace and Glory*. Aldershot: Ashgate, 2000.

8

Koreans' "New" Religious Concerns

Woo Hairan

Thirteen people sit in a circle around a room paying attention to a middle aged woman who is gently smiling and wearing a white dress of traditional Korean style. She is in charge of this four-week workshop and founder of a small organization called Hanvit Dowon as well.

She asks the participants to introduce themselves. All but two of them say that they are new to the group, having been informed of this workshop via Chŏngsin Segye-won, the first Korean New Age company, which has hosted various workshops and lectures since the beginning of the 1990s. The female master begins to tell a long history of her mental and physical disorder, which had brought her extreme pain and become more severe after her unhappy marriage, so that she was often tempted to commit suicide. But, she continues, *ki*-training (cognate with Chinese *chi*, life/cosmic force) changed her life totally. According to her, *ki*-training not only cured her chronic sickness and awakened her supernatural healing ability but also allowed her a series of mystical experience such as being unified with cosmic energy and realizing "the principle of the universe."

The first session focuses on "removing harmful spirits from the body." The mistress claims that everyone, without exception, is occupied by multiple spirits, among which harmful beings cause various mental and physical disorders. That is why true *ki*-training can only start after the participants' bodies are cleaned from these polluted spirits or energies. Some participants are rather hesitant about this kind of unfamiliar process. On the other hand, a group of people appeal to the mistress for priority treatment.

After several mats are spread on the floor and a small plastic bag is placed beside each mat, the mistress asks the first group to lie on their

Figure 8.1: *Participants in a* Qigong *Training for Spiritual Purification workshop. (Photo courtesy of* Hanvit Dowon.*)*

faces over the mats. The first person she will treat is a thin middle-aged man. She works up his body, stepping quite heavily on several spots from his legs to shoulders. After that, she asks him to turn over and lie on his back. She stands on him again and starts to step on his body. The man under her feet starts to groan with pain. No wonder, the mistress is a relatively heavy woman, and the spots she is treading on are quite sensitive. When, as the last step, her right big toe presses down the spot just beneath his throat, his face turns red, and he starts coughing from pain and the difficulty of breathing. The mistress gets down from him and asks him to spit what he gets in his mouth into the plastic bag which is laid besides him. He hawks up phlegm and looks relieved at last. The mistress tells him his general *ki*-condition as well as the disease he is supposed to have. Furthermore, she explains that what he spat out was impure *ki* or energy which she had released from his body.

After the mistress is finished with her treatment and diagnosis of the rest of the group, she looks exhausted. She confesses that this kind of treatment is quite an energy-consuming job. The reaction of those who went through the treatment vary. For some the treatment is quite painful, for others it is not so bad. Not everybody hawks phlegm. Some just spit saliva. Some feel much better instantly after the treatment is complete, while others feel no difference. The participants are asked to sit down in circle once again, and the mistress assures them of the positive effects of her treatment. All of sudden the mistress speaks to a female participant and reveals that her sickness is caused by the spirit of her aborted baby, which is possessing her body. She advises her to get out of the negative experience. The woman starts to sob, covering her face with both hands. The dramatic first session is closed with participants' deep bowing to each other.

The following three sessions are held once a week, each for three hours. These sessions focus on activating and experiencing *ki*. Every session begins and ends with certain exercises, like pounding on limbs and the lower abdomen, and trembling the whole body. This exercise is done under the guidance of a male assistant of the mistress and is said to relax the muscles and optimize the flow of *ki* in the body.

At first, the participants learn about the *ki*-channel which runs through the body as well as important spots which are located along the channel where *ki*-energy is gathered to a high degree. They are encouraged to sense those *ki*-spots, taking up various postures. To speed up this process, the mistress deals blows at particular parts of participants' bodies. Indeed her powerful hits enable some participants to feel high energy from those *ki*-spots. The participants also learn a breathing art called "hypogastric breathing" by concentrating on the lower abdomen. This breathing-method is said to be very effective in awakening and activating *ki*-energy in the body.

The last part of the *ki*-training contains "opening the *ki* spot on the crown of the head." This step is explained as essential for receiving and becoming one with cosmic energy in the end. The mistress requests the participants to attempt a sort of soul flight. This entails letting the soul free from the body and letting it fly as high and far as possible, while visualizing it as connected to the head with a long thin thread. After the "soul trip," the participants are asked to tell the group what they saw and how they felt while in the air. Some describe their wonderful journeys in the sky.

As the next step, the mistress asks the participants to sit in lotus position and instructs them to visualize golden shining heavenly energy pouring down through the *ki*-spot in the middle of their skulls into the *ki*-channel inside of the body, stretching to the lower abdomen. Some participants are successful in detecting such a powerful energy-flow in their body, and some fail at it, especially those who have not received any *ki*-training before. In addition, the participants get the chance to become acquainted with diverse practices, as such sitting in meditation, "*ki*-dance" (letting the body move to the natural flow of *ki*), dynamic dance (dancing freely to music), and others.

159

At the last session, she stresses that the participants should keep on exercising what they have learned from the workshop in order to attain real progress in physical and spiritual senses. She invites anyone among them who has a chronic disease to consult her individually at her organization. Even though a few participants show interest in getting together after the last session, this does not work due to the tight schedules of the majority. Eventually, people take their leave at the front of the building and scatter in all directions.

What Is "New Religion"?

The above description is of a workshop named "*Qigong* Training for Spiritual Purification" in which I took part in November 2005. The workshop illustrates many aspects which are identified as typical of "new religions" these days. These religions do not promote any community of believers, nor do they necessarily seek committed followers but rather paying clients (the fee of the above workshop was around $500). Furthermore, such religions stress "healing" in spiritual as well as physical senses and they are syncretic—in the case above, traditional *ki*-training and shamanist views of disease as possession of harmful spirits are combined.

Some readers may still wonder why the workshop above is introduced under the rubric "new religions," thinking that it is just about a workshop but not about a "religion" or religious group. Likewise, some may be disappointed to discover that large but notorious Korean new religions like the Unification Church (Moonies) are not treated in detail in this chapter. If so, then we have a good starting place for reflection on received concepts of "religion" and specifically, how the "newness" of religions can be appreciated. For a more flexible and practical approach to "religion" it is necessary not to lose sight of the diversity of contemporary religious culture as well as of the religious concerns of contemporary people.

The phrase "new religion" is, together with "new religious movement," generally used to designate religious phenomena that are seemingly not compatible with mainstream established religions. Here, traditional religions serve as criteria by which a certain religious group or movement is perceived as "new," sometimes an another expression of "exotic" or "deviant." For this reason, the term "new religion" is often criticized as a residual category, as the term is attached to a religious phenomenon that doesn't fit neatly in the generally accepted picture of "religion" in a given society, which itself is based on mainstream religions. Therefore, it is important not to overlook the fact that even though scholars of religion tend to make use of the term "new religion" as a value-neutral technical term, the word is entangled with religious hegemonic judgments.

   This is more evident in popular practices of naming religious groups. The word "cult" is preferred by opponents of non-mainstream religions as well as mass media in North America and carries pejorative connotations. "Cult" is mostly associated with those so-called negative, substantial "marks" of new religions: mental and material exploitation, indoctrination ("brain-washing"), authoritarian leadership, total commitment of followers, etc. As a consequence, the adjective "destructive" is often added to the word "cult." The same policy has been employed in South Korea. While the term *sin-jongyo*, "new religion," is used exclusively within academic circles, it has become a popular practice to call new religions *yusa-jongkyo* or *saibi-jonggyo*, which means "pseudo-" or "quasi-religion." Certainly, the Korean mass media have contributed to anchoring those words into popular discourse by primarily reporting or revealing scandals related to new religions. Under these circumstances all marginal (small, nascent, and foreign) religious groups are easily stamped as antisocial, deceptive and above all, not truly "religious."

   On the other hand, scholars of religion tend to employ a value-free definition of "new religion." Usually, they distinguish new religions from other religious collectivities based on some characteristics new religions supposedly share with each other. For instance, a strained relation between new religions and socio-cultural surroundings is often presented as a distinguishing mark of these religious groups. In the sociology of religion the way in which religious groups interact with a given society has served as an important criterion for classifying religious organizations. This started with the church-sect typology which originated in the work of Max Weber. The typology deals with changes religious organizations undergo. Here a "church" is conceptualized as having adapted itself to and sustaining a given social system, whereas a "sect" protests and criticizes wider society and therefore has the potential to steer social change.

   New religions were not part of this typology until Ernst Troeltsch, a theologian and church historian, presented three types of religious orientation as implicit in Christian teachings: church, sect, and mysticism.[1] Troeltsch predicted that a radical religious individualism based on the third type, "ideal mysticism" or "spiritual religion," would be of increasing importance in modern societies.[2]

   From these classical typologies of religious association, which took European Christian history as their background, evolved further typolo-

---

   1.   William H. Swatos Jr., "Church, Sect and Cult: Bringing Mysticism Back In," *Sociological Analysis* 42 (1981): 17-26.
   2.   Ernst Troelsch, *The Social Teachings of the Christian Churches*, trans. O. Wyon (New York: Harper & Row, 1960), 381.

gies where other types of religious collectivities are integrated, especially to be adaptable to the American situation. Richard Niebuhr added to the church-sect typology the concept of "denomination," which conforms to the society (like "church") but lacks the intention to dominate the society[3] The specific concept of "cult" was adopted into the church-sect framework, spurred by the appearance of a number of new religious movements in North America in the late 1960s and early 1970s. In Stark and Bainbridge's church-sect-cult typology, the distinction between "sect" and "cult" is drawn in terms of the condition of their origins: "sects" originate through schism, whereas "cults" "draw their inspiration from other than the primary religion of culture."[4] On the other hand, Meredith McGuire constructed the typology of church-denomination-sect-cult under the double criteria: the relationship between religious groups and the larger society, and the degree to which the religious group conceives itself to be uniquely legitimate. In this typology the "cult' or "cultic stance" stands for those groups which consider their legitimation to be non-exclusive. In other words, they pursue coexistence with other religious groups but at the same time stand in tension with the larger society, even though their dissent is less extreme because of their pluralistic viewpoint.[5]

Drawing a typology of religious collectivities is often criticized because the sheer diversity of religious collectivities does not allow them to be classified into a simple scheme. Even though a typology deals with "ideal types—pure abstract concepts which are derived from a few characteristics and elements of the given phenomenon and do not necessarily correspond to the real world—it is worthwhile to discuss whether those typological frameworks are grounded on value-free premises. Most of typologies mentioned above classify "new religions" primarily in terms of its uneasy relation to the larger society, corresponding with popular discourse about "cults." In other words, they are likely to strengthen a static and negative understanding of new religions running counter to the original aim of constructing typologies, which is to understand the dynamic or the change religious collectivities undergo in relationship to the larger society. Another problem concerns the univeral validity of these typologies. Given that the typologies initially refer to Western societies, we can ask whether they can be applied to religious collectivities in

3. H. Richard Niebuhr, *The Social Sources of Denominationalism* (New York: Meridian, 1929), 25.

4. Charles Y. Glock and Rodney Stark, *Religion and Society in Tension* (Chicago: Rand McNally, 1975), 245.

5. Meredith B. McGuire, *Religion: the Social Context* (Belmont, Calif.: Wadsworth: 2001), 154-58.

a society, as in the case of Korea, where one single religion never had as dominant a position as Christianity did in the West.

The difficulty of applying these typologies for non-Western religious culture is exemplified by the *ki*-training workshop introduced at the beginning of this chapter. According to the above mentioned typologies, the workshop could be classified as "cult" but with many problems. Korean *ki*-training groups are not in any visible tension with the larger society in general. This results from many factors: (1) they do not claim they are "religion," a deliberate strategy not only to avoid confrontation with established religions but also to ensure a broad spectrum of clients independent of their confessions; but (2) at the same time they claim that the worldview and practices that they offer stem from a traditional Korean culture of self-cultivation; and (3) *ki*-training is not a marginal phenomenon in South Korea any more but rather is absorbed in popular culture. Notwithstanding a recent attempt to classify "unchurched" or non-institutionalized religions (which are observed across the world), into subtypes like "audience religion," "client religion," and "creedless religious group,"[6] the problem still remains that a typology cannot be simply expanded *ad hoc* to meet every real religious situation.

There are also attempts to draw a line between "new" and "traditional" religions in terms of their starting date. Western scholars often identify "new religions" as having emerged principally since the Second World War and having come into prominence in the late 1960s and early 1970s.[7] But this periodization is irrelevant to those religious movements which arose outside of Western societies. In Korea, the first new religion, *Tonghak* (Eastern Learning), emerged in 1860 and soon established itself as a religious as well as political power in the country . It was followed by other influential new religions (e.g. *Taejong-gyo, Chŭngsan-gyo, Wonbulkyo*) at the outset of the twentieth century. In case of Japan, the first group of new religions (*Kurozumikyo, Konkokyo,* and *Tenrikyo*) appeared during the first half of the nineteenth century. Given the continued existence of all these religions today, they are now by no means "new." Indeed, some of them are well established (in Japan especially) even as forms of mainstream religion. Because the developmental history of Japanese and Korean new religions covers a long period, Korean and Japanese scholars of new religion tend to divide the period into several parts based on

6. Rodney Stark, Eva Hamberg, and Allan S. Miller, "Exploring Spirituality and Unchurched Relgions in America, Sweden, and Japan," *Journal of Contemporary Religion* 20 (2005): 10-12.

7. Swatos, "Church, Sect and Cult," 17; Elisabeth Arweck, "New Religious Movements" in *Religions in the Modern World*, ed. Linda Woodhead et al. (London: Routledge, 2002), 265.

the drastic social changes during the time which have also impacted on new religions.

A common periodization which is used to describe the historical development of Korean new religions is as follows:

- The period of the nation's opening (1860–1910),
- Under Japanese colonial rule (1911–1945),
- After the nation's independence (1946–1960),
- Under rapid industrialization (1961–1980) and
- Post-industrial period (1981–present).

The first period (1860–1910), which starts with the appearance of the first new religion, *Tonghak*, was a transition to modern society as the traditional social or class system of the Yi dynasty (1392–1910) slowly collapsed, and Neo-Confucianism, the ideological basis of the dynasty, increasingly lost its hegemonic power. This process was accelerated not only by the intrusion of foreign imperialist powers into the country but also by the introduction of Catholicism. This totally heterogeneous religious system caused a sort of cultural shock at that time. During this period *Tonghak* (founded 1860), *Chŏngsan-gyo* (founded 1901) and *Taejong-gyo* (founded 1909) emerged, subsequently serving as fertile soil from which a number of Korean new religions arose. These religions reinterpreted the Korean religious heritage (Confucianism, Buddhism, Taoism and folk beliefs) and developed coherent religious doctrines from various religious elements. At the same time, they showed a strong nationalist or anti-imperialist tendency. *Tonghak* followers led a rebellion in 1864 called the Tonghak Peasant Revolt, which initially targeted corrupt and exploitative officials but soon spread under anti-feudal and anti-imperialist slogans. Another new religion, *Taejong-gyo* (where *Tangun*, the mystical progenitor of the Korean people and nation, is the central figure of veneration), played an important role in the nationalist movement. Many of its adherents fought against the Japanese colonial regime in the following period. New religions during this period had a shared worldview, anticipating the advent of a new world to follow from the present era of social turmoil. This is expressed in the term *huch'ŏn-gaebyŏk*, "the beginning of the second world."

During the second period (1911–1945), when Japan had annexed the Korean peninsula as a colony, new religions that had already sprouted in the last decades began to split into many different groups, and a number of additional new religions appeared. *Tonghak* was reorganized into *Ch'ŏndo-gyo* after the revolution ended in failure, establishing itself as the largest new religion. It focused on campaigns for enlightenment until 1930 when the Japanese colonial government ordered the dissolution of *yusa-jongyo* (quasi-religion), as new religions were labeled. The Japanese government acknowledged only Buddhism, Confucianism, Christianity, and State Shinto as "religion," banning other religious groups that were suspected of being subversive of Japanese colonial power. Additionally, the Japanese colonial government carried out the separation of religion and state, and so the modern concept of "religion" was introduced into the country.

This changed policy drastically weakened the socio-cultural influence of Buddhism and Confucianism, which were traditionally closely related with ruling powers, but at the same time spurred a group of Buddhist and Confucian elites to reform the old structure of their religions. An attempt to reform traditional Buddhism was also undertaken outside of established Buddhism by *Wonbul-gyo* or Won-Buddhism (founded 1916), a new religion. The latter claimed to have reformed Buddhist teachings into more a modern, reasonable, and practicable form that better fit into contemporary advanced material civilization, independent of another declaration that it had combined the core essences of all religions into its teaching.

The end of colonial rule in 1945 and the following occupation of Korea below the 38th parallel by the the American Army in the Pacific again changed the Korean religious landscape to a great degree. The American occupation force issued a decree of religious freedom, freeing religious organizations from state control and encouraging free competition between them. On the other hand, under the United States occupation a pro-American, and anti-Communist standpoint developed as the dominant ideology in the country, and religious groups that supported that ideology obtained influence in society. Accordingly, Catholic and Protestant churches, which were openly hostile to Communism, gained both numbers and influence. In these circumstances, a group of new religions like Unification Church (founded 1954), the Olive Tree Church (founded 1954), and the Mount Yongmun Retreat (founded 1955) emerged and prospered. These reinterpreted Christian teaching by integrating Eastern ideas and autochthonous beliefs, while stressing a leading role for Korean people in the history of salvation. Conversely, old new religions such as *Ch' ŏndo-gyo* and *Taejong-gyo* which maintained traditional values and nationalist ideas and above all favored re-unification, became marginalized.[8]

In the 1960s the South Korean government proceeded with all-out economic development, and in the 1970s industrialization and urbanization were speeded up. The result was that the traditional social network based

8. Ro Kil-myung, "New Religions and Social Change in Modern Korean History," *The Review of Korean Studies* 5 (2002): 31-62.

on local and kinship ties was largely dissolved, and groups alienated from the process of industrialization increased in number. During the period a group of new religions came into being which put Christian eschatology (teaching about the end of this world) in the foreground but combined it with mystical elements of traditional Korean religions. Additionally, reform movement within old indigenous new religions formed new religions like *Chŭngsan-do* (founded 1972) and *Taesun Jinri-hwoe* (founded 1978), which as splinter groups of *Chŭngsan-gyo* later consolidated as an influential Korean new religion. The rapid growth of these religions is due to the reevaluation of traditional Korean culture in the 1970s and 1980s as a part of a protest movement against the rigorous modernization policy of the dictatorial regime of that time. It is noteworthy that college campuses were hotbeds of both the pro-democracy movement and of these religions, which were critical toward modern materialized society and offered alternative worldviews that have an affinity with traditional Korean religious culture. The new religions that appeared during the period have in common that they are urban-centered and lay particular weight on individual salvation.

Since the 1980s the tendency to seek "salvation" at the individual level has been strengthened. This tendency relates to material abundance as well as to the advanced fragmentation of society brought about by the "successful" industrialization or modernization of South Korea. Consequently, old new religions which propagate collective salvation—together with a concern for the good of the community as a whole—have declined. At the same time a totally new type of religious group surfaced. These differentiate themselves from the existing new religions by their non-hierarchical, loose organizational structure and the fact that they gather paying clients instead of committed believers. The appearance of these groups reflects the changed religious interests of modern people, who are particularly concerned with the present, seeking inner peace and well-being in daily life, and simultaneously pursing the maximization of their physical and mental capability to cope with the rapidly changing world around them. Accordingly, these new religious groups offer techniques that promise to produce a perfect harmony between body and mind, while activating previously latent human abilities. Certainly, the spread of this kind of self-centered and this-worldly religious activity outside of established religions is not confined to South Korean society but is a global phenomenon, observed especially in post-capitalist societies and generally named "New Age" or "new spirituality."

The first group which made individual "self-cultivation" popular is *Dahn-hak Sŏnwon* or *Dahn-hak* Meditation Center (founded 1986), which has had a huge impact on later *ki*-training groups, many of them directly modelled on its teaching and practices. The so-called *"ki*-syndrome" in the 1990s made it possible for diverse *ki*-training methods, including Chinese *qi-gong*, to be introduced in the market: *"ki*-training" became highly commercialised and developed into a lucrative business sector. As a result, certain *ki*-training groups expanded rapidly following the conglomerate format, as *Dahn-hak Sŏnwon* and *Suseonjae* (founded 1998) show.[9]

All indigenous *ki*-training groups rest on the so-called "traditional" Korean way of Taoist self-cultivation. In Korea Taoism has been never institutionalized, but rather it has been assimilated with folk beliefs. During the later part of the Yi dynasty, an attempt was made to systematize the philosophy and practices of a Taoist tradition named *Nae-Dahnhak* which aims to activate *dahn* (life-force in perfection) by focusing on self-training, including diet, breath and meditation, in order to be in tune with cosmic energy. Even though the tradition was not institutionalized and its teaching was not transmitted officially, all Korean *ki*-training groups insist that they originated in this Taoist tradition.

The popular Korean word *dosa* reflects the pervasiveness of a religious ideal of reaching the state of perfection on one's own. The term originally designated Taoist hermits or ascetics, especially those who gained supernatural powers through harsh self-training in seclusion in the mountains. There are still numbers of so-called *dosa* in every famous mountain in South Korea. Therefore, it is not surprising that many of the existing *ki*-training groups in South Korea were established by those who have a *dosa* career behind them. This means that contemporary self-centered or subjective religiosity is not totally "new" in Korean religious tradition. However, current *ki*-training is differentiated from its traditional form by having been made accessible to the general public via relatively well-structured groups which offer, for a fee, the necessary techniques.

Since the 1990s not only traditional arts of self-training but also diverse self-development programs have been offered. The latter usually combine the latest trends in Western psychotherapy with traditional meditation. Some of them demand quite a high price for their courses, which supposedly enable speedy "enlightenment" or total transformation of the self. A good example is the Avatar courses which were introduced to South Korea (the first Asia country to receive them) in 1993. The Avatar program is a product of Star's Edge Inc., which franchises the brand worldwide, supervising courses, fixing prices and licensing Avatar-teachers. A Korean counterpart is *Maum Suryon* or Maum Medi-

9. Woo Hai-Ran, "New Age in South Korea," *Journal of Alternative Spiritualities and New Age Studies* 4 (2008), forthcoming.

tation (founded 1996) which has grown rapidly, managing ninety-three meditation centres worldwide.[10]

A New Approach toward "New Religions"

In South Korea "new religions" in narrow sense, that is those with charismatic or authoritarian leadership, fixed doctrine and a community of committed believers, have been in a marginal position. This is despite the socio-cultural impact that a few older new religions as *Tonghak* (later *Ch'ondo-gyo*) once had. According to the census of the National Statistical Office in 2005 even the biggest new religion, *Wonbul-gyo* (Won-Buddhism), has only approximately 130,000 members (0.3 percent of 4.7 million South Koreans). Even when the members of well-known new religions, *Wonbul-gyo, Ch'ondo-gyo, Taejong-gyo, Chŏngsan-do,* and *Taesun Jinri-hwoe* are added up, they still amount to less than 1 percent of the general population. The number of Korean believers of the Unification Church (estimated to be around 35,000) is indefinable in official statistics because followers of the religion identify themselves as Protestants. In comparison with the weak presence of new religions, the statistics show that the power of traditional religions is quite firm and relatively stable. Among the people who answered that they are affiliated with a certain "religion" (53.1 percent of the general population), Buddhists represent 43 percent, Protestants 34.5 percent, and Catholics 20.6 percent.

However, what is not visible in the statistics is the increasing number of people who engage in various self-cultivation and self-development programs. Because the statistic narrows down "religion" to "institutionalized religion," such people are excised from the "religious population." There is unfortunately no statistical survey on them but there are rough estimates of over two million who are participating in *ki*-training and around five million who are registered in diverse meditation programs, including Buddhist ones.

Regardless of whether the above numbers are reliable, this signals that the general interest in seeking religious or spiritual experience outside of established religions is broadening. It must be also taken into consideration that many of the people affiliated to an established religion are also involved in various self-training and meditation arts, and do not necessarily feel conflict between their religious confession and any extra self-training they take up. This is based both on the long history of religious pluralism in Korea and on the claim of self-training groups that they are not "religions." Even though Korean Catholic and Protestant churches

10. Ibid.

condemn these groups as anti-Christian, they are not able to prevent their members from taking part in such alternative self-training which operates in the private domain exclusively.

I participated in three different workshops, including conducting questionnaire surveys, from 2005 to 2006: "*Qigong* Training for Spiritual Purification," "Speaking to your Body," and "First Step to NLP" (Neuro-Linguistic Programming). The first workshop—which was introduced at the beginning of this chapter—was organized by *Chŏngsin Segyewon*, a well known New Age company (founded 1984), and the other two by the *Minaisa Club* (founded 1997), which specializes in New Science.

The questionnaires which were collected from the worshop participants confirm the changing view toward "religion" or "religious concern." To the question "Do you think you can transform your life into a higher level without help of established religions?" the absolute majority of the participants answered "yes." Taking into consideration that a large number of them answered "yes" to the question "Are you affiliated to a established religion?" we can see that the authority of established religions is weakening, to a certain extent, while active pursuit of self-transformation is positively evaluated. In this context it is not difficult to guess that most of the participants who belong to particular religions answered "no" to the question "Does your religious belonging cause you any tension with the workshop in which you are now taking part?" To the question, "What is the ultimate concern for you?" most respondents chose "the ultimate meaning of life" and "peace of mind," followed by "enlightenment," and then "realization of the self," "mental and physical health," "mental training" and "development of potentialities," while only one person chose "material wealth." These answers show their ultimate concerns are nothing but "religious," even though they have a stronger tendency towards active involvement in self-development.

However, the increasing distance from established religions in the matter of self-development is not limited to those people who are actively engaged in self-training programs. According to an another questionnaire survey that I conducted in June 2006 among 135 students in their twenties, the majority answered "yes" to the same question, "Do you think you can transform yourself ... without help of established religions?" even though the rate is lower than among the workshop participants surveyed above. The result is quite interesting, since more than half of the students are Protestarian studying in a university with a Presbyterian foundation.

It is also significant that the workshop participants, independent of their religious belonging or non-belonging, most frequently chose Buddhism from among established religions as the most favorable religion, followed by Catholicism. The higher sympathy for Buddhism and Catholicism than Protestantism is to be explained by two facts: they also entail traditions of self-training like meditation or contemplation, and they have less rigid organizational structures than Protestant churches. These last have developed into quite hierarchical organizations in South Korea, especially when combined with Confucian patriarchal ideology.

To the question "Do you believe in reincarnation?" the absolute majority of the participants answered "yes." This result suggests that "reincarnation" or "rebirth," originally a Hindu or Buddhist idea, is broadly accepted in South Korean popular culture, especially by those who are engaged in alternative self-training, including Christians. A similar tendency is observed in contemporary Western society: more than 20 percent of Americans and Western Europeans believe in rein-carnation.[11] In addition, the result shows that the incongruity between official religious doctrines and the subjective religious world is rather a natural phenomenon.

To the question "Did you participate in other workshops or courses except the present one?" the majority answered "yes," and most answered regarding the number of visited courses "1–4," followed by "5–9." So the answer "yes" of the absolute majority of the participants to the question, "Do you intend to visit further workshops or programs?" is not surprising. These results indicates that the people who are interested in alternative self-training are "workshop-hoppers" who tend to experience and test for themselves as many different programs as possible. Because this kind of religious experiment requires money, time, and often some knowledge to understand the techniques which are offered, as the survey shows, the participants are mostly highly educated (university graduates), middle class, and largely self-employed. Nevertheless, it should not be assumed that alternative self-training is a privilege of better-situated people. A number of diverse *ki*-training and yoga courses are offered for public benefit by almost every regional community and apartment residents' association at minimal or no cost, although the standard of this popularized form of "self-training" is not very high.

In popular discourse as well as in some areas of religious studies the tendency to regard established religion as *the* model of "religion" still persists. Accordingly, non-mainstream or marginal religions, which are called "new religions," have often been measured and compared unfavorably to traditional established religions. Sometimes, non- or less-institutionalized religious groups are not accepted as "religions," and

11. Erlendur Haralsson, "Popular Psychology, Belief in Life after Death and Reincarnation in the Nordic Countries, Western and Eastern Europe," *Nordic Psychology* 58, no. 2 (2006): 172-6; David W. Moore, "Three in Four Americans Believe in Paranormal," http://www.gallup.com/poll/16915/Three-Four-Americans-Believe-paranormal.aspx

these groups' activities are hardly valued as genuinely "religious." But we should not overlook the fact that people are increasingly constructing their own identities by themselves, with the help of diverse methods and techniques offered in the religious marketplace. Even a person's affiliation with an institutionalized confession does not hinder this project.

The pursuit of subjective religiosity—in other words, attaining self-transformation freed from any religious institution—is not really "new"; rather, it has a long tradition in Asian religious culture. Still, the way to realize this is certainly "new." A broad spectrum of techniques and methods that are designed for the purpose have become available to the general public. What makes the contemporary religious landscape in South Korea interesting is the coexistence of religious individualism—exemplified by a booming *ki*-training industry—and the still influential established religions (Buddhism, Protestantism, and Catholicism). If the former satisfy personal growth needs, the latter satisfy people's need to belong to communities which not only ensure religious salvation, but also provide social networks that are increasingly of importance in a fragmented society. Even though these two different religious needs seem to be contradictory, they are not necessarily in tension with each other as the above survey shows. Individuals' religious worlds are quite complex, allowing some degree of autonomy over which doctrines of established religions—if any—have power.

To sum up, in order to understand the diversity and complexity of contemporary religious culture, more attention should be paid to the concrete experience of individuals rather than giving pre-made judgement on "new" religious phenomena, which are not really "new" when viewed at a close range.

Suggestions for Further Reading

Arweck, Elisabeth. "New Religious Movements." In *Religions in the Modern World*, edited by Linda Woodhead, et al., 264-88. London: Routledge, 2002.

Fuller, Robert C. *Spiritual, but Not Religious: Understanding Unchurched America*, New York: Oxford University Press, 2001.

Haraldsson, Erlendur. "Popular Psychology, Belief in Life After Death and Reincarnation in the Nordic Countries, Western and Eastern Europe." *Nordic Psychology*, 58 no. 2 (2006):171-80.

Lewis, James R. and J. Gordon Melton, eds. *Perspectives on the New Age*, Albany: State University of New York, 1992.

MacGuire, Meredith B. *Religion, the Social Context*. Belmont: Wadsworth Thomson Learning, 2002.

Ro, Kil-myung. "New Religions and Social Change in Modern Korea History," *The Review of Korean Studies* 5 no. 1 (2002): 31-62.

Shimazono, Susumu. *From Salvation to Spirituality: Popular Religious Movements in Modern Japan*. Melbourne: Trans Pacific Press, 2004.

Stark, Rodney, and William Sims Bainbridge. "Of Churches, Sects, and Cults." *Journal for the Scientific Study of Religion* 18 (1979): 117-31.

Stark, Rodney, Eva Hamberg, and Allan S. Miller. "Exploring Spirituality and Unchurched Religions in America, Sweden, and Japan." *Journal of Contemporary Religion*, 20 no.1 (2005): 3–23.

Woo, Hai-Ran. "New Age in South Korea," *Journal of Alternative Spiritualities and New Age Studies* 4 (2008), http://www.open.ac.uk/Arts/jasanas/.

9

Jews

K. Hannah Holtschneider

Sonja is in a pickle: it is her best friend's birthday on Shabbat, and she is invited for a garden party in the afternoon. Her friend lives at the other end of town. Sonja would need to walk for about two hours to get there. She would also have to walk back or ask for a lift from someone after dark. What should she do to honor both her religious obligations and her friendship?

To set the scene for this introduction to the study of Jews and Judaism, we begin with a case study: Jewish life in contemporary Germany. This will enable us to address better who and what may be part of the study of (religious) Jewish life, its history, and ramifications in the present. Finally, we will ask whether and how such a study of Jewish religious experience, can, should, or cannot or should not, be separated from investigations of Jewish history, culture, and literature which may be described as secular, indeed whether it is even possible to draw satisfactory distinctions between religious and "non-religious" Jewish self-expression.

The choice of the Jewish community in Germany as a case study arises from the following considerations: Most modern Jewish religious movements originated in Germany. Germany's Jewish community today is a very particular community in that it is both continuous (or at least strives for continuity) with pre-war German Jewish culture and religiosity, yet also radically discontinuous, with little to no interest in connecting with specifically *German* Jewish traditions. In addition, the Jewish community in contemporary Germany is often described as one of the least "religious" Jewish communities in the world, in particular when compared with the world's largest Jewish community in the United States.[1]

---

1. Marion Kaplan, "What is 'Religion' among Jews in Contemporary Germany?" in *Reemerging Jewish Culture in Germany: Life and Literature since 1989*, ed. Sander L. Gilman and Karen Remmler (New York: New York University Press, 1994), 77.

This makes for a challenging starting point in this religious studies exploration of Jews and Judaism, as it shatters assumptions about what it means to be Jewish, to live a Jewish life and to be a religious Jew.

While focusing on the Jewish community in Germany, this chapter treats its German context as a starting point for wider-ranging reflections on Jewish life and identity. Hence, when talking about religious practice and its foundation in texts and traditions, reference will be made to Jewish history in other parts of the world and distinctive ways of being Jewish which contrast with those of Jews in Germany. Of particular interest will be relations of Jews to the State of Israel.

Jewish Life in Contemporary Germany

Jewish life in Germany has a history of around 1,700 years, and its intellectual developments are significant for the history of the Jewish community in Europe as well as for contemporary Jewish life. The majority of contemporary Jewish religious movements originate in Germany, and its Jewish population played a significant part in shaping assumptions about what it means to be Jewish in secular states. Major changes in religious practice and notions of integrating this practice into a secular civil society whose members may be part of a variety of communities or of no religious community also originate with German Jews. And yet, despite this momentous history, until recently Jewish religious life in Germany was upheld by a dwindling number of people who had little connection with pre-war German Jews. Only recently, since German unification in 1990, has religious and cultural Jewish activity increased to occupy a more publicly visible role in shaping Jewish communities in Germany.

The rise of the Nazi party and the appointment of Adolf Hitler as chancellor in 1933 spelled the end of the German Jewish community as it had developed since the late eighteenth century.[2] At the beginning of World War II, in 1939, the majority of the approximately 500,000-strong German Jewish community (about 1 percent of the total population of Germany) had emigrated, thus escaping deportation and murder. In 1939, Jews in Europe mainly lived in the area of today's Poland, Byelorussia and the Ukraine, the Baltic states, Hungary, and the Balkans. In 1939, approximately 9 million of 15 million Jews in the world lived in Europe. With 3 million Jews, Poland had the largest Jewish population in Europe alongside Russia, where a comparable number of Jews lived.[3] The major-

---

2. For an authoritative history of German Jews from before the Enlightenment through the 1990s, see Michael A. Meyer and Michael Brennar, eds., *German-Jewish History in Modern Times*, 4 vols. (New York: Columbia University Press, 1998).

3. For detailed figures on the Jewish population in Europe, see Wolfgang Benz, ed., *Dimen-

ity of Europe's Jews, an estimated 6 million adults and children, were murdered in the Holocaust. After the war, the survivors largely decided either to emigrate to the United States, to the newly founded State of Israel, or to a smaller degree, the United Kingdom, or to return to their former homes, the latter option being chosen by a very small minority of survivors. Some neither emigrated nor returned to their pre-war homes, but made a life in the country to which they migrated after liberation and the end of World War II—Germany. Though mainly not of German Jewish origin, these liberated Jews found themselves on German territory. For a variety of reasons (economic, social, and educational) they stayed, revived old communities, and created new ones. They sat, as they said themselves, on proverbial "packed suitcases," ready to leave at any sign of danger. Although Jewish communities in the United States and Israel and the World Jewish Congress vilified them for living in the land of the murderers and for rejecting Zionist calls for emigration to Israel, Jews in post-war Germany nevertheless created a community for themselves. (Re-)migration of (often German) Jews to Germany began in the 1950s, and by the 1980s the Jewish population in Germany numbered about 30,000. Today, after the immigration from the former Soviet Union, the figure has tripled, now reaching to around 100,000.[4]

The Central Committee of Jews in Germany was founded in 1950 to represent the nearly 15,000 Jews then living in the country, following the pre-war principles of the *Einheitsgemeinde* (united community) which embraced communities following different religious rites under one umbrella institution. The title "Jews *in* Germany" was purposefully chosen, since the majority of Jews who found themselves in Germany after World War II came from Eastern Europe and did not share much culturally, liturgically, or religiously with the pre-war German Jewish community. Pre-war German Jews were, in the majority, oriented towards Liberal Judaism, a movement that privileged German as part of the liturgy, had introduced regular sermons, and included musical instruments in religious services. However, after the war, the majority of Jews who remained in Germany came from the more Orthodox Eastern European Jewish communities, and the character of the services changed to reflect this.

Jewish life in post-war Germany is still largely organized around religious events, such as prayer services and community events on the occasion of Jewish festivals. Religious instruction for children is also often

---

sionen des Völkermords: Die Zahl der jüdischen Opfer des Nationalsozialismus (Munich: R. Oldenbourg Verlag, 1991).

4 . Julius H. Schoeps, et al., *Ein neues Judentum in Deutschland? Fremd- und Eigenbilder der russisch-jüdischen Einwandere* (Potsdam: Verlag Berlin-Brandenburg, 1999), 9.

provided by the community, as are adult education programs.

The synagogue (literally meaning "assembly") is the building in which services and meetings are conducted, and this draws Jews together at set times. Most synagogues offer at least one service on Shabbat, the day of rest at the end of the week, either on Friday night, night-time being the beginning of the Jewish day, or on Saturday morning. Congregants attend for a variety of reasons. Faith may be one of them; alternatively the congregant might focus on the need to fulfill the *mitzvah*—meaning a "commandment" or "obligation," but one willingly and lovingly ful-filled—of communal prayer. Other reasons can be social or cultural. A service is a time at which meeting other Jews is guaranteed, hence getting together with friends and acquaintances during and after a service draws people together. Many communities will cater to the social character of a Shabbat service by providing snacks after the service and sometimes even a sit-down communal meal.

The synagogue also serves as a community center and remains a focal point for other activities, such as educational events, concerts, and other social occasions. Some seasonal festivals will be celebrated in and around the synagogue, as will events in the life of individuals such as weddings and coming-of-age celebrations—*bar mitzvah* for boys and *bat mitzvah* for girls—which signal the religious maturity of a boy at thirteen or a girl at twelve. Other life-cycle events that traditionally were more likely to be celebrated in the home now also often take place in the synagogue, for example, the circumcision of a boy (*brit*). The centrality of the synagogue in Jewish life also makes a point about the importance of the commu-nity of Jews that gathers there, as well as the importance of the notion of Jewish peoplehood.

Judaism

Judaism draws on a long textual and cultural tradition. From this tradi-tion it is possible to distil notions of normativity in world view and life-style that can be found in some form or other in the lives of most Jews today. While it is difficult to give an account of what Jews "believe and practice" and confidently to label this account normative, it is possible to enumerate elements which are likely to surface in the lives of many Jews across the world. It is useful, though, to bear in mind that the prac-tice of things distinctly Jewish does not necessitate a belief in a distinctly Jewish world view. Notions of what characterizes a life as "Jewish," or what makes a person Jewish, differ vastly. And while Jewish religious movements and other institutions such as national Jewish organizations apply a range of criteria to discern whether an individual is Jewish, these criteria are not necessarily consonant with the sense of Jewishness of the individual, though often they are. What follows is a description of aspects of Jewish textual and ritual tradition and their various embodiments in the lives of Jews.

Jewish founding narratives and many Jewish practices are based on biblical and talmudic texts. The first five books of the Hebrew Bible constitute the Pentateuch, or, in Jewish parlance, the *Chumash* (both literally mean "five"). These books narrate the beginnings of the world and the origins of the Jewish people, with G-d[5] singling out Abram/Abraham and forging a covenant with him, with his son Isaac, and with Isaac's son Jacob. The exodus of Jacob's descendants from Egypt and their liberation from slavery marks the story of the Jewish people proper. The journey of the Israelites through the desert into the promised land is accompanied by another covenant of the Jewish people with G-d through the giving of the Torah (literally "teaching"), with its commandments regarding civil, criminal, and ritual law. Therefore, the first five books of the Hebrew Bible are also called the Torah and are traditionally said to have been written by Moses who is said to have led the Jewish people out of Egypt.

As the first collection of laws and guidance for the lives of the Israelites, the Torah, in its narrow meaning of the *Chumash*, can be seen as the founding document or constitution of the Jewish people. The prophetic books and the collection of other writings which complete the canon of the Hebrew Bible report further episodes in the history of the Jewish people and contain moral guidance and spiritual poetry. As such, the Jewish people emerge on the scene of history as a people with a particular code of conduct and governance which is attributed to divine revelation.

While Jews have lived in the Diaspora, i.e. outside the land of Israel, at least since the Babylonian Exile (586 BCE), the destruction of the Second Temple in the year 70 of the Common Era (CE) led to a wide dispersion of Jewish people around the world in the exile (*galut*). Although a small number of Jews remained in the land of Israel, and community life there continued unbroken on a small scale until its expansion, thanks to Zionist immigration from around 1880 and the founding of the State of Israel in 1948. The term "diaspora" is of Greek origin and means "dispersion" from one's homeland. The Greek Jewish community is among

---

5. In Hebrew, the standard term for the divine is formed by four Hebrew letters, the Tetragrammaton (Greek, meaning "four letters"), the pronunciation of which is uncertain. Rather than mispronounce this four-letter word, and as a mark of the impossibility of grasping the nature of the divine, it is rendered simply as "the Name" (*Hashem* in Hebrew). In English, *Hashem* is commonly rendered as G-d.

the oldest communities of the Jewish Diaspora. Since the dispersion in the aftermath of the destruction of the temple in 70 CE, the majority of Jews has lived in the Diaspora, so that Diaspora has come to mean a permanent state of being for Jews, arguably even since the establishment of the State of Israel in 1948. Historically, significant Jewish communities developed in Southern Europe (Italy and Greece), the Balkans, and the Middle East. Jews migrated along the Silk Route as far as India and China. North African Jews were a strong community in the Middle Ages, and the Spanish peninsula had a varied and prosperous Jewish community during Muslim rule, which finally ended with the Christian conquest of Spain and the expulsion of Jews in 1492. France and Germany's Jewish communities were also flourishing at the time, though the German communities were hit hard by persecution and murder during the crusades of the eleventh and twelfth centuries. While these communities were able to re-establish themselves and continue to play a significant role in the development of Jewish spirituality and thought, the Black Death and persecution in mid-fourteenth century eliminated many communities. Waves of expulsions in the fifteenth and early sixteenth centuries initiated a demographic shift towards the east, while German Jews moved away from the cities to the countryside, where they remained until the nineteenth century. By the end of the fifteenth century, the majority of Europe's Jewish population had moved to Eastern Europe, notably to the territories of today's Poland and Russia, as well as to what is now Hungary and the Czech Republic. There Jewish life flourished until waves of mass emigration to Western Europe, the United States, and Palestine at the end of the nineteenth century following persecution and the Holocaust hailed the end of Jewish life in Europe as it was known until then.

Halakhah, the system of civil, ritual, and criminal law found in the Torah was further developed in compilations at the beginning of the Common Era such as the *Mishnah* (meaning "repetition" of the law) and the *Gemara* (meaning "completion" of the law), which are united in the Talmud. Both legal compendiums record a comprehensive legal system uniting civil, criminal, and ritual law, and also Jewish folk narratives which explore moral dilemmas. The *Mishnah* is the first attempt to codify Jewish legal tradition by ordering it into categories of law pertaining to particular problems, such as agriculture, rituals, women, etc. The resulting six orders (the main categories) of the *Mishnah*, edited in the second century CE, were then commented upon in the *Gemara* during the following three centuries. Two versions of the Talmud, named after their geographical origin (Jerusalem and Babylon) encompass the *Mishnah* and *Gemara*. With the addition of later, in particular medieval, commentators, a duly elaborated version of the Talmudic text was canonized in the sixteenth century at the time of the invention of printing. The components of the Talmud are known as the "oral law" or "oral Torah," by contrast with the written Torah, since before it was fixed in writing this body of teaching was passed on and developed as an oral tradition, whereas the Torah is connected to the notion of a direct revelation immediately secured in writing by Moses. The written and oral Torah together form the basis of distinctly Jewish forms of living.

Distinctive features are associated with Jewish life, such as Shabbat and festivals which commemorate seminal events in the history of the Jewish people. The weekly Shabbat, which lasts from Friday night through Saturday, reminds Jews of the completion of G-d's work of creation on the seventh day and the forging of the covenant between G-d and the Jewish people at Mount Sinai. *Pesach*, or Passover, in spring commemorates the exodus of the Jewish people from slavery in Egypt. Fifty days after this, *Shavuot* recalls the giving of the Torah at Mount Sinai. A number of festivals in the autumn continue the story of the relationship between the Jewish people and G-d. The New Year, *Rosh Hashanah*, recalls the creation of the world and at the same time inaugurates a period of renewal of the individual and the Jewish people. During the following ten days, Jews are called to examine their personal and communal conduct over the past year and to make amends for wrongs committed against other people. This period of repentance culminates in the liturgy of *Yom Kippur*, the Day of Atonement, at the end of which the "gates of forgiveness" are closed for another year. The cycle of festivals continues with the festival of *Sukkot* (booths), a reminder of how G-d provides for the Jewish people. Dwelling in temporary booths for a week, Jews are asked to remember the miraculous survival of the Jewish people on their journey through the desert after the exodus, sustained only by G-d's provision of sustenance.

Food plays a major part in differentiating Jews from non-Jews. What may be eaten and what is forbidden to Jews constitutes a complex system of rules designed to remind Jews of their status as chosen people, separated from non-Jews through a code of conduct applying only to Jews. The basis of these dietary laws, the system of *kashrut*, is the separation of meat and milk as well as refraining from seafood and certain types of meat. In order to qualify as kosher, permitted animals have to be slaughtered according to a particular method called *shechita*, which involves *inter alia* the cutting of the jugular vein of the animal to effect a quick and painless death and to drain the majority of the blood of the animal, which is forbidden to Jews. Jewish cuisine is traditionally regional and has adapted the recipes of a given region to the rules of *kashrut*. Today, "Jewish food" is often associated with Eastern European Ashkenazi cuisine introduced by immigrants to the United States and the United Kingdom but since then internationalized. At the same time "Jewish food" is also strongly associated with Israeli and Near Eastern cooking, which is replicated by Jews across the Western World.

Contemporary religious Jewish movements—notably Reform/Liberal, Conservative, and Orthodox (we will look at variants of these in greater detail below)—treat these texts and traditional practices in ways that signal their different understandings of "revelation," peoplehood, and commandment/*mitzvah*. Jews may be members of synagogues belonging to one or more of these movements, or they may not wish to express their Jewish self-understanding through membership in a synagogue congregation. Secular Jews have only recently begun to form their own organizations, such as Humanistic Judaism, paralleling the main religious Jewish movements. Secular Jews can be found in many Jewish cultural organizations, including synagogues, or may choose not to affiliate with any Jewish organization.

In Germany a majority of those who identify themselves as Jews can also be described as secular or not-observant. In English parlance, an observant Jew is someone who lives according to the *mitzvot* (plural of *mitzvah*). This can denote a strict adherence to a particular version of Jewish tradition, such as Orthodoxy, Conservative or Reform/Liberal. These traditions also describe different understandings of the relationship between the community (which can be as broad as the entire Jewish people) and the individual. While Orthodox Jewish practice demands the submission of the individual to the rule of the community, and many practices will be uniformly observed, Conservative, and Reform Jews each grant the individual a greater freedom in weighing up the different reasons and possibilities for observing particular practices. How is this played out in the lives of an individual? Let us imagine the preparation for and observance of Shabbat for four people, one with Orthodox, the others with Conservative, Liberal, and secular leanings.

Case Studies: Sonja, Tamar, Michael, and Anna

Sonja

Sonja is studying law in Berlin. She belongs to the Jewish student union and is active in one of the smaller traditional communities in the city. Thursday afternoon: Sonja leaves the library to do her weekly shopping. Later that evening she and her flat mate, Tamar, will begin to prepare the meals for Shabbat and will clean and tidy their flat, because both have a hectic schedule of lectures on Friday morning, and Shabbat is coming in early in November. Sonja needs to work to a tight timetable to manage her university commitments and the requirements of preparing Shabbat. From sundown on Friday night until sundown on Saturday night, no "work" can be performed and she needs to make sure that she has set up her small apartment for the requirements of Shabbat. Usually this means sharing the tasks of shopping, cooking, and cleaning evenly with Tamar, making sure that everything is accomplished before the set time for candle-lighting, seventeen minutes before sundown on Friday.

"Work" means any activities to do with earning money, but beyond that "work" describes a set of activities that was instrumental in building and maintaining the temple in Jerusalem in biblical times when the Jewish people were living in the land of Israel. In subsequent generations the rabbis (meaning "teachers") who contributed to the Talmud began to draw "a fence" around these activities and prohibited many more tasks on Shabbat, so that Jews should never come close to violating the actual prohibition. Hence, activities which may seem remote from "work" are part of the forbidden actions on Shabbat: the flicking of a light switch is connected to the prohibition of lighting a fire, as is driving a car. Similarly, all things to do with cooking are prohibited, and food needs to be prepared before the beginning of Shabbat and kept warm for its duration. Orthodoxy treats Torah and Talmud, written and oral law, as authoritative, since it is said to have been revealed in its entirety to Moses on Mount Sinai. Subsequent generations have the task of interpreting the law for the contexts they find themselves in—interpreting, but not changing the law. The whole of this tradition is treated as sacred and immutable, rendering contemporary rabbis the guardians of a tradition which may not be changed simply to fall in line with contemporary modes of life. Any change needs to be effected in faithfulness to the principles of *halakhic* (legal) decision-making rather than today's value systems.

Orthodoxy itself arose as a counter-movement to reforming changes introduced in Germany at the beginning of the nineteenth century. The term "Orthodox" signals a focus on a set of beliefs connected with the revelatory texts of the Torah. In the face of changes to traditional observance, Orthodox rabbis decided to issue a ban on any change. Today, the word "Orthodox" describes Jewish movements which adhere to this ban to varying degrees.

Preparing for Shabbat can sometimes be a mad rush before the Shabbat candles are lit on Friday evening, but both girls value the special time Shabbat brings for them. On a mundane level it gives them a prescribed, immovable rest from their studies, and thus provides a different perspective on life. Spending much of Shabbat in the synagogue, they may also socialize with their Jewish friends, who form such a small group in this big city that it would otherwise be quite possible to go without seeing them for long periods of time because of all the other commitments in their lives. Often they will invite friends and visitors to the synagogue to walk home with them and to share one or more of the three prescribed meals on Shabbat. When Sonja was looking for accommodation when coming to Berlin to study, it was important to her to choose a flat as close as possible to a synagogue, so that she would be able to walk to services on Shabbat and festivals.

Sonja is looking for a way to combine her deep attachment to traditional Jewish practice with her identity as a young woman who lives in a largely secular society. For a short while, she attended the services at the Adass Yisroel synagogue, a *haredi* community, but found that this did not satisfy her, despite the fact that the Eastern European Ashkenazi liturgy reminded her of her grandparents (*haredi* literally means "G-d-fearing" and denotes a very strict and exclusive Orthodox movement). She also spent some time at the Chabad Lubavitch synagogue which is part of a *hasidic* (mystical) movement which dedicates much time and resources to reaching out to young Jews and drawing them nearer to their particular way of Jewish observance. The strict segregation of men and women, not only during prayer services, but in all areas of life, has alienated Sonja somewhat. She finds this difficult to integrate into her life as a highly educated woman who is used to living alongside and in community with men. Sonja has as many non-Jewish as well as Jewish friends and wants to compromise neither her observance of the *mitzvot* nor her attachment to her non-Jewish friends. During the week, she spends time learning about the interpretation of Jewish scriptures, in particular about biblical texts. Sonja is active in her community, dedicating time to a Jewish youth group which fosters the relationship between young Jews in Germany and Israel, which is interpreted as their ancestral and future home as well as a spiritual concept that holds the Jewish people together.

Recently Sonja began dating a non-Jewish man. This has thrown her into conflict with her Jewish observance as well as with her family—whom she has not yet told of this recent relationship. Sonja grew up in a family who had quite a strong attachment to Jewish tradition. Her grandparents had ended up in Germany as so-called "displaced persons" after the end of World War II. They came from a small town in Lithuania with a vibrant Jewish life and were themselves steeped in the traditions of Lithuanian Jews. Both had a strong religious education and affiliated immediately with the synagogue community of a large city. There they were instrumental in building up the services the community offers to its members, not least prayer meetings and religious instruction. Their children were raised in this traditionally Orthodox environment.

Sonja's mother spent some of her youth in Israel and thought of making *aliyah* (literally "going up," i.e. immigrating to Israel) before she met her husband. Sonja's father is a German whose mother's family is Jewish and who developed an interest in this side of the family and Jewish religious practice as a teenager. The couple stayed in Germany and decided to raise a family there, Sonja being their eldest daughter.

Tamar

Tamar's preparations for Shabbat also begin early in the week, as she is sharing a flat with Sonja. Like Sonja's family her grandparents came to Germany in the wake of World War II from Hungary. Strongly affiliated with the Neolog movement, a movement which combines tradition and reform originating in nineteenth-century Hungary, like Sonja's grandparents they raised their children in Germany in one of the mainstream communities of the *Einheitsgemeinde*. While not exactly matching the Hungarian Neolog tradition, Tamar's grandparents were happy to be able to give their children a Jewish religious education at all.

As a young man, Tamar's father made *aliyah* and lived in Israel for a few years before returning to Germany with his Israeli wife for a job. Tamar's mother was born in Iran and emigrated to the State of Israel shortly after its establishment, when the situation for Jews in Iran became difficult due to political tensions with Israel. She grew up in a family who regarded Jewish religious observance as their culture, although they did not emphasize the religious education of their children beyond what was offered in the state schools. The family struggled to assimilate to Israeli life, which was dominated by Ashkenazi Jews who looked down on Persian and other Mizrachi Jews.

Ashkenazi literally means "German," but is used to describe Northern European Jews from France in the West to Russia in the East, united by the language of Yiddish, a composite of medieval German, Hebrew, and Slavic languages. Southern European Jews are known as Sephardim (meaning "Spanish," but referring to both Spanish and Portuguese Jews), although there were—and are—important Sephardic communities in Northern Europe, notably Amsterdam, Hamburg, and London. These groups are linguistically united by Ladino, a composite of Arabic, Hebrew, Spanish, and Portuguese. Italian and Greek Jews do not fit into this classification and form groups of their own, as do smaller Jewish ethnic groups such as Bucharan Jews, African Jews, and Chinese Jews. These Jewish groups distinguish themselves by variations in their religious practice, languages, and cultural habits. *Mizrach* means "east"; Mizrachim are oriental Jews, i.e. Jews of Arab and Middle Eastern countries.

Tamar was born in Israel and grew up in Berlin. She was raised bilingually and is now fluent in both German and Hebrew, but she no longer understands the languages of her grandparents: Hungarian, Yiddish, and Persian. She enjoys hanging out with other young Jewish people, and this is how she met Sonja, her current flat mate. Tamar enjoys the regularity of Shabbat and the opportunity it gives for socializing with a Jewish crowd that often includes Israelis. This gives her a feeling of belonging to more than one world, and she cherishes these opportunities to engage with Jewish tradition and culture. As an aspiring actress, she has cofounded a Jewish theatre group. Tamar describes herself as Jewish, German, and Israeli, with strong affiliations to all these parts of her identity. Living with Sonja has made her more aware of a distinctly religious lifestyle and she is engaged in more structured learning about Jewish practice and tradition. Recently she has begun going to the Conservative synagogue. This involves quite a long journey for her on Shabbat. But Tamar feels that involvement with this religious movement allows her a freedom she feels is lacking in the Orthodox community, a freedom she is used to from her youth and from visits with Sonja.

Conservative Judaism is a movement with German origins but which today is largely inspired by the large Conservative institutions of the United States. In its synagogues, men and women are equal in their access to all religious duties, and the alternatives of gender separation during services or mixed seating are left to the choice of the local community. Conservative Judaism tries to straddle a middle ground between faithfulness to the tradition of Jewish practice as expressed in *Halakhah* and faithfulness to the changed social and political circumstances of the present. Decisions about changes to the observance of *mitzvot* are authorized by the community after the consultation of experts in *Halakhah*. Hence some autonomy to determine Jewish practice is delegated from religious leaders to the community, which holds the authority to implement such practice. Connected to this is a notion of revelation which regards the *halakhic* tradition as sacred, but also subject to change in response to the various social contexts in which it is applied. While the principles of *halakhic* decision-making are derived from the traditional bodies of law (i.e. the Talmud), changing social and political circumstances and changing ideas about humanity are taken into account when Conservative rabbis make *halakhic* decisions and propose these to their communities. Faithfulness to *Halakhah and* the current needs of the community are the two principles held in tension in any Conservative *halakhah*. Thus it is permitted to switch on and off electric lights on Shabbat as well as drive a car to the synagogue, because even though these may be transgressions of the traditional law, for by permitting them more Jews are likely to observe Shabbat and attend communal services than if the stricter interpretation were upheld. Similarly, contemporary notions of what it means to be human include insights about the equal abilities and values embodied by both genders, and Conservative practice is now to grant access to all ritual and community functions to both men and women.

In this environment Tamar is able to explore her Jewishness, in particular as the Conservative movement holds notions of Jewish peoplehood and a strong attachment to the land of Israel and the State of Israel together with a commitment to living in the Diaspora as citizens and nationals of many different countries. Tamar can thus hold her identifications as Jewish, German, and Israeli together in a creative tension.

Michael

Michael is the president of a Liberal Jewish community. He is a teacher in his forties, married to a non-Jewish German woman. The couple has two children. Michael and his wife discussed how to introduce their children to their mother's Protestant Christian and their father's Jewish heritage. They want their children to know about the families from which they come and decided to enroll them in the Protestant religious instruction offered by their local primary school (in Germany Catholic and Protestant religious education is part of the curriculum which by law has to be offered by every state school, but parents and students can opt out of this), and they approached the synagogue to enroll their sons in the *heder*, the religion school. At the synagogue, they ran into difficulties as the boys have a non-Jewish mother and are therefore not considered to be Jews according to *Halakhah*. While the synagogue may be able to offer the children a place in religion school, they would not be allowed to participate in religious rituals as they were not seen as Jewish. Michael understood the argument, but at the same time did not wish his children to feel as if they had no right to belong. He began looking for alternatives and came across a newly established Liberal Jewish prayer group which met once or twice a month for Shabbat services. Enthusiastically Michael pitched in to establish this Jewish alternative which would offer his children the possibility of an education and himself the chance to reconnect with his own, long-buried, religious identifications.

Shabbat means family time to Michael, while Sunday is dedicated to the Christian side of the family. On Friday evening the family will gather for a festive meal at which each of them plays a part in the ritual, from lighting the candles to saying the blessings over bread and wine. Often there will be guests, friends and family, but also Jewish visitors who have asked the Liberal community whether there is a possibility of Shabbat hospitality. Saturday morning the family will go together to the Liberal synagogue.

In Liberal Judaism a great deal of the authority over the application of Jewish tradition in personal observance is given to the individual. The Torah is understood to contain divine revelation translated by humans into concepts and laws understandable at the time it was written down. Talmudic writings extend the interpretation of the original revelation of the Torah for another time and another place. Similarly Liberal Jews are asked to find ways of translating the "essence" of the Torah for today's world. Liberal Judaism grew as a movement in nineteenth-century Germany, not least through an interest in the Torah and other biblical texts as historical documents. Thereby Liberal Jews differentiate themselves from Orthodox and Conservative Jews, who link divine revelation closely to the wording and composition of the Torah and, to varying degrees, do not treat the Torah as a historical document of human authorship. While Liberal Jews focus on the divine essence of the revelation contained in the Torah, Orthodox Jews treat the Torah as literally revealed. In the nineteenth and early twentieth centuries, German Liberal Judaism was the strongest among the Jewish religious movements in Germany, boasting an important scholarly tradition. Traditionally anti-Zionist, the movement combined German nationalism with the reformulation of Judaism as a religion focused on ethics and spirituality, distancing itself from the concept of Jewish peoplehood and attachment to the physical territory of Zion, the land of Israel. The Holocaust destroyed this movement in Germany.

However, the American Reform Jewish movement, founded in the nineteenth century with significant support from German Liberal Jewish scholars who had migrated to the United States, is now extending its influence to Germany. Since the 1930s the American Reform movement has become more and more sympathetic to the Zionist movement, recognizing the need for a secure Jewish homeland. Similarly, the growing trend of intermarriage has led to a greater appreciation of mixed-faith couples and their needs. While Michael's family would not have found a home in Liberal Jewish communities before the war or even thirty years ago, the decision to bring up his children with knowledge of both their parents' traditions is valued by the movement. At the same time there continues to be a move to encourage the conversion of the non-Jewish partner, so that children are raised in a single religious environment. This is a particular feature of Reform and Liberal Judaism, since traditionally seeking converts is discouraged, and conversion should not be sought for the purpose of marriage but should arise out of the needs of the individual.

Immediately after the war, German émigrés from Nazi Germany to the United States returned to help build up the Jewish community in Germany. Small in number, the movement has grown in the last decade, due to the growing interest and initiative of people like Michael. The movement promotes equality of the sexes in all religious matters and accepts Jews in marriages with non-Jews by treating their children as Jews regardless of whether their mother or father is the Jewish parent. What matters is the desire for a Jewish education.

Michael's parents were born in Germany; his mother's family emigrated to Palestine in the mid-1930s while his father's followed a little later. Michael himself was born in Israel and grew up there until the family returned to Germany when he was ten years old. Like many of his parents' generation, his mother and father found it difficult to establish themselves as refugees from Nazi Germany, first in Palestine and then in the newly founded State of Israel. They were not Zionists by conviction: the Zionist movement had been small in Germany, never gaining much support from the Jewish establishment. When the opportunity to emigrate to Palestine arose, Michael's grandparents took it because this seemed the only opportunity to leave Germany and to take some of their assets with them, rather than having them expropriated by the Nazis. Religiously, the family was German Liberal, tracing their line back to the beginnings of the Jewish Enlightenment, the *Haskalah*, in the late eighteenth century. They were Germans as much as Jews, their national identity taking equal place with their religious affiliation. Germany was their mother country, German their mother tongue, and their synagogue membership expressed their religious but not their national identity. "Germans of the Mosaic faith" or "German Jews" were the labels Michael's grandparents would most likely have chosen for themselves, a designation that did not sit well with the Zionist ideology of the Jewish settlements in Palestine (the *Yishuv*) nor with the national identity proposed by the State of Israel, founded in 1948. Hence Michael's parents decided to move the entire family back to Germany in the 1950s.

Michael and his siblings were raised as Germans and as Jews, two identifications that did not (and still do not) sit comfortably with one another in the aftermath of the Holocaust. Michael's Jewish education outside the home took place in the local synagogue. However, due to an overwhelming majority of members being not of German Jewish, but of Eastern European Jewish ancestry, the rites and liturgy as well as the education given in this synagogue were anything but Liberal Jewish. Michael's parents and grandparents modeled their lives on the ideals of the German Liberal movement, instilling in him pride for his religious heritage. This heritage and Michael's identification with it were in tension with the synagogue. In addition, the youth groups in the synagogue were imbued with a Zionist ethos which encouraged youngsters to make *aliyah*. As an immigrant from Israel whose family intended to stay in Germany, Michael did not have an easy time there. His growing estrangement from the synagogue led to an almost complete break with any Jewish affiliation as an adult.

Anna

Anna has recently begun attending the congregation in which Michael is active. She emigrated from St. Petersburg in the middle of the 1990s when she was ten years old.

In Russia Anna's family was classed as Jewish by nationality, and her parents faced discrimination in their workplaces, not being able to progress in their careers on account of being Jewish. To enable their children to have the freedom to choose their professions in an environment free of antisemitism, they decided to emigrate soon after the collapse of the Soviet Union. They debated whether to go to Israel, as many of their friends had in previous years, or to take up the offer of immigration to Germany, something that had more recently been made possible by generous immigration quotas for Jews from the former Soviet Union.[6] The Jewish communities in Germany were keen to increase membership and with the help of the German government actively sought Jewish immigrants. In the end Anna's family decided to move to Germany as it seemed to offer better prospects for employment and education.

Anna's father comes from a Jewish family who originated in the Bucharan mountain region. Education mattered in her father's family, and he became an engineer, moving to Leningrad, now St. Petersburg. His educational options were limited by an unspoken quota of Jews in higher education, and he was not able to follow his real passion, the study of Russian literature. Instead he had to settle for a science degree, which enabled him to train for a job with no prospects of moving up the career ladder because his passport carried the nationality "Jewish." (In the Soviet Union ethnicities or nationalities were recorded in passports.) Anna's mother is not Jewish, but was not able to pass on her Russian nationality, which in Soviet times was inherited from one's father. As a result, the couple's children also suffered from the anti-Semitic discrimination experienced by their father, in particular when it came to educational choices.

Anna was brought up in a secular home with no religious identifica-

6. The legal context of this immigration movement is outlined at http://www.zentralratd-juden.de/de/topic/62.html.

tion. She knows she is Jewish, because of the stories of her father, his home and her grandparents, but does not connect this with any religious or cultural content. When the family arrived in Germany, the local Jewish community provided support, offering language courses and religious instruction for the children and adults. Anna was enrolled in religion school at the synagogue, but the family did not wish to take up an entirely different style of family life in order to accommodate alien religious customs. In particular, the hostility of parts of the community towards the non-Jewish mother and the subsequent declaration of the children as not Jewish alienated the family from the synagogue, adding another dimension to the experience of discrimination. As a young adult, Anna is now exploring her father's heritage. Feeling rebuffed by the traditional Jewish community, she now occasionally attends the Liberal community's services on Shabbat.

Current Issues for Jews in Germany Today

While immigration has repopulated and rejuvenated many communities, leading to the building of new synagogues and community centers, it has also split communities into groups of immigrants and groups of Jews previously living there. Very different interpretations of Jewishness may be at the root of this division between newcomers and "indigenous" Jews in post-war Germany. The interpretation of Jewishness as tied to religious identification (if not religious practice) that was common among those who have lived in Germany since the end of World War II contrasts with that of the majority of Jewish immigrants from the former Soviet Union, who would not describe themselves as religiously Jewish, but rather as Jews by nationality.

Another issue that is exercising the Jewish community is a growing religious diversity, which though not approximating pre-war diversity and only able to claim a tenuous continuity with pre-war Liberal Judaism in Germany, has been causing ructions in the community leadership since the early 1990s. Issues under debate here are the ability of the *Einheitsgemeinde* to contain such diversity and the consequences of a split into Orthodox and Liberal Jewish communities in terms of community and educational funding. Alongside the Protestant and Catholic churches, which are contractually linked with the German state, the Jewish community also enjoys the status of a religious community officially established in the state and as such collects the majority of its income from its members through taxation. In case of a split there would need to be a debate about the legal standing of Orthodox and non-Orthodox Jewish communities vis-à-vis the German state.

That the Jewish community in Germany is so small, fragmented, and embattled, internally as well as externally, makes it an ideal case study to explore how it is possible, from a religious studies perspective, to capture what is meant with the descriptor "Jewish." And what are the consequences of any such an identification?

Traditionally, a Jew is a Jew according to religious law, *Halakhah*, if his or her mother is a Jew and she or he does not profess another religion. That might sound very straightforward, identifying a person according to birth, rather than according to their own belief or practice. A pragmatic identification which, as a consequence, allows an ethnic classification of "Jew." For centuries this may have been a straightforward definition (though that is debatable too), guaranteeing the existence of distinct Jewish ethnic and religious communities in non-Jewish host countries in Europe and elsewhere. Jews living in exile among non-Jewish communities understood themselves as guests and were invited to settle by secular and religious powers alike, formed communities that enjoyed religious autonomy, and kept themselves—and were kept—distinct from their host societies, while at the same time existing in a mutually beneficial economic relationship. Movement between social classes and ethnicities was rare and tightly regulated, hence it is possible to argue that the definition of a Jew through the maternal line was sufficient to guarantee the survival of the community as well as separation from the host society. However, the dissolution of this fairly rigid social order with the onset of Enlightenment and the formation of European secular nation states in the wake of the French Revolution impacted on the ability of this definition of Jewishness to suffice.

Emancipation bestowed on Jews legal equality with their non-Jewish neighbors. At the same time Jews had to relinquish their communal autonomy, an interference with communal affairs many Jews did not see as a positive development, as it eroded communal cohesion and questioned the authority and cohesion of *Halakhah*. "Judaism" became a confession of faith and no longer was treated socially and legally as a complete way of life. When it became possible to leave the community and to found families outside of the juridical competence of the Jewish community, descent from a Jewish woman no longer determined that the person would also be counted on as a member of the community. Matters such as personal choice, actual observance of religious practice—indeed the very definition of Jewish practice as "religious"—became important for the definition of a Jew for community membership. At the same time, in the non-Jewish environment the notion of Jewishness as something that attaches to a person inherently and hence cannot be relinquished regardless of personal belief or religious practice gained currency. The rise of racist antisemitism joined the discussion about German nationalism and Jews were caught in the crossfire. The question arising at the end of the eighteenth century concerned the ability of Jews to join as equals the community of other European nations or whether a particular "Jewish character" would prevent Jews from being admitted to their host community. In the nineteenth century, racist antisemitism gained socio-political momentum in most European countries, so that Jews, though outwardly indistinguishable from non-Jews, were not seen as social equals or true fellow citizens.

Who is a Jew and What is Judaism?

For some, the suggestion that Judaism is a religion amongst other systems which can equally be labeled "religions" is a strange assumption, or even an offensive one. Some Jews would dispute that any definition of "religion" can be applied to Jews and/or Judaism. These Jews might argue that Jewish life should be guided by Torah and *Halakhah*, which give guidance for the formation of Jewish civilization. While this is a fairly traditional position, even those who do not identify with traditional Jewish practice or observance may not agree with the understanding of Judaism as a religion or the Jewish people as adhering to the religion of Judaism. Indeed, finding a term in the Hebrew language which appropriately translates the English words "religion" or "Judaism" is difficult.

So, if it is alien to foundational Jewish texts and the Hebrew language, where does the term "Judaism" come from? In fact, the English term "Judaism" derives from the Greek *Judaismos*, which is first found in the post-biblical books of the Maccabees and in the New Testament in Paul's letter to the Galatians (Gal 1:13f.). These texts were written in the first century CE. *Judaismos* describes what it means to be a Jew, and hence encompasses all that makes someone's life a Jewish life. The Hebrew equivalent to the English "religion," *Yahadut*, was not used until the Middle Ages and is a more practice-oriented term, describing the application of knowledge of the Jewish way of living. *Yahadut* is important in particular in texts that seek to distinguish what it means to be a Jew from what it means to be a Christian or a Muslim. Hence it is a term that came into greater prominence at a time when Jews were forced to participate in polemical disputes with Christians and Muslims. In modern times *Yahadut* is also used to describe the study of Judaism, or the study of Jewish history, again in the context of discerning "the state of being a Jew."

The Hebrew word *dat* describes a key element of what it means to be a Jew and in modern parlance has become synonymous with what outsiders may describe with the term "Judaism." The Hebrew word *dat* is commonly translated as "law" and describes not only Jewish law, but "the way in which Jews live." Rather than referring to an abstract set of rules, *dat* encompasses how Jews live, observe, and embody these rules or Jewish law as a whole in their lives. As such, *dat* is Judaism or "the reality of being a Jew." Many Jews whom others may describe as religious would describe themselves as observant. Observance of the commandments in the form in which Jewish law has determined is one of the features that distinguishes different ways of being Jewish. Jews may describe themselves as observant or non-observant, thereby indicating how they perceive their own relationship with Jewish law and its normativity—or lack thereof.

Many Jews and scholars who are engaged in the study of Jewish history, thought, and practice would not object to talking about Judaism and characterizing Judaism as a religion. Some may prefer Hebrew terminology, but it is generally accepted that a religion does not simply refer to a set of beliefs and can encompass many phenomena, including insider definitions of what it means to be a Jew. But what about Jews who reject any association with traditional elements of what it means to be Jewish? Where do secular Jews figure in these definitions which from both inside and the scholarly outside seem to suggest that being a Jew means to live in a certain way? And what of those who do not consider themselves Jewish while others do?

Definitions which include some and exclude others in the Jewish people or the community of Jews are part of Jewish discourse, and scholars of "Judaism" and Jewish studies are cognizant of these and need to work with them, just as scholars of religious studies need to position themselves to the various understandings of the term "religion."[7]

Suggestions for Further Reading

Bodemann, Y. Michal, ed. *Jews, Germans, Memory: Reconstructions of Jewish Life in Germany*. Ann Arbor: University of Michigan Press, 1996.

———. *A Jewish Family in Germany Today: An Intimate Portrait*. Durham: Duke University Press, Durham, 2005.

Brenner, Michael. *After the Holocaust: Rebuilding Jewish Lives in Postwar Germany*. Princeton, NJ: Princeton University Press, 1997.

Engel, David. *The Holocaust: The Third Reich and the Jews*. Harlow, UK: Longman, 2000.

Gilman, Sander L., and Karen Remmler, eds. *Reemerging Jewish Culture in Germany: Life and Literature Since 1989*. New York: New York University Press, 1994.

Gilman, Sander L. *Jews in Today's German Culture*. Bloomington: Indiana Univer-

7. Many thanks to Maria Diemling, Steven Sutcliffe, George Wilkes, and Melanie Wright for their insightful comments on earlier drafts of this chapter.

sity Press, 1995.

Goodman, Martin, Jeremy Cohen, David Sorkin, and Jonathan Campbell, eds. *The Oxford Handbook of Jewish Studies*. Oxford: Oxford University Press, 2002.

Gorelik, Lena., *Meine weißen Nächte*. Munich: Schirmer Graf Verlag, 2004.

Kaminer, Wladimir. *Russian Disco*. London: Ebury Press, 2002.

De Lange, Nicholas, and Miri Freud-Kande. *Modern Judaism: An Oxford Guide*. Oxford: Oxford University Press, 2005.

Peck, Jeffrey M. *Being Jewish in the New Germany*. New Brunswick, NJ: Rutgers University Press, 2006.

Solomon, Norman. *Judaism: A Very Short Introduction*. Oxford: Oxford University Press, 1996.

Wright, Melanie. *Understanding Judaism*. Cambridge: Orchard Academic, 2003.

10

Japanese Religionists

Katja Triplett

Celebrating the Year of the Water Monkey

The New Year (*o-shōgatsu*) is no doubt the biggest festival in Japan. The week-long celebrations bring family members together in their homes and also rouse a festive spirit in the local communities around Shintō (Shintoist) shrines, Buddhist temples, and other religious centers. Preparations for the New Year begin before the end of the calendar year, nowadays following the solar calendar, when the house is more thoroughly cleaned than usual and debts are paid off. Children are eagerly awaiting small (or more substantial) end-of-the-year money gifts from relatives. After visits to local religious centers during the first days after January 1, where friends and families engage in various transactions such as exchanging old amulets for new ones, drawing fortune slips, purchasing devotional objects such as evil-dispelling arrows and fastening votive tablets to a wooden trellis—all to ensure good fortune, health and happiness—the family gathers at home for a feast of traditional, "auspicious" foods. For the first seven days Japanese may continue to visit shrines and temples, but some may also engage in practices such as the "first brush" or the "first arrow," all related to traditional "way arts" or "dō arts" such as the path of writing or the path of shooting the bow. *Dō* is the reading of the Chinese character for "path, way, practice"; the character is rendered as *dao* in Chinese.[1]

The following scenes might be observed during this great festival of purifying the household and the nation in Japan:

Mr. Hashimoto and his wife and children are finally on their way to Kyoto, just an hour's ride on a crowded local train, then a taxi to the small

---

1. For more on Daoism, see Chapter 15, "Chinese Religionists."

village hidden from the main street by a steep hill covered in bamboo and underbrush. He estimates that they would arrive early at their destination, the village temple, Eikūin Temple (fictional), that has served the community for more than 350 years. The head priest of the village temple used to be Mr. Hashimoto's professor at Bukkyō University in Kyoto. He knows that Professor Kurodani likes his former students to arrive in a timely fashion, and Hashimoto likes to please his sensei (honorific for one's senior). Although trained to be a high school teacher at Bukkyō University, Hashimoto followed his interest in the teachings of Saint Hōnen (the revered founder of the Pure Land School or Jōdoshū), and took classes in Pure Land Buddhist doctrine with Professor Kurodani. He is now looking forward to greeting Amida Buddha with Sensei and the other guests, to the rhythmic toc-toc of the wooden fish-shaped drums and the multi-voiced calling of Amida Buddha's name (*nenbutsu*)— "Namu-Amida-Bu, Namu-Amida-Bu, Namu-Amida-Bu, Namu-Amida-Bu"—in the small prayer hall. Then there would be a feast, merry rounds of heated sake, cup after cup.

The Hashimotos finally arrive and are greeted by their hosts. They join Kurodani Jikoku Sensei in the prayer hall that in the summer opens to a small garden, so it can be approached by worshippers without going through the priest's living area. Now in the winter the wooden sliding door is closed, but still several portable gas heaters are battling the chill and emitting a hissing sound. Mrs. Hashimoto quickly finishes her greeting of Amida Buddha to assist the priest's wife and women from the community in the kitchen. The preparations are obviously underway since clouds of smoke escape from the grill into the neighboring rooms. The kitchen is actually connected to the prayer hall, the heart of the temple, via a small storeroom as well as a cozy sitting room.

Kurodani Jikoku Sensei interrupts his calling of the nenbutsu and tries to suppress a dry cough. "What are these women doing, I wonder; they'll be burning the whole house down next," he mutters. He is looking forward to the feast though and smiles at hearing an elderly neighbor's booming voice saying Amida Buddha's name over and over, drowning the squealing of the youngest Kurodani in the house, Sensei's first grandchild of his elder daughter. The informal greeting ceremony comes to an end, and the men and a few children make their way over to the gathering room.

Mrs. Hashimoto makes her way over to the dining hall carrying a tray with a sake pitcher and cups that rattle gently as she enters. She kneels next to the low table and sits it down noiselessly, smiling at the expectant faces of the guests already seated. She and the priest's wife and other women who helped in preparing the New Year's delicacies join in. There is a lot of catching up with Sensei's family and the other families of his former students. Mrs. Hashimoto admires the hanging scroll in the niche (tokonoma) dedicated to artistic objects celebrating the rhythm of the seasons. Kurodani Sensei explains that he chose this scroll because the calligrapher, his grandfather and former head of the temple, was ninety years old when he brushed the six characters of the "name" of Amida Buddha (南無阿弥陀仏 Na-mu A-mi-da Butsu). This year of the Water Monkey would be his hundredth birthday, so Kurodani Sensei selected the scroll to honor his grandfather. Mrs. Hashimoto nods in awe and then praises the delicate ikebana flower arrangement in the niche. The priest's wife thanks her, knowing that the praise is meant since Mrs. Hashimoto is an accomplished ikebana artist herself and practices the way of the flowers (kadō) at a Pure Land Buddhist convent in Kyoto. After this round of appreciation of the tokonoma exhibit, both guests and hosts turn to green tea and sake.

Japanese Buddhist Temples

Major temples (monasteries and convents) can consist of a large number of buildings following more or less a fixed layout that was developed in India and evolved in China before arriving in Japan from the Korean peninsula in the sixth century CE. Medium-sized and smaller temples nowadays are family businesses when they are led by men. Eikūin Temple, where we read of a New Year's gathering, is a typical example: the husband was trained in a seminary of his denomination (i.e. Buddhist sect or school). At the end of his training Kurodani Jikoku took his vows and became a monk. Because of his role as the leader of a religious institution who regularly conducts rites and ceremonies he should be referred to as a "priest" rather than as a monk, because one expects a monk to live a celibate lifestyle, which he clearly does not. Nuns, on the other hand, are not expected to marry and have families; therefore, nuns are sometimes seen as more traditional or "true" Buddhists living according to early concepts prescribing celibacy.[2] Temples in the True Pure Land Buddhist tradition (Jōdoshinshū), a denomination usually referred to as Shin Buddhism, are ideally headed by a married couple who are neither clerical nor purely lay practitioners.[3] The role of the husband is

2. Paula Kane Robinson Arai, *Women Living Zen: Japanese Sōtō Buddhist Nuns* (Oxford: Oxford University Press, 1999).

3. For more information see Richard Jaffe, *Neither Monk nor Layman: Clerical Marriage in Modern Japanese Buddhism* (Princeton, NJ: Princeton University Press, 2002); Esben Andreasen, *Popular Buddhism in Japan: Shin Buddhist Religion and Culture* (Honolulu: University of Hawai'i Press, 1998).

to perform the rituals whereas the wife, as the "protector of the hermit-age" (*bōmori*), is mainly involved in the pastoral care of the parishioners. At Eikūin Temple which belongs to an older strand of Pure Land Bud-dhism, the male offspring is expected to take over as temple priest.

This process of succession rarely runs as smoothly as many temple families would wish: Kurodani Jikoku's only son, Akira, for instance, refused to follow in the footsteps of his father, resulting in a family con-flict. Akira still joins in at the New Year because of his obligation to his parents. The solution to the inheritance problem was found in adopting the son-in-law, a trained Pure Land Buddhist priest, into the Kurodani family, so that in actuality the temple was passed on through the female line. This system of adoption of adult males so that they may carry on a business—or here a Buddhist temple—is not as popular as it used to be in earlier times, but in traditionally oriented families this is still a viable option to ensure the inheritance stays in the family of the wife's father. What would happen if the male priest died with children still not old enough to inherit? Can the widow in this case become the temple leader? Women used to be able to become heads of a temple only if there was no (or an unwilling) male heir. Recent discussions in the main Shin Bud-dhist administrative branches (the Honganji and Ōtani Temple branches) about this issue have led to a revision of succession regulations.[4]

Buddhist temples in Japan belong to transmission lineages that can be described as denominations (*shūha* in Japanese). The lineages were formed in China and Korea and introduced to Japan during different periods in history. Lineages also have emerged by foundation or schism on Japanese soil. Considering this, Japanese Buddhists seem to be firmly affiliated to one particular denomination (*shū*) and within the denomi-nation to a particular branch (*ha*). Indeed, this can be said to be true. Most Japanese when asked which denomination they belong to mention the place of the burial sites of their ancestors that are usually found at temples headed by a male priest. They also may refer to their daily prayer that broadly but clearly identifies the affiliation: "Namu Amida Bu(tsu)" points to a Pure Land Buddhist, "Namu myōhō rengekyō" to a Nichiren Buddhist, while the chanting of the Heart Sutra would denote a Shingon, Tendai, or Zen Buddhist affiliate. All Buddhist schools in Japan see them-selves going back to the historical Buddha. However, more important for the daily observance or the annual festivals is the person who is regarded as the founder or foundress of the present personal temple head's lineage. Pure Land temples, therefore, all hold statues of their central Buddha,

---

4. Simone Heidegger, *Buddhismus, Geschlechterverhältnis und Diskriminierung: die gegenwärtige Dis-kussion im Shin-Buddhismus Japans* (Berlin: Lit, 2006).

Amida, and images of the founder Saint Hōnen (Hōnen Shōnin), and in the case of Shin Buddhist sanctuaries we would find their founding figure, Shinran Shōnin.

How can one "become" a member of a religion in Japan? Membership is parochial in Japanese Buddhism. In the past there was a strict registration system to control the populace, and every household had to register at a temple (sometimes Shintō shrine). This is no longer practiced, but the old affiliations with the family temples one used to be registered with often remain intact. If affiliation goes through one's family, it is determined by the patrilineal affiliation. Indeed, the family Buddhist altar (*butsudan*) gets passed on (ideally) to the oldest son and with it the care of the graves that are located at a particular temple. The Buddhist house altar consists of a wooden case that holds images of Buddhist deities or character scrolls. The ancestor tablets are enshrined in this altar case that can be closed if not used and is usually placed in the largest room of the house so it sits in a prominent place amidst the living. There are also Buddhist groups of newer vintage that consist of members who entered the group as paying participants, e. g. the esoteric Buddhist Shin-nyoen (registered under this name in 1953).

Registering Religions as "Buddhist," "Shintoist," "Christian," and "Other"

Every year the Ministry of Education, Culture, Sports, Science, and Technology (MEXT) publishes statistics about religions in Japan based on numbers provided by registered religious corporations. Those can be both umbrella organizations as well as individual religious groups. The postwar Japanese constitution ensures religious freedom, but one is also free to be non-religious. A system of regulations treats religious corporations as non-profit charity organizations, and registration of such a corporation is relatively easy, although regulations were changed after a religious group, Aum Shinrikyō, killed a number of people in the Tokyo subway in 1995. The regulations are somewhat stricter now, especially in regard to controlling the finances of a religious group.[5]

Upon registration the organization can choose between four different categories, two of which represent the major religions in Japan, Buddhism and Shintō (Shintoism). The third is "Christian," which seems astonishing considering that Christians make up less than two percent of the population. The inclusion of this category may go back to political developments since the modernization of Japan and postwar legal

---

5. Robert Kisala,. "Japanese Religions," in *Nanzan Guide to Japanese Religions*, ed. Paul L. Swanson and Clark Chilson (Honolulu: University of Hawai'i Press, 2006), 3-13.

issues. The fourth is interesting because "All other, or various, religious teachings" (*shokyō*) includes religions that insist on the uniqueness of their faith and religions that may look like Buddhist groups from the outside but choose to go different paths. The extremely high number of registrations in this fourth category of "other" points to the fact that "other faiths" are popular in Japan. A closer look reveals that most of the larger groups and organizations were founded fairly recently and can be termed "new religions" (*shin shūkyō*). Also diaspora religions (Muslim or Hindu groups, for instance) find their home here in the fourth category.

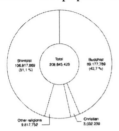

Whether a religion is from the ninth century CE such as Shingon or Tendai or newly emerged last week, the laws and regulations apply in the same way to both. This basically means that Japanese religions are in direct competition with each other. Some organizations may vie for members more than others because of a varying degree of inclusiveness: the more one religion belongs to a shared field of common religiosity the less there seems to be a need to propagate; the more universalistic and exclusivist the teachings and hierarchy of a given religion are, the fiercer the evangelization efforts seem to be.

Figure 10.1: *Numbers of members of registered religious groups as provided by the 2007 Annual Report on Religions (shūkyô nenkan) published by the Japanese Ministry of Education, Culture, Sports, Science, and Technology (MEXT) Agency for Cultural Affairs*

Features of a Shared Field of Common Religiosity

The wide spectrum of religious rituals, practices, and organizations in Japan are a direct result of a relatively flexible legal framework allowing for an extremely varied and complex pluralistic religious landscape. One approach to describing this religious landscape is to present Japanese religions in separate institutional bits, appetizingly presented like a colorful assortment of sushi on a finely lacquered platter. Every bit is unique and defined but only together make a complete and tasty meal. We may find attempts to order the pieces into the four categories mentioned above. More frequently though they are ordered and described according to the "three teachings" (a translation of two characters, 三 教, that are read *sankyō* in Japanese and *sanjiao* in Chinese). In China the three teachings are Confucianism, Daoism, and Buddhism. Other Asian countries that have a history of combining Confucianism, Daoism, and Buddhism besides China are North and South Korea and Vietnam. In Japan, Buddhism and Confucianism are combined with Shintō to form

200

Figure 10.2: *Pure Land Buddhist house altar, Religionskundliche Sammlung der Philipps-Universität Marburg, inv. no. Nu 134 (Copyright Rel.Samm.)*

the "three teachings".

What is easily overlooked in the "sushi approach" is that there are recurring, stable themes such as the ritual care for the ancestors ("ancestor worship") or the striving for good fortune and obtaining this-worldly benefits. Shared by most religionists are calendrical festivals such as New Year, the spring and autumn equinoxes, and the summer soul festival; the structuring of the days of the year into cycles of lucky and unlucky days according to almanacs; and frequent reference paid to the traditional Chinese calendar (*mannenreki* or *koyomi*) with its twelve animals of the zodiac. As to the ordering of space, pilgrimages—especially to mountains but also island sanctuaries—are popular during the holidays. We see here an overlapping of religious and secular travel culture. The leisure travelers may consider the religious outlook of the journey along one of the traditional circular pilgrimage routes more seriously and devote more time to religious transactions than previously planned. The pilgrimage routes very often include temples and shrines of historical importance, so travelers can be mainly motivated by the national treasures to be visited on the journey.

Combinatory Nature of Modern Japanese Religion

A Japanese person grows up naturally as a participant in different religious fields. A majority of Western introductions describe the nature of modern Japanese religion and religious life in Japan by stating that the two main religious traditions, which are defined as "Buddhism" and "Shintō," complement each other.[6] I would go further than supposing merely a complementary relationship between the two, and rather speak of a *combinatory system*. The emphasis here is on a shared field where we find practices belonging to two (or more) traditions but may be differentiated and need not be looked at as separate entities.[7] The recently published *Nanzan Guide to Japanese Religions* describes the nature of Japanese religiosity as being basically eclectic.[8] "Eclectic" may have a slightly negative tone because the described phenomenon appears as an unordered and somewhat untidy collection of elements forming a whole. In this context we often find the statement: "Born as a Shintoist, married as a Christian, died as a Buddhist."[9] The basis for this statement is the urge to explain the surprise—for students and scholars socialized in societies where religious institutions encourage complete commitment—that the perception of the Japanese is that they are continuously "changing" their religion during their lifetime. It seems from that statement that Japanese "convert from faith to faith." However, the statement is intended to indicate that Japanese can have multiple "faiths" at the same time. It explains the incredible fact that the numbers provided by religious corporations about their members add up to a figure exceeding the actual number of people in Japan. If a local Buddhist temple counts the families that have grave sites and celebrate memorial rites, and a Shintō shrine from the same village adds up all inhabitants of the village as parishioners because they constitute the local community that ought to attend shrine rituals, then you already have people counted twice. Also, religious groups tend to count people parochially, so they may include a member's family in their total.

"Born as a Shintoist" indicates the tradition of presenting new-born babies to the gods (*kami*) at a Shintō shrine. It also hints at the idea of all ethnic Japanese belonging to Shintō as a national faith (which is an idea greatly propagated by the umbrella organization of Shintō shrines, the

6. For example, Ian Reader, *Making Pilgrimages: Meaning and Practice in Shikoku* (Honolulu: University of Hawai'i Press, 2006).

7. Ian Reader and George J. Tanabe, *Practically Religious: Worldly Benefits and the Common Religion of Japan* (Honolulu: University of Hawai'i Press, 1998), 27.

8. Kisala, "Japanese Religions," 3.

9. Ibid. See also Ian Reader, *Religion in Contemporary Japan* (London: Macmillan, 1991), 7, 51.

Jinja honchō). "Married Christian" points to the popular "white weddings" styled after Christian ceremonies from Europe or America. The bridal business is huge in Japan, and purpose-built wedding chapels are often reminiscent of Christian church buildings. The last part, "died as a Buddhist," is associated with the image of Japanese Buddhism as "funerary Buddhism." Priests make a large portion of their living from the administration of death and memorial rites. If the deceased happens to be a lay person, the death rites are actually ordination rites whereupon the deceased receives a Buddhist spiritual name (called *kaimyō* or *hōmyō*). This posthumous ordination name can only be given by a Buddhist priest, and one often hears complaints on the side of the surviving relatives about the high cost of a such a name. The name is inscribed on an ancestor tablet (*ihai*) that is later stored on the Buddhist family altar.

Whereas the statement "born as a Shintoist, married as a Christian, died as a Buddhist" is not entirely wrong, it leaves out important points that may show Japanese religions in a more balanced way. I find the statement misleading because it seems to suggest that Japanese are somewhat opportunistic. They seem to switch religion on and off according to what is happening in their lives. When it is quoted as the main characteristic of Japanese religiosity, readers socialized within strict boundaries of one faith can think the Japanese to be disloyal, which gives a negative impression. In fact, the underlying pattern is a strong tendency for doing the right thing at the right time, and to do it according to one's best ability and with complete sincerity. The main loyalty is towards the family, which includes deceased relatives. This pattern derives from social structures of obligations diffused with Confucian ethics. The moral code of filial piety, for instance, is suffused within accepted social norms and is not institutionally framed in Japan.

As mentioned above, growing up in Japan generally means participating in different religious fields: as a child of a particular locality he or she is presented to the gods of the *local* shrine to obtain their attention and receive blessings. Often parents consult a Shintō priest about an auspicious name, who in turn consults a name almanac. The system of meanings of the characters in a name, in combination with the stroke count of the characters, is exceedingly complex and is an expert's endeavor. There are subsequent shrine visits according to the child's age, thus ensuring a smooth transition from age to age (in adulthood certain "danger years" require special ritual attention). Major shrines, including the powerful Meiji shrine in Tokyo, are also deeply involved in the wedding business, so that "married as a Christian" is a misnomer. Generally, a bride will first don a Shintō wedding gown, then change into a Western-style white dress, and possibly change one or even two more times during the day, according to the level of income and social standing. Many bridal agencies hire hotels or offer weddings at secular "chapels" that normally have no affiliation to a Christian church. Often, however, a Christian priest is hired to perform the main ceremony (although neither bride nor groom is baptized). Members of Buddhist clerical families or those who feel especially close to a Buddhist denomination marry in a Buddhist temple and receive their blessings there, so there are purely Buddhist wedding ceremonies. And not all Japanese die Buddhist: members of clerical Shintoist families mourn their dead in the Shintō style. The ancestor tablets placed in home shrine are called *reiji* in the Shintō world, which means "spirit seal".

To "die as a Buddhist" relates to so-called "funerary Buddhism" that definitely has a negative connotation and in Japanese is described as "dark and depressing" (*kurai*). Commonly, the reason given why Buddhist clerics make so much of their living by conducting rituals for the deceased is that when Buddhism entered Japan in the sixth century CE, it was put to the task of caring for the dead because the indigenous religionists at that time (who only in the fifteenth century called their practice Shintō) abhorred anything to do with death, which was thought to have highly polluting (*kegare*) properties, as do blood and animal remains. So a convenient division of labor, according to this model of explanation, ensued. It was convenient for the Buddhists because it gave them a continuous source of income and a *raison d'être*, and convenient for the Shintoists because they could concentrate more on ritual purity. This interpretation of Japanese religious history is a result of religio-political developments in the time after the Meiji Restoration (1868). A "clarification" and later a "separation" of two—to a large extent intricately linked—traditions was oftentimes violently pursued for decades starting at the end of the nineteenth century. The "restoration" relates to the political power of the Tennō that the Meiji oligarchs intended to "restore." In fact, the Tennō had been primarily a spiritual symbol and a figure of legitimization for political authorities (military leaders) for over a thousand years. *Tennō*, usually rendered in English as "emperor," literally means the "heavenly ruler," Strands of "Shintō " were also reformed and served the ultranationalists as their spiritual backdrop. This newly created state religion centered on the worship of the Tennō and the sun goddess Amaterasu ōmikami. Whereas the postwar constitution effectively prevents a resurgence of a Shintō state religion, the Association of Shinto Shrines (Jinja honchō) can certainly be seen as rather conservative. Religious corporations such as the Yasukuni Shrine in Tokyo, while not belonging to the Jinja honchō at all, include ultra-national aspects in their self-representation.

Figure 10.3: *Two sisters with their mother at a hall keeping the ashes of their deceased brother. They offer water in his personal tea cup and incense in front of the hall at Chion'in temple in Kyoto. (Photo by Katja Triplett.)*

Only recently has the extent of the combination of gods (*kami* or *shin*) and buddhas (*butsu*), retrospectively termed *shinbutsu shūgō*, especially in medieval Japan, been brought to light with research both in Japan and in the West. The forced separation of Shintō and Buddhism in the Meiji period (1868-1912) led to an organizational restructuring of sacred sites that included both shrines and temples, such as Itsukushima jinja on the island Miyajima with its famous vermillion *torii* gate placed in the bay to greet the gods. In recent years, this compulsory separation has become loosely reversed in some places, and there are ongoing discussions about territory and possession of religious artifacts, pilgrimage routes, sacred mountain-tops, and other matters among the religious institutions and local politicians. Sacred sites and culturally important objects are officially recognized as "cultural assets" because they attract large numbers of visitors who generate income even for quite rural places (some of the most popular pilgrimage destinations are in fairly inaccessible places

Figure 10.1: *A view of the Kagura hall of Izumo Grand Shrine with its spectacular rice straw rope marking the boundary of daily life and the realm of the Shintō deities* (kami). *(Photo by Katja Triplett, 2004.)*

even today). Visitors often do not care too much about the religious affiliation of the sites. They may consult one of the numerous guidebooks to help them find the right sub-temple or sub-shrine for a particular blessing or this-worldly benefit. In the Buddhist context these are called *genze riyaku*; in the Shintō world they are termed "divine virtues" or *shintoku*.[10] The aim of the pilgrim's visit is to conduct ritual transactions at the site to ensure a positive turn in one's life or those of loved ones, and in some cases for the entire nation or for the benefit of all living beings.

Obtaining this-worldly benefits is certainly a recurring theme in most Japanese religions but not all, and it is also not the only recurring theme. For example, Jōdoshinshū, the largest Buddhist organization in Japan, discourages its members from worrying about this-worldly benefits and rather concentrates on the teachings of the founder Shinran. It can be seen as one end of a spectrum. Shin Buddhist temples do not sell amulets and votive tablets. Jōdoshinshū is more inclined towards providing these services, as are most definitely the Zen Buddhist denominations. At the other end of the spectrum are the Esoteric Buddhist Shingon and Tendai

10. Reader and Tanabe, *Practically Religious*; Michael Pye and Katja Triplett, *Streben nach Glück: Schicksalsdeutung und Lebensgestaltung in japanischen Religionen* (Berlin: Lit, 2007).

schools with their very welcoming attitude to any conceivable kind of devotional object and ritual service. Shintō shrines in general sell Shintō-style devotional objects used for ritual transactions near the entrance of the shrine compound. The religionist enters the site and first of all finds out about his present life situation by drawing an oracle lot, which helps them to find out what can be done about possible obstacles. After the divination, the visitor then takes action to ensure that everything that can be done is done. This part is connected to his or her life management. There are convenient terms in Japanese for this dialectic movement: *unmei* ("one's destiny") and *kaiun* ("to open up destiny", usually translated as "good fortune"). Much of common Japanese religiosity hinges on this mechanism.[11]

A Visit to a Grand Shrine

One of the most frequently uttered wishes at religious sites could be to find a suitable partner, someone to "tie the knot with." In Japanese the term *enmusubi* is used, which means literally being tied to someone's karma. The idea is to meet someone with whom one has a special connection; the time and outer circumstances (*en*) result in a bond (*musubi*).

Ameno-san is a librarian with a decent job. She is twenty-nine years old and unmarried. Although she loves her work and is popular with her colleagues, the pressure to get married is mounting. Her boss, a well-meaning man, offered to assist her as a matchmaker. Ameno-san appreciates his offer. Her family wouldn't have to pay an agency, and to have an elder look for a suitable wife or husband is a normal social practice. Her family stopped asking her to become more active in looking for a spouse ever since her younger sister married and had their first grandchild. Ameno-san has not decided whether to seriously pursue the search and ask her boss. Her first step is to pay a visit to Izumo Ōyashiro Shrine in the distant Shimane Prefecture. The shrine is a Grand Shrine (ōyashiro or taisha), one of the oldest and holiest places in Japan and famous for granting worshippers a successful enmusubi.

The impressive shrine buildings are nestled into soft but steep forested hills, a short distance from the ocean. Ameno-san needs an entire day to reach Izumo from Kyoto. She enjoys the ride on the local trains and knows when she has entered sacred territory. This feels indeed like the place where all the myriads of gods gather once a year. She approaches the path leading to the main buildings, walking through the first *torii* gate

---

11. Pye and Triplett, *Streben nach Glück, 15.*

at the entrance to the park surrounding the buildings. Looking behind her, she admires the gigantic torii in the valley that marks the shrine visibly and therefore the presence of the kami for miles around. There are many modern bronze statues in the park playing on scenes in the ancient Japanese myths. Ameno-san recognizes them immediately but still reads the plaques explaining the statues. Soon she approaches the Oracle Hall with its famous shimenawa rice straw rope that weighs many tons. She joins other visitors and tries to throw a coin up into the rope. If it sticks in the straw it means good luck. Ameno-san then takes out her camera and has a fellow pilgrim take a memorial shot. Behind the Oracle Hall, in which she can see shrine maidens dancing in a ceremony, the main gate to the inner sanctuary can be seen. A group of Buddhists belonging to a Nichiren temple—Ameno-san can read their affiliation on the sashes they wear—are just about to leave from in front of the inner gate. After their prayer (go-kitō) is finished, she goes up to the fence behind which the god Okuninushi-no-kami has his shrine (among other gods) and bows and claps her hands following the ritual movements typical for the Shintō world.

Then Ameno-san walks over to the stall offering amulets, talismans, but also postcards, etc. and buys the most expensive votive tablet to put up for her enmusubi wish (she is a bit shocked at the price but after all this is Izumo Grand Shrine). The oracle written on a paper slip that she has drawn by lot says "to stay true to her course of action" and that her luck would not be too bad. Ameno-san ties the slip to the branch of the massive dark tree next to the inner sanctuary. The branches look like they are covered in snow when seen from afar, such is the number of paper slips. Also the large wooden trellises erected for this purpose are nearly covered. Ameno-san takes a few more pictures and returns to her hotel with a sense of accomplishment.

A pamphlet informs the visitor to Izumo Grand Shrine that the present chief priest from the house of Senge is the 84th in his line. Not only is this a very long lineage but it is claimed that the Senge are descendants of the second son of the Sun Goddess, Amenohohi-no-mikoto, who assisted Okuninushi-no-kami when the shrine was founded. The male heads of the Senge carry the title "Kokuso" or "Governor." As in Japanese Buddhism, the offices in the world of Shintō shrines are gendered. Men generally lead the ceremonies and women offer sacred dances (o-kagura) as shrine maidens (o-miko).

Izumo Grand Shrine is its own religious corporation and does not belong to the Jinja honchō, which is dedicated to the (somewhat competing) Ise Shrine and imperial lineage. One could even say that Izumo

Shrine has its own separate religion called Izumo Ōyashirokyō. The faithful English translation of the pamphlet (in a copy available from March 2004) says:

> It was in 1873 that Izumo Oyashiro-kyo Religion Order was organized by Takatomi Senge, the chief priest of Izumo Oyashiro and the 80th governor of the Izumo Province at that time. The doctrine is as follows; the human beings are wholly in the matchmaking power of Okuninushi-no-kami, in other words, his love. Their giving glory to him and making efforts to touch his love will lead them [to] a bright and happy life. The doctrine of this religion has been inherited by the lineage of Kokuso.

It is interesting to note that the translators used "religion"—for Japanese, *kyō*—which literally means "teaching(s)." Many religious organizations attach *kyō* to the name of their founder or another name to make a compound such as "the teachings of Buddha," *bukkyō*, which is usually translated as "Buddhism." Another possibility is to understand *kyō* as doctrine. To describe "religions" and "religion" systematically, Japanese use the term *shūkyō*. The *shū* is the same *shū* as in Jōdoshū and means denomination, school, or sect. *Shūkyō*, therefore, means the teachings or doctrinal content of a particular tradition that transmits and follows the teachings. To emphasize the ritual and cultic side within the framework of "religion," the term *shinkō* 信仰 is used, which literally means "trusting in (divine) assistance," and is usually translated as "faith" or "belief," as in *Kannon shinkō*, which could be rendered as the "trust in the helping power of Kannon."[12] Shintō as a generic term means "the way of the gods." Most Japanese feel that "Shintō " is not what they do at shrines; it is often felt to be an abstract and political term. In general, to visit a shrine or a temple is called "to humbly approach," *o-mairi* in Japanese.

Cosmological Aspects

Death and dying are linked with Japanese Buddhist practice as stated above. Still, the cosmologies informing the rituals are of a highly combined nature. Images of the beyond have been extremely productive culturally throughout Japanese history. As with other ideas and technologies, a look to China and Korea confirms that Japanese cosmological imagery is also informed by continental Asian culture and religion. It is tempting to search for elements associated with a major religious tradi-

---

12. Pye and Triplett, *Streben nach Glück*, 208. See also Chapter 16, "Buddhists," in this volume.

tion such as Daoism, Confucianism, Shintō, and Buddhism. In a popular ghost story one may easily point out motives from Chinese Daoist hell imagery, from an early story of a disciple of the historical Buddha who traveled through hellish regions in search of his mother, or from ancient Shintō mythology.

The fear of restless souls that wreak havoc among the living is a popular story motif around the world. The idea in Japan is that a person who died emotionally unstable is still too attached to this life to be reborn. They can and ought to be pacified by certain rituals. Those who cannot enjoy memorial rites because they died without relatives to conduct the rites may haunt the living. These kind of ghosts are called *muenbotoke*. The dead who do *not* have any connections or *en, mu-en*, are doomed, unless someone who performs rites for the dead includes them. The *botoke* part in *muenbotoke* is interesting in that it is the word for the Sanskrit term *bodhisattva*, the being that is to become a Buddha and vowed to assist all beings. When departing from this life, the wish of most Japanese Buddhists is to be not just reborn but to reach the Pure Land of Amida Buddha. In this Pure Land, imagined as a land of utmost bliss, fortunate beings enjoy ideal conditions to obtain Buddhahood. In common language, therefore, the dead are sometimes called Buddhas or Bodhisattvas.

Other Buddhist traditions in Japan emphasize practices that aim at obtaining Buddhahood or enlightenment here and now, while yet others claim that women have to be first born as men to become Buddha. Still, the majority of Buddhists make sure through rituals that the deceased can reach this goal. Especially important are the memorial rites performed every day for forty-nine days after death, then one year later and again in set intervals according to the respective tradition until the hundredth year is reached. After one hundred years the individuality of the deceased is thought to dissolve. Charts provided by temples help people remember to engage the priest on memorial days for one's relatives. The Buddhist house altar that contains the ancestor tablets also holds a small notebook for the purpose of registering the names and some bibliographical details of the ancestors who can be remembered and informed of what is happening in the family every day, not only on memorial days.

Here is another underlying theme: that the living can communicate with their ancestors. Not only that, but the living have the obligation to ensure the well-being of the dead relatives in the beyond. In Japanese Buddhism (in the majority of traditions) it is of great importance to perform what are conceived to be virtuous acts in the caring for ancestral spirits. Ideally this should not been done with an opportunistic motivation, but a well-cared-for ancestor will return the favors, so the living will benefit in the end. This exchange is referred to as the transfer of merit (*ekō* in Japanese). There is also the idea that a lack of care might result in illness.

Massively successful lay movements such as Reiyūkai (established in 1920) formed because their founders wanted to change the monopoly system by which only male Buddhist priests conducted these crucial rituals. The lay movements preach that everyone can or must care for one's ancestors. Other new religions were founded around the care of deceased children (including aborted fetuses), who are especially pitied because they did not have enough time to do the necessary virtuous actions that ensure a good rebirth, so they need extra protection in the netherworld.

Once a year all ancestors are invited for a celebration during the summer festival of *o-bon*. They are hosted for a few days, entertained with public community dances, and finally sent off again. O-bon has a Buddhist connotation, and there are again temple activities during that time; however, this festival is nearly as widely celebrated as New Year.

From the viewpoint of pious Japanese religionists, society is, to sum up, not only made up of the living but also of ancestors of different kinds. In the Buddhist context, deities (heavenly gods) and the various kinds of non-human beings living in the realms of rebirth (most traditions know six or ten realms) are all subject to suffering and ultimately strive for enlightenment. The Shintō gods, the *kami*, also fall under the Buddhist law, or dharma. For Buddhists, *kami* are thought of as Buddhas and Bodhisattvas in disguise. They manifested on Japanese soil to help the suffering and lead them to enlightenment. Shintoists naturally are not in favor of this system of assimilation. They tend to say that the *kami* pose as Buddhas to assist the Japanese, or that they are separate entities. This is a typical disagreement between theologically oriented Buddhists and Shintoists. Lay visitors are not too concerned with this issue. When they visit sacred sites they may not even know the name of the deities worshipped or enshrined there. This is most likely true in the case of Shintō deities who tend to have lengthy names consisting of characters with ancient readings that are hard to remember. The important thing to know is what kind of divine virtues (*shintoku*) the *kami* contacted at shrines have.

Religions Side-by-Side

Religions compete not only in the area of ancestor care but also in connection with questions addressing issues such as family crises, illness and how to manage life in general. To this end, new religions offer consultation and healing rituals. The present religious landscape in regard to new religions in Japan is far too varied and changeable to present an overview here. Still, it can be observed that newly formed religions often have teachings that seem to be variations on a theme of a shared field of religiosity. Some groups decide to offer their teachings and practices and regard their religious services as a certain way of life that may match someone's life situation and personality. Other groups have a more universalistic approach, either regarding their religion as the ultimate faith surpassing all others or as simply including all other faiths. A third type, the most critical towards the more loosely defined religiosity of most Japanese, claims to have the only true faith and that all others are wrong.

In this competitive climate, it is interesting to note that the more established religions react conservatively. Do they feel the urge to engage in a match of who has the better answers to life's problems? Japan is one of the world's most industrialized countries, and as technologically advanced as the nation is, the tendency to perform rituals and celebrate religious festivals has in no way fallen prey to "secularization." Japanese religionists effectively ritualize *concern and care*. Many Japanese ritualize the *resolve to do one's best*. Some put in great effort to visit a religious site commensurate with the importance of the matter at hand.

Religions in Japan, be they "Buddhist, Shintō , Christian, or Other," are in a constant movement of adaptation, invention, and reform, not only within the borders of the archipelago. Japanese religious groups, who are often enormously wealthy, are active proselytizing in Asian and non-Asian countries alike, mainly among ethnic Japanese immigrants. Buddhist denominations, for instance, serve parishioners in Brazil and other countries with a larger number of Japanese emigrants. Introducing Japanese religions in non-Asian countries is a fascinating subject, above all because of the specific problems that religionists encounter in cultures that do not share concern for ancestors and their well-being in the beyond.

Suggestions for Further Reading.

Anderson, Richard W. "Risshō Kōseikai and the Bodhisattva Way: Religious Ideals, Conflict, Gender, and Status." *Japanese Journal of Religious Studies* 21 (1994): 311-337.

Antoni, Klaus. *Shintō und die Konzeption des japanischen Nationalwesens (Kokutai). Der religiöse Traditionalismus in Neuzeit und Moderne Japans.* Leiden: Brill, 1998.

Astley, Trevor. "The Transformation of a Recent Japanese New Religion: Ōkawa Ryūhō and Kōfuku no Kagaku." *Japanese Journal of Religious Studies* 22 (1995): 343-80.

Bocking, B. "Of Priests, Protests and Protestant Buddhists: the Case of Sōka Gakkai International." In *Japanese New Religions in the West,* edited by Jeffrey

Somers and Peter Bernard Clarke, 117-131. Folkstone, Kent: Japan Library, 1994.

Breen, John. ed. *Yasukuni, the War Dead and the Struggle for Japan's Past.* New York: Columbia University Press, 2008.

Breen, John and Mark Teeuwen, eds. *Shintō in History: Ways of the Kami.* Richmond, Surrey: Curzon Press, 2000.

Bremen, Jan van, and D.P. Martinez. *Ceremony and Ritual in Japan: Religious Practices in an Industrialized Society.* London, New York, Routledge, 1995.

Covell, Stephen G. *Japanese Temple Buddhism. Worldliness in a Religion of Renunciation.* Honolulu: University of Hawai'i Press, 2006.

Davis, Winston. *Dojo: Magic and Exorcism in Modern Japan.* Stanford: Stanford University Press, 1980.

———. *Japanese Religion and Society: Paradigms of Structure and Change.* Albany: State University of New York Press, 1992.

———. "The Secularization of Japanese Religion: Measuring the Myth and the Reality." In *Transitions and Transformations in the History of Religions,* edited by T.M. Ludwig and F.E. Reynolds, 261-85. Leiden: E.J. Brill, 1980.

Dessì, Ugo. *Ethics and Society in Contemporary Shin Buddhism.* Berlin: Lit, 2007.

Earhart, H. Byron. *Japanese Religion: Unity and Diversity.* Belmont, California: Dickenson, 1969.

———. *Religions of Japan: Many Traditions Within One Sacred Way.* San Francisco: Harper & Row, 1984.

———. "Japanese Buddhism and New Religions: Buddhism as Power." In *Japanese Buddhism: Its Tradition, New Religions, and Interaction with Christianity,* edited by A. Miruara, 64-68. Tokyo and Los Angeles: Buddhist Books International: 1987.

Ellwood, Robert S. *Tenrikyō: A Pilgrimage Faith: The Structure and Meanings of a Modern Japanese Religion.* Tenri Oyasato Research Institute: Tenri University, 1982.

———. *Introduction to Japanese Religion.* New York: Routledge, 2007.

Fitzgerald, Timothy. "Japanese Religion as Ritual Order." *Religion* 23, no. 4 (1993): 315-341.

Grapard, Allan G. "Japan's Ignored Cultural Revolution: The Separation of Shinto and Buddhist Divinities in Meiji ("Shimbutsu Bunri") and a Case Study: Tonomine." *History of Religions* 23 no. 3 (1984): 240-265.

Hardacre, Helen. 1986. *Kurozumikyō and the New Religions of Japan.* Princeton: Princeton University Press, 1986.

———. *Lay Buddhism in Contemporary Japan: Reiyōkai Kyōdan.* Princeton: Princeton University Press, 1984.

———. "The *Lotos Sutra* in Modern Japan." In *The Lotus Sutra in Japanese Culture,* edited by George J. Tanabe and Willa Jane Tanabe, 209-24. Honolulu: University of Hawaii Press, 1989.

———. *Marketing the Menacing Fetus in Japan.* Berkeley: University of California Press, 1997.

Heine, Steven. *Zen Classics: Formative Texts in the History of Zen Buddhism*. New York: Oxford University Press, 2006.

Heisig, James W. and John C. Maraldo, eds. *Rude Awakenings: Zen, the Kyōto School, and the Question of Nationalism*. Honolulu: University of Hawai'i Press, 1994.

Higashibaba, Ikuo. *Christianity In Early Modern Japan: Kirishitan Belief and Practice*. Leiden: Brill, 2001.

Inoue, Nobutaka, and Mark Teeuwen. *Shinto: A Short History*, London: Routledge Curzon: 2003.

Kasahara, Kazuo. *A History of Japanese Religion*. Tokyo: Kosei, 2002.

Kisala, Robert. "Reactions to Aum: The Revision of the Religious Corporations Law." *Japanese Journal of Religious Studies* 22, no. 1(1997): 60-74.

Koepping, Klaus-Peter. "Manipulated Identities: Syncretism and Uniqueness of Tradition in Modern Japanese Discourse." In *Syncretism/Anti-syncretism: The Politics of Religious Synthesis*, edited by Charles Stewart & Rosalind Shaw, 161-77. London: Routledge, 1994.

Kornicki, Peter Francis and Ian James McMullen, eds. *Religion in Japan: Arrows to Heaven and Earth*. Cambridge: Cambridge University Press, 1996.

LaFleur, William R. *Liquid Life: Abortion and Buddhism in Japan*. Princeton, NJ: Princeton University Press, 1992.

Littleton, Scott C. *Understanding Shintō: Origins-Beliefs-Practices-Festivals-Spirits-Sacred Places*. London: Duncan Baird Publishers, 2002.

Ministry of Education, Culture, Sports, Science and Technology (MEXT), ed. *Shūkyō nenkan*. Tokyo: Gyōsei, 2006.

Mullins, Mark R. *Christianity Made in Japan: A Study of Indigenous Movements*. Honolulu: University of Hawai'i Press, 1998.

Mullins, Mark R., Shimazono, Susumu, and Paul L. Swanson, eds. *Religion and Society in Modern Japan: Selected Readings*. Berkeley, California: Asian Humanities Press, 1993.

Nagai, Mikiko. "Magic and Self-Cultivation in a New Religion: The Case of Shinnyoen." *Japanese Journal of Religious Studies* 22 (1995): 301-320.

Nelson, John K. *A Year in the Life of a Shinto Shrine*. Seattle: University of Washington Press, 1996.

———. *Enduring Identities: The Guise of Shinto in Contemporary Japan*. Honolulu: University of Hawai'i Press, 2000.

Offner, Clark B. and Henricus van Straelen. *Modern Japanese Religions: With Special Emphasis upon their Doctrines of Healing*. Leiden: Brill, 1963.

Pye, Michael . *Rationality, Ritual and Life-Shaping Decisions in Modern Japan*. Occasional Papers of the Marburg Centre for Japanese Studies vol. 31, Marburg: Centre for Japanese Studies, 2003.

———. "Shintō and the typology of religion." *Method and Theory in the Study of Religion* 1, no. 2 (1989): 186-195.

———. "This-worldly Benefits in Shin Buddhism." In *Gilgul: Essays on Transformation, Revolution and Permanence in the History of Religions; Dedicated to R. J. Zwi*

Werblowsky, edited by D. Shulman, S. Shaked, and G. G. Stoumsa, 191-202. Leiden: Brill 1987.

Reader, Ian, Esben Andreasen, and Finn Stefánsson. *Japanese Religions: Past and Present*. London: RoutledgeCurzon, 2002 [1993].

Shimazono, Susumu. "The Development of Millennialistic Thought in Japan's New Religions: From Tenrikyō to Honmichi." In *New Religious Movements and Rapid Social Change*, edited by by J.A. Beckford. London: Sage Publications, 1986.

———. 2004. *From Salvation to Spirituality. Popular Religious Movements in Modern Japan*. Melbourne: Trans Pacific Press, 2004.

Smith, Robert John. *Ancestor Worship in Contemporary Japan*. Palo Alto: Stanford University Press, 1974.

Suzuki, Kentarō. "Divination in Contemporary Japan. A General Overview and an Analysis of Survey Results." *Japanese Journal of Religious Studies* 22 (1995): 249-266.

Tamaru, Noriyoshi and David Reid. eds. *Religion in Japanese Culture: Where Living Traditions Meet a Changing World*. Tokyo: Kodansha International, 1996.

Tanabe, George J. *Religions of Japan in Practice*. Princeton: Princeton University Press, 1999.

Teeuwen, Mark. "From Jindō to Shintō : A Concept Takes Shape." *Japanese Journal of Religious Studies* 29 (2002): 233-63.

Traphagan, John W. *The Practice of Concern: Ritual, Well-being, and Aging in Rural Japan*. Durham, N.C.: Carolina Academic Press, 2004.

Yamasaki, Taikō. *Shingon: Japanese Esoteric Buddhism*. Boston: Shambhala, 1988.

11

Jains

Jeffery D. Long

One evening in April 2006, my wife and I drove to the Hindu temple in New Cumberland, Pennsylvania, just outside the state capitol of Harrisburg. We have been members of this particular temple, the Hindu American Religious Institute, since moving from Chicago to Elizabethtown, Pennsylvania, a few years ago. Through the temple we have met friends and have become connected to a surprisingly large Indian community, hailing not only from Harrisburg, but also from other nearby towns with names like Camp Hill, York, Lancaster, Mechanicsburg, and of course, Elizabethtown.

At least among Indians in the United States, there does not seem to be a hard and fast division between Hindus and Jains. I noticed the first time that I went into the temple in New Cumberland, in a niche in the wall—in a place of honor no less than that bestowed on mainstream Hindu deities like Shiva, Krishna, and Durga—a *mūrti*, or image, of Mahāvīra, twenty-fourth *Tīrthankara* of our cosmic era and putative founder of the Jain tradition, at least as it is known today. The particular event that we were attending that evening was the first in a week-long series of talks held in celebration of Mahāvīra Jayantī, possibly the holiest day in the Jain calendar, which commemorates Mahāvīra's birth.

The talk was preceded by a short ritual. First, at seven p.m., the *āratī* was held. At our temple, *āratī* is conducted daily at noon and again at seven in the evening. *āratī* is a ritual performed by both Hindus and Jains before the *mūrti* of a deity. At our temple, the central deity is Rāma, flanked on his left by his wife, Sītā, and on his right by his brother, Lakshmana. The *āratī* involves rotating a plate of five candles in front of the image of the deity and singing a song. Some people rotate the plate of candles clockwise an odd number of times, while others trace the Sanskrit character ॐ, "Om," in the air before passing the plate for the next person to offer their devotions.

Figure 11.1: *The Fourteen Dreams of Queen Trisala, from the Kalpasutra, 1475 (gouache on paper) by Indian School, 15th century. (National Museum of India, New Delhi, India: Lauros/Giraudon/The Bridgeman Art Library.)*

I noted that the Jains who had gathered for the event all participated in the *āratī*—singing and clapping their hands and offering the flames with as much evident fervor as the Hindus who were present. There appeared to be no conflict between being a devout Jain and offering the *āratī* to Rāma. Similarly, I recognized many of those who had come as Hindus, who had no problem with coming to celebrate a Jain holy day and listening to a spiritual lecture by a Jain *muni* (monk).

I was able to distinguish the Hindus from the Jains at this event only because I knew them personally. There were no distinctive sectarian marks or modes of dress that set the two communities apart from one another. Most of the participants were Gujarati, hailing from the western coastal state of India from which Mahatma Gandhi hailed. Most of the women wore traditional Indian dress. Some of the men wore the traditional Indian long shirt called a *kurta*, while others wore casual Western business attire: button-down shirts and slacks.

After the usual *āratī*, the community moved from the center of the temple to the adjacent wall niche where the image of Mahāvīra resides. In front of the image, a set of fourteen silver items had been assembled, which I recognized as the fourteen auspicious objects seen by Mahāvīra's mother, Queen Trisala, in a series of dreams that she had prior to his birth.

There another *āratī* was performed, dedicated to the Jina, the spiritual conqueror, Mahāvīra. I also noted that Jains greeted one another with the expression *Jai Jinendra*, "Victory to the Lord of the Jinas!" They also recited the universal Jain prayer:

Namo arihantānam
Namo siddhānam
Namo āyariyānam

Namo uvajjhāyānam
Namo loe savvasāhunam
Eso pañca namokkāro savvapāvappanāsano

This prayer, in the ancient Prākrit language of the Jain scriptures, is translated as:

I bow before the worthy ones [the Jinas, or *Tīrthankaras*].
I bow before the perfected ones [all who have attained *moksha*].
I bow before the leaders of the Jain order.
I bow before the teachers of the Jain order.
I bow before all Jain monks in the world.

After the *āratī* to Mahāvīra, the community assembled in front of a small stage where the guest speaker, a Jain monk, sat and delivered a lecture in Hindi. It consisted of highly practical advice on how to avoid unnecessary stress. Because of the traditional restrictions on travel for Jain monks, a new order of Jain monks has recently come into being, with fewer restrictions, thus making it possible for the now global Jain community to receive spiritual guidance and instruction. The monk we heard was a member of this order.

Who are the Jains?

There are today approximately 4.2 million Jains in the world.[1] Though there are Jain communities in the United Kingdom, North America, and elsewhere, most Jains live in India, as they have for millennia, as a small but highly influential minority.

A common stereotype of Jains is that they are all highly affluent merchants. Although many Jains are successful businessmen, there are also Jains who practice other professions, such as farming, and whose level of material wealth is relatively modest. Then there are Jain *munis* and *sādhvīs*, or monks and nuns, who have practically no material possessions to speak of, who live a life of deliberate simplicity and nonviolence. Indeed, the strict commitment to *ahimsā*, or nonviolence, which Jain monks and nuns embody is the source of another stereotype of Jains as a whole: that Jains wear a face-mask to avoid accidentally ingesting insects or that they carefully sweep the ground free of insects to avoid treading upon them as they walk. Only monks and nuns practice *ahimsā* to such a degree, and only two sects wear the *muhpattī* (face mask) at all times.

Jain identity, like all identities, is crisscrossed with a variety of affilia-

---

1. Adherents.com, http://www.adherents.com.

tions, such as class and profession—just mentioned above—caste, gender, and sectarian affiliation. Though Jainism, like Buddhism, arose partly in reaction to the caste system of Hinduism, Jains, like many other minority communities in India, are organized into castes—that is, endogamous, hereditary communities that practice a particular occupation.

Finally, Jains are also divided among sub-sects. The two most ancient ones, the Digambaras and the Śvetāmbaras, differ mainly on whether a monk should wear clothing and whether a woman can practice asceticism to the same extent as a man. Two more recent Śvetāmbara sub-sects, the Sthānakvāsīs and Terāpanthīs, differ from both the Digambaras and other Śvetāmbaras on *mūrtipūjā*, or the use of images in worship.

Are Jains Hindus?

What is the relationship of Jainism to the vast family of practices and worldviews that is designated by the term *Hinduism*? Are Jains Hindus? Or are Jains sufficiently different from Hindus to be regarded as a separate community?

This question is a divisive one for Jains, some of whom insist passionately that they are *not* Hindus, and some of whom are quite happy to be identified as Hindus, even to the point—particularly outside of India—of using Hindu religious facilities (though this is quite rare within India).

It is also a complex question, hinging ultimately upon how one defines the terms *Hindu* and *Hinduism*. Some define these terms very broadly, to encompass the range of traditions that have emerged historically from the Indian subcontinent. By this definition, not only the Vedic traditions generally understood as making up Hinduism—Vaishnavism, Śaivism, Śāktism, etc.—but also the non-Vedic traditions—such as Jainism, Buddhism, and Sikhism—are part of Hinduism, and their practitioners *Hindu* in this broad sense. But some argue that this is a hegemonic definition, imposing the term *Hindu* upon all Indians.

This is an issue that has become highly politicized in India. Passions can run very high when questions of religious identity are at issue. The wisest strategy, it would seem, would be to set the question of the "Hinduness" of Jains aside, leaving the question of whether Jains are Hindus for Jains to decide, noting only that there are significant overlaps and interconnections, as well as major differences and discontinuities, between the beliefs and practices of Jains and those of the Indic religious communities generally regarded as "Hindu."

Commonalities: What do the Jains Agree Upon?

We have already made some reference to divisions within the Jain community: between those who are affluent merchants and those who are not, between laypersons and ascetics (monks and nuns), between castes, between men and women, between Jain sects, and between those Jains who view themselves as Hindu and those who do not. But what makes a Jain a Jain? Mahatma Gandhi once famously said that there are in fact as many religions as there are people—that everyone, even members of the same tradition, will tend to interpret the beliefs and practices of their tradition differently, or pursue their practices in subtly different ways. But allowing for the inevitability that Jains, like other religious persons, will inevitably disagree amongst themselves on some issues, what can be said by way of generalization about the set of views and practices called *Jainism*?

One question around which Jains unite is that they practice the spiritual path set forth by Mahāvīra. Although they differ amongst themselves with regard to the specifics of what this path entails, all Jain communities orient themselves toward Mahāvīra as embodying the supreme ideals of Jainism.

But is Mahāvīra the *founder* of Jainism? In one sense the answer to this question is straightforward, but in another it is not. Most scholars, if asked to identify the founder of Jainism, would point to Mahāvīra, the "Great Hero," who lived around the fifth century BCE in the northeasterly region of India that was also home to the Buddha. But according to Jain teaching, Mahāvīra was not exactly the founder of Jainism, but the twenty-fourth in a series of *Tīrthankaras*, those who fashion or create a *tīrtha*, a ford or a crossing, over the waters of *samsāra*, the cycle of birth, death, and rebirth. A *Tīrthankara*, in other words, is one who makes it possible for others to attain liberation, or *moksha*, from the cycle of rebirth.

According to Jains, the universe is undergoing a beginningless and endless series of cosmic cycles. During each cycle, or *kalpa*, twenty-four *Tīrthankaras* appear. Mahāvīra is the twenty-fourth *Tīrthankara* of our current cosmic cycle. He was not, therefore, strictly speaking, the founder of Jainism, but its re-discoverer and re-initiator, after the path had declined during the period between his own time and that of the twenty-third *Tīrthankara*, who was named Pārśvanātha.

"Mahāvīra" was not Mahāvīra's given name. Like *Buddha*, "the Awakened One," Mahāvīra is a title of respect. Mahāvīra's given name was Vardhamāna, and his family name was Jñātriputra—rendered in the Prākrit language of the Jain scriptures and the Pāli language of the earliest Buddhist scriptures (in which he is also mentioned) as *Nātaputta*. In the

Buddhist scriptures, Mahāvīra is called *Nigantha Nātaputta*, "Nigantha," meaning "one who is without bonds," who has renounced all impermanent, worldly attachments.

The fact that Mahāvīra and the Jains—under the names *Nātaputta* and Nigantha, respectively—are mentioned prominently in the *Tipitaka*, the early Buddhist scriptures, is significant for historians of religion. Early Buddhist accounts of Mahāvīra and the Jains are sources of information about Jainism independent from the Jain tradition itself, and serve to confirm certain basic understandings Jains have of themselves: that Mahāvīra existed, that he was a contemporary or a near contemporary of the Buddha, and that he established a community of strict ascetics who practiced a rigorous path of detachment and purification of the mind in order to become liberated from the cycle of rebirth.

The mention of Mahāvīra in the Buddhist scriptures is significant in another sense as well. Jainism shares with Buddhism a number of assumptions, practices, and a system of philosophical terminology that is highly suggestive of the common social, cultural, and religious milieu from which both traditions are derived. Both Mahāvīra and the Buddha are supposed to have been born, lived, taught, and died in the north/northeastern part of India now made up of the states of Bihar, Jharkhand, and Uttar Pradesh (as well as, in the case of the Buddha, southern Nepal). Both men were critical of the Vedic traditions—later identified with Hinduism—predominant in northern India at the time. However, both also shared basic terms and assumptions with certain Vedic schools of thought, made positive reference to Vedic deities, and operated from a worldview close to views found in the later Vedic scriptures, the *Upanishads*.

Northern India during the time of Mahāvīra and the Buddha was in the process of undergoing a major social and cultural transformation. The Vedic traditions, centered in the northwestern region of India, were not as deeply rooted in the northeast. Also, Vedic traditions tended to be stronger—and this remains the case even today—in more agricultural and rural areas. But in the northeast, large urban centers were beginning to emerge, along with a prominent merchant class. The Vedic emphasis on caste, understood by the time of Mahāvīra and the Buddha to be a matter of birth, had less appeal for people of the new, urban merchant class than a philosophy based on the idea of improving oneself through one's own effort.

It was therefore in the northeast that a movement emerged that challenged Vedic orthodoxy and the spiritual supremacy of the Brahmans, the priestly caste responsible for upholding the Vedic traditions. Calling themselves *śramanas*, or "strivers," the leaders of this movement promoted spiritual paths emphasizing individual striving, or self-effort, over birth caste. In terms of their social vision, their philosophy is well summarized in the famous sentiment of the Buddha that it is not by one's birth, but by one's deeds that one becomes a Brahman. Individual merit, and not the caste of one's parents, should be the determinant of one's value and role in society.

The *śramana* movement was quite internally diverse, consisting of a great variety of teachers and schools of thought, some of which are delineated in the Jain and Buddhist scriptures. The only two *śramana* groups to survive to the present day are the Jains and the Buddhists. So Jainism and Buddhism are living continuations of the ancient *śramana* philosophy, thus explaining many of their shared characteristics.

The idea that Mahāvīra is not, strictly speaking, the founder of the Jain tradition, but the latest in a series of enlightened beings, is not without foundation external to Jain belief. Mahāvīra's predecessor, the twenty-third *Tīrthankara*, Pārśvanātha, is mentioned not only in the Jain scriptures, but in non-Jain texts as well. He probably lived about two centuries before Mahāvīra. According to the Jain scriptures, Mahāvīra's parents were Jains in the tradition of Pārśvanātha. Pārśvanātha is most often represented as a seated ascetic in yoga position (*āsana*) with a seven-headed cobra rearing up behind him and using its hoods to protect him from the elements as he practices his meditation. There is a similar story of the Buddha having been protected by the Serpent King, again suggesting the common cultural wellspring of Buddhism and Jainism.

Similarly suggestive are the stories of the lives of Mahāvīra and the Buddha, both of whom are depicted in the texts of their respective traditions as the sons of kings—and so as members of the *Kshatriya*, or warrior caste—who chose to renounce their worldly titles, wealth, and power in order to seek spiritual enlightenment.

The *śramana* movement was, above all else, an ascetic movement, based on the ancient Indic ideal of *sannyāsa*, or renunciation of worldly ties—and, as mentioned above, an ancient name for the Jains was *Nigantha*, one who is without worldly ties. The ideal of renunciation is also found in the early *Upanishads*, centuries before Mahāvīra and the Buddha. Again, it is not clear whether *śramanas* like the Jains and the Buddhists were in continuity with this earlier Vedic tradition of renunciation, or whether it was renunciation that came first, as a pre-Vedic institution that influenced the authors of the *Upanishads*.

Whatever its origins, the ascetic ideal is an ancient and powerful one in the Indic religious imagination. An ascetic, in any tradition, is one who gives up specific worldly goods in the name of spirituality. A Roman Catholic who gives up sweets during Lent or a Muslim who fasts during

Ramadan is practicing a form of asceticism. But *sannyāsa*, or renunciation in the Indic sense, is probably the most radical form of asceticism of all. And amongst the Indic renunciant traditions, Jainism stands out as the most radical in its asceticism. This explains the honorific title given to Mahāvīra—"Great Hero." For the asceticism of Mahāvīra was so great as to be regarded as heroic.

The image of the ascetic as spiritual warrior is frequently encountered in Jainism. The very name *Jain* means a follower of the *Jina*, "the Conqueror." This title, *Jina*, also bestowed upon the Buddha in the Buddhist tradition, designates one who has conquered not a physical territory, but the spiritual territory of the self, the ego. Mahāvīra and the Buddha, though born to the caste of warriors in the this-worldly sense, renounced their worldly status in order to become spiritual warriors, conquerors of the realm of the spirit. And asceticism—renunciation—is the primary tool, the spiritual weapon, by which they achieved their conquest—a conquest that consisted of self-mastery rather than mastery of the impermanent material world.

But what is the relationship between renunciation and spiritual realization in the Jain tradition? In order to understand the emphasis this tradition places on asceticism, it is important to understand the basic concepts of Jain cosmology.

In Jainism, as in Hinduism and Buddhism, one encounters a universe without beginning or end. According to this cosmology, we have all been undergoing a process of birth, life, death, and rebirth since time without beginning. The body is not what we really are, but the vehicle of that which is even more fundamental to us—the *jīva*, which corresponds roughly to what Western religious traditions call the soul.

Unlike the body, which is impermanent, the soul has no beginning and no end. In Indic traditions, it is the soul, not the body, with which we ought to be concerned. What will happen to us after the body dies? And where were we—if the soul is what we really are—before this body was born? How is the type of body we inhabit determined?

According to Jainism, a universal law called *karma*, which governs all action, determines the nature of our rebirth. Karma could well be compared to Newton's Third Law of Motion: For every action there is an equal and opposite reaction.

All we do, in other words, produces a corresponding effect upon us. But karma is not only a physical law. It is also a moral law. Every thought, word, and deed carries a degree of what could be called moral force, for good or ill. Just as applying force in the physical world produces an equal force pushing back upon us, similarly, the moral force of our thoughts, words, and actions comes back to us in the form of either pleasant or painful experiences, depending upon the moral character of the force we have exerted. Good deeds produce good effects; evil deeds produce evil effects. We reap what we sow.

Karma, the net effect of all our previous choices, produces the experiences of the present moment, in which we are now making the choices that will produce our future experiences. In effect, we are creating and re-creating the universe at every moment with our choices, including the type of body we inhabit. At the time of death, the karma of the soul will determine what kind of body the soul will inhabit next, including its location, its social circumstances, and so on.

One is therefore, in effect, choosing the nature of one's next rebirth all the time. Good karma, *punya karma*, will lead to a good rebirth. Bad karma, *pāpa karma*, will lead to rebirth in painful circumstances. Of course most of us, having a mix of good and bad karma, are born into circumstances in which we experience pleasure and pain, freedom and limitation, in various measures. All of this depends on our karma, which is changing at every moment, as we make moral choices and engage in action based upon them. It is not only in the afterlife that karma has its effects. These can occur in this life as well.

According to such a worldview, what should one do? Clearly, one should do good deeds so the karmic effects one experiences will be good ones. But the philosophy of renunciation is based on the insight that the highest good does not consist of making an endless effort toward bettering and maintaining one's karmic situation. Is there no rest for the soul? Is there no higher aim to give life purpose and meaning? Given that we are limited beings, will not even the most heroic good deeds produce karmic effects that will eventually wear out? The work of maintaining one's karmic state appears never-ending.

According to most Indic traditions, the highest good is liberation, or *moksha*, from the otherwise endless cycle of acting and experiencing karmic results, a cycle which we experience as the cycle of birth, death, and rebirth, or *samsāra*. But how, if karma is a universal law, is such liberation to be achieved? This is the central question on which the Indic traditions diverge. Each conceives of this basic cosmology in subtly different ways.

The distinctively Jain vision of karma, rebirth, and liberation conceives of the cosmos in a radically dualistic way, as consisting of two wholly different types of entity called *jīva* and *ajīva*—spirit and matter. *jīva*, or spirit, has unlimited knowledge (*jñāna*), bliss (*sukha*), and energy (*vīrya*). There are many *jīvas*—as many as there are living beings in the cosmos—but each is identical in terms of its three essential characteristics.

The differences among living beings are due to *ajīva*, or matter. Specifically, a particular type of *ajīva*, called *karma*, adheres to each *jīva*, producing the various kinds of experience that living beings have. In other words, karma, the universal law of cause and effect in the Indic traditions, is understood in Jainism to be a material substance that produces experiences in our souls according to certain regular patterns.

How does this process work? The *jīva*, in its ideal state, could be compared to a smooth body of water—like a lake on a windless day—clear and untroubled by turbulence or waves. But the *jīvas* of most beings, non-liberated beings, are not in their ideal state. They are like lakes whose waters are filled with waves and whirlpools, which correspond to emotional states called, in Jainism, the passions (*rāgas*). These passions can be seen as deformations on the smooth surface of the soul. These deformations attract particles of karmic matter to the soul, further deforming it. The passions are essentially reactions to experiences, and are of three basic types: attraction, aversion, and neutrality. We either like an experience, wanting more of it; we dislike it and so want to avoid it; or we are indifferent to it. Experiences are the result of karmic particles or "seeds" (*bīja*) coming to fruition. These experiences produce passions, which attract more karmic seeds, which come to fruition, producing more experiences, leading to more passions, and so on.

Put most simply, the goal of Jainism as a spiritual practice is to remove the karmic matter that obscures the true nature of the *jīva* and binds it to the cycle of rebirth in the material world and to prevent the further influx of such matter. Because it is the passions that attract karma to the *jīva*, an essential part of this process is to cultivate a disposition of detachment (*vairāgya*), of calm equanimity in the face of all of our experiences, both pleasant and unpleasant. For this reason, many Jains, like Buddhists and Hindus, practice a form of meditation. The distinctive Jain form of meditation is known as *preksha*, and has become a more prominent part of both lay and monastic Jain practice in recent times. (Acharya Mahapragya, the current leader of the Terapanthī Jain community, is widely credited with the rediscovery and promotion of this form of meditation.)

But while meditation and equanimity can help one avoid accumulating additional karmic matter, there are still karmic particles that need to be removed from the *jīva* if one is to achieve liberation. This is achieved by the undertaking of difficult ascetic activities, such as fasting. Such activities serve a double function in karmic terms. By helping the practitioner to exert a greater control over the passions through self-discipline, they aid in reducing karmic influx. But because such activities are inherently difficult, they in effect substitute for the unpleasant experiences that one's bad karma will inevitably create. One essentially pays one's karmic debt in advance by taking on such difficult practices and so accelerates one's progress toward liberation. In Jain texts, this is often called "cooking" the karmic "seeds" in the fires of asceticism. Just as a seed once cooked cannot sprout, in the same way a karmic seed has its effects negated by the voluntary suffering involved in the practice of asceticism. The seed is essentially brought to premature fruition and so removed from the soul.

The strict asceticism of Jain monks and nuns is closely connected with the ethical ideal of *ahimsā*, which is generally translated as "nonviolence," but which is actually much more radical than the English word "nonviolence" might suggest. It is not simply a matter of refraining from actual, physical harm. *Ahimsā* is the absence of even the desire to do harm to any living being. It is also not, according to contemporary Jains, a negative ideal of simply avoiding harm. *Ahimsā* involves compassion for all living beings. The centrality of *ahimsā* to Jainism is hard to exaggerate, though an exclusive focus on the ascetic *ahimsā* of the Jain monks and nuns can create a one-sided impression of the Jain community.

Why is *ahimsā* so central to Jainism? In terms of the Jain karma theory outlined above, a central Jain insight is that the worst passions, the ones that attract the heaviest, most obscuring karmic particles into the soul, are those involved in committing acts of violence. In order to ensure a good rebirth in which one is more likely to make spiritual progress, and certainly in order to purify the soul and reach liberation, it is essential that one avoid any thought, word, or deed that involves *himsā*, the desire to do harm.

According to a Jain understanding, however, it is very difficult to avoid doing any harm whatsoever to living beings. The universe is filled with microscopic organisms—a fact of which Mahāvīra, interestingly, was sharply aware in the fifth century BCE. Even the act of being physically alive therefore involves destruction of tiny life forms. Eating, digesting food, breathing, sitting, and moving about: all of these activities involve the destruction of organisms on a massive scale.

One could argue that because these activities are generally not carried out with the intention of doing harm, the requisite intent to do harm that attracts destructive karma to the soul—due to the passion with which this intent is normally associated—is absent from such activities, and that they must therefore be without karmic consequence. But this is not a traditional Jain understanding. Once one is aware of the existence of tiny life forms in the air one breathes, in the water one drinks, and on the surfaces on which one travels and rests one's body, one becomes responsible for the harm that one does. This is why the rules surrounding the conduct of Jain monks and nuns are so restrictive if compared to the standards of most religious communities.

Also, unlike Buddhist ethical thought, which typically sees motive as the chief determinant of the morality of an act—of whether it involves a good or a bad karmic result—Jainism teaches that the consequences of action, its actual destructiveness to living beings, are always a major factor.

Jain monks and nuns therefore spend a good deal of their time in the effort to have a minimal negative impact upon their environment. Jain asceticism consists primarily of curbing activities that might lead to the accidental destruction of life and of cultivating mindfulness of the life forms with which one shares the physical universe. A well-known symbol of this ascetic ideal is the *muhpattī*, a cloth that some Jain monks and nuns wear over their mouths to avoid accidentally inhaling or ingesting small organisms. (The *muhpattī* is sometimes worn by Jain laypersons as well, but only on particular ritual occasions directly involving a *mūrti*, or image, of a Jina. The purpose of the *muhpattī* on these occasions is in some ways the opposite of its use by ascetics—namely, to avoid *exhaling* any impurities onto the *mūrti*. Any piece of cloth can be used for this purpose.)

Central though the ascetic ideal of *ahimsā* is to the Jain community and its view of itself, it would be an exaggeration to suggest that all, or even most, Jains are constantly preoccupied with avoiding harm to microorganisms. There is a frank recognition in the Jain community, as in Buddhism, that most people are not yet at the spiritual level where they would wish to renounce life as a layperson and the activities that go with day-to-day existence.

So although the ascetic ideal informs even the life of the Jain layperson, it is not expected that the average Jain should follow the same strictures observed by Jain monks and nuns. Like Buddhism, Jainism involves a twofold morality, a set of rules observed to the letter by monks and nuns, but observed to the extent possible for a layperson. The basic moral principles of Jainism are expressed in five vows. Jain laypeople may take the following five *anuvratas*, or "small vows":

1. Nonviolence (*ahimsā*): to refrain from directly and deliberately taking the life of any animal or human being,
2. Truthfulness (*satya*): to tell the truth and to engage in honest business practices,
3. Non-stealing (*asteya*),
4. Sexual chastity (*brahmacārya*): to refrain from committing marital infidelity and to avoid pre-marital sexual activity,
5. Detachment (*aparigraha*): to avoid being possessive and materialistic.

Not all Jain laypersons actually take these vows formally, but they delineate the basic moral rules that inform all lay Jain practice. Monks and nuns take stricter versions of the same five vows, called, in their case, the five *mahāvratas*, or 'great vows':

1. Strict nonviolence in thought, word, and deed, avoiding even accidental injury to any living being,
2. Absolute truthfulness,
3. Non-stealing (literally 'not taking what is not given'),
4. Absolute celibacy,
5. Detachment to the extent of not owning any possessions whatsoever.

Controversies: On What Issues do Jains Disagree amongst Themselves?

The most divisive controversy in the Jain community regards the observance of the fifth *mahāvrata*—*aparigraha*, or detachment. How detached must a Jain monk or nun be? Is there any possession that a Jain monk or nun may own? Or must true detachment extend even to the clothing of one's body?

As mentioned earlier, the two most ancient sects of Jainism are the Śvetāmbaras and the Digambaras. The source of their disagreement is evidenced by their respective names. *Śvetāmbara* means "white-clad." Monks and nuns of the Śvetāmbara sect wear very simple white robes. In addition to these robes, a Śvetāmbara monk or nun will also typically carry a begging bowl, from which he or she will eat food provided by the Jain lay community, and a small broom for the purpose of gently brushing aside small insects that may be in their pathway.

Digambara, on the other hand, means "sky-clad." Digambara monks do not wear any clothing. They take the injunction of detachment, of not owning possessions, to be an absolute rule. They do not carry a begging bowl but eat only as much food as they can hold in their hands. Some do carry the small broom also used by the Śvetāmbaras for the purpose of protecting small creatures from accidentally being trodden or sat upon, but this is understood to be community property. In any event, the broom exists to protect other beings. But from a Digambara perspective, the wearing of clothing suggests that one is attached to one's own body—that one wishes to protect it, and that one has a sense of shame that implies a lack of spiritual maturity, of awareness that it is the soul and not the body that is of ultimate significance.

What of Digambara nuns? Though Digambara nuns do exist—there are actually more Digambara nuns than there are monks—they do not practice monastic nudity. They are, in fact, barred from doing so, due to fears that a wandering nude woman could be sexually assaulted and might otherwise be an occasion for scandal for the community.

Digambara insistence upon monastic nudity as a prerequisite for the attainment of moksha leads to another disagreement between Digambaras and Śvetāmbaras. According to the Digambaras, only a man may practice monastic nudity. Therefore, only men may attain moksha. A Jain woman must aspire to rebirth as a man in order to reach liberation.

From a Digambara point of view, Śvetāmbara monks and nuns are just very pious laypersons. Śvetāmbara monks are not true monks, from a Digambara perspective, due to their being too attached to their bodies to give up the wearing of clothing. They may be very evolved souls, but they will not attain liberation until they practice monastic nudity.

From a Śvetāmbara point of view, it is the attitude of detachment, rather than the actual practice of nudity, that is of ultimate importance in one's pursuit of liberation from rebirth. Women are as capable as men of attaining moksha. Indeed, Mallinātha, the nineteenth *Tīrthankara*, is believed by Śvetāmbaras to have been a woman—although this is regarded as the result of bad karma, so it is not exactly an endorsement of feminism.

Both the Śvetāmbara and Digambara ascetic communities are supported by and drawn from much larger communities of Jain laypersons, also known as Śvetāmbaras and Digambaras. These names, although they refer technically to the dress of ascetics, are used in practice to refer to both communities in their entirety: the ascetics and the laypersons who support them. A Śvetāmbara Jain or a Digambara Jain is therefore more likely to be a lay supporter of one or the other of these monastic communities than to be an ascetic him or herself, but will nevertheless refer to him or herself as Śvetāmbara or Digambara.

Two more recent Jain communities, both of which emerged from the Śvetāmbara community, are the Sthānakvāsīs and the Terāpanthīs. Though each has its distinctive history and practices, these two Jain groups share a common rejection of the practice of *mūrtipūjāpūjā* or the use of images in worship, and a common concern that the strictures of *ahimsā* be observed to the highest possible degree. Both groups derive their inspiration from Lonkā Śāh, a fifteenth-century figure who sought to reform the Jain practice of his time to bring it more into alignment with his interpretation of the Śvetāmbara scriptures. Although the ascetic use of the *muhpattī*, or protective mouth-shield, mentioned earlier, is referred to in ancient Jain texts and is not limited to the Sthānakvāsīs and the Terāpanthīs, these two groups are distinctive in their practice of wearing it at all times, and not only on certain ritual occasions.

The Sthānakvāsīs and Terāpanthīs emphasize mental worship (*bhāvapūjā*) over physical acts of worship using images (*mūrtis*), and it is the Terāpanthīs who have done the most in recent years to promote meditation, *preksha*, as a Jain practice. Like most Hindus, both Śvetāmbara and Digambara Jains practice *pūjā*—the act of giving worship to a deity through offerings of flowers, fruits, water, milk, a sacred flame, and various other sacred substances to the form (or *mūrti*) of that deity, usually through the medium of a statue. Unlike Hindus, whose worship is typically devoted to forms of divinity such as Vishnu, Śiva, or Śaktī (the Mother Goddess), Jain *pūjā* is devoted to liberated beings, such as Mahāvīra and the other *Tīrthankaras*, as well as to other respected ascetics of the Jain tradition. Some of the most beautiful and ornate temples in India are Jain temples, devoted to the worship of the *Tīrthankaras*.

The building of temples and monasteries, however, has not been uncontroversial in the Jain tradition. In favor of such construction, it has been argued that the spiritual benefits, particularly to laypersons, of visiting temples and worshiping the *Tīrthankaras* far outweigh the destruction of life necessarily involved in construction activities such as digging, carving, and so forth. Many Jains see *mūrtipūjā* as a form of meditation on the ideal of the liberated being.

The Sthānakvāsīs and the Terāpanthīs, however, argue that such rationalization is flawed, revealing an attachment to physical acts that is spiritually counterproductive. If one also takes into account the possibilities for destruction of microscopic life inherent in physical acts of worship, they claim, it is clear that a far more productive form of worship is to visualize and worship the enlightened Jinas mentally and internally rather than using physical means.

Further Controversies: On What Issues to Jains Disagree with Others?

On what issues do Jains tend to disagree with other communities? An ancient controversy between Jains and Buddhists regarded the relative importance of motive and consequence in determining the morality of an act.

As already mentioned, although motive is clearly important to the Jains, the destructive consequences of an action must be taken with great seriousness in evaluating its morality. This of course creates a very high standard of behavior, particularly when one takes into account the need to avoid the destruction of even very small life forms. From a Buddhist perspective, it is the motive that ultimately determines the morality or immorality of an act. This does not mean that consequences are unimportant to Buddhists, just as the Jain emphasis on consequences does not render motive irrelevant. But the different emphases of these two traditions in this regard have had practical consequences, with Buddhists emphasizing a "Middle Path" of moderation with regard to ascetic practice, while the Jains maintain that, at least for the aspirant to liberation, there can be no compromise with the ideal of *ahimsā*.

A point of divergence between Jains and many Hindus regards the existence of a divinity or Supreme Being. Jainism, like Buddhism, is not theistic, claiming the universe has always existed and that the effects of karma are sufficient to explain the regularities observable within the cosmos. Many Hindus, however—not unlike Jews, Christians, and Muslims—maintain that there is a Supreme Being who is creator, preserver, and periodic destroyer and re-creator of the universe, an idea reflected in the famous Hindu image of the *trimūrti*, or "three forms" of God: Brahmā, Vishnu, and Śiva. God is the coordinator of karma, the guarantor that each action will be followed by its inevitable result.

According to Jainism and Buddhism, however (and some forms of Hinduism, it should be noted), it is unnecessary to posit a divine being in order to explain the regular workings of the universe. This was a source of considerable controversy between Jains and Hindus in ancient India.

It is not the case, though, that most Jains—or Buddhists for that matter—are atheists in the full, contemporary sense of this term, which usually implies not only the denial of the existence of a creator and coordinator of the universe, but also the denial of a soul and an afterlife, and possibly of any ultimate meaning to human existence.

Jains believe quite fervently in the existence of what could be called a sacred reality of ultimate importance, and so in what could be called a "God" in a functional sense. This sacred reality is the *jīva*, or soul, in its pure, enlightened state. Some modern Jains even express this idea by referring to the soul as "God within," and referring to enlightened beings that have fully realized the soul in its purity as "God." The Jinas, like Mahāvīra, are, therefore, in this functional sense divine and are worshiped as such.

Another source of controversy between Jains and non-Jains is the practice of self-starvation—known as *sallekhanā* or *santhāra*—occasionally undertaken by Jain monks and nuns as the ultimate act of *ahimsā* and *aparigraha*. This practice—which, Jains emphasize quite strongly, is *not* a form of suicide, for it is not undertaken out of passion, because of despair or anger—can only be undertaken with the permission of one's spiritual preceptor, or *guru*. The guru ensures that one's motives in undertaking this fast to the death are pure, that one is doing it out of a genuine sense of detachment from the body and out of compassion for all the living beings that one will save by not continuing to eat, breathe, and consume resources. Such a holy death is seen as having great capacity to advance the soul on its path to liberation. The practice is of course controversial because it seems to be a religiously sanctioned form of suicide.[2]

The Jain Doctrines of Relativity

One of the most striking Jain contributions to Indian religious thought, and one of considerable relevance to today's world of inter-religious conflict, has been a complex of three doctrines that I call the Jain "doctrines of relativity." The first of these doctrines, anekāntavāda, claims that reality is complex, or anekānta (literally "non-one-sided").

The second doctrine, nayavāda, or the "doctrine of perspectives," is an epistemic claim. That is, given the complex nature of reality, any given thing may be known from a variety of nayas, or perspectives, that correspond to its many aspects.

This implies the third doctrine, syādvāda, or the doctrine of conditional predication (literally, the "maybe doctrine"), according to which the truth of any claim that one makes about a particular topic is dependent upon the perspective, or naya, from which the claim is made. A claim can be true, in one sense or from one perspective (the technical meaning of the Sanskrit verb syāt in a Jain philosophical context), false from another perspective, both true and false from another, have an inexpressible truth-value from yet another, etc.

The gist of these doctrines is expressed in the famous story of the Blind Men and the Elephant, first attributed to the Buddha. Several blind men are brought before a king and asked to describe an elephant. None of the men has ever seen an elephant, but an elephant is brought to them and they proceed to feel it with their hands. One, who grasps the elephant's trunk, claims that an elephant is like a snake. Another, grasping a leg, claims it is like a tree. Yet another grasps the tail and says it is like a rope; and another, feeling the elephant's side, claims it is like a wall. The blind men then proceed to argue amongst themselves about the true nature of the elephant. The moral of the story, of course, is that all of the blind men are partially correct—for an elephant does, indeed, possess all of the qualities that the blind men predicate of it—and partially incorrect, inasmuch as each denies the claims of the others.

Only someone who can see the whole elephant—like a Jina—is in a position to say, unequivocally, what its true nature is. The rest of us, with respect to the true nature of reality, are like the blind men. We can only

2. Narayan Bareth, "Another India Jain fasts to death," BBC News, 2 October 2006, http://news.bbc.co.uk/2/hi/south_asia/5400232.stm

say with certainty what we can apprehend from our limited perspectives—and be open to the equally valid insights of others.

That these Jain doctrines of relativity do *not* constitute a form of what is called, in contemporary Western thought, *relativism*—the view either that there is no truth or that "truth" is solely a matter of convention—is evidenced, again, from this story. There really is an elephant *there*, and it really does have particular characteristics and not others, and it is these characteristics that shape each blind man's perception.

A sighted person—again, for Jains, this would represent an omniscient Jina—is capable of apprehending the true nature of this reality. There is an ultimate truth in terms of which the claims of the blind men can each be evaluated and placed in their proper perspective—one is describing the trunk, one a leg, one the tail, etc.

The origin of the doctrines of relativity indeed seems to have been the claim to omniscience made by Mahāvīra (or on his behalf by his followers) in the earliest Jain scriptures—an omniscience that is an effect of the destruction of the knowledge-obscuring karmas that inhibit the unlimited awareness that is an essential characteristic of the soul. In these texts, Mahāvīra is represented as answering profound metaphysical questions (considered "unanswerable," or *avyākata* in the Buddhist tradition) with both a "yes" and a "no," depending on the perspective of the questioner. The soul is both eternal (in its intrinsic nature), and non-eternal (from the perspective of the karmic changes that it constantly undergoes); the world is both eternal (in the sense that it has no beginning or end), and non-eternal (inasmuch as it passes through cosmic cycles), etc.

Another rationale for these doctrines is to be found in the complex nature of the soul posited by Jainism—a nature extrapolated to apply to all entities. The soul has an unchanging, intrinsic nature; but it also experiences karmically conditioned states that come into being, exist for a while, and then pass away. According to *Tattvārtha Sūtra* 5:29, "Emergence, perishing and endurance characterize [all] entities." In other words, there is a sense in which all things come to be, perish and endure.

In later Jain philosophical texts, this understanding of reality came to be applied to the topic—endlessly debated between the Buddhists and the Brahmans—of the nature of reality as either permanent or impermanent. Contrasting themselves with the Buddhists, who upheld a doctrine of radical impermanence, and the Brahmans, who upheld a doctrine of permanence, the Jains claimed entities were both permanent and impermanent, in different senses and from different perspectives.

The potential use of the doctrines of relativity in resolving disputes between seemingly incompatible philosophical views has led to the view, held by many scholars (and Jains), that these doctrines are an extension of the Jain commitment to *ahimsā*—or nonviolence in thought, word and deed—to the realm of intellectual discourse. Though historically dubious, this characterization of these doctrines renders them attractive as a means for addressing the pressing question of remaining, on the one hand, committed to a set of religious and philosophical claims, while at the same time remaining open to diversity, to learning from the perspectives of others. They provide a way to argue in a logically coherent fashion for *religious pluralism*, the view that there is truth to be found in many traditions, and not only one. The difficulty with religious pluralism has always been reconciling the idea of truth in many traditions with the fact that religions say different things and often at least appear to contradict one another. But if they are simply describing different aspects of the same reality, like the blind men trying to give an account of the elephant, then the idea that they are all true can be defended.

Conclusion

Jains form a distinctive and important sub-community in the larger setting of Indic religious life. Their views on nonviolence have been particularly influential on the larger Hindu community in the midst of which they have traditionally existed. From the practice of vegetarianism to the political deployment of *ahimsā* by Mahatma Gandhi, the influence of Jains on the religious life of India has been profound. And this influence has been despite the relatively small number of people making up the Jain community.

To what can this influence be attributed? It is almost certainly due in part to the tendency of Jains to gravitate toward business professions. The wealth of the Jain community as a whole is considerable, and with wealth comes influence. Jain businessmen have long been and continue to be major players in Indian society. Their activities in the fields of both business and philanthropy have done a great deal to shape not only India's economy, but its cultural values as well.

But the reverence with which Jain monks and nuns are regarded by the various communities in the Indian subcontinent has almost certainly played a role in the extent of Jain influence as well. The difficulty and the rigor of Jain ascetic practices cannot but command respect in a region where asceticism and spirituality are closely linked across a wide variety of traditions. For Hindus as well as for Jains self-discipline and nonviolence are important spiritual ideals, which Jain ascetics embody to a degree that is difficult for many to even fathom, much less emulate.

Finally, Jains have formed a highly articulate community, producing numerous volumes of religious and philosophical writings over the centuries. In debate with both Buddhists and Brahmans, Jain philosophers have held their own, using their doctrines of relativity to present a perspective inclusive of both Buddhist and Hindu views. For all these reasons and more, the Jain community continues to thrive and to maintain its highly distinctive identity in the midst of the vastness of Hinduism.

Suggestions for Further Reading

Babb, Lawrence A. *Absent Lord: Ascetics and Kings in a Jain Ritual Culture*. Berkeley: University of California Press, 1996.

Bronkhorst, Johannes. *Greater Magadha: Studies in the Culture of Early India*. Leiden: Brill, 2007.

Chapple, Christopher Key. *Nonviolence to Animals, Earth, and Self in Asian Traditions*. Albany, New York: State University of New York Press, 1993.

———. *Jainism and Ecology: Nonviolence in the Web of Life*. Cambridge, Massachusetts: Harvard University Press, 2002.

———. *Reconciling Yogas: Haribhadra's Collection of Views on Yoga*. Albany, New York: State University of New York Press, 2003.

Cort, John, ed. *Open Boundaries: Jain Communities and Cultures in Indian History*. Albany: State University of New York Press, 1998.

Dixit, Krishna Kumar. *Jaina Ontology*. Ahmedabad: L.D. Institute of Indology, 1971.

Dundas, Paul. *The Jains*. London: Routledge, 2002.

Folkert, Kendall W. *Scripture and Community: Collected Essays on the Jains*. Atlanta: Scholars Press, 1993.

Jaini, Padmanabh S. *The Jaina Path of Purification*. Delhi: Motilal Banarsidass Publishers, 1979.

———. *Gender and Salvation: Jaina Debates on the Spiritual Liberation of Women*. Delhi: Munshiram Manoharlal Publishers, 1992.

Long, Jeffery D. *Jainism: An Introduction*. London: I.B. Tauris, 2009.

Matilal, Bimal Krishna. *The Central Philosophy of Jainism: Anekānta-vāda*. Ahmedabad: L.D. Institute of Indology, 1981.

Mookerjee, Satkari. *The Jaina Philosophy of Non-Absolutism: A Critical Study of Anekāntavāda*. Delhi: Motilal Banarsidass, 1978.

Umāsvāti. *That Which Is: Tattvārtha Sūtra*. Translated by Nathmal Tatia. San Francisco: Harper Collins, 1994.

Vallely, Anne. *Guardians of the Transcendent: An Ethnography of a Jain Ascetic Community*. Toronto: University of Toronto Press, 2002.

12

Indigenous Religionists in North America

Kenneth Lokensgard

Ralph is a busy man. He works at a Canadian federal government office as a liaison between that office and the Native American peoples of southern Alberta. He is well suited for this job: he is college-educated and highly respected by fellow members of his "tribe" or nation. Ralph often has to take time off from work, though, to conduct religious ceremonies for his people and for members of the other nations that comprise the Blackfoot Confederacy. Fortunately, Ralph's supervisors understand his occasional need to leave work, even if they do not really understand the Blackfoot religion.

Ralph is an "elder." This title does not simply refer to his age. Rather, it refers to the fact that Ralph spent many years caring for ceremonial materials called "medicine bundles" and mastering the ritual knowledge associated with that care. Years ago, Ralph transferred his bundles to new keepers. Those keepers, in turn, passed the bundles on again. Now, Ralph advises the current keepers about bundle care. In ceremonial contexts, Ralph is referred to as a "grandfather," and the current keepers, who represent a third generation of keepers beyond himself, are his "grandchildren." For these reasons, Ralph's title of "elder" is an appropriate one.

Ralph is particularly busy during the fall and spring, when the Blackfeet open their most important bundles during complex, daylong ceremonies. These ceremonies, like many other rituals associated with bundles, reflect the Blackfoot understanding that bundles embody other-than-human beings who possess the knowledge, skills, and powers to help humans. The bundle openings are a means of communicating to and thanking the beings in the bundles for the many times they use their gifts to help the Blackfeet live successful lives. The prayers spoken, sung, and danced during these ceremonies also honor the Blackfoot Creator, who gives all beings, human and otherwise, their abilities to aid others.

Rita, Ralph's wife, joins her husband at many of the bundle openings, just as she did when the two of them cared for their own bundles. In fact, Ralph could not live the life he does without his wife's support. Most bundles (not all) are primarily associated with men, because they were initially given to men by the beings embodied in them. The keeping of these bundles, however, which is really a sort of ritualized "care giving," requires more effort than a man alone can provide. Therefore, most bundles are looked after by husbands and wives. Shortly after Rita and Ralph married, they acquired their first bundle. Now, Rita, like Ralph, is a ceremonial advisor to the current generation of keepers, and she too must sometimes request time off from work to fulfill this role. Still, she is not as busy as her husband; because he is a man, Ralph is usually the first one approached by those who seek information about bundle keeping.

In truth, Ralph only became so busy as an elder in recent years. Many generations of Blackfeet were educated in European-American schools. There, they were introduced to and often embraced Christianity. Consequently, many Blackfeet turned away from their traditional religion. Ralph, on the other hand, grew up in one of the handfuls of families in each nation that clung to their indigenous religion, ignoring the pressures to assimilate into European-American culture. Certainly, there were times during Ralph's youth when those pressures were strong. Nevertheless, strengthened by his family's convictions, he remained an adherent to the Blackfoot religion.

In the 1970s, some younger members of assimilated families, inspired by the civil rights movements of the era, became interested in their people's "Old Ways." They turned toward Ralph and others like him for help in revitalizing their religion. Ralph pointed these young Blackfeet toward the few ceremonial elders who lived at the time. Since then, the traditional religion has grown in popularity among members of the Blackfoot Confederacy. Likewise, Ralph has grown in his own knowledge of the Blackfoot traditions. Today, he and Rita, to whom he has been married for twenty-five years, are elders themselves.

Of course, Ralph is pleased to see that so many people have returned to the traditional religion. Yet, he is concerned that some religious knowledge was lost over the years; many elders passed away before revitalization began, and their knowledge passed with them. He is concerned, too, that some younger traditionalists may not completely understand the Blackfoot worldview, since they are so deeply influenced by the white world. On the other hand, he knows that his ancestors, who first met the white men, had similar worries. Even so, the religion survived into the twenty-first century. For this reason, Ralph is ultimately confident the religion will continue to be embraced in some form by future generations.

Neither Ralph nor Rita is an actual person, but there are a number of Blackfoot elders like them. Indeed, there are people like them among all the Native American nations in Canada and the United States. These people are responsible for the continuity of North America's native or indigenous religions.

But what exactly are Native American religions? So far, the reader has heard a bit about Blackfoot medicine bundles, ceremonies, and religious change. In the following pages, we will explore these things further. Because Native American religions are many and diverse, however, we will explore many other topics too. First, though, as a means of introduction, we need to consider some more basic matters.

Land, Language, and Tradition

Native Americans are in many ways unique among the religious groups of the world. Their uniqueness derives from the fact that their cultures are centered around the landscapes, to which they are indigenous. These peoples are also known as American Indians. Much has been said and written about the usefulness and accuracy of both these terms. "American Indian" has often been identified as a blatantly inaccurate term, because it derives from the beliefs of early European explorers that Native Americans were the same as or similar to the peoples of the East Indies. The controversy surrounding this term has largely subsided; the indigenous peoples of the Americas have made it their own, and they often use it themselves. In this chapter, I rely more heavily upon the term "Native American," as it better captures the notion of location-based-culture that is so important to most forms of Native American religiousness. Normally, of course, Native Americans who practice the religious traditions passed down to them by their ancestors refer to themselves in their own languages, with the terms their ancestors used to distinguish themselves from other culture groups.

There is a second, controversial term that appears many times in this chapter: "traditional." My use of the term to describe some Native American religions may imply that the practitioners of these religions live in exactly the same ways their ancestors did. This is not so. While many Native Americans seek to maintain as much continuity as possible between the religious practices and teachings of today with those of the past, they have had to adapt to a changing world. Moreover, many Native Americans have embraced entirely new religions, such as Christianity and other "Pan-American" Indian religious movements. Some of these movements retain features of older Native American religions, but others do not. The focus of this chapter is upon these seemingly "older" religions, whose adherents, like the Blackfoot elder described earlier, are consciously trying to carry on the ways of their ancestors. It is these religions that I, and many Native Americans, refer to as "traditional." Despite the changes the Americas have undergone in the past few hundred years, and despite the fact that many Native Americans now practice less culturally specific religions, traditional Native American religions remain vital and meaningful to those who embrace them. This vitality and meaning are very much dependent upon the particular, living landscapes upon which Native Americans continue to live. As religions that have been orally communicated throughout most of their histories, the vitality and meaning of these religions are also dependent upon the native languages that give conceptual shape and life to their worlds.

Native American Diversity

There is a great variety of indigenous peoples throughout North, Central, and South America. Even in North America, to which our discussion is limited, this diversity is staggering. According to the census conducted by the United States government in the year 2000, approximately two and a half million Americans identify themselves primarily as American Indian or Alaska Native. Over four million more Americans identify themselves as part American Indian or Alaska Native.[1] Many of the persons holding these identities are enrolled in one of more than 560 federally recognized "tribes" or nations.[2] Others are enrolled in tribes that hold only state recognition, and others still, for a number of reasons, hold no legal affiliation with any tribe. The 2001 Canadian census recorded 976,305 Canadians as identifying with "at least one Aboriginal group," and 1,419,890 Canadians reported "Aboriginal Origin."[3] In Canada, there are over 600 recognized "bands" or nations to which the people claiming these identities might belong.

Neither census provides an accurate portrait of indigenous populations in the United States and Canada. Many individuals go unreported in the censuses because they would rather not participate or because they

---

1. Stella U. Ogunwole, "The American Indian and Alaska Native Population: 2000," *Census 2000 Brief* (Washington: Bureau of the Census, 2002).

2. Office of the Federal Register, "Notices," *Federal Register* 67, no. 134 (July 2002): 46328.

3. Statistics Canada, "Aboriginal Identity Population, 2001 Counts, for Canada, Provinces, and Territories," http://www12.statcan.ca/english/census01/products/highlight/Aboriginal/.

were never polled; some Native peoples live in remote places, particularly in Canada, and are not easily reached by census takers. Furthermore, the numbers recorded indicate only ancestry, and not culture. Nevertheless, the censuses point toward a very sizable population of people, who think of themselves as indigenous to the Americas. Such a population is inevitably diverse.

Indeed, the many indigenous peoples of North America practice a great number of distinct religions. Some practice the religions of their ancestors, but as indicated earlier, others practice Christianity or other religions to which they or members of previous generations converted. Whether they practice their people's traditional religions or not, contemporary Native Americans are now regularly affected by the mainstream, non-indigenous cultures of the U.S. and Canada. Thus Native American religiousness is diverse not only across specific tribes or nations, but within them as well.

Native American Religious Diversity

The respected scholar of religion Vine Deloria, Jr. proposed several categories that are useful in making sense of Native American religions.[4] Deloria was Native American (*Hunkpapa Lakota*) himself and was very familiar with these religions on both personal and scholarly levels. The first category of Native American religions he put forth is the "Old Ways."[5] This term refers to the religious practices and teachings passed down within a particular culture group. These practices and teachings are more or less unique to that people. Deloria's term, "Old Ways," thus refers to the type of religion that is most often called "traditional." Importantly, "Old Ways," like "traditional," should not be understood as referring to a static and unchanging religion. These practices and teachings may be rooted in the past, but they have also been adapted to the present; they are fluid and lively, but they also have distinct cultural histories.

A second category Deloria proposes is Native American Christianity.[6] Native Americans were the objects of tremendous Christian missionary efforts, especially in the late 1800s, when they were forced by the American and Canadian governments onto reservations and reserves. The American reservations and Canadian reserves were lands set aside for exclusive Native American inhabitation and use. Since these were

---

4. Vine Deloria, Jr., *For This Land: Writings on Religion in America* (New York: Routledge, 1999), 107-8. See also Sam Gill, "Native Americans and Their Religions," in *World Religions in America*, ed. Jacob Neusner (Louisville, Ky.: Westminster John Know Press), 8.

5. Deloria, *For This Land*, 110.

6. Ibid., 109.

usually smaller and often in different locations than the lands Native Americans previously inhabited, the reservation and reserve systems resulted in the passing of much land from Native American to European-American hands. For a period in the United States, the reservations were actually administered by representatives of various Christian churches. In both countries, Native children on the reservations and reserves were sent to boarding schools. These too were usually run by Christian representatives.

In general, white Americans and Canadians believed that Christianity was a marker of "civilization." Thus, they felt that if Native Americans were to enjoy the supposed benefits of European-American society, they needed to leave their "Old Ways" behind and embrace Christianity. What they did not realize was that Native Americans were not always attracted to the "benefits" of such a society at all. Regardless, many Native Americans turned toward one form of Christianity or another, usually the form to which they were introduced in boarding school, and it would be wrong to suggest this turn was always regretted. Many contemporary Native Americans find Christianity truly fulfilling. It is also the case, though, that many forms of Native Christianity incorporate, to varying degrees, Native themes and symbols. As a result, many forms of Native American Christianity resemble the Christianity of mainstream Americans and Canadians closely. Some other forms look quite different, and they often offer a powerful reinterpretation of Christian practices and teachings.

The Native American Church (NAC) is an example of this latter type of Native American Christianity. Members of the NAC rely upon the spineless cactus, peyote, as a sacrament. The practice of ingesting peyote for religious purposes probably arrived in the United States from Mexico in the mid-nineteenth century and later spread to Canada. It is thus a relatively new phenomenon north of the Mexican border. Today, peyote is classified as an illicit, hallucinogenic "drug" by the United States government, but a legal exemption is made in the Controlled Substances Act of 1970 for the use of peyote in NAC ceremonies.[7] Even so, NAC members have experienced conflicts on the state level because many state governments do not respect the federal exemption. Fortunately, Canadian NAC members face no legal obstacles, as there are no restrictions on the use of peyote in Canada. Still, many individuals, both Native and non-Native, consider peyote a drug, and the NAC movement remains controversial in both countries.

Many NAC opponents do not realize the NAC often incorporates

7. Controlled Substances Act of 1970, U.S. Code 21 (1970), s. 1307.31.

Christianity into its theology and rituals. The degree to which this happens varies, as the "churches" are only loosely organized, and meetings are influenced by the backgrounds of the "road men" who lead them. Regardless, NAC members use peyote strictly as a means to focus upon and commune with the Creator, God, Jesus, or to whomever each individual peyotist prays. This is done during all-night ceremonies, characterized by contemplation and song. The peyotists direct many of their prayers toward the sponsor of the ceremony, who may be seeking spiritual aid for himself or a loved one. Clearly, then, the non-addictive "drug," peyote, is not used recreationally in NAC ceremonies, as some opponents fear. In fact, a central teaching of all Native American Churches is the need to *abstain* from alcohol and other drugs, among which they do not include peyote.[8]

In addition to the "Old Ways" and "Native American Christianity," Deloria describes a category of religion that results from the rediscovery of Native traditions by those who were alienated from their traditions in the past.[9] Deloria does not offer a specific term for this category, but, increasingly, Native Americans and scholars alike refer to it as "neo-traditionalism."

Traditional Native American religions are passed along orally. Because of the power associated with oral knowledge, they are also passed along cautiously. Therefore, learning about these religions requires an individual to return to her or his native community and to follow the protocols that will grant her or him access to progressive levels of religious knowledge. Other religions in North America are not so difficult to explore; anyone who is interested can simply pick up a book and read about them or go to a local worship service. In the past, many assimilated Native Americans assumed that learning about tribal traditions was just as easy. Therefore, they read books about the practices and teachings of various culture groups, and they attended any ceremonies available to them, even if those ceremonies differed from or conflicted with those of their own people. The neo-traditionalism that resulted from this religious exploration now often translates into a generalized form of "Pan-American" Indian religion.

"Pan-Am" religions (a category not explored explicitly by Deloria) are those that are not specific to a particular culture group. Rather, they are practiced across cultural boundaries. The symbols and rituals found within them may be drawn from several cultures. For instance,

---

8. For further information on the Native American Church, see Omer C. Stewart, *Peyote Religion: A History* (Norman: University of Oklahoma Press, 1998).
9. Deloria, *For This Land*, 111.

each summer, certain Plains Indian peoples practice a form of the "Sun Dance," during which participants pierce themselves through the chest, tie those piercings to a central pole in a ceremonial space, and dance until the piercings break free. The precise logic behind this act varies across culture groups, but, generally, practitioners do this as a sacrificial sign of thanks for help needed or received from the Creator and to express gratitude for the earth's renewal each spring.[10] This type of Sun Dance is now found among culture groups that did not historically pierce during the annual ceremony or that did not practice a Sun Dance at all. Thus, the "piercing" Sun Dance has become a Pan-Am phenomenon.

One type of Pan-American Indian religion enjoys little support from any segment of Native America. This is the highly romanticized, Native American "spirituality" practiced by many non-Indians. Like neo-traditionalism, it derives largely from books, many of which are written by New Age writers, who misinterpret Native traditions as comprising a universal path toward the positive transformation of the world. It is also a highly commercialized form of religion. The New Age authors and other self-proclaimed experts, who usually have very tenuous associations with traditional Native American cultures at best, promote their services as healers, shamans, life coaches, and so on. Their services, like their books, can cost a great deal of money. Native Americans are thus left to balk at not only the appropriation and misinterpretation of their religious knowledge, but at the commodification of that knowledge as well.

Finally, in addition to those who practice neo-traditionalism, the Old Ways, and Christianity, Deloria points out there are those Native Americans who lead more or less secular lives. Like many mainstream Americans and Canadians, their primary concerns are supporting their families and perhaps even getting ahead materially or financially. Deloria goes so far as to suggest some of these latter people have become "materialistic capitalists."[11] He argues they have become so far assimilated into the mainstream American and Canadian cultures, that they have adopted the belief that material wealth is more important than anything else is. We might consider Deloria's somewhat controversial argument as a reminder that Native Americans now face the same choices, regarding religion, as everyone else in the contemporary world does; they can embrace the religions of their ancestors, they can reinterpret those religions, they can embrace entirely different religions, or they can become indifferent to what we normally consider religion, altogether.

10. For further information on the *Lakota* or "Sioux" Sun Dance, upon which many Pan-Am Sun Dances are based, see James R. Walker, Raymond J. DeMallie, and Elaine A. Jahner, eds., *Lakota Belief and Ritual* (Lincoln: University of Nebraska Press, 1991).
11. Deloria, *For This Land,* 108.

Traditional Religions

Of all the categories of religions practiced by Native Americans, the one that is most unique to them, as a whole, is the "Old Ways." For this reason, we will look at traditional religions more closely. As explained already, these religions are orally communicated and geared toward successful existence in particular places. This means every traditional Native American religion is, in many ways, distinct. Each religion may vary from the others according to the language or dialect through which it is passed along and according to the social and geographic environment in which it is practiced. It is thus important to remember there is no such thing as a single, traditional Native American *religion*.

Still, the fact that traditional religions are place-based and communicated orally means they share some broad themes. Plainly, a thorough examination of how these themes manifest in each tradition is beyond our scope. We can, though, examine the themes themselves and consider how they manifest in a few cultures. We will do exactly this in the remaining paragraphs. Before concluding, we will also reflect upon the implications for these religions of existing in a societal setting dominated by non-indigenous religions. Throughout, I will draw the bulk of my examples from the religious culture of the Blackfoot Peoples. The Blackfeet consist of four distinct nations. There are also the *Kainai*, or Bloods, and the *Siksika*, or Blackfoot Proper, and the *Pikanni*. The *Pikanni* are further divided into the *Aapahtosipikanni* and *Amskaahpipikanni*, or North and South Piegan. The *Kainai*, *Siksika* and *Aapahtosipikanni* reside on reserves in Alberta, Canada. The *Amskaahpipikanni* have their own reservation in Montana, on the American side of the border. I rely upon the Blackfeet for so many of my examples because they are the culture group with which I have the greatest scholarly and personal familiarity. Interested readers, upon finishing this chapter, can turn toward additional sources to familiarize themselves further with the Blackfeet and with the other Native American culture groups and religions mentioned in the following paragraphs.[12]

Traditional Religions: The Living Landscape and Personhood of Other Beings

Many Native American peoples have lived in specific areas for hun-

12. The Blackfoot data presented in this chapter derive from fieldwork conducted by the author with knowledgeable Blackfoot elders and ceremonial leaders between 1994 and 2007. For further information on the Blackfoot Peoples see Betty Bastien, *Blackfoot Ways of Knowing: The Worldview of the Siksikaitsitapi*, ed. Jurgen W. Kremer (Calgary: University of Calgary Press, 1994); Adolf Hungry Wolf, *The Blackfoot Papers*, 4 vols (Skookumchuck, BC: Good Medicine Cultural Foundation, 2006).

dreds or even thousands of years. Over time, they developed an intimate familiarity with their surroundings. In those surroundings, they observed carefully the movements of life—human, plant, and animal life cycles, the seasons, and even more drawn-out changes in the landscapes. They attributed a degree of vitality or life to these changes. This is not so surprising. Even those readers living in cities can look out their windows over the course of several days or weeks to see creatures such as squirrels or pigeons go about their respective businesses. On the boulevard, you might see leaves on trees grow or drop, or a patch of grass turn green or brown. If you observe long and carefully enough, you might even see a curbstone chip away from foot traffic, or wear away from rain. These changes are similar to those Native Americans learned to observe and interpret upon their own landscapes, over many generations. Native Americans did not simply regard the changes in their landscapes as reflecting life, however. They also regarded these changes as reflecting potential "personhood."

Personhood is something non-indigenous people rarely consider. The term, itself, can refer to the ability to interact intentionally with others. We generally attribute this ability to humans, alone, and we do so unconsciously. Yet, just as unconsciously, we are sometimes reluctant to grant it to those humans we regard as "other." Indeed, European explorers, settlers, and missionaries of the past did not always regard Native Americans as persons. Traditional Native Americans are more generous with this concept. They often believe the group of beings or things possessing the ability to interact socially includes many beings that are not human at all. In fact, they often believe this group can include things that the average non-indigenous individual does not even consider alive.

For instance, the traditions of the Blackfoot Peoples outline three basic categories of potential other-than-human persons, who inhabit and animate the landscape. First, there are the *sspomitapiiksi* or "above people." This category includes the sun, as well as the moon, planets, stars, and high-flying birds. Second, there are the *ksaahkommitapiiksi*, the "earth people." These are the low-flying birds, plants, animals, and even some rocks. Finally, there are the *sooyiitapiiksi* or "underwater people," which include the fish and wetland or riparian animals.

The "source" of vitality observed by Native Americans in their landscapes is the most powerful of beings or forces. This being or force is usually responsible for creation, but it is often believed to have received help from other figures. Many Native Americans refer to this being or force as the "Creator." Sometimes this being is thought of in personal terms, as a being with a distinct personality. Other times, it is thought of in much broader terms, as energy or another force that animates a group of particularly powerful beings, or even as a force that is manifest in all living things.

The Creator in Blackfoot culture is known as *Iihtsipaitapiiyo'pa* or "The One Through Whom We Live." Conceived of in this way, the Source of Life is the totality of energy that animates all beings. The Blackfoot Peoples, though, also equate the Source of Life with the sun, which they regard as a powerful person who plays a significant role in many ancient stories. Sun or *Naato'si* is, to be precise, the greatest manifestation of *Ihtsipaitapiyo'pa*. This makes sense from any cultural perspective, as the sun's rays give vitality to all the beings who inhabit the earth's landscape.

Traditional Religions: Reciprocity

In light of the preceding discussion, we can see that traditional Native Americans live in highly animate environments, densely inhabited by various beings and persons. These beings and persons may vary tremendously from culture to culture and from place to place. Their precise relationships to the Source of Life may vary too. But across cultures and geographies, they have in common their abundance and their ability to interact, both positively and negatively, with humans. Thus, Native Americans inhabit worlds in which their actions may affect and elicit reactions from many beings, both human and otherwise. There is a sense of interconnection in these worlds. Because of this feeling of interconnection, traditional Native Americans must always act with conscious recognition that their actions may be reciprocated by other beings—by persons, in fact, who may help or hinder humans. A Blackfoot ceremonial leader once summarized his conception of this to me with the old adage, "What goes around comes around." To this, he added, "Good takes a while. Bad will come back faster, but you'll still be the last to know."[13] What is implicit in his comment is that "good" and "bad" are visited upon humans by other beings, including the Source of Life, in response to our own "good" or "bad" actions. Other traditional Native Americans feel similarly; in all their worlds, there is a strong sense of ongoing "reciprocity," or give and take, between beings.

From the Native American perspective, every being (including humans) may possess unique knowledge, skills, and power. Every being, therefore, possesses the ability to help Native Americans live happy and healthy lives. These beings may even possess the ability to help humans live in

---

13. John Murray (Southern Piegan tribal member), interview by author, 26 September 2000.

closer relationship with the Source of Life. Thus, humans must respect the feelings and desires of other beings. Doing so demonstrates that humans are worthy of help and will offer something in return for the help they request or receive. Respect for other beings is expressed formally during ceremonies, when participants engage in ritual acts that honor the other beings and the Source of Life, who created those beings and gave them their special gifts. Indeed, a concern for reciprocity explains nearly every traditional Native American religious act.

Religious specialists among the Blackfeet enter into relationships with the knowledgeable, skillful, and powerful other-than-human persons of their landscape, by caring for their medicine bundles.[14] Other-than-human persons willingly place or embody themselves, or more precisely their "spirits" or life essences, into these bundles in order to be more accessible to the humans who depend upon them for help. Physically, medicine bundles are just that—bundles, and they contain such things as plants, rocks, earth paints, and animal parts. The things inside the bundles make present the beings with which they are associated. For example, a beaver skin may make present an actual beaver or, rather, all of his non-physical characteristics. That is, the skin makes present his personality, his ability to communicate, and so on.

The bundle-opening ceremonies, described earlier in this chapter, allow the Blackfeet to request help directly from the beings in the bundles or to give thanks for help already received. Again, for example, attendees may seek help from or give thanks to the beaver, who is particularly well endowed with useful knowledge, skills and power. The beaver, in turn, may offer healing energy to a human supplicant or know that aid he gave in the past is appreciated.

Attendees at the bundle openings seek help from and express gratitude to the beings embodied in the bundles through reciprocal acts. Most obviously, they bring gifts, such as food and blankets, to the ceremonies. The bundle keepers then distribute these gifts to other attendees in honor of the bundle beings. This gift-giving is a clear means of demonstrating a reciprocal attitude in response to the actions of the bundle beings; the gifts represent offerings made for things received or desired. Importantly,

14. I borrow the term "other-than-human" from influential psychological anthropologist A. Irving Hallowell. His linguistic work among the Algonkian-speaking Ojibwa revealed to European-American scholars that the Ojibwa live in a highly animate cosmos in which many "other-than-human" beings share the characteristics of personhood with humans. Hallowell also revealed to scholars that the Ojibwa and other Algonkian-speaking groups, including the Blackfeet, designate the potential for animacy and personhood linguistically. See A. Irving Hallowell, "Ojibwa Ontology, Behavior, and World View," in Barbara Tedlock and Dennis Tedlock, eds., *Teachings from the American Earth: Indian Religion and Philosophy* (New York: Liveright, 1975), 141-178.

the reciprocal acts engaged in by ceremonial attendees are also means of honoring *Ihtsipaitapiyo'pa*, as the source of the knowledge, skills, and powers—even the very life—behind the bundled beings.

In most traditional Native American cultures, the theme of reciprocity, and the respect it necessitates, is so important that it is considered a hallmark of personhood and cultural identity. This is because, in the densely inhabited Native American worlds, successful social interaction requires a conscious awareness of how one's actions affect others on the part of all individuals. Individuals who fail to display this awareness are often not regarded as persons at all.

Those humans who *do* act respectfully and reciprocally emphasize their personhood and their belonging to a larger group of respectful and reciprocal beings. This emphasis is often found in the names by which Native peoples identify their culture groups. For instance, one of the names the Blackfoot Peoples use to refer to themselves collectively is *Niitsitapiiksi*. This word means "Real Persons." A quick overview of other tribal names reveals similar examples. Members of many culture groups within the Athabaskan language family, such as the Navajo in Arizona, New Mexico, Utah, and Colorado, and the Chipewyan of northwestern Canada, call themselves *Dine*, or simply "People." The Northern Cheyenne, now located in Montana, are actually the *Tsitsistaseo*, or "Like-Minded People." Some indigenous tribal names further qualify the personhood of the people to which they refer as being oriented toward a particular landscape or lifestyle. For example, the Iroquois in the northeastern United States and eastern Canada call themselves the *Haudenosaunee* or "People of the Long House."

The list of indigenous tribal names emphasizing personhood is extensive. All of the names emphasize that the people to which they refer practice traditions that teach humans how to live properly in densely inhabited environments. Not surprisingly, among the many Native American culture groups throughout North America, there are those whose names do not emphasize personhood. This does not make their concern for respectful and reciprocal living any less important, though.

Traditional Religions: Kinship with Other Beings

In order to live successfully in social environments that include many beings besides humans, Native Americans must not only be mindful of others, they must also establish and maintain positive relations with those persons around them. What is the best model in the natural world for having positive relations with others? It is the family. Now, not every family is a healthy one. In those families that are, however, there is an understanding that one has special obligations toward her or his parents, grand-parents, siblings, children, grandchildren, and so on. In healthy families, members often go much further out of their way to support other family members in need than they do for strangers or mere acquaintances. Simi-larly, all of us probably go to greater lengths to support friends we regard "as sisters" or "as brothers" than we do to support friends with whom we are less close.

Traditional Native Americans, too, see close, positive relationships, whether they are biologically based or not, in familial terms. Indeed, kinship is an important theme in indigenous societies. Ancestors are often held in high esteem and familial organization and proper relations among living human relatives are strongly emphasized. Other beings with whom Native Americans have reciprocal relations are worked into the kinship system as well. For instance, creator beings are often regarded as fathers or grandfathers, the sustaining earth is often regarded as a mother or grandmother, and animals are sometimes seen as siblings.

For traditional Native Americans, it is understood that if you want to treat other living beings positively, so that they will treat you positively, you must treat them as kin. This is the case not only for humans, but for other members of the living landscape too. For nearly any person, human or otherwise, can help traditional individuals lead happy and healthy lives and can help maintain the vitality of each Native American culture, as a whole.

Traditional Religions: Effective Power of Language and Communication

All traditional religious insights, including the general ones discussed here as well as those that are more tribally specific, are communicated orally and lived daily by traditional Native Americans. Because their knowledge of the world and the quality of their lives is dependent upon their ability to communicate with others (as it is for all of us), Native Americans often associate communication with life itself. In fact, they remain more acutely aware of the importance of communication than many of us do.

Written languages, upon which non-indigenous peoples are so depen-dent, sometimes allow us to become lazy. In class, I often ask my stu-dents if they can recite more than two lines of a great text of Western Culture, such as one of the works of Shakespeare or the King James Bible. Rarely do I have more than one student in each class who can do so. This is because the students, like everyone else in the United States and Canada, can find Shakespeare or the King James Bible in the library or online, whenever they need to. They take it for granted that their cultural texts will always be available to them, precisely because those texts are recorded.

Not only do many non-indigenous peoples take the availability of recorded cultural knowledge for granted, they also take its impact, and the impact of all communication, for granted. This is reflected in sayings like "sticks and stones can break my bones, but names can never hurt me." We adopt this nonchalant attitude toward communication because we regard it as symbolic, as abstract. We regard our languages, spoken or written, as mere vehicles for ideas. Words, phrases, passages, and texts have no meaning, in and of themselves. Some concerted reflection, however, reveals that even if language is just symbolic, it still has real power and should be used carefully. The claim that "names can never hurt me" is simply untrue. In reality, names, and other words too, are very powerful. Native Americans know this. Therefore, they use words, as well as music, pictures, images—all things communicative—very carefully. As a matter of fact, many traditional Native Americans believe communication does more than just give expression to otherwise unspoken thoughts or ideas. They believe communication can also give shape to beings and forces. In other words, communication makes those things present not just in their minds, but in their lives as well.

For instance, Blackfeet avoid saying their word for "grizzly" in certain ceremonies; this word speaks the huge bear—or at least its power—into presence. Similarly, the reader has already learned that medicine bundles, which to most non-indigenous peoples would be considered mere symbols—pieces of so-called "primitive art"—are considered to manifest the beings whom they represent. Other Native Americans believe masks, much like pictorial words or Blackfoot bundles, bring other beings into presence and must therefore be respected. The Hopis of the southwestern United States feel this way about the *Katsina* costumes worn by ceremonial dancers; the dancers who wear these costumes embody the *Katsina* beings of Arizona's San Francisco Peaks temporarily, making them present to their fellow Hopis.[15] Throughout the rest of Native America, there are many other examples of spoken, pictorial and other images that bring beings into presence.

This may seem odd to some readers of this book, but language and communication have a degree of effective and representational power in *all* cultures. True, most non-Indians are unlikely to believe a word can actually make present another being. But we can certainly appreciate

15. The *Katsinas* are benevolent other-than-human beings. Some of them are associated particularly with rain, which is very important in the southwestern United States. For further information on traditional Hopi religion, see James D. Loftin, *Religion and Hopi Life* (Bloomington: Indiana University Press, 2003).

that language makes social reality possible—that it allows us to discuss, agree upon, or disagree upon the reality we share with others. Likewise, most non-Indians can appreciate that the misuse of language, something as simple as name-calling or gossiping, can have real consequences. Traditional Native Americans are just more aware of the power of language than many of us are. For them, language, like the living landscape, helps maintain the vitality of Native American cultures by keeping traditional knowledge alive and even by speaking that knowledge, and those beings who figure so strongly in it, into presence.

We have now considered some common themes in traditional Native American religions, and we have explored some examples that illustrate these themes. Before proceeding, though, it is important to remember that, despite the general features they share in common, traditional Native American religions are unique. This uniqueness results from the very themes they share in common. Traditional Native American religions vary according to particular living landscapes upon which they are practiced. They vary according to the human and other-than-human, familial communities surrounding those who follow the traditions. Furthermore, they vary according to the languages that help communicate Native American religious knowledge, shape Native American worlds, and allow Native Americans to have positive relations with others.

Native American Religious Freedom and Other Contemporary Issues

While many Native Americans feel they have some useful insights about the world to share with others, they do not proselytize or seek to convert others to their particular ways of life; they do not necessarily want others to practice their rituals. The diversity of Native American traditions means they are not generally available or even useful to people of other cultural and geographic origins.

Today, after years of being suppressed through missionary activity and governmental policy, Native American religious traditions have become attractive to non-indigenous peoples. The reasons for this are many. Some non-Indians are attracted to the close ties Native Americans hold to their environments. Others simply want to practice something very different from their own religions to protest what they perceive as deficiencies in those religions. Finally, some just want to capitalize upon the interest of other non-Indians. Being used to moving throughout their countries with little consequence for their identities, failing to understand the effective and evocative power of language consciously, and being most familiar with non-indigenous religions to which anyone can readily convert by claiming certain beliefs, they assume the adoption of traditional Native

American practices is easy.

This is not so. After all, it is hard to practice Blackfoot traditions if you are not part of a community whose members strive to live reciprocally. It is also hard to practice Blackfoot traditions if you do not speak the Blackfoot language, which helps shape Blackfoot reality. Even the other animals upon the Blackfoot landscape are presumed to speak Blackfoot, so conducting ceremonies involving them in any language other than Blackfoot will be difficult.

This is not to say that the Blackfeet or other Native Americans have a premium upon indigenous knowledge. To be sure, most European-Americans have distant, indigenous backgrounds in Europe. African-Americans have similar backgrounds in Africa, Asian-Americans in Asia, and so on. Additionally, some contemporary non-Indians have lived in the same place for many years and may have come to share views similar to Native Americans through a close observation of the land. Still, each indigenous tradition is uniquely and very complexly localized. Therefore, according to most traditional Native Americans, indigenous practices simply will not work out of context; if they do, they may have an unexpected or even dangerous effect (remember, language has power).

The failure of non-Indians to understand this fact has led to the popular misappropriation and misinterpretation of Native American intellectual culture or ritual knowledge by some segments of popular society. Many members of the New Age movement have adopted Native American rituals. Go to a New Age bookstore, or any bookstore, and you will see endless books teaching Pan-Am "spirituality." In some places, you may be able to buy a sacred pipe, a portable sweat lodge, a drum, a "smudge stick," or even a medicine bundle.[16]

From the Native American perspective, this is disrespectful. Native Americans do not want others profiting from the misinterpretation of their traditions. Furthermore, many Native Americans feel that rituals conducted improperly, if they have any effect at all, will bring anger from other beings, both to the New Agers and to the Native Americans who are responsible for protecting the traditions.

Sadly, the appropriation of Native American culture has a long history. In contemporary North America, it often is done out of a romantic fascination with Native American peoples. Historically, it has been done

---

16. Sacred pipes are common means of burning sacred tobacco as offerings to the Creator and other beings and as a means of having prayers carried to those beings. Sweat lodges are small domelike structures, common to many Native American cultures, in which participants sweat before hot rocks upon which they pour water. During these sacrifices of personal comfort, they offer prayers to the Creator and other beings. Finally, a "smudge" is a ritual burning of incense.

for other reasons, including academic ones. In fact, collectors of arti-facts and scholars of various disciplines are implicated in the misappro-priation and misinterpretation of Native American culture. Museums and private collections are filled with ceremonial materials, and these same things have often been dissected in scholarly books. Because many Native Americans believe ceremonial materials, such as the Blackfoot medicine bundles, embody other beings, they also believe these things require special care. If ceremonial materials do not receive this care, the embodied beings might be offended or become aloof, thus affecting the vitality of the culture to which the beings belong and offer aid.

After intense lobbying by Native Americans, the United States Con-gress passed the Native American Graves Repatriation and Protection Act (NAGPRA) in 1990. NAGPRA helps Native Americans repatriate ceremonial materials, funerary objects, objects of cultural patrimony, and remains of their ancestors from federally funded institutions.[17] The province of Alberta, Canada, recently passed similar legislation. The Blackfoot Peoples themselves and many other Native American nations are engaged in a great battle, using these pieces of legislation to repatri-ate their bundles from museums and private collections. All traditional Indians regard this political battle as being, at the same time, a religious battle to maintain their culture's vitality.

Repatriation, though, is only one of the most recent religious battles Native Americans have had to fight. During much of the reservation/reserve era, specifically from the 1880s until 1934 in the United States, and until 1951 in Canada, most traditional religious practices were banned. American citizens look toward the first two clauses of the first amend-ment of the United States Constitution for assurance of their religious freedom. These clauses read, "Congress shall make no law respecting and establishment of religion, nor prohibiting the free-exercise thereof."[18] Yet, Indians in the United States were not granted unconditional citizen-ship until 1924. And it was not until 1968 that Congress affirmed that the Bill of Rights, the first ten amendments to the Constitution, applied to Native Americans.

In Canada, Indians did not receive complete, enfranchised citizen-ship until 1960. This entitled them to religious freedom, as it was out-lined in the Canadian Bill of Rights of the same year.[19] This freedom, and many others in Canada, was strengthened by the Canadian Charter

17. U.S. Native American Graves Protection and Repatriation Act of 1990, US Code 25 (1990), ss. 3001–3013.
18. United States Constitution, First Amendment.
19. Canada Act for the Recognition and Protection of Human Rights and Fundamental Freedoms (Bill of Rights), S.C. 1960, c. 44, pt. 1. s. 1c.

of Rights and Freedoms of 1982 (part of the Constitution Act 1982).[20] Thus, Native Americans in the United States and Canada have only recently gained firm, legal protection for their religions.

Alas, there are many other ways, beyond those that are legislation or policy based, in which traditional Native American religions are impacted negatively. Nearly all of these result from the biased interpretation of religion, based upon the Christian and other Abrahamic ideas that are embedded so deeply in mainstream American and Canadian societies. As mentioned earlier, the majority of Americans and Canadians come from backgrounds that teach that religion is about faith or belief. No doubt, in both countries, you can *believe* what you want. The ability of each American and Canadian citizen to do so is constitutionally protected. This means that if you are Native American, you can believe your bundle is alive or that the land is animated. But getting that bundle back from a private collector, conducting a bundle ceremony upon a piece of living land owned by a developer, or convincing a non-Indian that he or she cannot conduct the same ceremony is another issue. In other words, each citizen's ability to *practice* religion freely is a more fragile in both countries.

Nevertheless, what is most essential to recognize about traditional Native American religions is that they remain vital and meaningful. True, these religions have faced many challenges in the past and even the present. This chapter emphasizes, however, that these religions are lived and spoken traditions, practiced consciously by people who believe their practices have consequences for them and for the others with whom they share their landscapes. Because of this, these religions are inherently responsive to the challenges placed before them.

Today, Native American peoples share their landscapes with many other Americans and Canadians, who practice or simply believe in very different religions, or who do not consider themselves religious at all. Whether or not these non-indigenous North Americans feel, like Native Americans do, that they share their social worlds with other-than-human beings, they must recognize that their countries are, at least, inhabited by a tremendous diversity of human beings. Native Americans are an integral part of that human diversity, and they always will be, precisely because their religions are so wonderfully adaptable.

Suggestions for Further Reading

Deloria, Vine, and James Treat. *For This Land: Writings on Religion in America,* New

---

20. Canada Constitution Act, S.C. 1982, sch. b, pt. 1, s. 2a.

York: Routledge, 1999.

Gill, Sam. "Native Americans and Their Religions." In *World Religions in America*, edited by Jacob Neusner, 8-23. Louisville, Ky: Westminster John Knox Press, 2003.

13

Hindus

P. Pratap Kumar

Madhavan Pillay is a fifth-generation South African Indian and his wife, Pramila Singh, is also a fifth-generation South African Indian. But they both come from different linguistic groups among Indians. Madhavan could have married a Tamil girl from any of the cognate groups (e.g., a Padayachi, Govender, and Moodley), or as a concession he could have married a Telugu Naidu/Naidoo or Reddy. Marrying outside his linguistic group is still rather unusual in South Africa. Similarly, Pramila could have married another Hindi-speaking Pandey, Maharaj, etc. But they chose each other as they met at the university and eventually got married in a ceremony that fused elements of both Tamil and Hindi cultures, a ceremony that is still new. Their case is certainly an exception rather than the norm. South African Hindus, although they do not marry along caste lines (as those boundaries have long been broken), still marry predominately along the lines of linguistic affinity. Tamils generally marry among Tamils and as a concession marry into Telugu families. Hindi-speaking Hindus generally marry among the same language groups.

Both Mandhavan and Pramila were raised in modern educated homes and settled into upper-middle-class life styles with high-achieving careers, yet they often felt the need to know more about their own cultural and religious backgrounds. Apart from doing some simple ceremonies at home such as lighting the lamp in the morning and evening, they are pretty much absorbed in their day-to-day busy lives. And they spend what little time they may get to be together with friends at the movies, theatres, and restaurants. Two years into their marriage, Pramila is expecting a baby girl. This certainly prompted them to know something about their culture and religion. Although they do not come from homogenous religious and cultural backgrounds, they are Hindus, and both are keen to introduce their soon to be born baby to their respective religious and cultural values.

Their obvious starting place was their parents and grandparents, then their neighbors, friends, and visits to the temples and religious centers. This start was not easy. There are far too many different things to practice and believe, and each temple, shrine, or religious organization has its own set of beliefs and practices. Added to this astounding variety, there are a great many new Hindu organizations and their literature which spells out their philosophies and doctrines.

Also, many books on Yoga are available (especially when New Age writings are included). Classically speaking, yoga is an Indian system of philosophy which emphasizes a practical approach to liberation using methods of concentration and discipline. Its philosophy is based on two fundamental principles: *Purusha* (Spiritual Principle) and *Prakriti* (Material Principle), which are considered eternally separate and never to be confused. According to the Yoga system, it is the confusion of the two that leads to suffering. Yoga introduces the idea of God (Ishvara) to explain the relationship between Purusha and Prakriti but sees no real role for God in the attainment of final liberation. Through meditative techniques, one has to achieve a proper understanding of the relationship between the Spiritual and the Material principles. As such the Yoga philosophy is described as a dualist system in that it upholds the two fundamentally separate principles.

Madhavan's and Pramila's parents and grandparents told them about where they came from, and who they came from (that is, their forebears). So they had some insight into how their forebears ventured into the unknown when they set sail in the mid nineteenth century (beginning in 1860) to come to Natal Colony in South Africa in the hope of earning gold coins. They came from a host of villages and suburbs from all over India. Those who came from South India used the port of Madras, and those who came from the north used the port of Calcutta (now known as Kolkotta). They did not come in any homogenous groups according to their castes and social backgrounds. They were lumped together by the ship master who obtained from them their details, such as their family names, religious affiliations, and so on. Most were illiterate and did not know what a family name was, let alone that their religion was being referred to as "Hindu". Some gave fictitious names, some changed their names, some gave their caste names, and some assumed new caste names. If that is not enough, when they arrived in various ships, they were allocated to different farmers in Natal, not necessarily according to their caste or religious affiliations but according to their abilities to do the job and the bidding of the farmers. This generally prevented families from living on the same farm, let alone being able to maintain their caste identity.

Figure 13.1: *A Shiva temple in Chatsworth, Durban (Built in 1960s). (Photo by P. Kumar.)*

Between 1860 and 1890 there were already a significant number of Hindus in Natal, and by the mid-1880s a new group of Indians known as "passenger" Indians began to arrive in Natal. These were mostly merchants from Gujarat who wanted to trade among the Indians. Most were Hindus of the Bania caste, but there were a substantial number of Muslims too. Gradually the Indian community moved beyond Natal and spread throughout South Africa, although the majority remained in Natal. Today at least 600,000 Hindus have made their home in what is now known as KwaZulu Natal province.

The indentured Hindus (those who came as laborers under the indenture system) built shrines and temples from the very early days of their arrival in South Africa. Today, there are scores of temples and small shrines, and many new Hindu organizations and new Hindu movements have made a home in South Africa. Generally, most Hindus in South Africa could be grouped into two broad branches, although such categories are not meant to be definitive. One group's historical and social affiliations could be associated with the worship of Vishnu, while the other is associated with the worship of Shiva, as may be represented by the two temples shown in figures 13.1 and 13.2. As a society, Hindus in South Africa have evolved into a highly diversified community, not only due to the various regional and linguistic differences that they brought with them, but more importantly through inventions of rituals, caste statuses, and localized customs of marriage and other rites. As explained earlier, many Hindus in South Africa did not generally maintain their caste status, due to the fact that the structures that were necessary to maintain a caste-based society could not be established in the new environment with its many social and political challenges. There is sufficient evidence in the immigration records that many Hindus moved up the social scale by adopting new caste names as their surnames or last names. While caste as a social structure could not be established with all its rules of conduct and so on, caste consciousness among early Hindus in South Africa did exist. For example, most of the names that they chose as their last names are were those of higher castes. The absence of any social structures to monitor caste-based conduct and behavior allowed people to adopt higher-caste names, usually from within the non-Brahmin castes. This occurred both among the south Indians as well as north Indians, with the Gujarati community being an exception. One consequence of such adoption of caste names is that it enabled a certain level of homogeneity among Hindus and thus helped in the process of establishing marital alliances. For instance, among south Indians, namely the Naidoos/Naidus, Reddys, Padayachis and Govenders, marriage alliances are possible as they are seen as cognate caste groups. Generally marriage alliances are less strict among South African Hindus.

However, notwithstanding the fact that there are four recognizable linguistic groups—Tamil, Telugu, Hindi and Gujarati—most commonly south Indians married among south Indians and north Indians married among north Indians. This is largely due to recognizable cultural differences in food, music, language, and other social practices and customs. The other consequence of inventing themselves into different linguistic and social groups is that dowry (a social phenomenon which to this day dominates Indian social life) could not be practiced among South African Hindus.

Beliefs and Practices: Vows, Fasts, and Celebrations

As most South African Hindus came from rural Indian backgrounds, they naturally brought with them belief systems that reflected those times and places. And they continue to share those beliefs and actively propagate them through rituals and festivals. Although most Hindus today would agree that they believe in one God (not being conscious of how much the colonial Christian thinking influenced their beliefs and ways of thinking), their rituals and practices do not necessarily reflect that. It is only when they intellectualize and rationalize their beliefs that they tend to suggest that their belief in and worship of the different gods and goddesses according to the seasons and festivals represent adherence to one ultimate principle or God. To understand their actual practice, it is perhaps less fruitful to engage in such philosophizing tendencies and instead to observe what they actually do and believe. Their beliefs are deeply entrenched in their rituals and festivals.

The various belief systems brought by north Indian Hindus and south Indians from ninetenth-century rural India are very popular and strongly pronounced. Often many Gujarati Hindus also take part in these festivals and rituals, even though in general they worship Vishnu/Rama/Krishna as the primary deities. Although from a classical perspective, Rama and Krishna are considered the incarnations of Vishnu, at the level of real worship it is hard to make such philosophical observations.

Central to the belief systems brought from the rural Indian background are the two goddesses that have become popular among the Hindus cutting across the linguistic boundaries: Mariamman and Draupadi. However, these two goddesses are specifically associated with south Indian groups, Tamil and Telugu speakers.

Hindu religious life in South Africa revolves around a set practice of observance of rituals and festivals. For most Hindus of south Indian background the religious calendar begins with the Tamil New Year (the Telugus and the Hindi-speaking Hindus have a different date for their New Year festival), which culminates in what is known as the Kavadi festival, occurring in the month of April.

Kavadi Festival

Kavadi literally refers to a horizontal pole used in rural India for carrying weights and water. It is an important tool in the lives of farming people, who carry their produce from the farms to the market places.

The Kavadi has become associated with the worship of Murugan, who in turn is associated with the worship of Shiva. Murugan is said to be the Tamil variant of the Sanskrit god, Skandha/Subrahmanya, who is considered the son of Shiva, along with his other son, Ganesha. Both Ganesha and Skandha are generally associated with Shaivism in that they are understood as sons of Shiva and Parvati. (Gods having spouses and children is an interesting concept of Hindu religious thinking.) Ganesha is viewed as a god who removes obstacles and hence his worship in any Hindu temple precedes the worship of the main deity in that temple. He is also known by other names, e.g. Vinayaka and Vignesvara. Skandha is also known as Subrahmanya and Shanmukha (in Tamil language, Shanmuga) which refers to the idea that he has six faces. In later Hindu theological developments, Skandha is also identified with the Tamil god Muruga. The worship of Muruga is very popular in the Tamil speaking region in India and also among the Tamil diaspora. In this sense, the Tamils could be in general associated with the worship of Shiva. However, it is a non-Brahmanical form of worship that does not require a priest from a traditional Brahmanical society. Rather, the priest could be anyone from the society who has been skilled in the rituals associated with the festival.

Kavadi is a ten-day festival. On the first day, the flag-hoisting ceremony takes place, which marks the beginning of the festival. Devotees take vows reflecting their particular circumstances, such as financial needs, health, or family needs. Those who take vows observe a fast until the day of the main festival, when they participate in an elaborate ceremony during which they would carry the Kavadi, which is beautifully decorated with flowers. Watching the ceremony is a harrowing experience, for the devotees carry heavy objects such as coconuts or limes, and some even draw the chariot of the festival with the hooks pierced through various parts of their bodies. It is believed that the devotees enter into trance and become the embodiments of the gods such as Murugan, Hanuman, and so on. (Although the worship of Hanuman takes special place among the Hindi-speaking Hindus in the context of the worship of Rama, it also is quite integral to the Kavadi festival.) Festival participants often offer devotion to the persons who claim to embody the gods by offering them fruits, washing their feet, waving the lamp, and receiving their blessings.

In anthropological terms, such acts of humans manifesting themselves as gods are usually seen as acts of transcending the normative social status. In caste society, one way a person can transcend one's social status is to "become an embodiment" of a god. Even if the person is from a lower level of society, the higher social groups have to offer devotion and reverence to them. In today's South Africa, where Hindus generally do not subscribe to caste rules, such acts could be seen not necessarily in terms of acquiring higher social status but rather as expressions of their personal power.

Mariamman Worship

The worship of the goddess Mariamman is common among Tamil and Telugu-speaking Hindus, as well as among many Hindi-speaking Hindus. One of the earliest Mariamman temples is built on a sugar cane estate outside the city of Durban in the northern suburb of Mt. Edgecomb. The other popular shrine of Mariamman is situated on the south coast of Durban, known as Isipingo Rail. For decades these two temples have played a vital role in providing for the religious needs of Hindus. Even to this day many Hindus from around South Africa still visit these temples not only because of their historical importance and their long association with these temples, but more importantly because of the belief that worshipping at these temples would bring special blessings and provide answers to their prayers.

Traditionally, Mariamman is believed to have manifested in various forms, and the physical phenomenon most commonly associated with such manifestations is the anthill. This explains the place of an anthill in the inner shrine of Mariamman. As is the case with many rural cultures in India, goddess worship is invariably associated with the earth and its vitality. The goddess Mariamman embodies the vital and fertile force that sustained the people who depended on the land for their daily living. In much of rural Tamilnadu and Andhra Pradesh states in India, Mariamman is worshipped whenever there is famine and other natural calamities. In particular, her worship is important for good crops every year. She also protects crops from perishing and prevents illnesses from affecting both cattle and people.

Although devotees can visit Mariamman's temple and pray to her any day, most of them visit mainly when they are in crisis situations—such as facing financial loss, disease, psychological suffering, social and family disputes, and so on. When people experience such crises in their lives, they take vows, and upon recovering from these crises, they visit Mariamman's temple to make offerings to the goddess for protecting them during their time of need. In the Indian villages, Mariamman is considered the protector of the village, and hence her shrines are to be found mostly on the outskirt of the village. She protects people from falling sick with smallpox, being deprived of crops, rain, and so on. The prosperity of the village is believed to be dependent on rituals performed annually to please the goddess. An angry goddess is believed to be a threat to the village.

All the Mariamman temples in South Africa become very busy during their annual festivals. In South Africa, the Mariamman festival takes place in August and is known as Porridge Prayers. Every Hindu household that worships the goddess Mariamman prepares a special sour porridge, which is offered to her along with fruits, milk, and coconut during their visit to the temple. The ritual begins with the worship of Ganesha and then Madurai Veeran (a male figure always associated with Mariamman), followed by the main prayers to the goddess. Some devotees, mainly those who have taken specific vows to do so, perform the optional circumambulation of the nine planet images. As Mariamman, Kali and

Gangamma are generally seen as of the same kind, some devotees also offer worship to Kali and Gangamma during the same prayers.

Draupadi Amman Worship or Firewalking Ritual

The goddess Draupadi is also commonly worshipped mainly by the south Indian devotees in South Africa. Like other festivals, hers is shared by other Hindus. Her mythology shares to a certain extent the narrative from the epic Mahabharata, one of the two popular epic texts—the other being the Ramayana—which have become significant religious resources for most Hindus today. The Mahabharata revolves around the deity Krishna and two families of cousins feuding for the control of their kingdom. Krishna plays an important role as a special advisor to the hero Arjuna and guides him in the battlefield. His dialogue with Arjuna before the war is recorded in the text known as the Bhagavadgita, which is perhaps on a par with the Christian Bible as far as Hindus are concerned. The Bhagavadgita became the central text for most Hindus today because of its emphasis on ethics and morality.

However, unlike in the classical Mahabharata epic, where she is a princess and Arjuna's wife, Draupadi in the Tamil variant of the mythology is considered a goddess. Her festival, which is popularly known as the firewalking ritual, occurs during the week of the Christian festival of Easter. During this period, the temples of Draupadi are specially prepared for the rituals associated with firewalking. A large pit is dug up in which wooden logs are burnt on the day before the devotees walk on the burning embers. As in the case of Mariamman worship, devotees take vows for various reasons and seek the blessings of the goddess Draupadi. Upon receiving those blessings, the devotees participate in the rituals and walk on the hot embers to prove their faith in her. Ostensibly no one suffers from burns except for an occasional mishap.

During the ten-day firewalking ritual, it is common in most temples to enact the epic story, especially the episode of the battlefield in which Draupadi kills her husbands' enemies and in order to demonstrate her chastity, walks on the burning embers. According to the epic, Draupadi was married to five brothers as a common-law wife, and she remained chaste in terms of her family custom of living with one husband at a time each year.

The ritual procedures and the various elements in both Mariamman and Draupadi worship are fairly similar and seem to fulfill similar expectations and beliefs of the devotees. Both are non-vegetarian communal rituals in which offerings of chicken, goats, eggs, and so on, are common.

264

Communal meals are an important feature of not only these two rituals, but in general most South African Hindu festivals.

Paratassi Prayers/Pitrapak

The period from 17 September to 17 October each year is called the month of Parattasi in the calendar of South African Hindus. This month is dedicated to the worship of Muruga. Almost all Hindus—and especially those who are non-vegetarian in their diet—fast during the month of Paratassi. They abstain from all forms of non-vegetarian foods, alcohol, smoking, gambling and so on. This fast mainly significant for the south Indian Hindus, while north Indian Hindus observe what is known as Pitrapak. While Paratassi is observed for a whole month, Pitrapak is observed for a ten-day period. Nevertheless, the common motif of both rituals is the remembrance of the dead. It is believed that the dead return every year during this time to visit their loved ones, and in return the living offer them food through ritual offerings. The meeting of the living and the dead through the medium of food is deeply embedded in a chain of beliefs in the soul, its transmigration, and rebirth in the course of its search for final emancipation. It is further deeply entrenched in a certain view of action—known in Indian terms as Karma. The soul, as it inhabits the body, performs actions, some good and some bad. As a result, it accumulates merits and demerits. When the soul departs from its body, the merits and demerits follow it, and in order to reap the consequences of those actions, it returns to take a new birth in a form befitting the type of merits and demerits it accumulated in its life on earth. Thus the soul is believed to transmigrate after its departure from the body and returns to take a new form of life. This transmigration carries on until the soul is able to break out of the cycle of birth and death either through its own self-realization or through divine intervention, depending on which philosophical view one takes. That is, if one takes a non-dualist philosophical view, then one is supposed to follow the path of self-realization through one's own effort. But if one follows the philosophy of devotion to God, then it is understood that God through his grace will intervene and rescue the individual soul. This latter is somewhat analogous to the Christian view of salvation. The role of observances like Paratassi or Pitrapak is to acknowledge the idea that the living have a responsibility to ensure that their departed forbears are on course through the process of transmigration.

Figure 13.2: *A worshiper kneeling in front of the Shrine of Vishnu. Vishnu is considered a deity who is mentioned in the Vedic texts, but became popular in the medieval period through the rise of devotional movement in India. The doctrine of Vishnu theology depicts him as the supreme God. There are several branches of Vishnu worship throughout India. Srivaishnavism in South India is a good example to understand Vishnu worship. In this tradition, Vishnu is always associated with his divine consort Lakshmi, the bestower of wealth. Photo by P. Pratap Kumar.)*

Navaratri Puja

Although in many parts of India (especially in Andhra, Karnataka and Maharashtra) Navaratri (nine nights) festival stands on its own—it is often known in Andhra and Karnataka as Dassara because of the ten-day ritual associated with it—in South Africa this special festival primarily focusing on the goddess Durga cannot be separated from Paratassi. It occurs towards the last phase of Paratassi and brings the fasting month to a close with a celebration of the goddess' victory over the demons on the last day, known as Vijayadasami. With the observance of prayers to the nine planets the final prayers are conducted to bring the fasting to an end. The formal closing of the Paratassi and the observance of the prayers of Navaratri in a way inaugurates the season of Diwali.

Diwali Festival

Diwali or Deepavali (arrangement of lamps in a row) is usually observed in the last week of October or first week of November, depending on the lunar calendar of the Hindus. As we have noted with regard to other festivals, because of the diversity of the Hindu community in South Africa the actual mythological narratives associated with the festival differ, but its broader significance is always associated with victory of good over evil. Both south Indian and north Indian Hindus in South Africa observe this festival. In the last decade, especially since the new democratic dispensation in South Africa, the observance of the festival has become a major event that attracts not only Hindus but also the general populace, not to speak of tourists, to the festival events in many parts of the country. In the city of Durban, the festival is observed on a large scale on the beach front, sponsored by the city council and big businesses. Festival processions and floats go around the city to mark the joyous occasion for Hindus.

The festival is associated with the return of Rama, the incarnation of the god Vishnu, to his capital, Ayodhya, after vanquishing his enemy, Ravana, thereby bringing joy to the people of his kingdom. This narrative is drawn from the Ramayana epic, which is most significant to the north Indian community. Like the Mahabharata epic, the Ramayana is another important religious resource for most Hindus, although it generally espouses the idea that Vishnu is the supreme god while Rama is one of the incarnations of Vishnu. Its story revolves around Rama, the hero who was sent to exile by his father in order to honor his word to his second wife. During the course of the exile, Rama's wife, Sita, is abducted by a demonic person called Ravana, and in the end Rama defeats him in the war and returns to his kingdom at the end of his exile. There are many regional translations of this epic story. Among the Hindi-speaking communities, the Tulasidas' Ramayana (Ramacharitmanasa) is very popular in South Africa, as it is in India and other places of the Hindu diaspora. However, some south Indians think of Diwali as a celebration of Krishna's victory over the demon King Narakasura, which is generally based on the Mahabharata. The popularity of these texts in parts of nineteenth-century India could explain why some diaspora Hindus associate the festival with one text and the others with another one. Be that as it may, the festival in itself is perhaps the only one that brings the whole Hindu community together, unlike many other festivals and rituals that are peculiar to different Hindu groups

Some General Comments

Thus far, we have mainly looked at the rituals and festivals that Hindus in South Africa observe as part of their religious life. When one thinks of Hinduism in South Africa, it is hard to think of it without these rituals and ceremonies. There are, nevertheless, many religious organizations and associations that teach Hinduism in various philosophical terms and expect their followers to subscribe to a particular philosophical view. For instance, the Ramakrishna Centre of South Africa generally subscribes to a certain modified non-dualistic Vedanta philosophy. Vedanta is one of the six systems of Hindu philosophy, and it developed into various sub-branches because of the various emphases by different interpreters. The philosopher Shankara developed a non-dualist interpretation of the Vedanta philosophy, according to which the ultimate reality or existence (viz., Brahman) is one and not two. He emphasized discrimi-

Figure 13.3: *The Trident of Shiva and his vehicle Nandi opposite the shrine of Shiva, the Bull. (Photo by P. Pratap Kumar.)*

nation and knowledge as the way to achieve the self-realization of Brahmanhood. Shankara's interpretation of Vedanta did not accommodate the idea of God, but other forms of Vedanta did.

The Divine Life Society of South Africa also subscribes to a type of Vedanta that allows for the notion of God, and the International Society for Krishna Consciousness (ISKCON, popularly known as the Hare Krishnas) preach the philosophy of Krishna consciousness and espouse the worship of Krishna as the highest form of religion.

Our focus on what people do and believe on a day-to-day basis—the sort of rituals and ceremonies that they perform—helps us locate Hindu religion within the empirically observable realm. As scholars and students of religion, it helps to focus on understanding what people do in their lives and how those acts regulate their life. Notwithstanding the fact that such acts are based on certain larger beliefs and philosophical views, the on-the-ground activities of people that we study allow us to also understand how their beliefs and philosophical views have been modified and adjusted to their changing circumstances.

Much of what Hindus do and believe has to do with their social and physical wellbeing. The fact that most of their rituals revolve around vows and fasts indicate that there is a close relationship between their beliefs and their day-to-day lives. What affects them is seen in relation to their beliefs in the gods and goddesses that they have come to worship following centuries of devotion by their forebears in India. There have been continuities and discontinuities in their Hindu way of life in South Africa. All of it is expressed in their rituals, ceremonies and celebrations.

Some Contemporary Challenges to Hindu Thinking

Hindus living in the diaspora face new challenges as they make their worldview relevant to the alien cultural world. One of their biggest challenges is to ensure their worldviews are transmitted to the next generation. For this reason, practicing Hindus take their children to the temples and the various devotional meetings and expose them to their religious ideas and activities. This is why they built shrines and temples representing their traditions from the onset of their arrival in South Africa. Another important aspect that generated a great deal of debate among many Hindu organizations involves temple priesthood. Unlike in India, Hindu priesthood in South Africa is not linked to membership in the Brahmin caste. Because most Hindus that settled in South Africa were from non-Brahmanical groups, usually from agrarian backgrounds, the Hindu priesthood evolved without any strict caste affiliations. Besides, the worship of gods and goddesses related to the agrarian cultures in India did not require a Brahmanical caste-based priesthood. And most of the Hindus that came to South Africa brought with them their village worship traditions in which priesthood is not necessarily linked to the Brahmanical castes. Anyone who had some specialist knowledge of rituals that he, or in some cases she, may have learnt from parents and other teachers could become a priest and perform rituals at both temples and at homes, officiating at marriages, funerals, and other rituals.

Since the early 1990s, however, more liberal immigration laws allowed the gradual arrival of priests from Sri Lanka, and the situation regarding the Hindu priesthood began to change. Some wealthy Hindu businessmen began to sponsor priests from Sri Lanka and helped them to be appointed at some major temples such as the Umgeni Road Temple, Cato Manor Temple, Havenside Road Temple, and others in the Durban metropolitan area. These new priests believed that their procedures were the correct way to perform Hindu ritual, which raised a few eyebrows initially and eventually led to a major debate about whether the existing ritual procedures and methods in South Africa should be changed to conform to those observed in India and Sri Lanka. This would mean also a reintroduction of the Brahmin caste-based priesthood in South Africa. Not only those who have been performing priestly duties for many decades but also the lay Hindus themselves often objected to the methods used by the Sri Lankan priests and expressed loyalty to their old traditions established by their forebears in the mid-nineteenth century. Just to indicate the nature of the objections raised by locals, perhaps we could consider the differences in the clothes worn by the two different types of priests. The South African priests have been used to covering their entire body, whereas the Sri Lankan priests always removed their upper garments, thereby exposing their body above the waist. Furious objections were raised by locals expressing the view that such exposure of one's body in front of the deity as well as the devotees, especially women, is unacceptable and unbecoming!

Another recent debate in South African Hinduism is about same-sex marriages. In November 2006 the South African Parliament adopted a bill permitting same-sex marriages to be officially recognized. Surprisingly, some prominent Hindu leaders came out in support, although they had indicated that they could not find scriptural testimony for such unions. Their support was based on the fact that modern society has been changing and that if two individuals of same sex wish to live together and have the same status as married couples, the law should not come in their way. Hinduism, according to them, should find a tolerant approach towards them and integrate them into the society. The president of the South African Hindu Maha Sabha, an umbrella organization for all Hindu organizations, however, expressed his view that although he had no difficulty with people of same sex living together, approving their marital status was not proper within Hindu view of life. For him, Hinduism upholds the view of marriage for purposes of procreation within an honorable and acceptable tradition.

Such debates, of course, indicate the changing circumstances within which Hinduism has to express itself meaningfully. The transmission of traditional Hindu values has to take into account the new and changing conditions of society. Such values need to be reinterpreted through the new social and political conditions. Observing how South African Hinduism has evolved since the first Hindu community arrived in South Africa in 1860 helps us to not only trace its many changing trajectories but also allows us to understand the new inventions of their social hierarchies, ritual procedures, and various social and religious customs. Returning now to the couple with whom we began this narrative, viz., Madhavan, who belongs to the Tamil culture and his spouse, Pramila, who belongs to the Hindi or north Indian culture, it would be interesting to see how they would continue their Hindu traditions and what new inventions and changes their generation would add to the South African Hinduism. In Hinduism, nothing seems to be cast in stone!

We have looked at Hinduism in its various manifestations in contemporary society. The approach here has been to underscore the idea that instead of presenting Hinduism through time-frozen texts, we looked at its manifestation far away from its homeland, in a society such as South Africa. Through globalization, today practitioners of virtually all religions are present everywhere, and Hindus are no exception.

Suggestions for Further Reading

Jacobsen, Knut A., and P. Pratap Kumar, eds. *South Asians in the Diaspora: Histories and Religious Traditions.* Leiden: Brill, 2004.

Knott, Kim. "Hindu Temple Rituals in Britain: the Reinterpretation of Tradition" In *Hinduism in Great Britain*, edited by R. Burghart, 157-79. London: Tavistock, 1987

Kumar, Pratap P. *Hindus in South Africa: Their Traditions and Beliefs.* Durban: University of Durban-Westville, 2000.

———. *Religious Pluralism in the Diaspora.* Leiden: Brill, 2006.

Richman, Paula. "The Ramlila Migrates to Southall." In *Questioning Ramayanas: A South Asian Tradition*, edited by Paula Richman, 309-328. Berkeley: University of California Press, 2001.

14

Christians

George D. Chryssides

Until recently, the English market town of Crossington was home to a small Roman Catholic book shop. Brigid, the manager, specialized in the local church gossip, which she shared with her customers, who included Anglicans and also Greek Orthodox Christians, who had a small local congregation. As well as books, the shop sold icons and statuettes, cards for confirmations, baptisms, and festivals, plus candles, incense, and church music. Above the bookshop is the CAFOD office—the Catholic Agency for Overseas Development—which aims to fight poverty and to seek social justice, particularly for the poor. Unfortunately, the bookshop suffered from dwindling sales, mainly due to competition from the Internet. Brigid never succeeded in appealing to the evangelical Protestants, who were unable to relate to much of the Roman Catholic imagery and who preferred to patronize the Wesley Owen chain of bookstores. The former book store is now a help center for Life, the Roman Catholic organization for the protection of unborn children.

Whatever their differences, Roman Catholics, Eastern Orthodox, and Protestants alike (Christianity's three major traditions) at least share the same Christian story. All would agree that Christianity is to be traced back to its founder-leader Jesus of Nazareth (4 BCE–30 CE). Foretold by prophets, Jesus' birth was heralded by the Angel Gabriel, who appeared to Mary, his mother-to-be, and announced that, despite being a virgin, she would give birth to the world's savior. Born in a stable in Bethlehem, his birth was announced by angels who appeared to shepherds, and he was visited by Eastern astrologers (Magi), who followed a star and presented him with gifts of gold, frankincense, and myrrh.

Jesus was baptized in the River Jordan, tempted by the devil, and emerged as a popular, although controversial, preacher, proclaiming the kingdom of God, teaching by parables, and performing miraculous healings. He gathered together twelve principal disciples, and his ministry ends with them sharing a final meal, commonly called the "Last Supper,"

Figure 14.1: *Orthodox church, Walsall, England. (Photo by George Chryssides.)*

around Passover time. Betrayed by Judas Iscariot, one of the twelve, Jesus was arrested, handed over to the Romans, whose governor Pontius Pilate sentenced him to crucifixion. Three days later, some women and two disciples—Peter and John—visited his tomb and found it empty. The resurrected Jesus appeared several times to his close followers and forty days later ascended into heaven. After ten days, his disciples re-assembled, and experienced the Holy Spirit descending on them—an event that is regarded as the birth of the Christian Church. The final part of the story is still to come: Jesus Christ will return to earth on the clouds, winding up human affairs, after which a final judgment will take place.

All this might be called the "rhetorical version" of the religion: it is the account with which followers are familiar and which is preached from Christian pulpits. However, different Christians regard it in different ways. Many take it literally, while many present-day Christian scholars are more skeptical. Although most Christians are unfamiliar with modern scholarship, many would hesitate to affirm the Bible story as literal truth. In practice, they draw on the story for guidance and inspiration, but do not hold firm views on matters of history or even theology. Even the clergy, who are trained theologically, tend not to disseminate the findings of scholarship to their congregations; in an Orthodox church, for example, the priest's homily is typically little more than a re-telling of the gospel passage that has been read earlier in the service.

Believers not only know this story, but it is acted out in the yearly cycle of the liturgical calendar. Sacred time is as important to the Christian as sacred story, and the two intertwine. The Christian festival year begins with Advent—not Christmas as one might have expected. In the Roman Catholic and Protestant traditions, Advent consists of four Sundays leading up to Christmas, and is a time of anticipation of Christ's coming— his second coming as well as his incarnation.

The Western churches celebrate Christmas Day on 25 December, while the Eastern Orthodox Church continues to

The Christian festival year

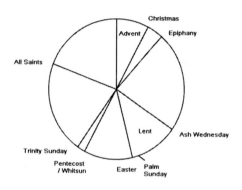

Figure 14.2: *The Christian Festival Year.*

apply the old Julian calendar, celebrating the festival on 7 January.[1] It is one of the most important Christian festivals, and marks the birth of Jesus: the date is traditional, but probably not the actual date of Jesus' birth, which the Bible does not define. The "twelve days of Christmas" end with Epiphany, which commemorates the visit of the Magi, who came to Jesus bearing gifts of gold, frankincense and myrrh. The word "Epiphany" literally means "to show forth," and it signifies the "manifestation of Christ to the Gentiles." The Magi, being astrologers from the East, are reckoned to have been Gentiles rather than Jews, and hence the festival highlights the Christian understanding that Christ's coming is an event of significance for the entire world and not merely for the Jewish people to whom he belonged.

Lent follows some time after Epiphany: its exact timing varies, since the date of Easter varies from year to year. The Eastern and Western churches differ somewhat in the dating of Lent and Easter, on account of the calendrical differences. Usually, but not always, Lent and Easter

1. The Orthodox Church in America celebrates Christmas on 25 December, but uses the Julian calendar to determine the dates of Lent and Easter.

fall at slightly different times for each tradition. Lent is a forty-day period (excluding the Sundays), marking the forty days Jesus spent in the desert, fasting and being tempted by Satan, before beginning his earthly ministry. It is a subdued, somber period in the Church calendar, and many Christians endeavor to make some personal sacrifice, demonstrating that they can control their earthly desires. On Ash Wednesday, Roman Catholics (as well as some other Christians) mark this first day of Lent by going to church and receiving the sign of the cross, made from ash, on one's forehead. The final week of Lent, known as Holy Week, commemorates Christ's passion. It begins with Palm Sunday, which marks Jesus' triumphal entry into Jerusalem, mounted on a donkey, and hailed by crowds. The ensuing week focuses on Jesus' imminent death, with Good Friday as the most solemn day in the Christian calendar. During Holy Week many churches hold extra services recalling incidents in Jesus' last days. The Thursday of this week (Maundy Thursday) marks the celebration of the Last Supper, and many churches celebrate Holy Communion. Since the Bible records that Jesus washed the feet of his disciples before the meal, a ritual foot-washing is sometimes incorporated into the liturgy. On Good Friday some churches follow the "stations of the cross," enabling the faithful to follow the incidents from Jesus' death sentence to his burial.

The solemnity of Lent highlights the exuberance of Easter, which is the high point of the Christian calendar, marking the day of Christ's resurrection. Some churches hold Easter vigils, either on the preceding night or in the early hours of the morning, commemorating the watch that was kept over Jesus' tomb and recalling his resurrection at the dawning of Easter Day. Forty days after Easter is Ascension Day, always on a Thursday, commemorating the return of Christ into heaven. Ten days from this brings Christians to Pentecost (also known as Whitsun), recalling the coming of the Holy Spirit. The following Sunday is Trinity Sunday. This day summarizes the key events in the Christian tradition, which have involved the Father, the Son, and the Holy Spirit, and highlights the completeness of the godhead.

The ensuing Trinity season is a lengthy period of over twenty Sundays without major festivals. (Some churches count the Sundays from Pentecost instead of Trinity.) All Saints' Day, popularly observed as Hallowe'en, occurs at the end of October, and its particular emphasis on the dead reflects the concept of the church as including Christians of the past, as well as those of the present and future. Other festivals falling in this season are not part of the Christian story, and are therefore not strictly liturgical festivals. These include Thanksgiving in the United States, known as Harvest Thanksgiving in the United Kingdom, at which God's goodness in providing food is celebrated. Remembrance Sunday is celebrated in the United Kingdom on the Sunday nearest 11 November and commemorates the two world wars.

The Bible

The story which Christians act out liturgically is found in its key scripture, the Bible. Although "Bible" literally means "book," the Bible is not a single book, but is an anthology of sixty-six writings. It is divided into two sections, commonly called the Old Testament and the New Testament. The Old Testament contains the same books as the Jewish scriptures, but in a different order. Christians believe that their faith inherits and completes the Jewish story, beginning, they teach, with the story of Adam and Eve, how they disobeyed God ("the Fall") and were cast out of the Garden of Eden. The Israelites made various attempts to regain their forfeited favor with God, and God entered into a "covenant" with various patriarchs, notably Noah, Abraham, and Jacob, promising a return to favor, if they obeyed his commandments. Moses led the Israelites out of bondage in Egypt, in which they had become captives, and they received God's law at Mount Sinai during their desert wanderings. They finally reached their promised land of Canaan, where they prospered for several centuries, but were later exiled in Babylon. Following the Persian conquest of Babylon, the Jews were allowed to return to and rebuild their country. At the time of Jesus' birth, Judaea was once again under foreign occupation, this time by the Romans. It is in this context that messianic hope arose: there emerged a popular belief that God's messiah (meaning "anointed one'") would come and re-establish the kingdom as it was in the days of King David.

The New Testament, consisting of twenty-seven books, picks up the story by proclaiming Jesus as the messiah. The four gospels (Matthew, Mark, Luke, and John) begin the anthology, presenting Jesus from slightly different perspectives. The first three are clearly interdependent, having much common material. Traditionally Matthew was regarded as the first gospel, but most present-day scholars have come to regard Mark as the original one. John writes independently, and his work is much more theologically oriented than the three "synoptic" writers. Whether any of the gospel writers were eye-witnesses of Jesus' ministry is disputed: Matthew and John purport to be members of Jesus' inner circle of twelve apostles. Mark and Luke make no such claims, but seem to be known to the apostle Paul.

The Gospel of Luke has a sequel, the Acts of the Apostles, which begins with Jesus' ascension and tells the story of the early Church, focusing primarily on Paul, who made four extensive missionary journeys, taking the newly founded Christian faith into the world of the Gentiles, traveling as far as Rome. Paul's writings form the next part of the New Testament: twelve letters are attributed to him: nine of these are addressed to early Christian communities in the Gentile world, and four are to individuals, although many scholars believe that not all of them are authentic. The Letter to the Hebrews—really a theological treatise rather than a letter—makes no claim to Pauline authorship. A number of short letters follow, attributed to Jesus' disciples James, Peter, John, and Jude, the last of whom claims to be James' brother. The final book is Revelation (sometimes called the Apocalypse), which is a series of visions of signs of the end-times and of the heavenly "New Jerusalem" to be established in heaven and on earth. The imagery of the book is obscure, and few Christians would claim to understand it. Because of its cryptic nature, it has given rise to a wide variety of interpretations; many Protestant fundamentalists hold that it unfolds a timetable of imminent events on earth, leading up to the final "Rapture"—a happening at which Christ will return and gather up his faithful into heaven. A number of American Protestant novels have endeavored to envisage such events, most notably the *Left Behind* series by Tim LaHaye and Jerry B. Jenkins.[2]

In addition to the 66 books comprising the Old and New Testaments, there exists a body of literature known as the Apocrypha. These come from Jewish sources, but were written in Greek rather than Hebrew. Some are historical, some are hagiographical (recounting pious legends), while others are apocalyptic (prophesying a dramatic end to human history) or philosophical. In many cases, their exact origins are unknown. This body of literature is found in the Latin Vulgate—Saint Jerome's translation of the Bible (384 CE)—and hence has found its way into the Roman Catholic and Eastern Orthodox canons of scripture. It is not accepted by Protestants, although some parts are occasionally read in Protestant churches.

Mention was made earlier of the two testaments—the Old and the New. The word "testament" in this context is perhaps somewhat misleading: the Greek word *diathēkē* means "covenant," and the two "testaments" are fundamentally about two "agreements" between God and his people. The new covenant does not demand obedience to the Jewish law. Christians, particularly of the Protestant variety, have emphasized "justification by faith"—a key theme in Paul's teaching. "Justification" means "making straight" (as in "justifying a margin" when typing); Christians teach that it is not possible to "get right with God" by obeying his com-

---

2. Tim LaHaye and Jerry B. Jenkins, *Left Behind: A Novel of the Earth's Last Days* (Wheaton, Ill.: Tyndale House, 1995).

mandments, because sin is more than simply a series of human misdeeds. Traditionally, Christians have taught that when Adam and Eve sinned, they became subject to "original sin," which is a condition, not merely a disobedient act. This condition must be reversed, and Jesus Christ accomplished this, being the "second Adam," living a life of perfect obedience to God, and paying the price of the world's sin, by dying on the cross. Believers can now experience forgiveness and gain everlasting life. Christ's death is an act of grace on God's part, and thus "grace" (undeserved favor) is a key concept in Christianity.

Key Tenets

The belief that humanity owes the debt for sin, and that only God can pay it, has caused the Church to insist that Jesus was fully God and fully man, not half-god and half-man. As the Athanasian Creed puts it:

> As God he is equal to the Father,
> as human he is less than the Father.
> Although he is both divine and human
> he is not two beings but one Christ.

Christians have formulated a number of creeds, which serve to define the person of Christ. The best known and most used are the Apostles' Creed and the Nicene Creed, although the former is not used within Orthodoxy. Despite the name, the twelve apostles did not write the Apostles' Creed, although there is an apocryphal story that each of the twelve contributed a line on the day of the first Pentecost. Its genuine origins are uncertain: its earliest appearance in its definitive form is in the early eighth century. It runs as follows:

> I believe in God, the Father almighty,
> creator of heaven and earth.

> I believe in Jesus Christ, his only Son, our Lord,
> who was conceived by the Holy Spirit,
> born of the Virgin Mary,
> suffered under Pontius Pilate,
> was crucified, died, and was buried;
> he descended to the dead.
> On the third day he rose again;
> he ascended into heaven,
> he is seated at the right hand of the Father,
> and he will come again to judge the living and the dead.

I believe in the Holy Spirit,
the holy catholic Church,
the communion of saints,
the forgiveness of sins,
the resurrection of the body,
and the life everlasting.
Amen.

The Church and the Sacraments—Baptism and the Eucharist

The creed refers to "the Church," and, theologically speaking, there is only one church. In common parlance, one frequently uses the word "church" to mean a building or a denomination, but the theological definition of "church" (often signaled by an initial capital 'C') is "all Christians everywhere." The creeds relate the church to the concept of "the communion of saints": hence the church does not merely consist of its present members, who are still alive on earth, but of all Christ's followers, past, present, and future. A "saint" is not necessarily the spiritually advanced individual who has been canonized by a pope and who is depicted with a halo: a "saint" is one who endeavors to follow Christ on earth and who is part of his kingdom.

Mention was made of the notion of "covenant," and the necessity of physical signs to testify to it. A number of the church's principal rites make use of physical matter to signify the way in which God guarantees his promise of salvation to the faithful. These rites are known as sacraments, and despite certain differences in understanding and practice, baptism and the eucharist are accorded special importance in all Christian traditions. There are two exceptions: the Quakers (or Society of Friends) and the Salvation Army. Emerging as a more radical part of the Protestant Reformation, the Quakers abandoned all externalities in worship, preferring simply to sit in silence at a Quaker meeting and to allow any member who feels prompted by the Spirit to speak spontaneously to the gathering ("giving ministry"). The Salvation Army takes the view that the believer can place absolute trust in God's grace in Jesus Christ and that no external signs are needed.

The Catechism in *The Book of Common Prayer* defines a sacrament as "an outward and visible sign of an inward and spiritual grace given unto us, ordained by Christ himself, as a means whereby we receive the same, and a pledge to assure us thereof."[3] Christians make use of two sacraments:

3. Church of England, *Book of Common Prayer* (London: Collins, 1968 [1662]).

baptism and the eucharist. To these, Roman Catholicism and Ortho-doxy add a further five: confirmation (called "chrismation" in Ortho-doxy), penance, anointing the sick, taking holy orders, and marriage. The question of whether all seven rites or only two should be regarded as sacraments was a point of contention at the time of the Protestant Refor-mation. Protestantism takes the view that, in order to qualify as a sacra-ment, the rite must be instituted by Jesus himself. According to the Bible, Jesus instructed his disciples to baptize (Matthew 28:19) and to celebrate his last evening meal (1 Corinthians 11:23-26), but he gave no instruction to perform the other rites. Although Jesus' presence at the marriage at Cana, where he is said to have turned the water into wine (John 2:1-11), suggests his approval of the institution of marriage, he gave no instruc-tion that men and women must marry.

Most Christian churches practice infant baptism, at which either water is sprinkled on the baby's forehead, or the sign of the cross is made on the head with water. In Eastern Orthodoxy, babies are baptized by total immersion in water. In all traditions, the celebrant uses the Trinitarian formula, naming the child and saying, "I baptize you in the name of the Father, and of the Son, and of the Holy Spirit." The Baptist and Pente-costal churches take the view that baptism should only be administered to adults who have a firm personal commitment to following Christ, which clearly a baby cannot have. In these two denominations, baptism is by total immersion.

The second sacrament is the Eucharist, the celebration of the last meal that Jesus had with his disciples before his arrest. The rite goes by differ-ent names in different traditions.

"Eucharist" is a generic name, although some Protestant Christians may not recognize it since they are more accustomed to the term "Holy Communion." "The Mass" is the Roman Catholic term —decidedly avoided in Protestant circles, who wish to distance themselves with beliefs and practices that have been associated with it. Some minor Protestant groups, such as the Brethren, prefer the phrase "The Lord's Supper"—an expression used by Paul.[4] Originally the Eucharist was intended to be a symbolic common meal, signifying that the Christian Church was "one body, for we all partake of the one loaf."[5] However, the Eucharist has become the source of much division within Christendom. On account of the historical splits in Christianity, the validity of clergy's ordination has been questioned. Eastern Orthodoxy and Roman Catholicism have insisted that their clergy must be ordained by a bishop whose lineage can

4. 1 Cor. 11:20.
5. 1 Cor. 10:17.

be traced back to the apostle Peter, whom Jesus said was the "rock" on which he would build his Church.[6] (The name Peter—*petros* in Greek—means "stone" or "rock.") Protestantism departed from this practice, and Orthodoxy and Catholicism stem from rival sees. Hence there is dispute about who may legitimately celebrate the Eucharist, and who is eligible to receive it.

Figure 14.3: *Corpus Christi celebrations in a square in Bordeaux, France. (Photo by George Chryssides.)*

There is also disagreement in theological understanding of the Eucharist. Roman Catholicism has traditionally held that, in a real sense, the bread and wine become the body and blood of Christ, since Jesus said, "This is my body."[7] Obviously, the change is not believed to be a physical one, but rather a metaphysical one, and the doctrine is known as "transubstantiation." If the eucharistic elements become Christ's body and blood, then it follows that when the priest raises them above his head, he is offering Christ up once again as a sacrifice. The doctrines of transubstantiation and the sacrifice of the Mass were emphatically rejected by the Protestant reformers. There is no agreed theology of the sacrament in Protestantism, but most Protestants view Holy Communion at least as

6. Matt. 16:18.
7. 1 Cor. 11:24.

an act of thanksgiving (which is the literal meaning of the word "eucharist") for Christ's atoning sacrifice and as a memorial to his life, death, and resurrection. Protestants have also held to the doctrine of Christ's "real presence," acknowledging that in some spiritual sense he is present with his followers, although not through any miracle of transubstantiation.

Orthodoxy rejects transubstantiation but contends that something real takes place. However, what happens is a mystery and hence does not admit of precise explanation. Indeed, Orthodoxy prefers to talk about the "seven mysteries" rather than the seven sacraments. The word "Orthodoxy" can mean "right praise" as well as "right doctrine," and Orthodoxy is more concerned about proper and authentic modes of worship. Hence the Orthodox are more concerned about the way in which the mystery is celebrated than about its theology. The Orthodox hold that the Last Supper was not a Passover meal, and hence Jesus and his disciples would have used leavened rather than unleavened bread. Accordingly, they use ordinary table bread (*azumē*) rather than the eucharistic wafers that are common in Roman Catholicism and Anglicanism. The bread is crumbled into the wine, and communicants receive both elements together on a long spoon, administered by the priest.

The Church and its Divisions: the Great Schism

Although the church is one church, we have already noted that Christendom's many divisions. The split between Roman Catholicism and Eastern Orthodoxy took place in 1054 and is known as "the Great Schism." As Christianity grew, the status of the Bishop of Rome increased. However, there was another city whose bishopric was regarded as important: Constantinople, also known as Byzantium (now modern Istanbul in Turkey). Byzantine Christians regarded their own bishop as the supreme source of authority, and there was rivalry between the two sees. Eager to establish Constantinople's supremacy, Byzantine leaders sought to demonstrate that Roman doctrines were inauthentic, and the main controversy between the rival factions related to the Trinity. Eastern Orthodox Christians hold that the Holy Spirit proceeds only from the Father, while Western Christians affirm that he proceeds from the Father and Son.

Christians are insistent that they are monotheistic, and that the notion of the Trinity does not imply that there are three gods. However, God is three "persons": these are not parts of God, neither are they simply aspects or manifestations. The doctrine can be more easily understood once it is explained that "person" should not be understood in the colloquial sense of "individual." The word is related to the Latin word *persona*, whose original meaning came from ancient drama and meant "mask."

283

Actors typically wore masks to indicate their role, and an actor who had more than one part in a performance would change masks off-stage and come back with a different *persona*. The Christian Trinity is to be understood somewhat in this way. Just as we can say that an actor "is" the part (for example, "Helen Mirren is Queen Elizabeth II"), so God is the Father, the Son and the Holy Spirit—all three, each of whom are equally God. This idea is often expressed in the form of a triangle, sometimes depicted in churches (often in Latin rather than English).

One important difference between the Trinity and the actors in a drama is that God is not to be construed as simply acting a part in being Father, Son, and Holy Spirit. God really is all three, and each member of the Trinity is fully God. The average Christian would probably be unable to explain the doctrine, however, acknowledging that God's nature is mysterious, not wholly amenable to human comprehension.

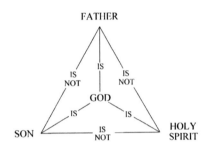

Figure 14.4: *Visualizing the Trinity.*

The theological occasion for the East-West split concerned the position of Holy Spirit in the Trinity. Anxious to demonstrate that the doctrines of Roman Catholicism were less than sound, the Eastern churches pointed out that the phrase in the Nicene Creed concerning the Holy Spirit—"who proceeds from the Father and the Son"—was inauthentic. The words "and the Son" (*filioque* in Latin) did not appear in the original text, and were added, mainly in sung versions of the Creed. If it is asked why such a fine point should be of importance, the Orthodox would affirm the importance of maintaining the tradition of the Church without alteration and also insist that there needs to be one single fount of divinity, not two.

Protestantism

The Catholic-Protestant split came around five centuries later. Protestantism is characterized by its emphasis on the Bible and its doctrines of salvation by faith and divine grace. Protestants typically regard themselves as having a faith that comes from the heart, with direct access to God. Almost all Protestants will at least have heard of Martin Luther (1483-1546), with whom the rise of Protestantism is usually associated, and even if they are unfamiliar with the writings of the Swiss theologian

John Calvin (1509-1564), many of Calvin's ideas find expression in the preaching and worship in Protestant churches.

Martin Luther was a monk and an academic, and his study of scripture brought him to the conclusion that "we have been justified by faith,"[8] not by good deeds or by the use of intermediaries such as the saints or the Virgin Mary. One key Protestant notion is "the priesthood of all believers," which highlights each believer's direct access to God. (It does not imply that Protestants do not have clergy, which most Protestant denominations have.) Luther's quarrel with the Roman Catholic Church began with an attack on its system of "indulgences"—financial donations to the Church for the purpose of rebuilding the ornate St Peter's Basilica and the Vatican's Sistine Chapel. Luther's critique of Roman Catholicism went further, however, and on 31 October 1517 he nailed his "Ninety-five Theses"—ninety-five objections to the beliefs and practices of the Church—to the main door of the church at Wittenberg. The ensuing controversy caused Luther finally to deny the authority of the pope, which marked the beginning of the Protestant movement's secession from Rome.

Protestant reformers aimed to make the Bible available in the language of the people, rather than in Latin, which was the language of the Roman liturgy. The desire for a religion based on faith led to a removal of "aids" to devotion such as icons and statues depicting the saints or the Virgin Mary. Protestants tend to object to statues and crucifixes, viewing them as a violation of the second of the Ten Commandments: "You shall not make for yourself an idol."[9] Stained glass is acceptable, being two-dimensional, and also serving a didactic function where the glass depicts scenes from the Bible. The focal point of a Protestant church tends to be its pulpit—important for preaching God's word—and frequently a plain, empty cross is prominent. Not only does the plain cross not contain a "graven image": it is a reminder to the worshipper that Christ does not remain dead on a cross, but that the cross is empty since Jesus has risen from the dead.

Worship is simpler within Protestantism. Roman Catholicism and Eastern Orthodoxy have an elaborate predetermined liturgy. By contrast, Protestant churches tend to have no uniform pattern of worship, with the order of service tending to follow local practice rather than any denomination-wide blueprint. In England, under King Charles II, Parliament passed the Act of Uniformity in 1662, requiring the Book of Common Prayer (approved by Queen Elizabeth in 1559) to be fol-

8. Rom. 5:1.
9. Exod. 20:4.

lowed in all churches. Some two thousand clergy rebelled and were removed from office—an event known as the Great Ejection. Many of these clergy established their own congregations, becoming the "Non-Conformist Churches" or "'Free Churches." The Baptists had already established their own identity. While Orthodoxy and Roman Catholicism make the sacrament available as the principal service each Sunday, the main service in Protestantism is not necessarily a communion service. It consists of readings, prayers, and a sermon, interspersed with hymns. Holy Communion is celebrated less frequently: hearing God's word on a regular basis is more important.

Christianity is complex, and there are denominations that are difficult to place within the three-fold distinction of Eastern Orthodoxy, Roman Catholicism, and Protestantism. The Anglican tradition is one. Anglicanism is a worldwide tradition, originating from the Church of England. (In the United States Anglicans are known as Episcopalians, and in Scotland the denomination is known as the Scottish Episcopal Church.) The English Reformation stemmed from King Henry VIII's appeal to the Pope for annulment of his marriage to Catherine of Aragon. The Pope's refusal ultimately led to Henry's assumption of headship over the Church, and, ever since then, the reigning monarch has been the Church of England's titular head. The Church of England retains Roman Catholicism's episcopal hierarchy, consisting of bishops and archbishops (of which there are two—the Archbishop of Canterbury and the Archbishop of York), but not cardinals or a pope. Although, unlike Roman Catholicism, the Church of England established the practice of having its worship in the language of the people, the pattern of the service follows the Roman model. Whether the Church of England is "Protestant" is a moot point: it often describes itself as "catholic and reformed."

Mention here should be made of Methodism. Founded in 1784 by John Wesley (1703-1791), with the aid of his brother Charles (1707-1788), the movement gained its rise from Wesley's itinerant preaching throughout England. It was unusual for Church of England clergy to evangelize outside their parishes, and since many churches closed their doors to Wesley, much of his preaching was in the open air. The split from the Church of England was occasioned by John Wesley's ordaining his own ministers: the Church of England only permits ordination by a bishop. Although the Methodist liturgy bears some similarity to Anglicanism, the denomination's organizational structure is different, being grouped in circuits, each with a Superintendent Minister, and overseen by District Synods and the Annual Methodist Conference, which is the denomination's authoritative body. Methodism is particularly associated with singing, which plays a major part in worship. John and Charles

Figure 14.5: *St. Michael's (Anglican) church, Walsall, England. (Photo by George Chryssides.)*

Wesley were prolific hymn writers, and Charles Wesley's son and grand-son—Samuel Wesley (1766-1837) and Samuel Sebastian Wesley (1810-76)—were organists and composers.

Like many religions, Christianity has been male-dominated for the greater part of its history. In Roman Catholicism, women have been able to gain admission to monastic orders, but without the priestly powers of presiding over the sacraments or pronouncing absolution for sins. Eastern Orthodoxy and Roman Catholicism have had an entirely male priesthood throughout their history. Within the last 150 years or so, Protestantism has given increasing recognition that the priesthood of all believers includes women, and in 1853 the first woman—Antoinette Louisa Blackwell (1825-1921)—was ordained to the full ministry in the Congregationalist Church in the United States. Until the mid-twentieth century women's ordination was rare, but then grew steadily. In 1992 the Church of England formally approved women's ordination. Not all Prot-estants approve of women's ordination: some of the more conservative denominations refer to Paul's statement: "I do not permit a woman to teach or to have authority over a man; she must be silent."[10] Accordingly,

---

10. 2 Tim. 2:12.

the Southern Baptist Church in the United States and the Independent Evangelical Church—to name two examples—do not allow women's ordination.

Christian Ethics

All religions provide guidance for life, and Christianity has its moral code in common with all other religions. Unlike the other traditional religions of the world, Christianity does not have distinctive "special obligations." While, for example, Jews and Muslims avoid pork, most Christians believe they have permission to eat anything.[11] There is no prohibition on alcohol or tobacco, although the Bible teaches that one's body is "a temple of the Holy Spirit,"[12] and hence that due regard should be paid to one's health. While there are Christian vegetarians, they avoid meat through personal choice rather than from any religious requirement. Some Protestant groups are opposed to alcohol: at one time Methodists avoided it on principle, although many Methodists now drink.

Although Christianity is based on a "new covenant," Christians do not totally reject the law of Moses. All Christians accept the Ten Commandments, and—in common with all people of integrity—are opposed to murder, stealing, adultery, lying, and so on. If asked about Christian ethics, many Christians would think of Jesus' Sermon on the Mount.[13] In this discourse Jesus comments on the Mosaic Law, although Christians are not altogether agreed about what his stance was. Some think that Jesus was asserting himself as a higher law-giver than Moses, while others see him as offering a heightened interpretation of Mosaic standards. For example, Jesus taught that anyone who has lustful thoughts is an adulterer and that anyone who becomes angry is guilty of murder.[14] In Christianity ethical standards apply to one's thoughts as well as one's actions, although no doubt most Christians find this a rather tall order.

Apart from the Roman Catholic priesthood and monastic orders, the vast majority of Christians live a conventional lifestyle, like other members of society. A few communities have followed the early Church's example of community living and sharing of possessions, but this is uncommon: most Christians accept the Bible's teaching, that they are "in the world" but "not of the world."[15] This entails living in a world that has inherited Adam's original sin, but not living according to worldly practices, such

11. Acts 10:9-16.
12. 1 Cor. 6:19.
13. Matt. 5-7.
14. Matt. 5:21, 27.
15. John 17:13-19.

288

as telling untruths, committing adultery, or putting personal ambition before the welfare of others.

In recent times, matters of sexual morality have aroused debate. Christians of all traditions regard marriage as a serious commitment, not to be entered into lightly, and not to be dissolved without very good reason. The marriage vow commits the couple to living together "till death us do part." However, Christians are not unrealistic and realize that marriages often go wrong, and not merely as a result of adultery—the one reason Jesus specified for permitting divorce.[16] Roman Catholicism does not permit the re-marriage of divorcees, even civilly. Anglicanism allows the remarriage of divorcees, but not in church, although a couple can request a Church blessing ceremony, as happened when the Archbishop of Canterbury blessed the civil marriage of Prince Charles and Camilla Parker-Bowles at Windsor Chapel in 2005. Eastern Orthodoxy permits the re-marriage of divorcees in church on two further occasions, while Protestant churches do not have formal restrictions.

In Western society, the idea of confining sexual relationships to marriage is coming under question. Many couples live together without undergoing any official ceremony, and this is increasingly tolerated. Homosexuality remains a thorny issue within the Christian faith, and attitudes vary markedly. Some conservative Christians disapprove thoroughly of all gay and lesbian relationships, while at the other end of the spectrum a few clergy in the Anglican and Protestant traditions will provide religious blessings for same-sex relationships, although not on church premises.

In general, all Christians would claim to base their ethics on the teachings of the Bible, although with differing degrees of literalness. For the Roman Catholic and the Orthodox Christian, the Church tradition is an additional source of authority, and Roman Catholicism has codified the Church's pronouncements on ethics in its canon law. Because Protestants reject papal authority, they would possibly lay greater emphasis on the importance of conscience in matters of morality. Paul spoke of conscience as a law written on one's heart,[17] arguing that the Gentiles of his time could not plead ignorance of the Mosaic law. However, the authority of conscience in no way implies subjectivity, or that "anything goes" in matters of morality. In the Protestant tradition, Christian ethics has been popularized by the "What Would Jesus Do?" (WWJD) movement. The slogan originates from a nineteenth-century book by Charles

16. Matt. 5:32.
17. Rom. 2:15.

M. Sheldon, entitled *In His Steps: What Would Jesus Do?*[18] Sheldon was an American Congregationalist minister and one of the leaders of the "social gospel" movement. Towards the end of the twentieth century, the book was brought back into print, and WWJD paraphernalia marketed, mainly within evangelical circles, although the popularity of these goods is not by any means confined to this tradition.

Modern Trends in Christianity

The last two centuries have witnessed some major changes within Western Christianity. The European Enlightenment created an emphasis on reason rather than faith, and the rise of science presented a challenge to the Christian faith. The principal challenges to traditional Christianity in the nineteenth century came from Charles Lyell (1797-1875), whose *Principles of Geology*[19] suggested that fossils were millions of years old—much older than the traditional date given for the world's creation: 4004 BCE. Charles Darwin (1809-82) published his *Origin of Species* in 1859,[20] and the theory of evolution still causes disquiet in conservative Christian circles. The idea that *Homo sapiens* and apes may have had a common ancestry not only militates against the notion that the Earth was created in six days, as described in the Bible, but also contradicts the doctrine that humanity was a special divine creation, the culmination point of God's creative work.

The Enlightenment caused critical reflection on the part of scholars of religion as well as scientists. German scholars began to ask questions about the sources of the Bible, arguing, for example, that the first five books of scripture were not written by a single author (assumed to be Moses) but edited from writings by at least four authors, representing different perspectives. "Higher criticism" was not confined to the Old Testament, but applied to the New. Not only were questions raised regarding authorship, but about whether the Gospels could be regarded as a reliable historical account of the events they described. In some respects the New Testament proved to be more vulnerable than the Old, since it records many more miracles, which appeared to be unscientific and contrary to reason. The "quest for the historical Jesus" continues, with no sign of any substantial consensus. Some scholars have seen Jesus as primarily a teacher, since his teachings cannot be countered by scientific and historical evidence; others have contended that the Gospel miracles are

18. Charles M. Sheldon, *In His Steps: What Would Jesus Do?* (London: Walter Scott, 1896.)
19. Charles Lyell, *Principles of Geology* (London: Penguin 1997 [1830]).
20. Charles Darwin, *On the Origin of Species* (London: Odhams, 1859).

merely embellishments of historical happenings. More recent scholars, such as Rudolf Bultmann (1884-1976), have suggested that the Gospel accounts do not hark back to any real historical happenings to any great degree, but reflect answers to controversies that were occurring within the early Church.[21]

One major problem raised by the "Jesus of history" debate is that the resurrection is a miracle, and scholars who reject miracles on principle therefore appear to be removing the principal salvific event from the Christian story. It was by way of response to Christian liberal scholarship that Christian fundamentalism emerged. A number of conservative scholars organized a Bible Conference at Niagara, New York, in 1895, and formulated five principles of fundamentalism: (1) the literal inerrancy of the Bible; (2) the divinity of Jesus Christ; (3) the Virgin Birth; (4) the substitutionary theory of atonement; and (5) the physical resurrection and bodily return of Christ.

For some Christians, a return to the Bible involves more than simply subscribing to its teachings. It records people performing miraculous healings and "speaking in tongues," and some Christians held the view that modern-day believers should be doing this as well. Speaking in tongues ("glossolaliation") is a phenomenon that harks back to the early disciples' experience at Pentecost. The Pentecostal movement took its rise in 1906 at a revivalist meeting at Azusa Street, Los Angeles (commonly referred to as the Azusa Street Revival), where people met to pray and study. As the intensity of their devotion built up, members found themselves speaking ecstatically in a language that was not recognizable as any human speech. The movement spread through the United States and Britain, and became institutionalized in various Pentecostal denominations, the most prominent of which are the Elim Foursquare Gospel Alliance, the Apostolic Church, and the Assemblies of God.

Pentecostal Christians lay considerable emphasis on prophecy—one of the "gifts of the Spirit" mentioned by Paul.[22] Some Pentecostal churches have a designated prophet, but all of them allow members of the congregation to speak in tongues and to offer any message that they believe the Holy Spirit has placed on their hearts. Pastors, who have oversight of congregations, tend not to be formally trained, but to be chosen from the congregation, since wisdom and knowledge are also gifts of the Spirit, rather than skills learned at theological seminaries. Services at Pentecostal churches therefore tend to be exuberant and spontaneous. Members may feel constrained to read a Bible passage of their choice or give a

21. Rudolf Bultmann, *Jesus and the Word* (London: Collins, 1958)
22. 1 Cor. 12:10.

testimony of what God has done for them. It is common practice for a service to end with spiritual healing, where members may come forward and receive "the laying on of hands" by the pastor.

Many "black churches" are Pentecostal. When black immigrants first came to the West, many initially attended mainstream churches in the United States and the United Kingdom. Regrettably, many felt less than welcome, sometimes being victims of racist attitudes within the churches, and often feeling that Christian worship was formal and restrained. They therefore decided to form their own Black Pentecostal churches, the best known of which is the New Testament Church of God. It is important to put on record that, although racism has undoubtedly been found in Christian congregations, the Church has also done much to combat it. One high-profile campaigner was Martin Luther King (1929-1968), a Baptist minister, and one of the leaders of the American civil-rights movement, who was assassinated by an opponent.

Recent and Future Trends

This account of Christianity has endeavored to encompass many of the vastly differing expressions of the Christian faith. Although there have been many occasions throughout history where Christians have been in conflict with each other, politically, theologically and institutionally, it is a matter of concern that the Christian faith, although theologically "one Church," should have so many divisions. It is a matter of considerable embarrassment that a religion that is committed to Christ's commandment of loving one's neighbor should find itself made up of so many rival factions, who question the validity of each other's ordination, eligibility to receive the Eucharist, and how the sacraments should be administered. At times rivalry has even generated physical conflict, as in Northern Ireland.

The ecumenical movement has been an attempt to address the problems of denominational rivalry, and can be traced back to the nineteenth century. Within the Protestant tradition a number of inter-denominational youth organizations took their rise, such as the Young Men's Christian Association (YMCA, 1844), the Young Women's Christian Association (YWCA, 1855), and the World Student Christian Federation (1895). In the United States the Federal Council of Churches was formed in 1908. Of particular importance was the Great Missionary Conference held in Edinburgh in 1910, attended by some 1,200 delegates representing 160 missionary societies. After 1910 the ecumenical movement gathered momentum, particularly among Protestants, with the formation of other national Councils of Churches, and the setting up of the World Council of Churches in 1948.

Not all branches of the Church have wished to be drawn into ecumenical activity, however. Initially the Roman Catholic Church declined to be part of the World Council of Churches, arguing that there was only one church, not "churches" in the plural. Historically, Roman Catholicism has defined the church as consisting of those who "are joined in the visible structure of the Church of Christ, who rules her through the Supreme Pontiff and the bishops."[23] At the other end of the spectrum, there are evangelical and charismatic Protestants who are opposed to Roman Catholicism, frequently for reasons that hark back to the Protestant Reformation. These evangelical Christians, particularly Pentecostals, are concerned about the liberal attitudes of other Christians, as evidenced by their toleration of homosexuality and their abandonment of biblical literalism, and prefer to participate in their own inter-denominational organizations, such as the National Association of Evangelicals (NAE) in the United States and the Evangelical Alliance in the United Kingdom.

Some ecumenical activity has involved attempts to devise means of recognizing each other's ordination and sacraments. Ecumenical activity has encompassed a variety of projects, including Bible translation, aid work in developing countries, environmental activity, and the search for worldwide peace and justice. On the institutional front, there has been progress. One particular success was the formation of the United Reformed Church in 1972 in England and Wales, a merger of the English Presbyterians and the English and Welsh Congregationalists; the Reformed Association of the Disciples of Christ merged with them in 1981.

Mission and Other Faiths

Despite their origins in missionary concerns, many Christian churches are now less concerned with working ecumenically for proselytizing purposes. As globalization has brought together the world's various faiths on a more equal footing than that of the nineteenth century colonial missionary heyday, many Christians seek to explore inter-religious dialogue, rather than convert members of other faiths who were described as "heathens" or "pagans" in previous generations. In the wake of Darwin's evolutionism, some missionaries, such as J. N. Farquhar, suggested that other

---

23. *Lumen Gentium* (1964), cited in *Catechism of the Catholic Church* (London: Geoffrey Chapman, 1994), para.837.

faiths might be a step on the evolutionary scale, culminating in Christianity.[24] Other writers, such as the Roman Catholic theologian Karl Rahner, have suggested that Jesus Christ could in some sense be present in other religions, offering salvation through them.[25] Such opinions have proved controversial: some Christians believe it is patronizing to claim that other faiths are less "evolved" or that members of other faiths are being saved through Christ without knowing it. Evangelical Christians, however, particularly fundamentalists, continue to remain adamant that an explicit act of repentance and turning to Christ is necessary for salvation.

In contrast to those who continue to argue about the position of adherents to other faiths, there are Christians who contend that Christian mission should no longer be directed against "false religion," but that the Christian's real enemies are materialism, secularism, injustice, poverty, and a variety of social ills, and that their task remains to redeem a fallen world. It is unlikely in the foreseeable future that Christians will reach any agreement about the nature of Christ's kingdom, and how it might be brought about. The "kingdom of God" is a multifaceted and a contested concept: while agreeing that it involves justice and truth, different believers continue to attach different understandings and degrees of importance to each of these components.

Suggestions for Further Reading

Bowden, John, ed. *Christianity: The Complete Guide*. London: Continuum, 2003.

Chryssides, George D., and Margaret Z. Wilkins. *Christians in the Twenty-first Century*. London: Equinox, 2009.

Hill, Jonathan. *The History of Christianity*. Oxford: Lion, 2007.

Klein, Peter. *The Catholic Source Book*. Dubuque, Iowa: Brown-Roa, 2000.

Lindberg, Carter. *A Brief History of Christianity*. Oxford: Blackwell, 2006.

Taylor, Richard. *How To Read a Church*. London: Rider, 2003.

Ware, Timothy. *The Orthodox Church*. Harmondsworth: Penguin, 1963.

24. J.N. Farquhar, *The Crown of Hinduism* (Oxford: Oxford University Press, 1913).

25. Karl Rahner, *Theological Investigations* (London: Darton, Longman and Todd, 1965).

15

Chinese Religionists

Shawn Arthur

If you ask typical Chinese people "Are you religious?" most will answer "No." However, if you follow them throughout their lives, you will find that many pray and light incense at various Daoist and Buddhist temples, embody subtle Confucian principles, and participate in a range of popular religious practices.

Unless they are members of a formal religious organization, Chinese people generally do not identify with a particular religion. Rather, as circumstances of need arise throughout their lives, the Chinese show interest in parts of various religions in a fluid manner—regardless of their primary interest in being non-religious, atheist, Daoist, Buddhist, Christian, Muslim, Jew, or something other.

To call Chinese religionists "believers" is to say they are claiming to take part in a relationship of "mutual trust" (*xiangxin* 相信; the term translated as "believer") with another. In other words, people are taught that all proper social relationships have demands of mutuality and reciprocation placed upon them; therefore, people have the idea that performing ritual actions with the proper intent will bring about changes in their lives because the deity who receives the offering will be obligated to help them. Furthermore, Confucianism (a moral and intellectual socio-political system whose focus is to create a harmonious society by producing individuals who act properly in all social circumstances) teaches people to treat deities "as if" they were real—if people are to go to a temple to make an offering or prayer, they need to believe in the efficaciousness of their actions, even if the concept of supernatural agency is questioned.

According to religiously inclined Chinese, Buddhism can help alleviate life's suffering, Confucianism deals predominately with education and social harmony issues, and Christianity is well-known for its beautiful wedding ceremonies. On the other hand, Daoists deities are thought to be particularly efficacious when dealing with issues related to long life, health and illness, and uncontrollable situations, as well as death and the afterlife.

In this way, the Chinese historically have had an inclusive understanding of religion. Individuals who have not taken vows to formally associate themselves with a particular religion can choose to participate in any religion at any given time because it is commonly recognized that each religious tradition addresses different circumstances in peoples' lives. How does this happen? Let us begin our examination of lived Chinese religions with Daoism, China's major remaining indigenous religious tradition. If people need divine intercession for themselves or on behalf of a loved one, they often will visit a Daoist temple or shrine to pray for help and health.

Visiting a Daoist Temple

When a Chinese visitor walks into a Daoist temple in modern China, after paying a small

Figure 15.1: *Daoist Guardian of the East with the Green Dragon.*

admission fee, they must first pass through the main gate building, at the south end of the temple complex, which houses statues or paintings of the temple's guardians on either side of the entrance. These two figures, the Green Dragon in the east and the White Tiger in the west, symbolize the primordial powers of yang and yin, respectively.

The term yang 陽 originally meant "the sunny side of a hill," and it came to refer to the active energetic principle of the cosmos, and thus yang correlates to life, sunrise, rapid movements, lightness, and forcefulness. On the other hand, yin 隱 originally referred to "the shady side of a hill," and it came to refer to the more stable, subtle energetic principle of the cosmos, and thus yin correlates to death, sunset, slow and deliberate movements, heaviness, and carefulness. Yang and yin are *not* equated with the moral principles of good and evil. An imbalance between these two forces is considered bad, not the forces themselves. The traditional Chinese worldview argues that every ideal situation should have a balance between yang and yin, since these are the two most fundamental manifestations of the Dao 道—literally "the Way," but understood as the Way the universe works, the ultimate cosmic principle, the vast and eternal mother of all things, and the principle at the heart of all transformations. Thus the Daoist temple guardians have the attributes of balancing the subtle energies of all who enter the temple complex, as well as protecting the temple and its inhabitants from chaotic or harmful influences.

The gate buildings of many religious temples throughout China, as well as the areas just outside the gates, contain small shops and stalls that sell deity statues and religious paraphernalia, but more importantly they sell bundles of musky-scented incense sticks, sheets of colored tissue paper, and red candles. People who visit the temple to pray or worship are expected to purchase a set of these ritual combustibles that are burnt at the appropriate time during prayer.

Once through the entrance gate, visitors enter a large courtyard from which the layout of the temple complex becomes evident. For Daoist and Buddhist temples across China, the main gate is typically located in the south and the main deity halls are along the central north-south axis, while shrine halls to minor deities and important Daoists, the tea house or vegetarian restaurant, administrative offices, living quarters for the monks and nuns who work at the temple, and various other buildings are aligned to the east and west sides of the main temple buildings. The significance of this layout is twofold: first, it mimics the structure of the Chinese imperial palace, where the emperor sat in the north looking out towards his kingdom to the south. (Following this standard, ancient Chinese compasses and maps were also oriented to point southward.) Second, the Daoist pantheon was conceived of as a celestial counterpart of China's traditional bureaucratic model of government. This celestial bureaucracy has the Jade Emperor residing in the supreme position in the North Star, corresponding to the actual emperor, with the other deities residing in throughout heavenly realm and having jobs that are significant to the harmonious operation of the cosmic and earthly realms—such as the Director of Destiny, the Director of Health, the Director of Fertility, and the Director of Weather. Many Daoist temples house shrines to these deities.

In addition to the compass orientation, Daoist temples have many significant symbols crafted into their structures. For example, the main temple buildings are generally square in shape, symbolizing the Earth, while the central portion of the inner roof of the main building is round,

Figure 15.2: *Daoist temple building with dragons, pearl, and mountain shape. The laypersons are lighting candles and incense before entering the shrine. (Photo by Shawn Arthur.)*

symbolizing the celestial realm where the deities are thought to reside. The temple complex itself and the steeply pitched roofs of the temple buildings represent the sacred mountains where the Dao is thought to manifest in its most pure forms. The main gate of many temples, for example, is called the Mountain Gate, and entering the temple is symbolic of beginning a journey to climb a sacred mountain. In fact, there are many mountains in China that are considered culturally significant and sacred, and many are home to a large Daoist temple or monastery complex.

At the apex of many temple roofs sit two ceramic dragons facing each other with a flaming pearl in between them. This image represents an important goal for the temple and its monastic inhabitants: the cultivation of purified energy symbolized by a pearl of *qi* 氣 (the organic material energy that is found throughout the cosmos and is the basis for life) through the balance of yin and yang energies (the dragons). Ideally, the perfected *qi* emanating from the temple will not only help restore any cosmic imbalances, but it will also help the human social realm to become more harmonious, and it will improve the health and longevity of each visitor and resident. But who visits Daoist temples, and what do they actually see and do there?

Laypersons and their Worship Rituals

There are three major types of people that can be found at religious institutions across China: social visitors, laypersons, and clergy. Social visitors go to temples with little or no interest in becoming involved in any religious activities and ideas. Some of them meet with friends for tea and relaxation; others are interested in the spectacle of the religious adherents or in the beautiful art and ornate architecture of the buildings. Other social visitors are the tourists who travel to historically and culturally significant places yet who know little about the religious traditions themselves. A great deal happens in a temple of which social visitors remain unaware as they look at burning incense, people prostrating themselves, and the artistic and architectural elements in their midst.

Laypersons (non-clergy believers and devotees) on the other hand actively participate, thought not necessarily often, in temple-oriented religious activities such as attending religious festivals and worshipping and praying to the deities. These are the temple visitors who are described throughout this chapter. Some laypersons have rudimentary training in key ideas, beliefs, and practices by Daoist clergy. Some people in this category also include curious visitors who take part in the actions of worship although they might not understand or fully believe in the reality of the divine or in the effectiveness of their practices. Many millions of people who grew up during the Cultural Revolution (1966-1976), as well as their children, have been indoctrinated into an active dislike for religious ideas. However, as China's policies have changed, many people have developed a curiosity and interest that allows them to suspend their disbelief and rediscover a hope for divine assistance. This is a large subset of the laity in contemporary China, as it has been throughout China's history, which includes a wide range of people from students praying for assistance in exams to adults praying for prosperity, fecundity, or health for their aging parents. To be part of the Daoist laity has no formal requirements, although lay worshippers are expected to follow the precepts (such as proscriptions against killing, eating meat, drinking alcohol, lying, and having elicit sexual encounters) to their best abilities.

How does this differ from the experience of Daoist clergy? When people are called "Daoist" in China the term generally refers to the men and women who are formally initiated into the tradition, who receive the tradition's formal teachings and training, and who function as clergy members, ritual leaders, and adepts of self-cultivation. Their understanding of the religion's beliefs, practices, symbols, and rituals is significantly more sophisticated and detailed than non-initiates. This group represents what "Daoism" means in a more official capacity. Daoist clergy and Daoist laity are not equal participants in the religion, although both groups may hold similar worldviews and utilize similar prayer techniques.

When lay worshippers approach a temple building containing a deity statue, they first light a few sheets of the appropriate colored paper— yellow when prayers are uttered for assistance and red when prayers of giving thanks are said—and place them in a large cauldron in the building's courtyard. Second, they light a candle and place it in the large steel candle rack that catches the dripping wax. From the candle flame, practitioners then light three sticks of incense and place them in the large sand-filled incense burner that sits in the courtyard directly in front of the shrine building under the "watchful gaze" of the deity statue. The significance of the number three relates to the Daoist cosmological view which places humanity at the center position between the cosmic realm and the earthly realm. It is also symbolic of the practice of Daoist priests who write petitions and prayers in triplicate so that they can be buried in the earth, submerged in water, and consumed by fire so that the smoke can rise to the heavenly realm.

The worshipper then enters the shrine hall, which is basically one large room with the deity statue in the center of the back wall. As with terrestrial bureaucracy, the deities have celestial attendants to hold their ritual implements, to carry and read special texts, and to act as their advisors and messengers—and these smaller figures are located along the side walls.

Once inside the building, practitioners kneel down onto cushions that are on the concrete floor in front of the statue. This is the time when prayers are uttered and thanks are given to the deity represented by the statue. Worshippers then prostrate themselves three times—by bowing down and placing their hands on the floor with their forehead touching the back of their hands—to show their reverence, respect, and humbleness to the deity. This set of actions will be repeated at each of the major temple shrine buildings.

In larger temples, the main deity halls will have a monk or nun in attendance who will ring a large bowl-shaped bell every time adherents prostrate themselves in front of the deity. This is done to alert the deity of the presence of the practitioner worshipping them. The need for a bell is indicative of how believers understand deities and their temple statues. Daoist clergy and laity do not worship the statues themselves: they recognize that the carved figures in the temple are only symbolic approximations of divine reality, thus their focus is on the cosmic component of the deity that is represented by the statue. According to Daoist ideology, the deities are busy working in the celestial bureaucracy, and the bell is used as a gentle signal to interrupt their activities so they will pay brief attention to the concerns of the human realm.

Signaling a deity to wake up and notice humanity is done in many other ways in Daoism. For example, every morning and evening Daoist monks and nuns perform rituals to request that the deities pay attention to the temple and its inhabitants throughout the day. During the morning ceremony, the doors to the main temple buildings are opened, and the deities are "aroused from their slumber" with chanting and offerings of tea, fruit, and rice. This means that the cosmic deities are asked to send a small portion of themselves to take up temporary residence in the statues when the shrine bell is rung, thus opening a gateway from the cosmic realm to the earthly and human realms. As deities are entities that manifest a primordial form of the Dao, this allows for the influence of the Dao to become more prevalent on Earth.

Confucianism in China Today

The formalized prayer ritual outlined above is similar to traditional Confucian practices of showing filial piety to one's elders and ancestors through reverence and respect that often took the form of prostration and the giving of food. Confucian practices were never particularly interested in deities, but reverence for elders and ancestors was of paramount importance because of their crucial role in the present moment coming to fruition.

Many textbooks present Confucianism as China's predominant religion, but in actuality, much of its overt influence is in the past. To see Confucianism in modern China, we must look beyond Confucian religious institutions because the few that remain open today are museums, not temples. Instead, we can see the lived reality of Confucian ideals in the subtle rules of social etiquette, family and business interactions, and the government's bureaucratic structure, since all of these are rooted in Confucian ideas and practices. For example, Confucian reverence can be seen in action when laypersons bow slightly when they encounter a Daoist monk or nun.

This tradition can be traced to Kong Fuzi 孔夫子, the "Great Master" Kong (551-479 BCE), whose name has been Latinized as Confucius. He was a scholar with frustrated political aspirations. However, due to his lack of success, he developed a "consciousness of concern": an attitude that one should always strive to do one's best and to be concerned for others although ultimate perfection and success is uncertain. This attitude propelled him to work diligently, to carefully observe the norms of polite behavior, and to always help others. Ultimately, Confucius wanted people to learn how to be more than ordinary social beings. For him, "being religious" meant to be engaged in the process of being fully human, living a moral life, and improving the whole of the human community. This meant cultivating proper virtues, striving for the best possible education for self and society, cultivating proper manners and respect, enacting one's social roles properly, and developing a strong sense of social responsibility.

The central features of Confucian thought and practice are social virtues enacted in community settings. The two most important Confucian virtues are *ren* 仁 and *li* 禮. *Ren* means humaneness, benevolence, or consideration for others, and is meant to be the attitude that underlies all social conventions and human conduct in relationships. According to Confucius, a conscientious attitude for the self and for others is the basic aspect of being human, and therefore it must be cultivated within each person if they are to strive for their highest potential. *Li*, on the other hand, means propriety, courtesy, or etiquette. The most important practice according to Confucius is to act in accordance with *li*—to do what is correct in the proper manner in the proper situation, time, and place. The ethical actions and civil conduct of *li* are the means by which *ren* is put into practice.

The ideal Confucian acts with *ren* and *li* while exhibiting other vital virtues such as filial piety, loyalty, social responsibility, mutuality, and sincerity. As mentioned above, filial piety is crucial to developing virtue, because it enables people to develop concern for family members above the self. For Confucius, the crucible that forges the human being is the family; therefore, children should learn to respect their parents and elders. Ideally, as filial people mature, they will learn that they have responsibilities to the entire human community, and it is in "acting properly in human relationships" that Confucianism is most easily recognizable.

Although Confucianism forms the cultural DNA of China, it did not gain popularity until it was adopted as the official state policy in the early Han dynasty (c. 135 BCE). Over the next thousand years, the tradition became China's civil religion and the dominant force in education, ethics, politics, and the primary means to enter civil service. For most people through China's history, Confucianism has functioned as a sociopolitical philosophy, with some religious elements, such as State offerings to heaven and its deities, a strong moral component, and veneration of Confucius and other important ancestors; however, it remained a this-worldly tradition mostly uninterested in supernatural matters.

These teachings are propagated in the *Analects*—the collected sayings of Confucius and his conversations with many of his followers—and in other ancient classics such as *The Book of Rites* (rituals and rules of propriety) and *The Book of Changes* (the divination text called the *Yijing* 易經). The Confucian Canon introduces distinct realms of social interest—including art, morality, religion, science and technology, philosophy, politics, and history—and how to best interact with and appreciate each. However, after the Qing dynasty ended and the Republic period began in 1911 (followed by Communism in 1949), Confucianism was actively suppressed for being overly conservative, superstitious, and a detriment to modernization; however, the tradition has remained prevalent in Japan, Korea, and Vietnam.

Since the 1980s a modern intellectual movement called New Confucianism has begun to revitalize Confucianism by making it relevant to modern concerns, developing answers to problems of modern Western influences, adopting an ideology of equality and mutual respect with regards to social relations and gender concerns, and teaching that people need to recognize their moral responsibility to the human community. Only since 2005 is Confucianism again being taught in public schools— as a government-sponsored program to teach young people proper ways to act in society. The Confucian tradition claims that with proper education, people can learn to be good, humane, just, and kind. It is through repetition of actions which accord with ideal virtues that people learn to become good in each social situation that they encounter. These ideas remain part of Chinese culture, and they inform social and family interactions. However their association with Confucianism is understated throughout much of contemporary China.

Deity Halls and the Three Primes

Building upon the Confucian model of an ideal bureaucratic political system, Daoist religion envisions a corresponding celestial bureaucracy that oversees the working of the cosmos. At the top of the celestial bureaucracy sits the Jade Emperor, with the Three Primes immediately below him as the anthropomorphized manifestations of the three major divisions of reality into the cosmic, earthly, and human realms. The Three Primes are central to the Daoist pantheon, and statues of this trinity of deities are housed in the largest building at the center of most Daoist temple complexes.

These three deities are also symbolic of a significant facet of Daoist ideology and practice. When Daoist clergy and serious lay devotees take vows to follow certain precepts, they understand that part of their vows include the moral imperative of facilitating and maintaining a harmonious balance between the cosmic, earthly, and human realms. One of the major means by which this goal is accomplished is through worship of the deities, who are thought to be embodiments of the primordial Dao. The other major way is to perfect the self in order to become a human conduit for the Dao to manifest in the natural world. As Daoists practice the religion, they are able to attune themselves to the Dao; and by working to emulate its patterns in the natural world, they become human embodiments of the harmonious Dao.

The Queen Mother of the West, who is married to the Jade Emperor, is the most important goddess in Daoism. She is thought to reside to the west of China, high in the Himalayan Mountains of modern Tibet. She lives on a spirit mountain called Kunlun, which is surrounded by water on which nothing can float, thus making her realm inaccessible to mortals. Stories of her exploits, her miraculous powers, and her luscious gardens are found throughout Daoist texts and Chinese folk literature. Many popular tales tell of her special trees that bloom once every thousand years, producing peaches whose nectar bestows immortality. Subsequently, there are many historical sources that explain how emperors and wealthy aristocrats paid Daoists to travel to western China in search of immortals who would bestow the secrets of immortality on their behalf.

The statues of important deities such as the Jade Emperor, the Three Primes, and the Queen Mother of the West are generally quite large—between three and five meters in height—and they are painted in brilliant colors or are covered in gold paint to indicate their cosmic significance. These figures are housed in the major buildings along the temple's central axis. Typically, minor deities such as those overseeing fecundity, health, or deaths, and statues of influential Daoists are slightly larger than human sized and are found in the smaller buildings around the temple complex. Most deity statues are surrounded by ornate carvings, detailed paintings, and smaller one-to-two meter tall figures of their various celestial attendants. Furthermore, deity statues are almost always surrounded by protective glass or walls that symbolize the celestial grottoes (caves) in which the actual deities are thought to reside.

Shrines to Important Daoists—Laozi and the Daodejing

Most Daoist temples have a special shrine building dedicated to the deified Laozi, one of the most important figures in Daoism. Laozi 老子, whose name means "Old Master," is the legendary founder of Daoism, and he generally is sculpted or pictured as an old man with a long beard but with boyish facial features and lively, wise eyes. Laozi shrines also often contain images associated with his legendary teaching and travels.

People visit shrines to Laozi in order to pay respect to the mythological founder of Daoism, who is thought to be the best human embodiment of the principles of the Dao. Most Chinese, whether urban or peasant, have grown up hearing and sharing stories of these idealistic ways to improve life's harsh conditions and to live a simpler and more content existence in peaceful harmony. Therefore, many people pray to Laozi to help them recover from chaotic, imbalanced, and seemingly uncontrollable circumstances in their lives and for inspiration to deal with difficult problems.

Based on the figure of Lao Dan, a court archivist toward the end of the Spring and Autumn Period (770-476 BCE), Laozi is credited with writing one of the most influential Daoist texts, the *Daodejing* 道德經 (The Classic of the Virtue of the Way). As the Daoist tradition grew, legends of Laozi emerged. Some say that as he was leaving China and traveling to the Himalayan Mountains via the southwest gate at either Luoyang (outside of modern Xi'an in central China) or Chengdu city (in southwest China's Sichuan province), he was stopped by a border guard, Yin Xi, who recognized his spiritual attainments. The guard would not let him pass without sharing his insightful teachings. Laozi then wrote a text of approximately five thousand

Figure 15.3: *Daoist priests praying in front of a shrine to Laozi, which is surrounded by talismans of health and protection. (Photo by Shawn Arthur.)*

characters in eighty-one short poems, the *Daodejing*, and gave it to the border guard before riding an ox out of the country. Both Luoyang and Chengdu currently are home to large Laozi-focused temples.

The *Daodejing* remains one of the most important and influential Daoist texts, and it is the second most widely translated book in the world—with only the various versions of the Christian Bible being translated into more languages. The text is attributed to Laozi, but its authorship remains in question. Internal linguistic evidence of the earliest extant copies of the text suggests that the text was compiled by a group of proto-Daoists from 400-350 BCE.

This dating places the text during the Warring States period (475-221 BCE), at the end of the Zhou dynasty when there were 144 small kingdoms that fought one another in attempts to gain land and wealth. By the end of this era, there were seven remaining kingdoms, and it took Qin Shihuangdi (reigned 221-206 BCE), the ruler of the Qin kingdom, to unite them for the first time under a single dynastic rule with himself proclaimed as China's first emperor. The Warring States period was also called the "Period of One Hundred Philosophers" because there were so many people attempting to attract the attention of the various rulers in order to suggest means by which their constant political struggles could be replaced with harmonious and peaceful social interactions. Confucius is also thought to have lived near the same time as Laozi, and he also addressed many of the same concerns. Similar to Confucianism, Daoism sees social order coming through individual self-perfection; however, harmony and self-cultivation are not accomplished through social ethics, rites, laws, and education, but through developing naturalness, following the patterns of the cosmos, and spontaneity.

Historically, the *Daodejing* has been interpreted as a political strategy that emphasizes a utopian vision of small non-competitive communities that act in simplistic harmony with nature. In some ways, Laozi's utopian vision helped to legitimize the acceptance of Communism throughout China. The text also is understood as a metaphysical treatise that puts emphasis on sagehood—acting in accordance with the Dao while promoting simplicity, teaching by example, and controlling the self. The sage directly influences society and the world because he/she embodies the principles of the Dao in a way that people will want to emulate, and thus the Dao becomes more manifest in the human realm. These ideas remain cogent for many contemporary Chinese, who visit Daoist temples hoping to receive the beneficial effects of the Dao. The text also remains popular among trained Daoists, who are required to memorize the text, and laypersons who read it as a guide to proper living.

The *Daodejing* teaches that in order to attain a peaceful state, people must learn to recognize the Dao's patterned manifestations in the natural world, attune themselves to the Dao, and emulate the Dao's actions throughout their own lives. It is here that the Dao is conceptualized as more than a mere path or way of doing things, but instead as the way that the universe works—the fundamental reality which existed prior to and gave rise to the physical universe and all things in it. However, the Dao is amorphous and ultimately unknowable because it is vast, eternal, ineffable, constantly changing, and has no personality or consciousness. Since it is fairly difficult to define the Dao, the *Daodejing* explains that people can learn about the way it functions through close examination of its manifestations in the world around them: as the harmonious, orderly, and selfless cyclical transformations and patterns found throughout the natural world—such as the ever-changing seasons, the way water flows downward and around obstacles, and in the way yin and yang balance themselves in the world. Many of the symbols found in Daoist temples reflect these ideas.

According the *Daodejing*, living a simple life, maintaining a tranquil and clear mind, and working spontaneously to harmonize one's actions with the natural world is key to attuning oneself to the Dao. This can also be accomplished by acting like a mother who cares, nurtures, and is gentle toward others. Therefore, sages and rulers should follow the yin-based example of water and seek a lowly position while being supple and yielding to barriers rather than working to attain lofty titles and wealth, using force and determination to conquer that which is in the way of one's goals.

This ideal practice is described by the term *wuwei* 無為, which literally means "do not act acting" and which is more adequately translated as "non-intervening action." *Wuwei* is a way of acting in the world that does not force oneself in situations, but where needed jobs are completed while the doer remains moderate and selfless. A modern example of *wuwei* is surfing—and this is one sport that has influenced the spread of Daoist ideas in the West through popularizing such ideas as "going with the flow."

Once a surfer lies down on the surfboard and paddles out to sea, there are three main ways to return to shore. First, a person could lie on the surfboard and wait hours for the waves and tide to push them ever so slowly back to the beach. This is the complete avoidance of action, which is not *wuwei*. Second, the surfer could paddle straight back to shore. This is a flagrant attempt to exert and exhaust oneself to accomplish the goal, and therefore it is not *wuwei*. The third method is, of course, to wait for the perfect swelling of water that indicates the development of a wave, to jump up onto the surfboard and balance oneself at just the right moment, and to actually surf back to shore. Surfing is a useful example of *wuwei* because surfers learn to recognize, follow, and utilize the natural patterns of the circumstance to their best advantage without forcing themselves onto the situation, without attempting to control the situation, and without causing harm to others or the situation itself.

In other words, when confronted with any given situation, especially when a person is in an authoritative position, the *Daodejing* argues that the best actions will be those which do not work to promote ego-driven desires, to intervene unnecessarily in peoples' lives, or to advance goals that were detrimental to a peaceful, harmonious social system. In this way, Laozi's ideas foster a laissez-faire style of government and anarchic political theory in which society is better without powerful rulers, extensive laws, and forced morality. This continues to be an attractive idea for many contemporary Chinese who live under oppressive social conditions.

Zhang Daoling and Celestial Masters Daoism

Another key feature of many Daoist temples is a shrine hall dedicated to Zhang Daoling, who is not worshipped by the laity as much as he is venerated as an important ancestor. In 142 CE, Zhang Daoling founded institutionalized religious Daoism in southwest China (near modern Chengdu in the Sichuan province). Zhang claims to have been meditating in a cave when he had revelations from Laozi, who introduced himself as Lord Lao—the personal manifestation of the abstract, impersonal Dao. Lord Lao gave Zhang the title of *Tianshi*, "Celestial Master," which also became the name of the school associated with Zhang's teachings.

This is the first official school of Daoism, the Tianshi Dao 天師道 (The Way of the Celestial Masters). In the contemporary world, this tradition is transmitted along a patriarchal lineage, and many Tianshi Dao clergy are able to have families and live at home. They embody their official capacity as mediators between the cosmic, earthly, and human realms during rituals, which are often paid for by the lay community. The current patriarch of the Tianshi Dao School, who is sixty-fourth in the direct lineage of masters beginning with Zhang Daoling, resides in Taiwan, where this school remains popular.

Many Daoist temples across China have a shrine to Zhang because of his importance to the development of the Daoist religion. Visiting his shrine and reading the available information about him and his school is one significant way that visitors and tourists can learn about Daoism and its history, while paying due respect to the historical founder of the Daoist religion.

Zhang integrated Laozi's political vision, early self-cultivation practices, popular religious belief in ghosts and ancestors, divination, ancient mythology, Chinese medical theories of the body, and ideas of correlative cosmology to create a liturgical and ritual tradition. Additionally, the *Daodejing* became an important meditation guide, a source for the development of Daoist ethical proscriptions, and a liturgical text that was memorized and chanted during ritual. For example, the *Xiang'er Commentary* interprets the *Daodejing* in such a way as to develop nine prescriptive practices (such as being truthful, yielding, and generous) and twenty-seven proscriptive admonishments (such as avoiding deviance, injury to self and others, and egotistical desires). Even today, all initiated members of the Celestial Masters School of Daoism are meant to follow these rules.

Zhang also was influential in the development of the idea of a celestial bureaucracy of deities and immortals modeled after the governmental structure of the Han dynasty. The name Celestial Masters Daoism was appropriate because Zhang taught male and female clergy ritualized methods for worshipping and communicating with the various deities in order to petition them for help, healing, and protection for community members. Initiated clergy members were also taught how to master control of lesser spirits such as ancestors and ghosts, so that they would not be able to cause sickness or suffering among the community.

This religious community of co-ed laypersons and priests lived together, could marry and have children, and mutually worked toward creating the seeds of Great Peace for the community and the world. To attain this idealized state, Celestial Masters Daoists created complex rituals to restore and maintain cosmic and social balance. They also actively intervened via ritual into the starry realms of the deities and the earthly realm of the dead on behalf of the salvation of the community's members—both living and deceased. Ancient Celestial Masters rituals such as these can still be witnessed in Daoist temples across China and Taiwan.

Based on the model introduced by Zhang Daoling, three types of formal Daoist practitioner emerged: literati, communally oriented, and self-cultivation practitioners. Literati Daoists are part of the educated, literate elite in China, and as early as the fifth century CE literati Daoists began to collect and compile Daoist scriptures, commentaries on scriptures, and hagiographies. Text-collecting continued periodically throughout history and culminated with the Ming dynasty publication in 1445 of the *Daozang*, the Daoist canon, which contains approximately 1,500 individual texts.

Communal Daoists are closely related to Daoist organizations such as the Celestial Masters and neighborhood temples. These Daoists tend toward clergy roles whose religious expressions are through ritual practices such as liturgy, prayer, chanting, and the use of talismans—complex symbols thought to embody certain healing or protective powers. Organized Daoist groups rely on their surrounding communities for support; therefore, many Daoists have taken on roles as funeral leaders and soothsayers to generate money and interest among China's peasant population.

Daoists interested in self-cultivation form a significant subset of the religion. Historically, they codified the ancient Chinese preoccupation with longevity and perfect health with various prevalent self-cultivation techniques—such as meditation, prayer, breathing practices, grain-avoidance diets, sexual control, stretching exercises, and alchemy—into specific regimens. Additional self-cultivation practices that are often seen in Daoist temples include *qi*-manipulation exercises such as calligraphy, painting, music, meditation, and the martial arts.

These practices of nurturing life are meant to facilitate adepts' health, to help them better communicate with deities, and to perfect themselves to such a degree that a state of immortality—permanent existence—is attained. Daoist immortals are humans who perfect themselves physically, spiritually, and morally to such a degree that they are able to garner the attention of the deities, who then either grant them an extended life or invite them to hold minor jobs in the celestial bureaucracy. Ideally, to be a Daoist, especially to be part of the initiated clergy, one should follow all three of these patterns: adherents should study the Daoist worldview, should be socially responsible, should perform rituals and pray to Deities, and should undertake self-cultivation for health and spiritual advancement.

Wang Chongyang, Complete Perfection Daoism, and Immortality

After Zhang Daoling, there have been many important Daoists and Daoist schools, but none more important than the Quanzhen Dao 全真 道 (The Way of Complete Perfection) School founded by Wang Chongyang in 1167 CE. Wang claimed to receive a series of revelations from two immortals in 1159, and following their admonitions, he subsequently founded five monastic Daoist communities in eastern China (in modern Shandong). These institutions expanded the precepts and regulations that had been developed by Zhang Daoling and his followers, and a much stronger emphasis was now placed on avoiding harm to the self and others, maintaining a vegetarian and alcohol-free diet, mandatory living in or being associated with a monastic community, and maintaining a celibate lifestyle focused on balancing and strengthening one's internal *qi* energies.

This school has subsequently become the largest official Daoist school in contemporary China, with its headquarters currently located in the White Cloud Temple in Beijing. Most Daoist temples in contemporary China are associated with Quanzhen Daoism. They contain shrine halls dedicated to Wang Chongyang and his disciples, the woman and six men known as the "Seven Perfected" who were instrumental in spreading this new form of Daoism throughout China.

Quanzhen represents a new type of Daoist monasticism that closely integrates personal self-cultivation goals for its inhabitants with a social agenda centered on meeting the spiritual needs of the laity and facilitating social and cosmic harmony. To accomplish these goals, Quanzhen Daoists adopted inner alchemy as a way to focus on spiritual development through the combination of Daoist religion, various health-related longevity techniques such as controlled breathing and meditation, cosmological correlative ideas, and symbols used by Chinese alchemists of the second century BCE to the sixth century CE.

Inner alchemy began in the sixth century CE but became widespread during the Song dynasty (960-1279 CE)—a time of dramatic religious and cultural development across China—and remains popular today as a means to attain longevity and spiritual development. Adepts utilize an extensive set of metaphors and symbols to understand the landscape of the body (a composite image that corresponds to the primordial workings of the entire cosmos) and to create visualizations to refine the body's qi into a perfected immortal spirit body that is not confined to the earthly realm. During rituals, this spirit body is thought to travel to the deities in the stars or to help the deceased in the realm of the dead. Ideally, upon the death of the physical body, the immortal spirit will be able to take up residence in the celestial bureaucracy or will be able to merge into the oneness of the Dao. Although this spirit immortality is an ultimate ideological goal of Quanzhen Daoism, it is generally limited to the few men and women living in monastic institutions who are able to devote the time and energy necessary for such an endeavor. Not every Daoist is interested in going to this extreme.

Interestingly, the correlation between immortality and unifying with the abstract, cosmic Dao has been a significant feature in support of achieving this state: as human beings attune themselves to the Dao and let it manifest through them, the Dao then resonates throughout the world bringing cosmic and social harmony as natural results. Similarly, Daoist temples also function as the loci of concentrated Dao due to the amount of self-cultivation and ritual taking place there. For experienced lay practitioners, entering a temple complex comes with an awareness of a more rarified energy that is both powerful yet soothing—the manifested Dao first presented in the *Daodejing*.

Daoism under Communism

Although most temples and monasteries in China have extensive historical lineages, almost all of them were destroyed during China's Cultural Revolution—a time when the Communist party actively worked to eliminate "feudal" and "superstitious" traditions and their material representations. Throughout Chinese history, Daoism has not been widely supported by the political system of China. From the time communism became the official political system of China on October 10, 1949 until the late 1970s, the government sought to eradicate religious practices across the country. During the Cultural Revolution, most of China's religious institutions were destroyed or turned into factories, schools, and public parks; and their inhabitants were made to rejoin the peasant working population. Since the late 1970s, the government slowly has begun to recognize that religious ideas remain popular among much of the populace and has begun to relax religious prohibitions. More recently, temples have been rebuilt and slowly reopened, and this trend is accelerating as the Chinese government is realizing the importance of these temples for (1) the revenue generated by tourist dollars, (2) promoting peaceful interaction among community members, and (3) preservation of Chinese culture and its remaining artifacts. Therefore, most of the physical structures, statues, and art that visitors encounter in contemporary China are relatively new reproductions of antiques.

Although Daoism is regaining importance in Chinese society, the monks and nuns that reside in the temples across China are employed by the government. Each person living and working or living in a temple complex is assigned a specific job: from shrine attendant to ritual musician, from temple historian to divination specialist. The only jobs that necessitate significant Daoist religious training are those related to formal ritual performances—which require the perceived ability to contact and interact with the Daoist pantheon because it is with this type of intercession that Daoists hope to facilitate and maintain the harmony between the cosmic, human, and earthly realms. In this way, Daoist religious ideas continue to be propagated under the control of a government that sees religion as superstition. In modern Daoism, as with all religion in China, government committees such as the China Daoist Association oversee religious matters and limit the size of monastic institutions, monastery finances, the overall activities of the inhabitants, and the number of monks and nuns that they employ. Therefore it can be difficult for a visitor to recognize the differences between the various forms of lived Daoism when walking around a temple and observing temple life.

Why Visit a Daoist Temple?

There are many reasons for laypersons to visit a Daoist temple. Many older people go to Daoist and Buddhist temples for the same reasons that they frequent local parks: for socializing with their friends and neighbors over a cup of hot tea or finding a relaxing place to read the newspaper—after all, temples are manicured landscapes that act as idyllic places outside of social realities. However, the typical person's religious proclivities speak to many additional reasons for visiting a Daoist temple, including worshiping, asking for divine assistance, improving one's fortune, and practicing Daoist arts.

Often laity attempt to barter with the deities using an economic model of religious practice: if the deity does something for me, then I will promise to provide some set of offerings, worship, and donations for the deity. Therefore, visiting a Daoist temple, it is easy to find many people worshipping and thanking the particular deity with whom they made an oath. Due to this model of interaction, some people have developed relationships with a particular god or goddess, and it will be to that deity that the majority of their reverence and worship is directed; however, the other deities will not be ignored since they are part of a larger interrelated pantheon. Typically when a visitor buys incense, candles, and paper for worship, they receive enough to share among many of the different shrine halls in the temple complex.

One of the most common reasons for visiting a Daoist temple, however, is to garner good fortune. This is done in many ways by visitors, from prayer to touching efficacious objects to divination. Daoist temple patrons pray for an increase of good fortune when they burn offerings to the deities. Merely being present at a Daoist temple, especially on days associated with major festivals, deity birthdays, or communal rituals, is thought to be particularly efficacious for generating good merit. Additionally, many temples have good-fortune symbols (the Chinese words for luck, wealth, fecundity, and longevity) or excerpts of the *Daodejing* carved into a wall. Visitors stand well away from the wall, cover their eyes, and turn themselves around in circles to lose their bearings. Then, with their eyes tightly closed, they will walk toward the "fortune wall and will reach out attempting to touch one of the large carved characters. Devotees claim to receive benefits in accordance with the fortune symbol that is touched.

Divination is also popular at many Daoist temples. One form is the oracle block: a pair of crescent-shaped wood pieces each of which has a flat (yang) side and a rounded (yin) side. After making offerings of incense and spirit money (paper printed with designs of otherworldly money that, when burnt, is thought to become tangible cash for the receiver in the spirit realm), the person asks the deity a question and tosses the blocks onto the ground in front of them. If there is a balance of one yang side up and one yin side up, the answer is considered to be positive. If both yang sides are up, the deities are thought to be angry; whereas if both yin sides are up, the deities are thought to be laughing.

The other major form of divination is based on the *Yijing* (The Book of Changes), the ancient Confucian divination manual that purports to explain the patterns of yin and yang energetic flow throughout the cosmos as well as in the situation being questioned. In contemporary temples, visitors are able to borrow a canister of bamboo sticks to perform the divination. After making offerings to the deities, the person focuses on their question as they gently shake the canister in a rhythmic pattern. Eventually, a single stick will emerge and fall to the ground. The number on the stick is noted and taken to the person in charge of divination who provides the devotee with a piece of paper explaining their fortune—for a small fee.

After the visitor is finished worshipping, praying, and performing divinations, they are free to wander the temple grounds, to watch any rituals being performed, to sit in the tea house, or to relax while sitting on a bench near one of the many fragrant, flower-filled gardens. As Daoist temples are meant to recapture the naturalness that has been lost due to the developments of urban areas and large-scale civilization, their atmospheres are tranquil and relaxing places for reflecting on the peace and harmony represented by the Dao.

Suggestions for Further Reading

Berthrong, John H. *Transformations of the Confucian Way*. Boulder, Colo.: Westview Press, 1998.

Dean, Kenneth. *Taoist Ritual and Popular Cults of South-east China*. Princeton: Princeton University Press, 1993.

Despeux, Catherine and Livia Kohn. *Women in Daoism*. Cambridge, Mass.: Three Pines Press, 2003.

Hymes, Robert. *Way and Byway: Taoism, Local Religion, and Models of Divinity in Sung and Modern China*. Berkeley: University of California Press, 2002.

Ivanhoe, Philip J. *Confucian Moral Self-Cultivation*. Indianapolis: Hackett Publishing, 2000.

Kohn, Livia. *Daoism and Chinese Culture*. Cambridge, Mass.: Three Pines Press, 2001.

Kohn, Livia, ed. *Taoist Meditation and Longevity Techniques*. Ann Arbor: University of Michigan Center for Chinese Studies, 1989.

Laozi and Red Pine (Bill Porter). *Lao-tzu's Taoteching*. San Francisco: Mercury House, 1996.

Neville, Robert Cummings. *Boston Confucianism: Portable Tradition in the Late-Modern World*. Albany: State University of New York Press, 2000.

Slingerland, Edward, trans. *Confucius: Analects*. Indianapolis: Hackett Publishing, 2003.

Tu, Wei-ming. *Confucian Thought: Selfhood as Creative Transformation*. Albany: State University of New York Press, 1985.

Wang, Yi'e. *Daoism in China: An Introduction*. Warren, Conn.: Floating World Editions, 2006.

16

Buddhists

Eve Mullen

Figure 16.1: *Tibetan Buddhists protest the Chinese occupation of Tibet. (Photo by Eve Mullen.)*

On the steps of San Francisco's City Hall, Tibetan Buddhists living in northern California are gathered to protest the Chinese occupation of Tibet.

In 1949 China invaded Tibet and in 1959 officially occupied Tibet. Repression of Tibetan Buddhism and the partly religious governmental system of Tibet began. In front of the City Hall on a beautiful California day, maroon-clad monks and nuns from the Vajrayana tradition, the type of Buddhism that originated in Tibet, hold banners and signs with slogans such as "United Nations, We Want Justice," "Negotiate with the Dalai Lama," and "Free Tibet." Tibetan laypeople march around the block, also carrying homemade signs. A group from the Tibet Justice Center holds placards reading, "Lobsang Dhondup, 1975-2003. Murdered" to bring special attention to the human-rights situation in their homeland: Lobsang Dhondup was a young farmer executed for protesting against China in Tibet. Human-rights activist groups are present at the demonstration in San Francisco, handing out black cloths for people to wear over their mouths in order to symbolize the voicelessness of Tibetans inside Tibet. Guest speakers from local Tibetan Buddhist and Tibetan aid organizations take the megaphone to inspire the crowd. Many remind those gathered that the Panchen Lama, the second most powerful Buddhist authority in Tibet, next to the Dalai Lama, is missing. His true whereabouts are unknown, and most Tibetans believe he was kidnapped or killed as a child by the Chinese government. Reporters and cameras record highlights from the day for the local news stations.

The day is March 10, an important date in Tibetan history that has become an annual day of remembrance and demonstration for Tibetans in exile around the world. On March 10, 1959, Tibetans in their homeland protested the Chinese occupation of Tibet. It was an uprising that ended in much bloodshed for the Tibetan demonstrators. Now in cities across the world, wherever Tibetans can be found, "March 10 Uprising Day" is a day of gathering and opposition, a new, distinctly Tibetan Buddhist tradition and duty, as many Tibetans describe it; it is a day of telling others about the plight of loved ones still in Tibet, of bringing attention to the human rights situation in Tibet, and of giving voice to those who are voiceless in Tibet so that the world may not forget them. March 10 Uprising Day has become for many Tibetans a new Buddhist ritual, one that encourages and reinforces the greatest of all Buddhist religious virtues: selfless compassion.

Anatman

It is this selflessness that the Buddha himself embodied in the sixth century BCE. Tibetan Buddhism is one of many Buddhist traditions that range from the conservative Theravada, or "Way of the Elders," in Southeast Asia to the more varied and adaptable Mahayana, or "Great

Vehicle," flourishing from Tibet to Japan. Both of these main forms as well as the many sub-forms of the Mahayana are found throughout the world today. What all types of Buddhism share in common, however, are the basic teachings of the founder of the religion, Siddhartha Gautama, a prince who would become known simply as the Buddha.

The "Buddha," a title taken from the Sanskrit for "awakened one," discovered that the self or soul does not exist. Like all else in the universe, the human self is impermanent. In short, the ego is an illusion. Our personal desires are thus also illusory, and living a life of selfishness is thus nothing more than following a false path as a slave to one's own wants. This leads only to suffering. The Buddha's realization of this basic truth is known as enlightenment, the goal of Buddhist meditation. When one realizes *anatman*, or "no-self," one is then freed from *samsara*, the world of birth, death, and rebirth. This enlightenment can be attained in a human life, and selfless compassion is both a virtue to be cultivated in Buddhist practice and the quality gained upon realization of *anatman*.

Siddhartha Gautama, The Buddha

Key to this selfless behavior is nonattachment. It follows logically that if everything in the world is impermanent, and if the self or ego is also impermanent, then forming personal, clinging attachments to things, people, even the Buddha's teachings themselves, is an error. Consider the useful metaphor found in the very life story of the Buddha. Born to a king and queen of the Shakyas in what is now perhaps Nepal or the foothills of the Himalayas in India, Prince Siddhartha is said to have stated even as a mere baby, "For enlightenment I was born, for the good of all that lives. This is the last time that I have been born into this world of becoming."[1] His childhood, however, was spent in his father's luxurious palace, purposefully isolated from the outside world. The king, disturbed by the seer Asita's foretelling that the prince would never become a king himself but would instead become a great teacher, lavished upon his son a life of such pleasures that Siddhartha would never wonder about the world beyond the palace walls. The prince was given a life without suffering. Upon reaching young adulthood, however, Siddhartha's inquisitiveness prevailed, and upon visiting the world outside his youthful experience, a world filled with illness, old age, and death, he abandoned his family and royal life, including his new wife and child, to become a wandering ascetic. He thus began his journey on the path to end suffering for all creatures, vowing not to stop trying until reaching that goal. His enlight-

---

1. Edward Conze, trans., *Buddhist Scriptures* (New York: Penguin, 1959), 36.

enment successfully attained after much hardship, the Buddha returned to his kingdom with a new realization of no-self to enlighten others and establish his *dharma*, his teachings of truth that have been the basis for the Buddhist religion for centuries.

The first part of the Buddha's extraordinary biography provides a useful lesson itself: selfish attachments to the world are obstacles, problems. It can be no coincidence that the name of the son he left behind as he entered the ascetic life was Rahula, or "hindrance." Walking away from his family was surely difficult. And the temptation to remain within the luxuries that palace life offered was no doubt overwhelming. Yet the prince did leave and ultimately discovered an invaluable truth. If he had given in to desire and attachment, these jewels of discovery would have remained hidden. The story does not end with Siddhartha's exit, however. In the classic hero's motif, Siddhartha discovers a great treasure, the path to liberation, and returns to his community to share that discovery with all. When Siddhartha Gautama, alone in the forest meditating, became enlightened, he simply could have blinked out of existence and escaped the world of suffering immediately. Yet he returned to his people to teach them the truths he discovered. The Buddha's vow was to end the suffering of all sentient beings. His example, then, is one of perfect compassion toward the world without specific attachment to it.

What the Tibetan people and their supporters do each March 10, too, is exemplary of Buddhist selflessness: in order to end the suffering of others, namely those living under Chinese oppression in Tibet, they gather to call for change. Also exemplified in the Tibetan Buddhist case is a selflessness that leads to action in an impermanent world. Buddhist selflessness is often an engaged compassion working in the world. The Buddhist worldview is not a nihilistic one. To be Buddhist does not mean to shun the world or other human beings as impermanent, but to embrace the impermanent world so that suffering may end for all beings living in it.

Karma, Samsara, and the Four Noble Truths

The Buddha, in his sixth-century BCE Indian context, operated within a *karma*-based assumption about the nature of the universe. *Karma*, "action" or the law of justice in the universe, is that force of individual action that drives *samsara*, the world of rebirth. A helpful simile is that of *samsara* as a vast engine of birth, death, and rebirth, and *karma* as its fuel. All action, good or evil, returns to the individual who acts with attachment, with the wish for selfish gain. *Karma*, action done with attachment, itself causes rebirth. Thus, any action performed selflessly, without attachment to a selfish end, gains no karma and causes no rebirth. Again, nonattachment is key to the Buddhist concept of compassion: Buddhist compassion is action done out of selfless motivation, not out of egoistic, attached, desirous motivation. With this understanding, activism for others, such as holding a protest on the steps of City Hall in San Francisco for Tibet, can be ideal Buddhist action. What is unacceptable above all else is an absence of action when people are suffering.

Siddhartha Gautama found an end to rebirth in this world of suffering. His teachings, known as the *dharma* in Buddhism, can be summarized in the Four Noble Truths. These truths were the fruits of the Buddha's introspection and meditation. The four begin with the declaration that life is "suffering," *dukkha*. To put it simply, our lives in *samsara* are burdened with the constant search for happiness and comfort, yet this search results only in unhappiness. Even when one has found pleasure in life, that pleasure leads to further displeasure once more because comfort is not a permanent state. In fact, everything in existence is temporary and fleeting. For example, consider how comfortable you are sitting in your chair, reading this paragraph in your book. If you were forced to hold that position, now so satisfying, for one hour without moving, then a day, then a week, the comfort you experienced before would turn to pain and possibly even a crippling condition. Just as we constantly move about in order to stay comfortable, so do we also leave one fading happiness for another in a constant attempt to keep up with fleeting, impermanent pleasure in the world.

This leads logically to the second truth: the cause of suffering is *tanha*, craving or desire. We crave to be comforted over discomforted, sated over hungry, quenched over thirsty. We desire happiness over unhappiness. Again, we as a result eagerly wander from one thing to the next, or one idea or person to the next, hoping for that ever-elusive satisfaction. Thus far, the Four Noble Truths may seem a bit pessimistic: life is suffering, and we are slaves to our own desires, without the ability to escape our suffering. But the Buddha's teachings offer reassurance and hope. While the first two truths state the human condition and problem, the third and fourth provide the cure.

The third Noble Truth is *nirvana*. The Buddha tells us that an end to suffering is possible, and it is *nirvana*. *Nirvana* is a "blowing out," just as a candle flame is extinguished in the wind, from our lives in *samsara*. It connotes an end to rebirth, an end to life itself. Thus, there is a way out of the suffering, a liberation from our lives of craving and desires. The path to *nirvana*, to the end of suffering, is the Eightfold Path to enlightenment, the fourth truth.

The Eightfold Path as the Ideal Buddhist Life

In all religions, patterns of moral behavior can be discerned, and we refer to the collection of these guidelines for action as ethics. Buddhist ethics are defined in the Eightfold Path, the final of the Four Noble Truths. A Buddhist following the Eightfold Path is leading the ideal Buddhist life.

The Eightfold Path is like a prescription given to a patient with a good prognosis. There is a cure to suffering, according to the Buddha, and the treatment of action toward that cure is a mode of living that dwindles the earning of more *karma* and that can eventually lead to *nirvana*. The Eightfold Path is a set of guidelines from the Buddha to help us overcome suffering and desire. Briefly summarized, the eight medicines, so to speak, are correct understanding, correct thought, correct speech, correct action, correct livelihood, correct effort, correct mindfulness, and correct concentration. This Eightfold Path contains three major virtues and practices that the individual should nurture. Wisdom is attained in correct understanding and correct thought. Ethical conduct is reached via correct speech, action, and livelihood. And the central Buddhist religious practice, meditation, relies upon mental discipline honed through correct effort, mindfulness, and concentration.

Correct understanding refers to the right understanding of the nature of reality, namely the assumptions about the universe contained in the Four Noble Truths. Being equipped with a clear awareness that our suffering is caused by desires from a false ego should lead one to at least two main conclusions: first, the self is only illusion and should not be the driving force in one's life, lest further suffering arise. Second, in the knowledge that there is no self, no ego, a natural equanimity with others should begin to grow. In other words, when one lets go of one's own self, then the boundaries between "self" and "other" become more blurred, allowing compassion for all creatures to arise. This leads us to the next element in the Path to be discussed, correct thought. The compassion cultivated ideally means that gentleness, generosity, and goodwill replace violence, greed and ill-will in one's views toward the world. Together, correct understanding and thought are said to lead to *prajnaparamita*, perfect wisdom.

Correct speech means avoiding hurtful language toward others, including lies, exaggerations, useless chatter (such as gossip), slurs, and vulgarities or angry words. With correct speech, we begin to see how inward virtue should be reflected in outward behavior, particularly in gentleness and compassion toward others. Correct action draws most directly upon the concept of *ahimsa*, "no harm," and presupposes no killing, no harmful sexual acts, and no stealing. For monks and nuns, correct action more dramatically means no sex and no handling of money, both considered to be acts that encourage attachments to the world. Correct livelihood refers to how one can make a living as a lay person in as ethical a manner as possible. If a livelihood necessitates killing, as a butcher's or soldier's life does, then such a livelihood is detrimental and wrong. In addition, work depending upon lying—for the Buddha this was false palmistry, astrology, and magicians' tricks—is unacceptable. These three together—speech, action and livelihood—make up ideal ethical conduct, the correct outward manners of conducting oneself.

Correct effort may also at first sound like a prescription for outward action but is much more connected to the concept of intention, an inward effort. Effort can mean the intention to earn good *karma* over bad. It can also mean earning no *karma* and overcoming the trap of both good and bad *karma*. When one is suitably nonattached to action or *karma*, then no *karma* is earned. For example, your neighbor may trip and fall down on the sidewalk in front of you. Several thoughts may cross your mind: you might think that if you help your friend up, he will like you more. You might want him to do you a favor, and you wonder if helping him would make that more likely. At worst, you might kick him when he is down out of anger at some transgression in the past. In the Buddhist view, our intentions earn us *karma*, good or bad. The ideal is to reach that state of selflessness in which compassion flows naturally: we do not think how we might benefit from helping others, we are simply urged to help. One helps a neighbor because the neighbor needs help, with no thought to one's personal gain or desires. While good *karma* earned is better than bad, no *karma* earned is the ideal.

Correct effort is acknowledged as a mental discipline, vital to the Buddhist practice of meditation, just as correct mindfulness and correct concentration are. Correct mindfulness means to become alert in contemplation. In meditation, the practitioner must be watchful and attentive to the thoughts, feelings, body, and mental objects that are the main categories of focus. And for Buddhist meditators, correct concentration refers to a one-pointedness, a perfect unification or focus of mind, which is the essence of meditation. Without correct concentration, the practice of meditation is hindered. With right concentration, meditation is supported, and liberation is possible.

A Modern Meditation

An ordinary man sits by his open apartment window. Outside on the street below is a typical urban scene: people hurry to their destinations, the noises of buses and cars fill the air, and pollution wafts from exhaust pipes and sewer grates, acrid to the senses. The man sits quietly in meditation through all these assaults to the ears, eyes, and nose. He purposefully chooses this setting for meditation: the challenge of concentration amidst such distractions is, he calmly claims, the best cultivation for the focused mind. If one can achieve a one-mindedness within an environment of screeching brakes, car horns and roaring engines, then the task of meditation is complete. It is the ability to cut through such distractions that allows true insight into the nature of Buddhist reality. What better place is there to nurture such mindfulness, then, than a busy, noisy street?

The practice of meditation can take many forms and occur on many levels of cultivated concentration. One does not need to be a wizened monk or nun with years of isolation in a forest retreat to benefit from meditating. In fact, the goal of one-pointedness is common to all meditators, regardless of place or level of practice. Whether a Soto Zen nun in a rock garden or an ordinary lay person by a city window, the Buddhist meditator seeks to calm the mind and tame the senses so that a penetrating realization of no-self might be achieved. It is not the "I" which thinks, ponders, or reacts to a taxi's door slamming on a busy street; the meditator should conclude that these thoughts and reactions arise and fall by themselves.

Figure 16.2: *A Buddhist college student meditates in a campus setting. (Photo by Eve Mullen.)*

With this scene of modern meditation in mind, we should beware of oversimplifications of Buddhist practice. Too often scholars have tried to pit monastic practice against lay practice, with the greater authority given to monastic, "elite" life over a lesser, "folk" tradition. It would be an arrogant assumption to say that lay Buddhists are only interested in earning good *karma*. On the contrary, non-monastic Buddhists also meditate, study, and seek enlightenment. The old, stereotypical dichotomy between the monk on the mountaintop and the lay person steeped in superstition is a false one. *Nirvana* is the ultimate goal for all.

Seeking the Self and Not Finding It

Through inward-looking meditation a Buddhist practitioner focuses on reality, sees through the illusions of craving and desire, and finds liberation. When a Buddhist meditates, contrary to many stereotypes about Buddhists, he or she is not "thinking nothing." Honing one's skills of concentration can be hard work, and many forms of meditation have objects of concentration to be deconstructed or contemplated, or upon which to be single-mindedly focused. A Buddhist novice may simply attempt to focus attention upon the breath flowing in and out of the nostrils. Any thoughts that arise, such as a passing worry or wish, are to be considered not as "my thoughts" but as evidence that there is indeed no self: even in concentration, desires and cravings arise, detached from any self or soul. The Western philosopher René Descartes may have insisted, "I think, therefore I am," but for Buddhists, thoughts come and go by themselves. Therefore there is no "I" and no "I am."

Deconstructing objects to which we easily become attached is another element of Buddhist meditation. A vital treatise in some Mahayana canons is from the early Indian Buddhist adept Nagarjuna. He attempted to argue logically that the state of the world is emptiness. Connected to the idea of impermanence, emptiness refers to the lack of inherent existence in all things. Nothing lasts forever. The strongest of rocks will crumble, and the mightiest of oceans will eventually disappear and become land. What exists is only a series of connected moments in time, often accepted as continuity, but in reality in flux and possessing no stability or permanence. Attempting to find a thing in itself results in the realization that the thing does not inherently exist. To use Nagarjuna's classic example, a chariot exists on the mundane level only: we see a chariot and can touch a chariot. We can attach a chariot to a horse, hop in, and ride away into the sunset. But the Buddhist teaching is that we cannot define the chariot via its parts, shape, or collection of parts. Analysis shows only parts, parts which themselves are not permanent, and a shape that is not itself the object, for a shape of a chariot could be simply a drawing of a chariot, not an actual, functioning chariot. In short, Buddhist analysis concludes that everything, like the chariot deconstructed by Nagarjuna or the sunset into which we ride, is emptiness.

While it may be easy to think of a chariot, or even a car, a television, or another mere object as empty of existence, a person, perhaps a loved one or one's own illusory self, makes the task of deconstruction more difficult. Some meditation exercises involve contemplating rotting corpses. Again, meditation can be a hard task.

Chandrakirti, the great seventh-century disciple of Nagarjuna, expanded Nagarjuna's reasoning, producing what is for Tibetan Buddhists, an important, more complete, logical argument for emptiness. What is established once again is the impermanence of all, emptiness.

> Chandrakirti's Sevenfold Reasoning, a deconstruction of objects and an argument for emptiness. (paraphrased from Chandrakirti's *Autocommentary on the "Supplement to Nagarjuna's Treatise on the Middle Way"*)

> 1. Is the chariot inherently the same as its parts?
> No, just as there are many parts, so there would also be many chariots.

> 2. Is the chariot inherently different from its parts?
> No, for if the chariot were different from its parts, then we would be able to observe it separately from its parts. We would be able to find a chariot with no parts, or we would have to call the mere idea of a chariot, separate from the physical world, a chariot.

> 3. Does the chariot inherently depend on its parts, or
> 4. Do the parts of a chariot depend upon the chariot?
> No, for dependence would mean that the chariot and its parts would have to be inherently different, and we have already refuted this.

> 5. Does the chariot exist as inherently possessing its parts?
> No, for possession would mean that the chariot and its parts would have to be inherently different, and we have already refuted this.

> 6. Is the chariot the collection of parts?
> No, for then any heap of the parts of a chariot could be called a chariot.

> 7. Is the chariot inherently the shape of parts? No, it is not feasible for the shape of the collection of parts to be the chariot, for then any shape resembling a chariot, regardless of its function or lack of function, could be called a chariot.

In the end, Chandrakirti concludes,

> That chariot is not established in these seven ways
> Either as its own suchness or in the world,
> But without analysis it is designated here
> From the viewpoint of the world in dependence upon its parts…
> Parts, qualities, passion, definition, fuel and so forth…

These do not exist in the seven ways when subjected to the analysis
of the chariot;
They exist through worldly renown which is other.

Chandrakirti, known as Dawa Dragpa in Tibetan, does not conclude
that the chariot is not there. Buddhists do not deny the existence of
objects; only the imagined, elevated status of objects. Thus in Buddhist
analysis, objects are only established nominally. The chariot then exists
mundanely, not ultimately. What is established once again is the impermanence of all, emptiness.

Perhaps it is true that the self is the most difficult "object" to decon-
struct in this way. But "no-self" is the Buddhist truth about human beings
and must be confronted. In reality, there is no "I," no "me." Instead,
personal identity is demarcated in five components of mind and body,
called the five *skandhas*, or "aggregates." These are form, feeling, mental
discrimination, consciousness, and conditioning factors that include the
emotions. Like the parts of a chariot, these parts of a person are constantly in flux and empty.

Wrongly understanding, we believe that the self is real and lasting,
or perhaps that there is even an eternal soul, like the *atman* that those in
the Buddha's Hindu-Brahmanical context believed exists. In Buddhist
reality, however, the self is nothing more than a falsely interpreted continuity of moments in constantly moving time. The figment of self or
ego must be overcome, for it is this delusion that misleads the individual
toward a life of craving and desire. The Buddha taught that to find liberation from suffering is to recognize that there is no self to satisfy. No
ego needing feeding exists. To blow out the flame of birth, death and
rebirth, we only need to be enlightened to this basic truth, and meditation is the primary tool for comprehension of no-ego. The ultimate goal
in meditation is to become enlightened, to see and know reality as it is.
One must inwardly search for the self, and, ideally, not find it. With this
knowledge, ignorance is defeated and replaced with deep wisdom. As
the second-century teacher and poet Rahulabhadra wrote in his *Hymn
to Perfect Wisdom*,

As the drops of dew in contact
With the sun's rays disappear,
So all theorizings vanish,
Once one has obtained [Perfect Wisdom].[2]

2. Conze, *Buddhist Scriptures*,169.

Craving and desire have no hold over one who has conquered the self: who can say "I want," "I need," or most importantly "I hate" when there is no "I"? *Anatman* is not only the key to perfect, selfless action, it is also the key to enlightenment, to ultimate Buddhist liberation.

While the undertaking of meditation may not be an effortless one, it is the primary praxis of Buddhists, both monastic and lay. As a young woman who works a stressful job as a nurse in San Francisco said, "I don't think meditation is an easy task, but it is an excuse to get away from the maddening crowd. It is very healing to practice meditation."[3] Her words emphasize the curative power of meditation, not the hard work that meditation often is. This is the Buddhist Four Noble Truths in action again: our sickness is suffering caused by craving, but the cure is possible. Even the journey to *nirvana*, following the Eightfold Path with awareness, eases our pain.

Losar

It is the Tibetan Buddhist New Year, called Losar, in New York City. A meeting hall at the Ukrainian East Village Restaurant has been rented by the New York New Jersey Tibetan Association, a group of Tibetan immigrants or "transnationals"—a word which perhaps better describes the physical and psychological "traveling" immigrants experience between new and former cultures—and others who assist Tibetans in the United States with immigration issues. At the front of the hall is an altar of sorts with a framed photo of the Dalai Lama, the spiritual and political leader of Tibet and the *bodhisattva* who returns through many lifetimes to lead the people of Tibet. He is a most beloved and respected leader and a Nobel Peace Prize winner, now leading his people in exile outside of their homeland. It is part of his mission as a leader to draw the world's attention to the Tibetan situation. Throughout the day's celebration, the *kathas*, or Tibetan scarves of greeting and respect, offered to the photo of His Holiness the Dalai Lama begin to obscure the frame on the table.

Some representatives from the Office of Tibet's New York headquarters open the celebration with a Buddhist prayer, asking for peace and a return to the homeland for all Tibetans. Throughout the day, the children's groups offer presentations with traditional dance, music, and costumes to the people gathered. Speakers offer readings from the Heart Sutra. The chairs and tables set up in the room allow a good view of the performances and speakers to everyone. Lama Pema Dorje, the older monk from the Palden Sakya Center in the city, sits and chats with some

---

3. Interview with meditator, 19 March 2003.

Figure 16.3: *Photo of His Holiness the Dalai Lama almost completely obscured by scarves of greeting. (Photo by Eve Mullen.)*

of the children who are his students. They meet each week to work on the intricacies of the Tibetan language and to hear some Buddhist lessons as well. The noisy meeting hall is a change from their usual classroom at the Office of Tibet and Tibet Fund where the room is decorated with protest placards and banners used on March 10 and other days. At the entrance of the hall begins a line of food and refreshment tables that stretches across the room: the women have stayed up all night, in keeping with traditional gender roles, preparing everything from dumplings and vegetables to the beverages for the party. Next to the food tables at the entrance are petitions to be presented to the United Nations, asking for recognition and help for Tibet. Also present are guests from human rights organizations such as Students for a Free Tibet. Not everyone celebrating Tibetan Buddhist Losar is Tibetan or Buddhist, but the work of human rights groups is seen as a vital part of being both Tibetan and Buddhist. Anyone who is active for the Tibetan cause is welcome at the gathering. The fete lasts all day and into the night with more dancing, speakers, napping children, and conversation. The Tibetan community is not a closed one, but it is one in which social unity is imperative. Many of the Buddhists at Losar, and indeed at any other Tibetan gathering such as March 10 Uprising Day, the Dalai Lama's birthday, or any other, would have been members of fiercely competing schools of Tibetan Vajrayana in the past. Now, in the face of exile and with the priority of maintaining

327

Tibetan unity, differences between Gelukpa and Nyingma, Kargyu and Sakya, are all but forgotten.

The Ideal Buddhist Personhood

In Theravada Buddhism, the conservative Buddhist tradition of South-east Asia, the ideal personhood is known as the *arhat*. An *arhat* is one who has attained enlightenment but has no obligation to help others to that end. The *bodhisattva* of Mahayana Buddhism is a contrast to the *arhat*. The *bodhisattva*, literally "body of light," is an enlightened being who returns to the unenlightened out of the compassionate motivation to enlighten all sentient beings. He or she, for the *bodhisattva* can be male or female, sometimes changing in form, embodies wisdom and compassion. Upon entering the Buddhist path, a novice monk or nun might take the *bodhisattva* vow: at its most basic in any Mahayana sect of Buddhism, it is, "May I attain enlightenment for the benefit of all sentient beings." The example of the Buddha Siddhartha Gautama suffices in the Mahayana: one's path to *nirvana* is not to be a selfish path. To return to the unenlightened is the sign of the truly liberated. In Tibetan Buddhism, the Dalai Lama is considered to be Avalokiteshvara, the *bodhisattva* who has continually returned to the Tibetan people since perhaps the sixteenth century or earlier. In China, Kuan Yin is the female appearance of Avalokiteshvara. In Japan she is known as Kannon.

There is a story about Kuan Yin in China that exemplifies the role of the *bodhisattva* in Mahayana Buddhism: a rich governor asked an artist to carve a beautiful representation of Kuan Yin for him. The artist did so, and the finished work was very good. The rich governor was so moved by the excellent work of the artist that he gave his prized horse to the artist as payment. Some time later, the rich man changed his mind and wanted his horse back. He sent one of his servants to kill the artist and steal the horse. The servant shot the artist with arrows, killing him, and returned the prized horse to the governor. When the rich man went to his altar for Kuan Yin to view the beautiful carving, however, what he saw was the *bodhisattva*, her breast pierced with arrows, weeping. He immediately felt great remorse and knew the terrible error of his ways.

The story is one of a great lesson without wrath, without force. Kuan Yin is not a lofty deity quick to punish or strike down a murderer. She puts herself in another's place, with arrows in her chest just as the artist suffered arrows in his, as a being who is not above others but interchangeable with others. To be kind or cruel to any person is to be kind or cruel to Kuan Yin. The lesson is powerful: Buddhist *anatman* means that boundaries between self and other are as false as the notion of a soul is. To be compassionate toward all beings is the greatest virtue. Kuan Yin is a gentle teacher of just this lesson.

In Tibet, the Dalai Lama was the spiritual and temporal authority. For the current Dalai Lama, fourteenth in the line, the titles of "god-king" ascribed to the position in the past are matters of inaccuracy and discomfort; he prefers to be known as a "simple monk" and states as much in many of his interviews. It is not only his humor or dedication, proven repeatedly in difficult situations, which earn him respect from Tibetan Buddhists worldwide. It is his inspiring humility, as well. In *Ethics for the New Millennium* he states,

> The work of a person laboring in some humble occupation is no less relevant to the well-being of society than that of, for example, a doctor, a teacher, a monk, or a nun. All human endeavor is potentially great and noble. So long as we carry out our work with good motivation, thinking, "My work is for others," it will be of benefit to the wider community. But when concern for others' feelings and welfare is missing, our activities tend to become spoiled. Through lack of basic human feeling, religion, politics, economics, and so on can be rendered dirty. Instead of serving humanity, they become agents of destruction.[4]

It is clear that the Dalai Lama's role is more than a political leader. He is a religious leader and moral compass. He is a diplomat to China and elsewhere, champion of human rights, and perhaps most important for Tibetans in exile today, a source of hope.

For Tibetans, the *bodhisattva* found in the figure of the Dalai Lama is a symbol of survival for Tibetan Buddhist culture and religion. All *bodhisattvas* are symbols of the potential in everyone for enlightenment and perfect selflessness. And all *bodhisattvas* receive prayers from those wishing for liberation and peace.

Diversity and Contentious Issues

The majority of Tibetan Buddhists may have shunned their historical differences and religious differences for unity today, a necessity in the struggle for rights in their homeland, but throughout the Buddhist world many divergent ways of being Buddhist are lived each day. Even within the Vajrayana many conflicts are found. One, for example, involves the Dalai Lama and a deity known as Dorje Shugden. This centuries-old conflict is over the figure of Dorje Shugden, revered as beneficent by some and cursed as a demon by others. The Fifth Dalai Lama, a lama

---

4. Bstan-'dzin-rgya-mtsho, Dalai Lama XIV, *Ethics for the New Millennium* (New York: Riverhead Books, 1999), 174.

of the Gelukpa school of Tibetan Buddhism who lived in the seven-teenth century, was also known to engage in the practices of a competing school, the Nyingma. Dorje Shugden was thought to be an incarnation within the Nyingmapa school of a wrathful though protecting god. In the many years after the Fifth Dalai Lama's rule, a dramatic controversy over Shugden's authenticity and Gelukpa and Nyingmapa ideological disparity arose: doctrinal differences regarding Dorje Shugden in the two schools became a strongly divisive force. In 1976 the current Dalai Lama banned the worship of Dorje Shugden, citing the divisiveness the figure stirred among his people. Up to that point, the Dalai Lama had offered daily prayers to Shugden himself; the decision must not have been an easy one. To placate Shugden devotees' uncertainties, he assured all that he alone would face any challenge presented by the deity and that no harm would come to anyone.[5] The tensions he sought to ease continue, however. The minority of Shugden devotees today protest against the Dalai Lama and what they regard as an encroachment on their religious rights. They are sometimes found in small groups where the Dalai Lama may be speaking publicly, alongside the protests and human rights dem-onstrations for Tibet against China.

While the Dorje Shugden controversy within Tibetan Buddhism is a peripheral one, fueled by a small minority within the tradition, other more basic and common differences are reflected in the main divisions of the Buddhist religion. The Theravada tradition is highly patriarchal, conservative, and more orthodox than the multivalent Mahayana. The Mahayana is characterized in part by the vast diversity of Buddhist tra-ditions, varying from country to country or culture to culture. Thera-vada Buddhists often see themselves as holders of tradition, allowing for fewer adaptations of the religion. Geographically, the Theravada is most common to Southeast Asia, while the Mahayana is found from Tibet and China to Japan. In modernity, the two main divisions of Buddhism cross such physical boundaries and are both found throughout the world, including in Europe and the Americas.

The place of women in monastic life is, for instance, a point of much debate within the Buddhist world. While in the Mahayana women are nuns, often however subjugated to the official authority of their male counterparts, the struggle even to enter the monastic life is far greater in the Theravada: Theravada Buddhism does not permit women to become nuns. Denied access to a life of renunciation for centuries, many Theravadin women today handle the matter independently and under-

5. Stephen Batchelor, "Letting Daylight into Magic: The Life and Times of Dorje Shugden," *Tricycle: The Buddhist Review* 7, no. 3 (Spring 1998): 60-66.

take renunciant life as well as they can. In Indonesia, for example, one community of world-renouncing women has found some success on the island of Java near Solo. Their survival depends upon donations from the surrounding villagers. The need to supplement that subsistence often leads them to humble business ventures, thus forcing them to break the precept against handling money. Still, the motivation to practice nonattachment in an ideal Buddhist way is strong, and they persevere under the disapproving and often patronizing eyes of the Theravada Buddhist authorities in Indonesia. Their petitions to be recognized officially have yet to be accepted. Most commonly within the Theravada, authorities recognize such women not as *bhikkhuni*, or nuns, but only as *mae ji*, "intellectual servants" to the *bhikkhu sangha*, the community of monks.[6]

Another difference between the two main divisions of Buddhism is canon. The sacred texts of the Mahayana are as varied as the schools of Buddhism within the Mahayana. The Tibetan, Chinese, and Japanese canons emphasize different forms and contents, and one tradition, Ch'an, also known as Zen in Japan, is largely anti-textual in nature, favoring immediate experience over intellectual study as a means toward liberation. The canon of the Theravada, however, is more uniform, consisting of a Pali-language *Tripitaka*, or "three baskets." The three sections of the Theravada *Tripitaka* are the *Vinaya Pitaka*, a code of ethics for the early monastic community, the *Sutta Pitaka* with accounts of the Buddha's teachings, and the *Abhidharma Pitaka* consisting of philosophical arguments and psychological analyses of Buddhism. The Mahayana texts are considered to be an open canon, that is, one for which additions are not uncommon. The Theravada canon is closed, and while new commentaries are composed all the time, no additions are made to the orthodox *Tripitaka*.

Perhaps unique among Buddhist practices is Pure Land devotion, found within the Mahayana and most popular today in Japan. According to this tradition, a great Buddha, once a disciple of Gautama Buddha, vowed to save all living beings, and in doing so created a paradise world called the Pure Land as a refuge for those with abundant *karma*. This Buddha, known in Sanskrit as Amitabha, is understood to be a grantor of liberation. One need only recite his name and call upon his grace to receive liberation from *samsara*. In China, he is called upon as Omituo; in Japan he is Amida. Before final *nirvana* from a last human life, his devotees are said to spend a lifetime of bliss in the Pure Land. This pietous

---

6. Wilis Rengganiasih Endah Ekowati, "Official DeNUNciation: Theravāda Buddhist Nuns in Indonesia: Struggling to Define Identity," paper presented at the annual meeting of the American Academy of Religion, San Diego, California, 18 November 2007.

form of Buddhist practice is a contrast to the meditative forms found elsewhere: instead of looking inward to realize truth and reach enlightenment, the practitioner need only to ask for liberation from a powerful, outside source. As a result of this basic doctrine, Pure Land Buddhist religious activity is characterized by hymns, prayers to Amitabha, worship, and other distinctly devotional practices.

Selections from the *Heart Sutra* (translated by Edward Conze):

"... in emptiness there is no form, nor feeling, nor perception, nor impulse, nor consciousness; no eye, ear, nose, tongue, body, mind; no forms, sounds, smells, tastes, touchables or objects of mind; no sight-organ-element, and so forth, until we come to: no mind-consciousness-element; there is no ignorance, no extinction of ignorance, and so forth until we come to: there is no decay and death, no extinction of decay and death; there is no suffering, no origination, no stopping, no path; there is no cognition, no attainment, and no non-attainment."

"Therefore, O Sariputra, it is because of his indifference to any kind of personal attainment that a Bodhisattva, through having relied on the perfection of wisdom, dwells without thought-coverings. In the absence of thought-coverings he has not been made to tremble, he has overcome what can upset, and in the end he attains to Nirvana."

Conclusion: Buddhist Practices in the World Today

With these examples of the multiplicity of Buddhist life, one can see clearly that the religion we call "Buddhism" is not one static, unchanging tradition but a vibrant, dynamic one. The religion is one of diverse peoples and practices, as well as of a long history of differing cultural movements and developments that continue today.

Like all religious traditions, Buddhism is a system of practice and, ideally, a means for fulfilling one's true potential as a human being. For Buddhists worldwide the ultimate human potential is for enlightenment. In this worldview, human beings are best-equipped for reaching the goal: we can learn, contemplate, and cultivate awareness of our emotions and desires in order to conquer them. Regardless of the particular school or sect, all Buddhists regard liberation as the ultimate goal of religious life. And on the journey toward final liberation, the virtues cultivated are invaluable: compassion, selflessness, and wisdom define true Buddhist liberation. It is these virtues that are found in almost every aspect of Buddhist religious practice. Enlightenment, then, can be understood as a personal awakening via lived practice, a very real transformation from a selfish life to a selfless one.

Suggestions for Further Reading

Bstan-'dzin-rgya-mtsho, Dalai Lama XIV. *Ethics for the New Millennium*. New York: Riverhead Books, 1999.

Batchelor, Stephe. "Letting Daylight into Magic: The Life and Times of Dorje Shugden." *Tricycle: The Buddhist Review* 7, no. 3 (Spring 1998): 60-66.

Conze, Edward, trans. *Buddhist Scriptures*. New York: Penguin, 1959.

17

Baha'is

Peter Smith

On 29 April 2008, a thousand delegates from 153 countries met in Haifa to elect the Baha'i faith's international governing body, the Universal House of Justice. Almost five hundred others who were unable to attend sent postal ballots. Particularly missed were delegates from Iran, the religion's birthplace, where the Baha'is are presently denied fundamental human rights. In addition to the election—held prayerfully with no candidates, nominations, or electioneering—the delegates also met to discuss the progress of the faith throughout the world, providing an important means of promoting a common vision and cementing international solidarity within a global community.

Baha'is are followers of Bahá'u'lláh (1817-92), whom they revere as God's messenger for the present day. There are about five million Baha'is worldwide, with Baha'i groups and communities established in every country apart from North Korea (and the Vatican city state). Baha'is believe that theirs is a religion of global unity and celebrate the enormous diversity of their membership, drawn from all major religious and ethnic backgrounds.

Despite certain commonalities, the experience of being a Baha'i varies considerably around the world. In Iran, the religion's birthplace, the 300,000 or so Baha'is remain a persecuted minority, with more than two hundred Baha'is having being murdered or "disappeared" for their beliefs since the 1979 Islamic Revolution, and the remainder suffering from often severe limitations on their personal freedoms. Iranian Baha'is are not allowed to legally marry or attend university; Baha'i school students are routinely humiliated in front of their classmates by their teachers; courts have dismissed murders of Baha'is as non-crimes; Baha'i holy places and burial grounds have been desecrated and destroyed.

Elsewhere, in those countries in which the Baha'is are free to practice their religion (almost every country outside the Middle East), there

Figure 17.1: *The final home and shrine of Bahá'u'lláh at Bahji, Israel. (Photo by Graham Harvey)*

are some differences between those Baha'is who live in the Third World countries in Southern Asia, Africa, and Latin America and those who live in the "'developed" countries of North America, Europe, East Asia, and Australasia. Most Baha'is now live in the Third World, where Baha'i concerns with socio-economic and community development naturally play a more important role. By contrast, in the developed world, the Baha'is benefit from their high rates of literacy and the ready availability of modern amenities to play a more forward role in Baha'i administration and scholarship.

This said, the similarities of experience worldwide are considerable: Baha'is are strongly encouraged to become literate and to read the religion's key texts for themselves and there is effective central direction from the Universal House of Justice, whilst local and national Baha'i communities arrange regular meetings to promote a commonality of vision and practice.

Being a Baha'i: Aspects of Baha'i Life

The key elements of practice can be summarized under the headings "the spiritual path," "Baha'i law and practice," "Baha'i community life," "Baha'i administration," and "Baha'i activities and the wider world."

The spiritual path

For Baha'is, spirituality and morality are linked together in the concept of the spiritual path, whereby the individual believer strives to develop greater spirituality and acquire spiritual-moral qualities. Rejecting the conception of a division of the world into "saints" and "sinners," Baha'is see the challenge to "live the Baha'i life" as an ongoing daily struggle to try to live up to the spiritual and moral demands of what is required of a "true Baha'i." By so doing, each individual is able to discover the realities of their own souls and progress towards God.

The Baha'i teachings in this regard generally take the form of statements of general principle rather than a detailed set of rules to obey, with the idea that individual Baha'is should use their own consciences and understanding to apply these principles in the particular contexts of their own lives. Essentially, everyone is called upon to find their own salvation, and each individual is made responsible for his or her own spiritual life. Each individual faces his or her own spiritual challenges and difficulties in pursuing this path, fighting their own spiritual battles and striving to develop a good character that is ultimately the only true source of human glory.

Turning to God

Central to progress on this path is the "mystic feeling" which unites man with God. Baha'is should therefore turn to God and seek to commune with him, finding the divine light that is present within all human beings. To this end, they should regularly read and contemplate the Baha'i scriptures, and develop a sense of spirituality and prayerfulness in their lives, aware, however, that the purpose of prayer is to draw the believer closer to God and to uplift the soul and not to weary it through an excess of piety. (There are many Baha'i prayers—most by Bahá'u'lláh and his eldest son, 'Abdu'l-Bahá—available for use). Ideally, an attitude of devotion should pervade the thoughts and actions of the believer's daily life— although not to the extent that Baha'is lose contact with the everyday world. Rather, prayer should lead to a transformation of character and greater strength in overcoming moral weaknesses. Again, Baha'is should review their own actions, bringing themselves to account each day—ere death intervenes, and it becomes necessary for them to give an account of themselves before God.

Baha'is should try to free themselves from the "prison" of self and the "fetters" of worldly attachments. Worldly possessions and dominion are seen as transient and worthless, and faithful believers should instead seek "God's enduring bestowals," placing their "whole reliance" on him and submitting themselves to him. They should be content with little, developing the qualities of humility and patience, and being ever mindful of their own nothingness before God. As they fear God, they should not be overwhelmed by earthly fears.

It is also necessary to control one's passions, striving to lead a chaste and holy life, and to be modest, pure, temperate, decent, clean-minded, and moderate in one's dress, language, and amusements. At the same time, no one should ever pride themselves on their piety—no individual ever knows what his or her own spiritual fate will be, and asceticism and excessive puritanism are to be avoided.

Relations with others

Relationships with other people are a crucial part of the spiritual path. Baha'is should strive to become the manifestations of divine love: in "spiritual communion" with their fellow Baha'is and loving all human beings of whatever religion, race, or community. They should be loyal, courageous, magnanimous, generous, compassionate, forbearing, meek, selfless, considerate towards others, courteous, amiable, and forgiving; succor the dispossessed and the destitute; and be kind to animals. They should completely avoid iniquity, envy, malice, backbiting and covetousness; not breathe the sins of others nor be a cause of grief to them. Truthfulness and trustworthiness are particularly praised as being foundational qualities on which other virtues depended. Correspondingly, lying is seen as the worst possible human quality.

Baha'is should be tolerant of others, particularly in matters of religion, associating with all the peoples of the world with "joy and radiance" and with the followers of all religions in a spirit of "friendliness and fellowship." They should free themselves of all prejudices in their dealings with those of a different race, class, or religion. Fanaticism and "unreasoning religious zeal" are condemned, as are the practices of shunning other people because of their religious beliefs or regarding them as ritually unclean (both common practices in nineteenth-century Iran).

Baha'i Law and Practice

Being a Baha'i also involves following Baha'i law. This includes the following:

Personal obligations towards God

Bahá'u'lláh prescribed a number of spiritual obligations for his followers, notably daily prayer and reading of Baha'i scripture (there are set obligatory prayers); an annual nineteen-day fast from sunrise to sunset for those who are fit and well; and payment of *Huqúqu'lláh* (the "Right of God"), a form of tithe on capital gains for those who are sufficiently wealthy. These practices are regarded as a means for the individual to draw closer to God and to develop spiritual qualities.

Marriage and family life

Baha'i teachings emphasize the importance and sanctity of marriage and family life, both for the individuals involved and for society as a whole, and Baha'is are encouraged to marry. All Baha'i marriages require the consent of both the couple and their parents—this latter permission being required so as to strengthen ties between family members and to prevent any enmity in the family. Baha'i marriage is monogamous. Divorce is permitted, but strongly discouraged. The importance of parenthood and the responsibilities of parents to ensure the education of their children are greatly stressed. All forms of injustice and violence within the family are condemned.

Aspects of individual life

The most distinctive regulations regarding Baha'i personal life relate to sex, alcohol and drugs. Thus, whilst sexual attraction and activity are regarded as a natural part of human life, and of value both to the individual and for the procreation of children, the Baha'i teachings insist that the sexual impulse can only be legitimately expressed in heterosexual marriage. All forms of pre- and extra-marital sexual relationships are thus forbidden, as is the practice of homosexuality. As to alcohol, opiates and other psychoactive drugs, these are seen as leading the mind astray and weakening the body, and they should thus be absolutely avoided unless prescribed by a physician. Tobacco smoking is discouraged but not forbidden.

Other regulations include the practice of burial rather than cremation of the dead, and a requirement to write a will. 'Abdu'l-Bahá commended vegetarianism, but Baha'is are free to eat what they wish, and there are no prohibited foods. There is no required use of Baha'i symbols of identity—no distinctive names or forms of dress, although many Baha'is wear a Baha'i ring, place 'Abdu'l-Bahá's picture in their home, or hang a copy of a calligraphic evocation of the name *Bahá* (God's Greatest Name) on their wall, and Iranian Baha'is in particular often use the salutation *'Alláh-u-Abhá'* (God is Most Glorious) when greeting each other.

Relationship to civil society and the state

Baha'is are required to follow the law of the countries in which they reside unless these laws require them to deny their faith or violate fundamental Baha'i principles; they are to be loyal, honest, and truthful in their dealings with their government; strictly to avoid sedition; and to avoid any partisan political involvement. Baha'is can vote, become members of neighborhood councils, and hold administrative office in government service if this does not entail partisan political involvement. Baha'is in public employ should be exemplary in their honesty, integrity, trustworthiness, justice, and service.

Whilst Bahá'u'lláh stated that it was better to be killed than to kill, Baha'is recognize that it may be necessary to use force in some circumstances, such as to defend their own lives and those of others against attack by criminal assailants. They should not allow defense to deteriorate into retaliation, however. At a national level, Baha'is should be willing to be inducted into the military forces of their country, applying for non-combatant status (e.g. as medical orderlies) where this is possible and not being afraid to risk their own lives to try to save the lives of others.

Sanctions

In general, observance of most Baha'i laws is regarded as a matter of individual conscience, and it is only when there are relatively extreme and public breaches of the law that any sanctions are applied—normally in the form of depriving the individual of the right to participate in Baha'i elections and such activities as contributing to the Baha'i funds. Only Baha'i "national spiritual assemblies" (elected councils which govern Baha'i activities in each country) can deprive an individual of his or her voting rights, and as such action is regarded as very serious, it normally only occurs as a last resort after careful fact-finding and extensive consultations with all involved. Other than this, assemblies are instructed to be compassionate towards human frailty—offering counsel rather than blame.

Aspects of Baha'i Community Life

Being a Baha'i also involves membership of the Baha'i community, seen both as a worldwide family, and in its local expression in a particular Baha'i group. To become a member of a Baha'i community requires formal registration, normally on a membership list maintained by the national spiritual assembly of the country in which the believer resides.

Those who are born into Baha'i families must also at some point register as full members of the community. This is often done at the age of fifteen, which Bahá'u'lláh established as the age of social and religious maturity.

The Baha'i year

One focus for Baha'i identity is the variety of activities organized by local Baha'i communities. Of particular formal importance are the regular Nineteen-Day Feasts and the commemorations of the Baha'i holy days (below), but many communities also organize devotional and social meetings; children's, youth, and adult study classes; informal discussion groups for enquirers; and public meetings and other campaigns for proclaiming the Baha'i teachings. Neighboring local communities may also collaborate in organizing joint meetings and activities, whilst national assemblies and their committees organize national and regional conferences and schools. Many Baha'is also meet regularly as members of locally-elected Baha'i councils ("local spiritual assemblies") and their various committees.

Baha'is have their own calendar, consisting of nineteen months each of nineteen days (361 days), with four or five "intercalary days" to make a solar year. Each month is named after a divine quality ("Glory," "Beauty," 'Grandeur," etc.), and the beginning of each month is marked by a Nineteen Day Feast in which members of the local Baha'i community come together to pray, consult on matters of concern, and socialize. The new year is the ancient Iranian new year of *Naw-Rúz* (Persian, "New Day"), normally 21 March at the spring equinox. The last month (*'Alá'*, Loftiness) is the Baha'i month of fasting. The first year of the calendar is 1844, the year of the Báb's declaration (see "A Short History," below), so the Baha'i year 165 began at Naw-Rúz 2008. There are also eleven holy days over the course of the year, including the new year festival; the commemorations of the births of the Báb and Bahá'u'lláh and their declarations of mission; the martyrdom of the Báb; the passing of Bahá'u'lláh and 'Abdu'l-Bahá; and the establishment of Bahá'u'lláh's covenant of succession. The "Rezván period" (21 April-2 May), commemorating Bahá'u'lláh's declaration of mission, is normally the time at which elections for Baha'i local and national spiritual assemblies are held.

Baha'is also often meet each other outside their local communities at institutes and courses of learning ("Summer Schools," weekend institutes, and the like) where they can study their religion in more depth. Specialist conferences concerned with specific issues and interests—such as the arts, music, education, women, youth,

Figure 17.2: *Seat of the Universal House of Justice, Haifa, Israel (Photo by Graham Harvey.)*

socio-economic development, health, and scholarship—are also organized.

Holy places and pilgrimage

Various sites associated with the Báb, Bahá'u'lláh, and 'Abdu'l-Bahá are considered holy by Baha'is, the most important being the various holy places at the Baha'i World Centre in the Haifa-Akka area of what is now Israel, and many Baha'is endeavor to make a pilgrimage to these sites at least once in their lifetimes. Some of these places are also open to the general public, the 'Baha'i Gardens' in Haifa, in particular, having become a major tourist destination. The Shrine of Bahá'u'lláh at Bahjí is the Baha'i *qiblah*, the "point of adoration" to which Baha'is throughout the world turn when the say their daily obligatory prayers.

Important Baha'i sites in Iran are either inaccessible or have been destroyed by the authorities since the establishment of the Islamic Republic.

Baha'i Administration

The various local and national Baha'i communities are structured around the Baha'i Administrative Order, now under the overall guidance and direction of a supreme Baha'i council, the Universal House of Justice. The Order essentially comprises two branches: the system of elected local and national spiritual assemblies, which organize and administer the collective lives of the Baha'is in their communities, and the various "institutions of the learned" (an International Teaching Centre in Haifa, and appointed individuals at continental and local levels), which are concerned with enthusing and advising the Baha'is.

The Baha'i writings frequently emphasize the need for the Baha'i administration to embody a specific "spirit" and not operate purely as a bureaucratic structure. Thus, assembly members are reminded of the spiritual responsibilities of their work (including "extreme humility" and selfless devotion); warned of the dangers of personalistic leadership and of over-administration; and urged to gain the support and affection of their fellow believers. One key element here is held to be the principle of consultation, which is regarded as an essential means whereby individual voices can be heard and a variety of views examined dispassionately. For Baha'is, genuine consultation occurs when every individual feels able express their views with absolute freedom in an environment of mutual respect and fellowship rather than merely voicing personal opinions and trying to win debating points. There are also appeals procedures for those Baha'is who wish to question the decisions of their local and national spiritual assemblies.

Funding for Baha'i activities comes from both the *Huqúqu'lláh* system (above) and the voluntary contribution of the Baha'is to various funds at local, national, continental, and international levels. Whilst individuals are encouraged to support these funds as a spiritual blessing to themselves, all contributions are a strictly personal matter, determined purely by the dictates of conscience. Only Baha'is are allowed to contribute to funds supporting the direct work of the faith (e.g. administration and teaching projects), but non-Baha'is are able to contribute to separate Baha'i funds devoted solely to charitable and socio-economic development work.

Baha'i Activities and the Wider World

There are two main aspects of Baha'i involvement with the wider world: the mission of expansion and social involvement.

The mission of expansion

All Baha'is are encouraged to "promote the faith" and gain new adherents through the teaching and proclamation of the Baha'i teachings. This teaching work should be non-disputatious. The central importance of spirituality in teaching is much emphasized: ultimately it is only the moral quality of Baha'i "teachers" which will vindicate the claims of the faith and attract outsiders to it. Some Baha'is spend often considerable periods of time as "travel teachers," traveling from one place to another to teach their
, whilst others "pioneer" to commence or support Baha'i activities in new locations. There are no full-time professional Baha'i promoters of the faith, although some teaching activities may be subsidized on a short-term basis. Individual Baha'i communities seek to deepen the knowledge

and faith of those who become Baha'is through various forms of study programs, devotional meetings, and classes for children and youth.

Social involvement

There is also a lot of Baha'i activity in support of the faith's multi-faceted vision of social reconstruction, some elements of which Baha'is seek to implement within their own communities, whilst others they promote to the wider world. Areas of particular concern include internationalism and support for the United Nations; the promotion of religious tolerance and the coexistence of ethnic groups; the advancement of women; the development of education (there are a number of Baha'i schools and colleges worldwide); literacy training; and socio-economic development—with particular emphasis on sparking change at the grassroots level.

A Short History

The Babi movement

The Baha'i faith developed out of the earlier Babi religion, and Babism in turn emerged as a movement within Shi'i Islam, particularly as it had developed in Iran. Shi'i Muslims are those who believe that the rightful successors of the Prophet Muhammad were a series of *Imáms* drawn from the Prophet's own family. These claims are rejected by the majority of the world's Muslims (the Sunnis), but Shi'ism has come to predominate in several parts of the Middle East, most notably Iran, where "Twelver" Shi'ism (following a succession of twelve *Imáms*) has been the state religion since the sixteenth century. According to the Twelvers, the last of these *Imáms* disappeared mysteriously whilst still a boy in the Iraqi city of Sámarrá in AH 260 (873-4 CE), remains hidden, and will eventually reappear as the *Mahdí* (rightly-guided one), battle the forces of evil in a final apocalyptic battle, and herald the day of judgment.

The Babi religion centered on Sayyid 'Alí-Muhammad Shírází (1819-1850), a young Iranian merchant from the southern city of Shíráz, who after a series of visionary dreams made a claim to religious authority which was at first widely understood to be that of being the *Báb* (Gate) to the Hidden Imam. Therefore, 'Alí-Muhammad came to be frequently referred to as the Báb, and his followers were labeled as "Bábís." Following the conversion of his first disciple in May 1844, a movement rapidly developed, Babi missionaries spreading his teachings throughout Iran and neighboring areas of what was then Ottoman Iraq. The Babis' activities were widely seen as a challenge to the power of Islamic leaders and were soon opposed, at times with force. Meanwhile, the Báb's attempts to secure the allegiance of the king, Muhammad Sháh, were unavailing, and he was instead sent as a prisoner to a fortress in the remote northwest, close to the Ottoman border. Here, he made claim to be the Mahdí himself, implicitly the supreme ruler of the Shi'i world.

Meanwhile, local tensions between the Babis and their opponents had developed in several parts of the country, finally leading to armed conflict close to one of the northern towns in the confused conditions following the death of the shah in September 1848. Fighting defensively, and inspired by the tradition of heroic martyrdom characteristic of Shi'ism, several hundred Babis fought off government forces for seven months until the survivors responded to a false truce and were massacred. Two further conflicts erupted in May 1850, prompting the prime minister of the new shah to order the execution of the Báb (on 8/9 July) in the hope that this would stem the religious fervor of his followers, which he blamed for the disturbances.

The Bábi's execution, the killing of most of the Babi leaders, and the persecution of the Babi groups that remained forced the Babis into a secretive existence with different individuals assuming leadership of various factions. In August 1852, one of the Babi factions in Tehran determined to revenge their losses by attempting to assassinate Násiru'd-dín Sháh (reigned 1848-96). The attempt proved to be a fiasco, but provoked a lightly-wounded shah to seek to extirpate the Babis altogether. Accordingly, many Babis were arrested and killed, including prominent Babis who had had nothing to do with the radical faction responsible for the attack.

Bahá'u'lláh and the reanimation of Babism, 1853-63

It seemed as if the Babi movement had been utterly destroyed. That this proved not to be the case was largely due to the activities of Mírzá Husayn-'Alí Núrí (1817-92), eventually generally known by his title "Bahá'u'lláh" (The "Glory of God"). The son of a formerly powerful government official, Bahá'u'lláh was one of the most socially prominent of the Babis. Although himself opposed to the Babi radicals, he was amongst those arrested in 1852. Thrown with other Babis into an underground prison in Tehran—the "Black Pit"—Bahá'u'lláh languished for four months in circumstances of terrible suffering and degradation before being released and forced into exile. Traveling across the western mountains in the winter of 1852-3, Bahá'u'lláh and his family settled in Baghdad, in Ottoman Iraq.

After a prolonged period of spiritual retreat in the mountains of

Kurdistan (April 1854-March 1856), Bahá'u'lláh set about reviving the demoralized and fractious Babi remnant, writing extensively to his core-ligionists in Iran and attracting a growing circle of disciples in Baghdad. Although not yet making any explicit claim to leadership, Bahá'u'lláh was increasingly seen by many as a natural leader of the Babis, a situation which appears to have evoked the jealousy of his own younger half-brother, Mírzá Yahyá (1831/2-1912), known generally by his Babi title, "Subh-i Azal" (the "Morn of Eternity"), who explicitly claimed leader-ship of the Babis but led a secret existence separate from them.

Much of Bahá'u'lláh's prominence at this time was due to his writings. These strongly conveyed his own sense of the divine presence—in part it would seem as a result of a series of visions he experienced during his imprisonment in Tehran. As such they bore authority, and gave renewed hope and purpose to the demoralized Babis. They also gave them a new vision of their religion, Bahá'u'lláh emphasizing in particular the impor-tance of the spiritual-mystical path and the ethical demands of belief—themes which were of interest to Sufis as well as Babis. He also provided the Babis with an explanatory framework whereby they could see the persecution and execution of the Báb as the latest chapter in human rejection of God's messengers, caused as in the past by the superficial-ity and fanaticism of those who awaited but eventually persecuted their promised one, and by the fears of religious leaders that they might lose their power.

The resultant reanimation of the Babi movement attracted the atten-tion of the Iranian government, which requested the Ottomans to returnBahá'u'lláh to his native land. Instead, the Ottoman government invitedBahá'u'lláh to travel to Istanbul, initially showing him favor -- perhaps in the hope that he would become their tool, but subsequently rejecting him and subjecting him to further exile—to the city of Edirne in Rumelia.

The emergence of the Baha'i faith, 1863-92

The four and a half years Bahá'u'lláh spent in Edirne (12 December 1863–12 August 1868) marked a crucial point of transition. Just prior to leaving Baghdad in April 1863, he had confided a claim to divine authority to his immediate disciples. In Edirne, after the breach with his half-brother became open (Azal tried to poison him), Bahá'u'lláh made open claim to be the promised Babi messianic figure of "He Whom God Shall Make Manifest," and invited all Babis to become his follow-ers, taking his name as "Baha'is" (1866). Sending emissaries to the Babis in Iran, he soon gained the allegiance of most of them, leaving only a minority as followers of his brother ("Azalis"). Further exile followed, with Bahá'u'lláh and most of his immediate followers being transferred to the prison-city of Akka (Acre) in Ottoman Syria, and Azal and a few others dispatched to Famagusta in Cyprus. Initially held in Akka prison, Bahá'u'lláh was later allowed to live under effective house arrest in the city, and then, from 1877, in country mansions in the vicinity. In one of these (Bahjí), he died in 1892.

During these last three decades of Bahá'u'lláh's life, the Baha'i faith took shape as an organized religion. Bahá'u'lláh continued to write extensively, revealing his own code of divine law in his book, the *Kitáb-i-Aqdas* (c.1873); outlining his vision for a united and just world; and sending a series of letters to some of the major world leaders of the time (the Ottoman Sultan Abdulaziz, Násiru'd-dín Sháh of Iran, Napoleon III of France, Queen Victoria of Britain, Alexander II of Russia, and Pope Pius IX) proclaiming his mission. Meanwhile, Baha'i migrants and teachers established Baha'i groups in various parts of the Ottoman Empire, as well as in Egypt, Russian Turkistan, and British India and Burma. Effective organization ensured that the now multinational Baha'i groups remained in close contact with Bahá'u'lláh and that copies of his writings were widely distributed. There was also some printing of Baha'i literature in India.

Baha'i leadership since 1892

Bahá'u'lláh appointed his eldest son, "Abbás," *'Abdu'l-Bahá* (the "Servant of Bahá," 1844-1921) to lead the Baha'is after his death. 'Abdu'l-Bahá was then almost fifty, well known to the Baha'is, and greatly respected as his father's chief assistant, so the appointment was readily accepted, despite opposition from his own half-brother, Muhammad-'Alí (1853/4-1937), and a small band of supporters.

The almost thirty years of 'Abdu'l-Bahá's leadership was a crucial period of change for the Baha'i faith, most dramatically with the growth of small Baha'i communities in North America and Europe. Although only a few thousand in number, the new Western Baha'is vividly demonstrated the international nature of the faith and became an extremely active element in Baha'i publishing and teaching activities. 'Abdu'l-Bahá himself was able to visit the Western Baha'is in two lengthy tours in 1911-13. Meanwhile, in Iran, despite worsening persecution, the Baha'is were able to impress an increasing number of "progressive" Iranians with the relevance of their ideas of social reform, as well as successfully establishing a number of Baha'i schools and furthering the emancipation of women within the community.

With no living sons of his own, 'Abdu'l-Bahá was in turn succeeded by his eldest grandson, Shoghi Effendi Rabbani (1897-1957), who served as the first in a projected line of "guardians" of the faith from January 1922 until his death. At the time of his succession, Shoghi Effendi was still a student in Oxford, but despite his youth, proved to be a strong and effective leader, consolidating a system of elected local and national Baha'i councils ("spiritual assemblies") to administer the affairs of the faith; producing a number of significant English-language translations of the writings of Bahá'u'lláh and 'Abdu'l-Bahá; defining matters of Baha'i doctrine; and overseeing the extension of the buildings and gardens of the Baha'i World Centre in the Haifa-Akka area. He also directed a series of increasingly ambitious expansion plans to spread the faith throughout the world.

Shoghi Effendi died suddenly in 1957. He had no children, and a body of twenty-seven senior Baha'is whom he had recently appointed as "Hands of the Cause" assumed temporary leadership of the faith pending the election of the Universal House of Justice (an international council referred to in the Baha'i scriptures) in 1963. Since 1963, the Universal House of Justice has continued the programs of global expansion and administrative consolidation set in motion by Shoghi Effendi, as well as overseeing the further expansion of the Baha'i World Centre and more translations of the Baha'i writings into a diversity of languages.

Aspects of Baha'i development since 1892

The most obvious characteristic of the modern Baha'i faith is perhaps its internationalization, particularly since the 1950s, when a series of expansion plans led to the establishment of Baha'i communities in virtually every country in the world and the gaining of converts from an enormous diversity of cultural and religious backgrounds. Although the Iranian Baha'is (themselves severely persecuted since the establishment of the Islamic Republic in 1979) remain an important part of the global Baha'i community, the Baha'is can now rightfully claim to be a worldwide religion, with particularly large memberships in India and parts of Africa and Latin America. Linked to this development is an increasing range of Baha'i literature addressing a great variety of religious and secular issues.

A second characteristic is the maintenance of the religion's unity. All religious movements face a potential crisis of leadership when their founders die, and many split into competing sects as a result or alternatively lose their original dynamism. In the Baha'i case, development of the doctrine of a covenant linking each of the successive leaders back to Bahá'u'lláh has played a significant role in maintaining the religion's unity and dynamism, with internal opposition to each of the leaders being small in scale and relatively transient—direct opponents of the successive leaders being expelled from the faith as "Covenant-breakers."

A third characteristic, evident in Iran since the late nineteenth century and elsewhere particularly since the 1960s, has been the increasing importance of educational and other socio-economic development projects within the faith.

Beliefs

Baha'i texts

The Baha'i faith is very much a religion of "the Word," its authoritative teachings being derived from the original writings of the successive leaders of the faith, and in the case of 'Abdu'l-Bahá, approved transcripts of his public talks. Some eyewitness accounts of what the leaders said and did are widely circulated for their inspirational value, but they are explicitly discounted as sources of Baha'i doctrine. It is relatively easy for all Baha'is to identify official Baha'i teachings, and there is now an extensive archive of original writings which comprise the religion's canonical texts.

Given that a very large part of the Baha'i writings was originally composed in Persian or Arabic, authorized translations are of great importance, those by Shoghi Effendi into English having the highest status because of his official status as an appointed interpreter of the teachings of the faith. Although much still remains to be translated, there are already over forty volumes of the Baha'i writings in English (including twelve from the writings of Bahá'u'lláh, eight from those of 'Abdu'l-Bahá (excluding the unauthenticated extempore oral translations of some of his talks), fifteen from Shoghi Effendi, and five from the Universal House of Justice. There is only one (a compilation of extracts) from the Báb. The Universal House of Justice's Research Department also prepares compilations of Baha'i writings on various subjects.

There is no Baha'i sacred or liturgical language. Arabic, Persian, and English have a special status as the languages of the original writings of the Baha'i leaders, but access to and understanding of the texts is what is regarded as of primary importance, with the result that extensive translation programs of Baha'i scriptures and other literature have been an important part of Baha'i endeavor ever since the faith began to spread outside of its Middle Eastern heartland. All Baha'is are also strongly encouraged to become literate (and to ensure that their children become literate), in part so that they can have access to the faith's writings.

Baha'is recognize that individuals will have their own particular understandings of the Baha'i teachings, but are warned not to allow differences in interpretations of the Baha'i writings to become a cause of disunity. Each individual has a right to his or her own understanding, but no one has a right to force their views on others. There should be respect and tolerance for differences of viewpoint, but also a humble recognition of the limitations of human understanding. Dogmatism and fanaticism are to be avoided.

There is a massive Baha'i secondary literature in many languages, particularly in English, including commentaries on Baha'i texts and expositions on numerous aspects of the Baha'i belief and practice, but none of them have any authoritative status as guides to Baha'i belief.

Theology and Metaphysics

God and the manifestations of God

The Baha'i faith is strictly monotheistic. Some understanding of God can be gained from "his" names and attributes ("his" is merely a convention as God has no gender). These are numerous, and include Almighty, All-Sufficing, All-Loving, King of the realms of justice, Inspirer, and Help in Peril. More generally, all existence is seen as reflecting his image, and every created thing in the whole universe as a sign of God's sovereignty. Ultimately, however, God in essence is unknowable. He is exalted above human understanding so that all human conceptions of God are mere imaginations, which some individuals mistake for reality. Therefore, knowledge of God is primarily to be achieved by way of his messengers: the "Manifestations of God."

According to the Baha'i view, these Manifestations of God represent the divine presence to humankind. They include the Biblical-Quranic figures of Adam, Abraham, Moses, Jesus, and Muhammad, as well as Zoroaster, Krishna, and the Buddha, and for the present age, the Báb and Bahá'u'lláh. Distinct from God, they mirror his glory and reveal his attributes. They are the primary means through which human beings can approach God. They are the bearers of divine revelation and law, and a source of transformation and empowerment in the lives of their followers. Whilst each has his own specific mission—which leads their followers to see them as different from each other—they share an essential unity which transcends the diversity of the world's various religions. Each is authoritative and infallible.

Various other figures—"lesser prophets" in Baha'i parlance—also provide divine guidance to humanity under the shadow of the Manifestations of God (as, for example, the Biblical prophets Isaiah, Jeremiah, and Ezekiel). Again, it is believed that some Manifestations appointed successors to guide their followers after their deaths—most notably in the case of the Baha'i leaders succeeding Bahá'u'lláh under the doctrine of the Covenant and the Shi'i *imáms* in Islam.

The diversity and continuity of religions

For Baha'is, the development of the Baha'i faith forms part of a single overarching history of religion on this planet (symbolically starting with Adam, seen as the first known Manifestation of God). The major religions recognized by the Baha'is (Zoroastrianism, Judaism, Christianity, and Islam in the West; Hinduism and Buddhism in the East) are incorporated into this schema and their founders honored as divine Manifestations with a fundamental unity of mission. As God is believed to have guided all the peoples of the world, the existence of other religions and revelators is assumed, but there is no official list of these (At a popular level, many Baha'is are evidently willing to add, for example, various Native American prophets to their personal lists of divine messengers).

The unity of these religions is seen as both recurrent and progressive. Thus, on the one hand, each of the divine religions expresses eternal moral and spiritual truths which are proclaimed and renewed by their founders, each new Manifestation representing the coming of new spiritual springtime, bringing new life to a world made spiritually cold and dead by people's neglect of the teachings brought by the previous Manifestation. At the same time, each religion represents an evolutionary stage in a single and eternal religion of God, progressively revealed to humankind (a process which Baha'is term "progressive revelation"). This schema also accounted for differences between the religions, in that each of the Manifestations of God brought divine teachings appropriate to the spiritual capacity of the people of their own particular time and place, so that there were certain aspects of religious truth that were relative to their recipients and not absolute. For example, whilst all religions enjoin honesty and piety and condemn murder and theft, they might have different laws concerning social institutions such as marriage and the treatment of criminals, as well as employing different conceptual frameworks to present theological and metaphysical ideas (many of which, according to Baha'i belief, are essentially beyond human comprehension).

Some of the religions are also linked together by prophecy, with the coming of the next divine messenger being predicted in the scriptures of the past—most notably in the case of Bahá'u'lláh, whose coming is believed to be foretold in all religious traditions.

Creation and knowledge

Of Baha'i descriptions of the nature of reality, the most striking perhaps is the view that evil has no objective reality other than in the evil deeds of human beings. There is no devil or Satan, nor evil spirits nor demonic possession. Rather God's creation is good, and the material universe is pervaded by the Holy Spirit (the logos; the "Primal Will"). It is human rebellion against God which generates evil.

As to the Baha'i conception of knowledge, this is multi-faceted and incorporates a certain natural tension between what we might term "authoritarian" and "anti-authoritarian" elements. The notions of the absolute authority of the Manifestations of God and the infallibility of the successive Baha'i leaders suggests a strongly authoritative conception of knowledge. Yet, at the same time, the Baha'i writings emphasize the importance of human reason and scientific enquiry in a manner that is intrinsically anti-authoritarian and anti-dogmatic. Not only is true religion proclaimed to be subject to the test of reason, but opposition to knowledge and science is described as a sign of ignorance and is to be condemned. From this standpoint, to oppose reason in the name of religion is a sign of superstition, and at the present time, it is held to be ignorance, not science, which threatens the foundations of religion. Contemporary irreligion and the growth of secularism has developed because of the dogmatism and irrationality of many religious people.

This said, the Baha'is maintain that there are limits to human understanding. We should always seek knowledge, but be humble in the realization that there are some matters—God, creation, the human mind itself—which are ultimately beyond our complete understanding. Correspondingly, we should be tolerant of a diversity of understandings of such matters.

Being Human

The soul and its development

For Baha'is, human beings possess both a physical body and a non-material rational soul. The soul is the essential inner reality of each human being. It is unlimited and immortal. It comes into existence at the time of conception and enters a new existence after death. All human beings have an inherent spiritual potential, but this can only be revealed if we decide to turn to God and seek to acquire spiritual qualities. Each individual has God-given free will and the ability to make moral and spiritual choices during their lives. They can choose to commit good or evil actions, and whatever they decide to do will have existential consequences.

Baha'is believe that human beings are innately selfish, but not that they are innately evil (they reject all notions of original sin). The development of a moral sense therefore requires moral education and training from childhood onwards so that individuals can be motivated to make moral choices, control their baser instincts, and spiritualize their lives. In so doing, people will discover their own true selves. Again, turning towards God in prayer and study and meditation on the Baha'i teachings will strengthen the individual to resist their own selfish tendencies and the immoral influences of wider society.

Individuals achieve different levels of spiritual development as a consequence of their choices. These levels are symbolically described in terms of "heaven" and "hell"—in reality states of soul rather than physical places. Thus, those who are close to God are in "heaven," whilst those who are distant from him are in "hell," a distinction which applies in both this life and the afterlife. To come closer to God fulfils the divinely ordained purpose of human existence and raises the individual to a heavenly state of "eternal life." By contrast, those who are faithless and turn away from God, become victims of "self and passion," and, perverting the God-given purpose of their own lives, finally sink in the depths of degradation and despair. From this standpoint, "sin" is simply disobedience to God and his laws. A sinful life separates the soul from God, hindering it from attaining its natural potential. Specific sins include anger, jealousy, disputatiousness, lust, pride, lying, hypocrisy, fraud, worldliness, self-love, covetousness, avarice, ignorance, prejudice, hatred, and tyranny.

It is of note that in Baha'i thinking the powers of the human intellect are seen as expressions of the soul and as God's greatest gift to humanity—linking the soul to the quest for knowledge and understanding which is enjoined on all Baha'is.

Suffering

For Baha'is, much suffering is a result of our own actions, and as such can be avoided, either by obedience to divine law or simple common sense (e.g. avoiding some health problems by not overeating). Again, some suffering results from harmful emotional states such as anxiety, depression, envy, and rage, which we should seek to avoid. However, Baha'is should realize that a lack of a spiritual life is also a source of suffering: by its very nature, the material world is transient and unsatisfactory, and the only true happiness is to be found in reliance on God and detachment from material concerns. Looking at the world in this way also enables us to avoid the fear of such realities as death. Again, Baha'is can see suffering as a divine test, and as a means to draw individuals closer to God (as in the Biblical story of Job). Whilst Baha'is should not be fatalistic—taking all wise precautions against adversity and working to eliminate poverty and disease—they should also seek to develop fortitude and patience in response to suffering.

Death and the afterlife

Baha'is believe in the immortality of the soul and its eternal spiritual progress, but the Baha'i writings do not give a clear picture of the afterlife: it is presented as beyond the understanding of those who are still living, just as the present world would be incomprehensible to the unborn fetus. In this perspective, death and the decomposition of the body are a natural part of human life. Accordingly, whilst we may lament the death of those we love, we should also realize that death represents a potential liberation for them, freeing their eternal souls from the fetters of material existence. We may pray for the spiritual progress of those who have died.

In the afterlife, it is believed, individuals will become aware of the consequences of their actions and choices, those who have walked humbly with God being honored, whilst those who have lived in error will be filled with fear and consternation. The doctrine of reincarnation is rejected, as is the belief in "earth-bound souls" or ghosts.

Social Teachings and the Vision of a New World Order

For Baha'is Bahá'u'lláh came to unite all the peoples of the world, to bring together the followers of the world's religions, and to establish the future millennial age which has been prophesied in all religions. The Baha'i teachings then include a vision of a future world of peace and justice (the "Most Great Peace") whilst at the same time outlining what are seen as practical means to accomplish that objective. Baha'is see the growth of this "New World Order" as partly an evolutionary process occurring now as a twofold process, with humanity increasingly forced to accept the realities of global interdependence and the need for an effective international order, and the Baha'is themselves creating a global community dedicated to spiritual objectives. Such a transformation is far from straightforward, however, as evidenced by opposition to both the Baha'i faith and to rising globalism—impedimenta which are seen as major factors in present global disorder and suffering.

The main elements of the Baha'i millennial and social vision can be summarized as follows:

(i) *The achievement of world peace in a united world* in which all peoples are seen as the citizens of one country. Ideally, this would be the religiously-based "Most Great Peace" referred to by Bahá'u'lláh, but the Baha'i leaders also referred pragmatically to a "Lesser Peace" that could be achieved by existing governments learning to work together effectively to achieve more limited goals, including peace keeping, armament reductions and a system of collective security (Baha'is have therefore supported the work of the United Nations despite its evident weaknesses and have advocated that its powers be strengthened to counter the negative consequences of unfettered national sovereignty). The fostering of tolerance and freedom from all religious, racial, political, economic, and patriotic prejudices and the adoption of a universal auxiliary language are seen as further important elements in the achievement of a united world.

(ii) *The establishment of social order and justice.* Again, ultimately, Baha'is believe that this can only be achieved through a religious reformation of the whole human race, but pragmatically advocate the adoption of means to build up good governance, the rule of law, and the protection of the poor and downtrodden at a national and international levels. All barriers to a just society—such as tyrannical rule, exploitation of the people by their rulers, corruption, and extreme disparities of wealth and poverty—are condemned. Constitutional monarchy—or at least some form of representative government with a separation of powers—is seen as the ideal political form.

(iii) *The advancement of women.* For Baha'is, men and women are equal in the sight of God, and the importance of achieving gender equality in almost all areas of human life is repeatedly stressed in the Baha'i writings, the main exceptions being opposition to allowing women to become combat soldiers or be elected to the Universal House of Justice. The oppression of woman, so characteristic of many societies, is seen as a primary factor retarding the progress of humanity as a whole. Women are seen as a potential driving force in the anti-war movement.

(iv) *Education.* Baha'is emphasize the importance of both religious and secular education for the individual and for society as a whole. Children need to gain a sense of morality and the fear of God, but they also need to learn how to read and write and to study for a career. Baha'i parents are under an obligation to ensure that their children are educated, and universal access to education is a fundamental right. The education of girls—as potential mothers and hence their own children's first educators—is of prime importance. Education is regarded as essential to social-economic development and the creation of a just society. (Without education, the common people are not able to act effectively against misgovernment.)

(v) *The role of religion.* Baha'is emphasize the importance of combining "spiritual" and "material" solutions to the world's problems. Whilst praising many secular goals as a proximate means of improving an imperfect world, they hold that it is only through pure and revived religion—shorn of fanaticism, bigotry, and superstition—that the necessary fundamental changes in human society can be achieved. In this context, the Baha'i social vision is ambivalent towards certain aspects of modernity, embracing what we might see as a liberal social reformism whilst at the same time strongly opposing materialism and secularism as destructive social forces in the modern world.

Suggestions for Further Reading

Esslemont, John E. *Bahá'u'lláh and the New Era.* London: Bahá'í Publishing Trust, 1974.

Ferraby, John. *All Things Made New: A Comprehensive Outline of the Bahá'í Faith.* London: Bahá'í Publishing Trust, 1987.

Hatcher, William S., and J. Douglas Martin. *The Bahá'í Faith: The Emerging Global Religion.* San Francisco: Harper & Row, 1984.

Huddlestone, John. *The Earth is But One Country.* London: Bahá'í Publishing Trust, 1976.

Momen, Moojan. *The Baha'i Faith: A Short Introduction.* Oxford: Oneworld, 1996.

Momen, Wendi, and Moojan Momen. *Understanding the Baha'i Faith.* Edinburgh: Dunedin Academic Press, 2005.

Smith, Peter. *The Babi and Baha'i Religions: From Messianic Shi'ism to a World Religion.* Cambridge: Cambridge University Press, 1987.

———. *The Bahá'í Religion: A Short Introduction to its History and Teachings.* Oxford: George Ronald, 1988.

———. *A Concise Encyclopedia of the Bahá'í Faith.* Oxford: Oneworld, 2000.

———. *An Introduction to the Baha'i Faith* .Cambridge University Press, 2008);

Warburg, Margit. *Baha'i.* Salt Lake City: Signature Books, 2003.

———. *Citizens of the World: A History and Sociology of the Baha'is in Globalization Perspective.* Leiden: Brill, 2006.

Websites

Baha'i Library Online (http://bahai-library.com).
Bahá'í Reference Library (http://reference.bahai.org).
Bahá'í World News Service (http://news.bahai.org).
One Country (http://www.onecountry.org).

Index of Names

Breinigsville, PA USA
15 January 2010
230832BV00003B/1/P